Chechnya

Chechnya

From Nationalism to Jihad

JAMES HUGHES

PENN

University of Pennsylvania Press

Philadelphia

10   9   8   7   6   5   4   3   2   1

Published by
University of Pennsylvania Press
Philadelphia, Pennsylvania 19104-4112

Library of Congress Cataloging-in-Publication Data

Hughes, James, 1959–
    Chechnya : from nationalism to jihad / James Hughes
      p. cm.
    ISBN-13: 978-0-8122-4013-9 (alk. paper)
    ISBN-10: 0-8122-4013-8 (alk. paper)
    Includes bibliographical references and index.
    Contents: The causes of the conflict—Russia's refederalization and Chechnya's
secession—A secular nationalist conflict—Dual radicalization: the making of jihad—
Chechnya and the meaning of terrorism—Chechnya and the study of conflict.
    1. Nationalism—Russia (Federation)—Chechnya. 2. Radicalism—Russia
(Federation)—Chechnya. 3. Chechnya (Russia)—History—Civil War, 1944–. I. Title
DK511.C2 H84   2007
947.5'2—dc22   2006050037

Auferre trucidare rapere falsis nominibus imperium, atque ubi solitudinem faciunt, pacem appellant.
To theft, massacre and plunder, they give the lying name of government, and where they create a wasteland, they call it peace.

From the speech of Galgachus before the battle of the Graupian Mountains, A.D. 84, Tacitus. *De vita et moribus Iulii Agricolae* 30.

Contents

Preface

The wars in Chechnya of 1994–96, and 1999–present, rank alongside those fought over Bosnia-Herzegovina and Iraq as the most bloody and costly conflicts of the contemporary era. The destructive depth and sustained nature of the violent conflict in Chechnya over the fifteen-year period 1991–2006 make it the most protracted of all the violent post-Soviet conflicts. Much of the capital of Chechnya, Grozny, was reduced to rubble by the fighting, mainly by Russian air and land bombardments. The modern infrastructure of Chechnya—its economy, communications, health and social services, and cultural institutions—was devastated. Its society was uprooted as the conflict displaced the bulk of its people from their homes. As we shall discuss later, the human costs of the conflict are bitterly disputed. Estimates of the casualties vary widely from tens of thousands to several hundred thousand. Few Chechens escaped the trauma of suffering violence personally, whether through direct war injury or as victims of abuses by Russian forces and their local Chechen militias, and by the loss of relatives and property.

The role of territorialized ethnicity in the drive for secession allows for comparisons between Chechnya and some of the other violent post-Soviet conflicts, such as the presently frozen conflicts of Nagorno-Karabagh, Transdnistria, and Abkhazia, but one of the unique features of the conflict in Chechnya is its very location. It is the only large-scale violent conflict to have occurred within the Russian Federation since the collapse of the USSR. It is also the only case where Russia has employed military power to resist secession, and it is the sole case where secessionists militarily resisted Russia's attempts to reimpose its sovereignty. Moreover, the violent conflict in and over Chechnya has caused significant spillover attacks in Russia itself, as well as episodic violence in the neighboring regions and republics of the Russian Federation, which increasingly threatens to cause wider political instability in the North Caucasus region.

The conflict has seen some of the world's worst terrorist atrocities. I define "terrorism" as the deliberate and indiscriminate targeting and killing of civilians. This definition would cover those acts perpetrated by Chechen extremists at the Budennovsk hospital, Dubrovka theater, and Beslan school, and by the Russian military in the bombing of Grozny. Equally, the main protagonists have engaged periodically in attempts to reach a settlement by dialogue and negotiations. Indeed, the "peace process" in Chechnya is littered by a "truce," a "treaty," and several "agreements." Why has a final peace "settlement" to the conflict been so elusive?

While the study of the collapse of the Soviet Union is by now much plowed terrain, the reasons why this collapse was followed in Chechnya and so many other places by large-scale political violence, and elsewhere was substantively and remarkably peaceful, are much less well understood. Most theories and studies of conflicts tend to focus on two strata: explanations of the causes, and prognoses about potential solutions or forms of managing conflict. What tends to be overlooked is the impact of how the conflict is fought on the conflict dynamics. Studies of conflict that seek to uncover root causes will establish the range of contributing factors and then reorder them in hierarchical importance. By examining the temporal phases of a conflict, however, we can identify more clearly the development of the key issues and changes in the protagonists. The focus on the dynamic of conflict is critical for understanding the parameters of any potential agreement. For what might have been the basis for compromise and a settlement at one stage of the conflict may be made redundant by the conflict dynamics as new dimensions and new actors become more salient over time, while previously established ones become less salient.

Explanations of the causes of the surge of nationalist and ethnic conflicts in the former Soviet Union in the 1990s, as in the Balkans, tend to follow two broad patterns. First, in the case of the conflicts in the Caucasus region during and after the fall of the Soviet Union, some studies reflect a historicist inclination (in the Popperian sense of historical determinism) and attribute the conflicts to the warlike "nature" of the peoples of the region, and to the way ethnic "traits," "propensities," "belligerence," and "ancient hatreds" contributed to the conflicts. Others focus on how the contingent factors of systemic collapse, such as the clash of interests that characterized the post-communist transition, impinged upon the development of conflict. What is normally studied as "the conflict," however, may in fact be several conflicts, occurring in interactive simultaneity. How the core constituents of conflict interact, oscillate, and are transformed over time in a dynamic process is critical for understanding causes and providing remedies. I am not simply referring to the oft-cited "escalator," "ratchet," or "feedback" effects in the way that a conflict develops, in particular as regards the intensity of violence. Rather, the protracted dynamics of the conflict in Chechnya must be analyzed as a key part of the causation chain, for they interacted with and altered the fundamental constituents of the conflict over time, such as the principal protagonists, the salient issues, and how the conflict is framed.

The conflict began as a clash between competing nationalist ideologies, and between two core principles: the right of the Chechen people to national self-determination (and secession) versus the Russian Federation's right to protect its territorial integrity and statehood. What began as a mainstream secular nationalist struggle over territory in the early 1990s was transformed and radicalized by the second half of the 1990s into a struggle driven largely by ideas based on religious and racial exclusivism. This book explains this transformation by focusing on the dynamics of the conflict. It also offers a new way of thinking about ethnopolitical and other conflicts—by focusing on conflict dynamics as part of the causation chain in a conflict. I will show how the roots of the conflict have been regularly reframed and revised by the protagonists as they have been radicalized by the way that the conflict has been fought.

At the outset, the demand for self-determination was justified by Chechen nationalists as legitimate in the context of the collapse of the Soviet empire, as it was an assertion of the right to decolonization—a right guaranteed under international law. They also emphasized their right to secede under the Soviet constitution, because Chechnya had legally acquired this right by constitutional changes enacted before the dissolution of the USSR. The Russian political elite's narrative, by contrast, generally offers a threefold rationale for the roots of the conflict in Chechnya: structural, ethnic, and ideological. The structural causes are seen as deriving from the region's poverty and backwardness. The ethnic roots of the conflict are attributed to the oft-cited "historical enmity," a historicist interpretation equally favored by Western journalists. In Russia and Chechnya historicist views can rarely be categorized as informed cognition, but rather reflect racist stereotypes: the Russian view of the Chechens stresses their supposed propensity for violence and criminality, and the notion of "Caucasian bloodlust." The ideological factor in the conflict has received increasing attention from Russians as the conflict has evolved, and presently borders on a paranoid fear of the grip of Islamic radicalism on the Chechen resistance. Consequently, the conflict is frequently interpreted in Russia as one of Samuel P. Huntington's "fault-line" wars between "Orthodoxy" and "Western civilization" and "Islam." It is evident that this kind of threefold rationalization of the conflict by Russian elites, stressing backwardness, race, and religion, is not particular to Chechnya. It is a common pattern in the framing of anti-colonial struggles by imperial incumbents.

This book aims to avoid stereotypical, historicist depictions of the

Chechen conflict. Chapter 1 balances the salience of historical experiences and structural legacies with the potency of Chechnya's claim to national self-determination in the context of the collapse of the Soviet empire and post-Soviet Russian state-building. It analyzes the elite politics of the period, and demonstrates how elite circles in Moscow and Chechnya mobilized nationalist political conflict, which spiraled out of control into military confrontation.

Chapter 2 places Chechnya's demands for secession in the context of Russia's post-Soviet re-federalization. The Russian federation is an anomaly for those analysts of Soviet-type federations that stress their "subversive" institutional characteristics, as it is the only socialist-era federation that has survived. Chechnya also represented the exception to Yeltsin's strategy of asymmetric federalism in the 1990s, based on the personalized bilateral power-sharing treaties that he negotiated with the leaders of the key ethnic republics. This chapter explores the combination of geographical, structural, historical, and identity-based factors that made Chechnya the only effective and authentic secessionist challenge to the completion of Russian "statehood" on the whole territory inherited from the RSFSR.

A clash of presidential personalities between Dudaev and Yeltsin is widely seen as a major cause of the first Chechen war of 1994–96. Chapter 3 critically assesses this thesis and stresses an alternative explanation that focuses on the political factors, and specifically the secular nationalist struggle over competing visions of statehood. It provides an assessment of the nature of the Dudaev regime and debunks the Russian-propagated myth that what occurred in Chechnya in the early 1990s was a criminal group's "power-grab." The conflict was instrumentalized by both leaderships to achieve several key political objectives: as a tactical lever to outmaneuver opponents in the institutional struggles between president and parliament of the early post-Soviet transition period, to maximize their electoral appeal, and to assist their consolidation of power through authoritarian means. The first war was characterized by war crimes by both sides, but in particular by Russia's disproportionate and indiscriminate use of its overwhelming military force. This factor, more than any other, had a radicalizing effect on Chechnya. Signs of the radicalization included the increasing resort to the use of terrorism by the Chechen side, the growth of Islamic religiosity, and the shift from secular nationalism to Islamic fundamentalism as a mobilizing idea for important elements of the Chechen resistance. Russia's surprising military defeat in the first Chechen war led to the only genuine attempt at comprehensive peace negotiations: the Khasaviurt Agreement of 1996, followed by a peace treaty in 1997 that brought Russia very close to the de facto recognition of Chechnya's claim to self-determination. Why did this seemingly accomplished secession fail?

Explanations for the failure of Chechnya's president Maskhadov to establish state capacity in Chechnya in 1996–98 are examined in Chapter 4. The power vacuum in Chechnya is widely attributed to the rise of the influence of foreign militant Wahhabi Islamists, who, through their connection with Chechnya's legendary field commander Shamil Basaev, assumed an influence in Chechen politics that was disproportionate to their numbers and popular support in the country. The Wahhabis attempted to transform the core issue from secession, a concept that was grounded in a territorialized idea of the nation-state, into one based on a concept of the theocratic solidarity of the Muslim community (*ummah*) across the wider North Caucasus region. There were other dimensions to the failure of Maskhadov's nascent state-building project. Despite the legitimacy provided by the democratic elections of early 1997, Maskhadov received little international support. The deadlocked negotiations with Russia over the question of Chechnya's permanent status provided Russia with an excuse to block financial assistance and economic relations, and much of the aid was lost to corruption, mainly in Russia but also in Chechnya.

The second Chechen war from 1999 onward has been marked by the dual radicalization of the protagonists in Russia and in Chechnya. In Russia the conflict was framed by Vladimir Putin first as a "counterterrorist operation" and later as part of the global "war on terror." Russia's military success against the Chechens, secured by an even more resolute use of disproportionate and excessive military force, was critical to Putin's victory in the "khaki" presidential election of March 2000 and to his reelection in 2004. On the Chechen side the second war saw a steady shift from secular nationalism to radical Islamization and the idiom of *jihad*. Russia has increasingly relied on Chechen proxies, notably the Kadyrovs, and a policy of Chechenization to reduce its own losses and to put itself at one remove from the most brutal forms of repression. War has demodernized Chechnya, and reconstruction efforts are minimal. As a result, the scope for conflict resolution has continuously narrowed, while the potential for broader regional instability and spillover attacks in the North Caucasus has increased.

Chapter 5 examines the Chechen conflict within the wider global discussion about the nature of terrorism. It demonstrates the high degree of politicization surrounding the concept of terrorism in Russia and internationally, and how the politicization of the term has intensified after 9/11. I suggest that to define terrorism in a less politicized and more useful way it is more constructive to focus on the nature of the acts perpetrated rather than attempt to brand organizations and individuals selectively as "terrorist." In most conflicts acts of terrorism (in the most meaningful sense of indiscriminate attacks on civilians) are generally only a minor part of the repertoire of violence by all parties, however spectacular and horrific they may be. They do, however, play a key role in radicalizing protagonists and framing the conflict. By analyzing how terrorism has been used tactically and strategically by the Chechen resistance throughout the period of conflict with Russia since 1991, the book also places the violence of the conflict in a comparative perspective.

In Chapter 6 the common features of the concepts and theories of nationalism, democratization, and secession are examined to provide insights into locating the conflict in Chechnya within the comparative study of national and ethnic conflict. These theories share a central focus on the active role of the state in nation-building, regime change, and conflict resolution. The homogeneous nation-state is viewed as the most stable political unit, while multiethnicity is generally regarded as precarious. International law, and the mainstream theories of democratization, are vehemently opposed to secession and consider it acceptable only under very exceptional political conditions; almost without exception it requires at least nominal agreement of the state concerned. A strong current of theory argues for the management of divided societies by institutional forms of multiculturalism and power-sharing, autonomy, federalism, and consociation. Most mainstream theories, however, suggest that the homogeneous versus heterogeneous dilemmas of a state's demographic content should be "ended" by the assimilation or integration of minorities into the values of the hegemonic ethnic group (though they would never openly express matters this way). Adherents of such policies of assimilation and integration tend either to view them in essence as part of a wider strategy of control by a hegemonic group, which normally rests on subtle forms of coercion (sometimes termed "incentives") as opposed to crude force, or to be naïve as to the consequences. For assimilation is not a panacea and can cause and exacerbate ethnic and social antagonisms and grievances just as readily as the more brutish forms of discrimination. Moreover, there is no known case of comprehensive peaceful assimilation occurring among a people living in its historic homeland. Secession is, therefore, a defense against assimilation as much as to engage in a state-building project.

This book focuses on both the context and the process of the conflict between Russia and Chechnya as the keys to understanding why it has become one of the most violent and protracted of the contemporary post-communist conflicts. What began as a localized secular national conflict over territory became steadily infused by the global ideas of Islamic fundamentalism, internationalism, and jihad. While the conflict remains concentrated in Chechnya, it has escalated into a broader regional conflict in the North Caucasus. This shift was largely the result of a radicalization induced by the brutality of Russia's military response to what was, and remains, a political problem. What is the conflict in Chechnya about? The answer to this question, as this book attempts to demonstrate, is that conflicts mutate and actors and issues change accordingly.

Map 1. Chechnya.

Map 2. Main oil pipelines in the Caucasus.

Map 3. Federal districts of the Russian Federation.

Chapter 1
The Causes of Conflict

There is no a priori reason to assume that ethnic conflict in Chechnya was inevitable or would be more intractable than in other post-communist states or elsewhere in the world. While it is important to give due recognition to historical factors in the conflict, it is equally important to avoid an overly historicist interpretation of the causes of the conflict. In contrast to previous studies of the conflict in Chechnya I explore in depth the role of contingency in sparking the conflict. There is now a significant literature on how the contingency of the period of liberalization during Gorbachev's perestroika energized the idea of national self-determination and impelled the opposition to Soviet control in the countries of Central and Eastern Europe and among the peoples of the Soviet Union.[1] Scholarly works may vary in their emphasis on the relative weight of the political, economic, social, ideological, institutional, and international aspects of the collapse of the USSR, but there is an accepted consensus that the reforms undermined the authority of the center and eroded the will of the Soviet communist elite for sustaining their rule by coercion. The demonstration and spillover effects of the nationalist resurgence accelerated the momentum of nationalist mobilization within the Soviet Union itself, and tipped the Soviet system into collapse.

Since it was the combination of control and quasi-federal institutional constraints that had managed national and ethnic historical antagonisms in the Soviet Union, it was inevitable that with the end of the Soviet empire, and the breakdown of the control regime, there would be challenges to the institutional architecture of the Soviet settlement of the nationalities question. How the Soviet institutional legacy for managing multi-ethnicity was disassembled during the collapse, and what attempts were made to reassemble it as part of post-Soviet Russian state building, are crucial elements of the contingent causation of the conflict in Chechnya. For the conflict in Chechnya arose as part of the wider struggle between competing secular nationalisms and mobilizations for national self-determination within the postcommunist states of Eastern Europe and the Soviet Union.

There are also by now a large number of studies of the conflict in Chechnya. For the most part, they can be organized into two categories: accounts by journalists, generally derived from their transient experiences in the field; and academic studies which focus on the history of Russo-Chechen relations as the principal context for understanding the current conflict. The dominant explanation in both categories is that the present conflict is "about" a historically rooted Chechen experience of resistance to Russian conquest, oppression, and control. The conventional wisdom is that the conflict should be primarily understood as part of a continuum of "ethnic" conflict between Russians and Chechens that originated in the era of Russia's colonial expansion into the North Caucasus in the early nineteenth century.

Historicism and the "Ethnic War" Account

Many recent accounts have emphasized a recurrent theme that focuses on the primordial roots of the conflict by manipulating mythic elements of "ancient hatreds" and historical "ethnic enmity" in the relations between Russians and Chechens.[2] Insights have been shaped by the work of Soviet and Russian ethnologists and anthropologists, which is often strongly derivative of stereotypes dating from the nineteenth century. Journalists also have had an immensely important role in shaping general perceptions of what the Chechnya conflict is about. Their works range from inchoate "diaries" and "notes" to decent attempts at reportage and analysis, but often the reader is lured into the "fog of war," with impressionistic narrative flashes of how the conflict is fought but little understanding of its causes. The media coverage of the conflict in Chechnya inevitably concentrated on the most intense periods of war and spectacular episodes of violence. Many journalists wrote up their notes into book length accounts.[3] The common problem in the journalistic accounts is that they assume that inherent truths about the causes of the conflict can be found by recording daily life in a conflict zone, whether it is from sharing a billet, a tin of fish paste, and a bottle of vodka with Russian troops, taking tea with Chechen fighters, or everyday conversations with local contacts, drivers, and their families and neighbors. Such reportage is not insignificant, for it provides us with many illustrations of the ordinary responses to a conflict environment, but we should attach no more importance to these observations for the explanation of the conflict than we would to the musings of an infantryman stuck in a trench on the Somme in the search for the causes of the First World War. Moreover, the reconnaissance nature of contemporary journalism, driven by deadlines and headlines, does not lend itself to nuanced analysis, perspective, and the explanation of complexity.

Many male journalistic accounts are shaped by "Boys Own" fantasy-like projections. While I am not aware of any Western journalist who actually took to wearing the *cherkesska* when covering the contemporary conflict in Chechnya, many were mentally so adorned. Many were inspired by the work of the Edwardian British journalist John Baddeley, who did like to "go native" and be photographed in the *cherkesska* with a *kinzhal* at his waist. A correspondent for the *Observer*, Baddeley wrote a narrative Romantic history, *The Russian Conquest of the Caucasus*, published in London in 1908, which provides the background to the core narrative of many contemporary Anglo-American journalistic accounts of the conflict in Chechnya.[4] The war in Chechnya of 1994–96 also coincided with the cinematic mythologizing of highlanders and resistance to colonialists through the "Braveheart" phenomenon of the mid-1990s.[5] The maps in the journalistic literature are also, on occasion, Tolkienesque.[6]

Most of the academic and journalistic accounts of the post-1991 Chechen resistance to Russia exaggerate and romanticize the enduring pre-modern nature and "highlander" clan bonds of the organization of contemporary Chechen society. These non-Chechen understandings of the role of clan in contemporary Chechnya are strongly influenced by the work of Soviet-era anthropologists, which tends toward romanticized descriptions. Chechen ethnologist Mahomet Mamakaev drew on Lewis Henry Morgan's controversial studies of the Iroquois, a North American indigenous people, to apply "classic" markers of a hierarchy of kin lineages, clans, and tribes, and thereby established the view of the traditional Chechen clan (*taipa*, usually Anglicized as *teip*) structure as one that was characterized by these features, and that was the foundation of Chechen institutions, including a political role. This view endures as a popular conventional wisdom, but is much disputed by academics. The Chechen word *taipa* is itself not indigenous but is an import from Arabic, suggesting prima facie a foreign concept. Recent work suggests that the pre-modern *teip* kin structure among the Chechens was fragmented by population movements and social change in the seventeenth and eighteenth centuries as communities abandoned highland communal pastoral territories and dispersed to settle and farm the lowlands and steppe area. Russian colonization from the late eighteenth century further weakened the traditional "kin" basis of the *teip* through military conquest, genocide, deportation, and commercialization, while it also attempted to reinvent and affirm the concept as a useful tool for the administration and management of the conquered territory. Thus, the modern notion of *teip* is largely an invention of Russian nineteenth-century military colonizers and bureaucrats who forced the Chechens into an artificial, territorialized notion of "teip" identity.[7]

The work of Russian anthropologist Sergei Arutiunov follows Mamakaev's model and has become widely and uncritically cited in many of the studies of contemporary Chechnya. Arutiunov argues that the traditional *teip* structure consists of about 150 *teips* organized into about nine larger "tribal" groups called *tuqums,* all of which are based around extended kin networks. Arutiunov suggests that Chechnya is a kind of "military democracy, e.g., like the Iroquois in America or Zulu in South Africa (sic)": "In peacetime, they recognize no sovereign authority and may be fragmented into a hundred rival clans. However, in time of danger, when faced with aggression, the rival clans unite and elect a military leader."[8]

In the search for understanding of the development of Chechen society, some authors have drawn comparisons with other highland clan cultures on the periphery of empire, for example, the Berbers of North Africa. Yet when they have looked for the contemporary influence of the *teip* in Chechnya, the search has been largely futile.[9] Oddly, comparisons are not drawn with historic Gaelic clan societies in Ireland or, in particular, in highland Scotland, from which culture, after all, the word clan itself originates.[10] Perhaps this is because there is no anthropological foundation for understanding contemporary Scottish or Irish society through clan referents. Indeed, it would be absurd to do so, for as a form of social organization they were deliberately physically eliminated over the sixteenth to eighteenth centuries by British colonialism, in cooperation with commercially minded local co-opted elites. The residues of these quintessential clan societies, where in fact territorial communal identity was as important as loosely defined and often imagined lineage and "kin" ties, were dispersed by the Industrial Revolution, the flight to towns, famine, poverty, and mass emigration. In these societies clan undoubtedly has a contemporary symbolic or lyrical cultural resonance in the arts, but it is of virtually no importance to social connection, and certainly exercises no political significance. This is a much more convincing point of reference for understanding the symbolic resonance of the *teip* in contemporary Chechnya.

Ekaterina Sokirianskaia's recent study of the role of *teip* in the "Vainakh" republics of Ingushetia and Chechnya debunks many of the myths surrounding the concept.[11] She found that there was no shared understanding of the meaning of *teip.* She identified two broad uses of the concept. First, it denominated a large-scale imagined territorial and shared-lineage identity. The Chechen *teip* "benoj," for example, which is associated with the pro-Russian forces of Akhmed and Ramzan Kadyrov, supposedly accounts for 15 percent of the population of Chechnya. This broader *teip* identity is more symbolic, lyrical, and anonymous. It is associated with iconic oral histories and myths of ethnogenesis and genealogical lineage in historical personages, places, and monuments, for example, "our" stone battle towers in the highlands. Second, *teip* refers to a small-scale social network of extended families related by blood and usually in direct contact, often through male family members. Sokirianskaia persuasively argues that while the narrow *teip* plays a role in political clientelism, which is to be expected, the broader concept of *teip* plays no role in state building and politics.

Rather, she focuses on the operation of "political-military groupings" in contemporary Chechnya, which may have kin-based and territory-based elements, but are mostly organized around shared political ideals and "personalistic" clientelist ties.[12] Her findings are confirmed by the subordinate place of "clan" in the idiom of Chechen politics. Chechen political groups and networks are either ideological, territorial (based around village of origin), or personalistic. Chechen politicians speak and write about political "clans" as patron-client networks and name them accordingly—"Zavgaevtsy," "Khadzhievtsy," "Arsanovtsy," and so on.[13] As we shall discuss later, the current role of the "Kadyrovsty" is another manifestation of this kind of clientelism. This is far removed from the notion of kin-based "clan" ties as a basis for political activity.

The notion of contemporary Chechnya as a clan-based society has little basis in sociological fact. If *teip* ever did communicate a direct social connection as the basis for politics, this was destroyed by a century of social upheaval and fragmentation resulting from Russian colonization in the mid-nineteenth century, Tsarist and Soviet modernization, in particular, state policies of industrialization and secularization, the Bolshevik Revolution, and collectivization, culminating in the genocidal deportation of the Chechen people in 1944. While social change eroded such identities, the deportation (discussed below) killed many of the older generation, where the values of traditional society were strongest. The Russian ethnographer Valerii Tishkov is a vocal critic of the distorting influence of the "ethnographic romanticism" of some scholars and journalists on the nature of Chechen ethnicity and the role of history in the Caucasus. Tishkov blames Arutiunov and other Russian ethnographers for having "contributed to the forging of myths of a unique Chechen civilization," which were readily consumed by Western journalists such as Lieven. He has described this genre as a "reification of Chechenness," an attempt to forge them out of "ethnic trash," and a "nationalistic narcissism" impelled by "superficial historicity and cultural fundamentalism." Equally, we must note that it is important for Tishkov's overall thesis on the present conflict in Chechnya to deny the Chechens an identity as a "nation," to downplay the extent of a "national revolution," and to overstate the appeal of a secular "Soviet" identity in Chechnya prior to the beginning of the conflict in 1991.[14]

Anatol Lieven emphasizes the "noble military tradition" of the Chechens, their "antiquity" as an ethnie, their "epic" and "warlike" spirit and "highlander camaraderie."[15] The Chechen fighters of the 1994–96 war, according to Lieven, were like "Homeric heroes," comparable to "Aeneas with the RPG" or "Achilles with a rocket propelled grenade," and characterized by "archaic championship . . . dash and elan."[16] Much cruder stereotyping is evident in the simplistic white hat-black hat representation of the protagonists in the work of other journalists. Bird's writing is typical in this respect, as Chechen fighters are portrayed as "slim and fit," with "eagle"-like faces, whereas Russian officers and their Chechen collaborators are "paunchy," "fox-eyed," with "jackal"-like grins.[17]

The "ethnic" chic attached to the contemporary conflict in Chechnya has infected policy-makers as well as journalists. I witnessed a classic example of this kind of absurdity at the highly respected Royal Institute of International Affairs (Chatham House) on 10 March 1998, when, after delivering a speech on the subject "Chechnya: our future as a free nation," a bemused Chechen President Aslan Maskhadov was presented with an antique traditional dagger (*kinzhal*), with decorative motifs supposedly of Chechen craftsmanship, by an Oxford don. It occurred to me as I watched that this was the equivalent of presenting Gerry Adams, the leader of Sinn Fein, with a *cliath mhor*.

This incident is emblematic of the Orientalism which permeates Western and Russian attitudes to Chechnya. Much of the contemporary stereotyping of "Chechen-ness" or "the Chechen" reflects the historical pattern of ambivalence of colonizers toward the colonized. The idea of framing the colonized as exotica has ancient roots and is illustrated by a long line of literatures from Livy to Kipling. The empathizing and glamorizing metaphor of the "noble savage" is ubiquitous in the romanticization of conquered and colonized peoples by colonizers. Its alternate is the notion of the "wild" "primitive," and "cruel" savage, whose nature is irredeemable—an interpretation generally favored by the generals and the genocidists. Orientalism, as Edward Said explained in his classic study of the subject, is a discourse by which the unequal power relations inherent in imperialism are actively reproduced in political, cultural, intellectual and moral life. As such it "is—and does not simply represent—a considerable dimension of modern political-intellectual culture, and as such has less to do with the Orient than it does with "our" World".[18]

The Russian form of Orientalism is inextricably embedded in its nineteenth-century colonial experience in the Caucasus. Pushkin, Lermontov, and most notably Tolstoy, the latter two of whom served long tours of duty as military officers in the Caucasus, fashioned the most imaginative and enduring of the romanticized metaphors for the Caucasus in Russian culture. In particular, Pushkin's *Kavkazskii plennik* ("Prisoner in the Caucasus") and Tolstoy's "moral" novel of the "Murid" war, *Hadji Murat*, along with Baddeley, seem to have framed contemporary Western journalists' and policy-makers' understanding of contemporary Chechnya. Tolstoy's moral tragedy is set in the early 1850s during the Russian military "pacification" of the territory of present-day Chechnya. It tells the story of the Avar resistance leader Hadji Murat, who, tired of struggle and anticipating Russian military victory, defects to the Russian side, only to become disillusioned by Russian ignorance and cruelty, and ultimately be killed in a shoot-out with Russian forces.

Historicist approaches tend to freeze the patterns of behavior discussed above that are associated with Chechen communities by eighteenth- and nineteenth-century Russian colonizers, and project them forward to the late twentieth century. Thus, there is an emphasis on the mythical ethnogenesis of the Chechens as a group of highland clan communities, with a society based on a pastoral economy that was supplemented by brigandry on the precarious trade routes over the Caucasus Mountains and against the plains peoples (who were increasingly Russian in the nineteenth century). It was a society where customary law ('$\bar{a}d\bar{a}t$) prevailed over strict observance of Islamic law (shari'a), and where blood feuds and hostage-taking was the norm. The brigandage is usually interpreted as an innate expression of the martial spirit of the Chechens that found its full expression in the resistance to Russian colonial expansion in the nineteenth century. This resistance is also seen as being directed by the episodic religious "fanaticism" of Islamic "holy war" (jihad).

Let us examine more closely the two substantive elements in the historicist approach. First, the claim is made that the conflict is rooted in the particularly coercive nature of Russian colonization of the Caucasus in the nineteenth century. Russian imperial expansion into the Caucasus began as early as 1722, when Peter the Great annexed the regions of the Caspian Sea littoral of present-day Dagestan. By 1730 the Russian Empire established the Terek as the boundary between Europe and the Asiatic Caucasus.[19] It was the start of a century and a half of military engagement and colonization, as the Caucasus became a frontier of strategic and cultural-religious competition between the Orthodox Christian Russian and the Islamic Ottoman empires. The brutal policies of subordination of Christian and Muslim peoples in the North and South Caucasus became political causes célèbres in both empires, and provided a "just cause" for intervention on behalf of coreligionists when required. After the Napoleonic Wars, the northern Caucasus area became a highly militarized frontier zone. The Russians adopted classic colonial tactics and established a "line" of blockhouses (fortified military garrisons), with paramilitary Cossack settlements in support, behind which settler-colonists farmed the fertile plains areas. The aim was to isolate the indigenous highland peoples, including the Chechens, in the less agriculturally viable upland and mountainous areas to the south of the Terek River.

As with many colonial conflicts, these wars were long and bitterly fought, and both sides forged a historical mythology of brutal and unremitting conflict, with little quarter given by either. The scholarly historiography has tended toward polarized treatments, focusing on either the Russian colonial "advance" into the Caucasus or the highlanders' resistance. Nuanced approaches to the complex interaction of colonizers and natives, and the sophisticated socioeconomic interdependencies and blurring of identities that emerged on the frontier, are highly exceptional.[20] As was the pattern in many colonial occupations, when confronted by an overwhelming and technologically superior, modern professionalized Russian military, the Chechens rationally resorted to the hit and run operations of guerrilla war, thus tactically exploiting their local knowledge of the forests and mountains, but they were strategically doomed by their own form of restrained and traditional nonprofessionalized warfare.

The struggle was framed by dichotomies at the level of both cultural references and policy-making. In the literary-cultural sphere, topoi alternated between "primitive despot" and "noble savage."[21] For Russian policymakers the contrast was one of modernization and civilization through incorporation into empire, captured by the notion of spreading *grazhdanstvennost'* (citizenship), against the "fanaticism" of peripheral and backward "mountaineer" (*goretz*) peoples.[22] Susan Layton has dissected the hypocrisy of the enchanted mirror of empire by observing of the Russians: "while accepting the conquest of the Caucasus as a civilizing mission, late nineteenth-century Russians idealized themselves: they created a noble savage of Asia who threw back to the 'European' beholder a flattering image of the self as a humane, generous-spirited civilizer, rather than a perpetrator of genocidal warfare."[23] As is commonplace in the history of colonialism, such framing allowed Russia to apply ruthless and extreme "pacification" measures, most infamously under General Yermolov in the 1820s. Yermolov ordered the wholesale physical destruction of villages, deforestation to remove ground cover, and a scorched earth policy to reduce Chechen morale and resistance by starvation, and finally ethnic cleansing by expelling Muslim peoples from across the Caucasus into the Ottoman Empire.[24] The question is whether we should view this and other historical episodes of the colonial era as having an ongoing hold over Russian-Chechen relations, or as providing a pool of symbolic referents that could be selectively revitalized to assist the nationalist mobilization in the specific context of 1990–91.

Second, related to the colonial experience, the contemporary conflict is seen as a serious fissure in a wider cultural conflict that is articulated in an essentialist form similar to Huntington's influential vision of the "clash of civilizations." The Caucasus is part of the fissure in the Huntington map of the world between the Islamic and Orthodox Christian spaces. Huntington's argument is that Orthodoxy is somewhat less antithetical to Western "civilization" compared with Islam, which is not only incompatible but has an "inherent propensity toward violent conflict". Huntington deduces from the coincidences of conflicts in 1993–4 that "Islam's borders are bloody, and so are its innards", and he places the Chechnya conflict within his general pathology of "Muslim" violence.[25]

The history of colonial resistance in Chechnya is widely viewed as a critical foundation that shapes the present-day struggle for Chechen independence and the growth of Islamist fundamentalism across the North Caucasus. Consequently, references to the traditional nature of contemporary Chechen society not only stress the *teip* structure, and the role of *ʿādāt*, but also the importance of the historical legacy of Islamic resistance and Sufism as contexts for understanding the contemporary conflict. The periodic anticolonial uprisings against Russia were often led by Islamic religious leaders, imams, who were not only local spiritual leaders but also military commanders in the resistance. The Chechens and Ingush are Sunni Muslims of the Hanafi School, a form of Islam that spread from the ʿAbbasid caliphate (present-day Iraq) and that was accommodating of the role of local custom in Islamic law. Sufism, a form of Islam based on orders or traditional paths of mysticism (*tarīqa*), and organized into brotherhoods (*virds*), became embedded in Chechen society contemporaneously with the social turmoil of colonization and resistance in the middle of the nineteenth century. Historically, two orders of Sufism were of importance in Chechnya: the Naqshbandiia order, which fused religion and politics to frame the resistance to Russian colonialism in terms of a "holy war" (*ghazavat*) against the Russian infidels, and the more mystical and "otherworldly" Qadiriia order.[26] The Chechen Sheikh Mansur who led the revolt against Russia in 1785–91, and the Avar Shamil, who led the "Murid" revolt against Russia in the 1840s, were adherents of the Naqshbandiia order. Shamil's jihad, moreover, was driven by the goal of expelling the Russians and also of purifying and spreading "true" Islam and building an Islamic society based on shariʿa.[27] There was, however, a century of historical development between the resistance to Russian colonialism and the contemporary conflict that must be accounted for.

The Modernization of Chechnya

By the late nineteenth century the Chechens were essentially pacified. In the 1860s, following the defeat of Shamil's revolt and the exhaustion of violent resistance, there was a general drift away from the Naqshbandiia order in Chechen society, particularly in the highland areas.[28] Modernization in the late nineteenth century saw the building of towns, roads, railways, schools, and industry, to complement the extensive plains farming of Russian peasant settlers, whose inward migration to the Caucasus accelerated after pacification. The breakdown of *teip* social networks by

modernization and secularization led to the emergence of new mutually reinforcing territorial, socioeconomic, and political cleavages among
the Chechens: along a north-south territorial divide between highland
and lowland, between agricultural/industrial settlements and mountain-
pastoral communities, and between the secular modernized and more
assimilated communities whose elites were coopted, and the peripheral
highland communities where traditional values were conserved. Thus,
modernization added to the complexity of the cleavages in Chechen society: secular/religious, Russified/traditional, insider/outsider. One of the
most fundamental transformations brought about by modernization was
demographic change through large-scale Russian migration. What had
been the Russian-named military blockhouse "Terrible" (in the sense of
terrorizing), Grozny, became the capital for a region that was an important part of the Russian oil boom in the 1890s. Rather than assimilate,
however, many Chechens went into exile into the Ottoman Empire.[29]

After the 1917 revolution there was a brief attempt to create a North
Caucasus emirate on theocratic lines, but this was quickly suppressed by
the Bolsheviks, though small-scale guerrilla warfare continued into the
1920s.[30] The historic "Vainakh" lands were divided into Soviet national-
territorial "autonomous regions" within the RSFSR, for the Chechens in
1922, and for the Ingush in 1924. The two regions were formed into the
Checheno-Ingushetia Autonomous Republic in 1936. Russian labor migration continued under the Bolsheviks and during the Stalinist industrialization of the late 1920s and 1930s. By the time of the 1937 census Russians
accounted for 28.6 percent (190,000) of the population of Checheno-
Ingushetia. The culmination of the logic of colonial enmity in the Russian-
Chechen relationship, it is often argued, was Stalin's elimination of the
Republic and genocidal deportation of the whole of the population of
Checheno-Ingushetia to Central Asia in February 1944. The deportation
was not unique to the Chechens, as several peoples of the North Caucasus,
some 600,000 people (though the large majority, 400,000, were Chechens),
were deported to Kazakhstan and Kirghizia, supposedly for collaborating
with German forces against the Soviet Army. The episode resulted in an
estimated 100,000 deaths and led to an ingrained historical memory of
genocide among the Chechens.[31]

The deportation, which is within living memory for many Chechens,
was a defining event for the reinforcement of a Chechen identity for both
Russians and Chechens. As the Russian nationalist dissident writer Aleksandr Solzhenitsyn observed of the deported Chechens, "No one could
stop them from living as they did. The regime which ruled the land for
thirty years could not force them to respect its laws."[32] The question is the
exact impact of the deportation on Chechen identity? Did it construct a
new form of identity around the bitter experience of deportation, or did

it reconstruct a traditional identity around the idea of resistance to Russia? How was the impact on identity manifested? Rather than exhibit a "propensity" for violence, the return of Chechen deportees and the reestablishment of the Autonomous Republic of Checheno-Ingushetia at the height of Khrushchev's de-Stalinization campaign in 1957 seems to have resulted in no significant acts of violence or resistance.[33] Even during Gorbachev's liberalization of the mid-1980s, as we shall discuss later, Chechen nationalism was a late developer.

During the Soviet oil industry expansion of the 1950s and 1960s there was a further influx of Russians (and to a lesser extent Ukrainians and Belorussians), primarily technical specialists, who concentrated in the capital, Grozny, which was a major oil pipeline terminal, petrochemical center, and transshipping point on the Baku-Novorossiisk pipeline. Much of the concrete residential infrastructure that has become so familiar worldwide through its destruction by the Russian military in early 1995 and late 1999 was constructed in the Soviet building boom between the 1950s and 1970s. According to the 1959 census Slavs, mainly ethnic Russians, made up half of the population of Checheno-Ingushetia. By the 1979 census they had fallen to around 30 percent. Between 1979 and 1989 there was a dramatic demographic shift, partly caused by a steady flow of returnees of deported Chechens from Central Asia, but mostly by an explosion in the birth rate of Chechens (not unusual among post-genocide populations), benefiting from the Soviet welfare state (see Table 1 below).

Chechens began to reverse a century of population shifts by migrating from the overpopulated highland areas to lowland steppe towns, drawn by employment, education, and cultural opportunities. They were displacing Russians in areas that had been Slavic-populated for one hundred and fifty years or more. This accelerated a kind of "White flight," known in Russian as "return" (*obratnichestvo*), as ethnic Russians and Slavs who were disconcerted by the demographic shifts moved to Russia.[34] Consequently, by the 1989 census Chechen society had become much more

TABLE 1. DEMOGRAPHIC CHANGE IN CHECHENO-INGUSHETIA, 1979–89

	1979	1989	Growth rate (percent)	Percent outside Republic
Total Chechens in USSR	785,782	958,309	26.8	23.4
Total Chechens in Republic	611,405	734,501	20.1	
Total Slavs in Republic	350,346	308,985	-11.8	

Source: *Itogi vsesoiuznoi perepisi naseleniia 1989 goda.*

ethnically homogeneous and was dominated by younger generations, who were thoroughly Sovietized, secularized, and urbanized (about half the population lived in towns, and one-third of the population lived in Grozny (where about 55 percent identified themselves as "Slav"). Equally, the census revealed an exceptionally high retention of the Chechen language compared with other "ethnic" territories, with 98.79 percent of all Chechens citing Chechen as their first language. Poverty and the search for better quality of life had also forced many Chechens to migrate to other parts of the USSR, with over 23 percent of all Chechens residing outside the republic. Almost 60,000 lived in neighboring Dagestan, but this was a historically rooted community that had been dislocated by Soviet territorial changes. A further 50,000 lived in Kazakhstan as a residue of the deportation.[35]

It is extremely difficult to assess the extent and significance of Islam, in particular Sufism, in Chechnya by the time of the Soviet collapse. In the late 1980s Chechnya was outwardly among the most politically stable parts of the country. Identifying the scale of religious identity is difficult because Islam was severely controlled and Sufi orders were suppressed by the Soviet regime. Furthermore, the orders themselves are secret and allow pragmatic deception by members to avoid detection. There were just six official mosques, staffed by no more than twenty mullahs.[36] Some have argued that the trauma of deportation strengthened religious identity and "parallel Islam," and there is a good deal of evidence of underground Sufi activity being punished by the Soviet regime.[37] Of particular note is the fact that sociological research conducted in Chechnya under the communist regime in the mid-1980s found that in the highland Vedeno district "almost half of the school children sympathize with Islam."[38] Vedeno is the native village of Shamil Basaev, who would have been about fifteen at this time, and who came to play a leading role in the Islamization of the national resistance struggle against Russia during the 1990s.

If the historicist account had purchase, one would expect some acts of violent resistance and revenge after the return from exile. Certainly, the Soviets retained a profound mistrust of Chechens. This was reflected in the exceptional arrangement of the power structure in the republic after its restoration in 1957. The conventional Soviet arrangement was carefully crafted to ensure centralized control, subdue nationalist tendencies, and guarantee Slav ethnic dominance. The norm was for a "dyarchy of native first secretary and Russian second secretary," with the latter usually in charge of cadres.[39] In Chechnya, however, as Rywkin shows from his examination of data for 1985–86, the Party setup was one of "intensive Russian control" and "political probation." Compared with a neighboring Muslim republic, Dagestan, Russians or Slavs saturated the key appointments in the party apparatus at most levels in Checheno-Ingushetia: the regional party committee (*obkom*) secretary, one of the three "third" *obkom* secretaries, seven of thirteen *obkom* bureau members, all the leading positions in *obkom* departments, about 47 percent of the *obkom* committee membership, and even the first secretaries of the major city party committees (Grozny and Gudermes), and most districts (67 percent).[40] No ethnic Chechen was appointed *obkom* secretary until 1989, when the "second" secretary Doku Zavgaev was appointed to the top post—by which time the Soviet system was disintegrating.

While the arrangement of Soviet power in the republic was exceptional, Soviet policy was typical in that the indigenous elites were cultivated and co-opted into the Soviet nomenklatura, and the main societal goal that was promoted was upward social mobility and consumerism. The ethnic Chechen nomenklatura elite, like Zavgaev, tended to be recruited from the lowlands steppe district of Nadterechny (Above-the-Terek) and its main town Znamenskoe, lying to the northwest of Grozny. Traditionally, caught between the Russians and the Murids of the highlands, the so-called "Terek" elite network learned to navigate pragmatically between the two. While this area was the last traditional stronghold of the Naqshbandiia order in the latter nineteenth century, by the 1980s it was the most secular, and Russified part of Chechnya.

Journalists have tended to see the use of symbols associated with the resistance struggles of the nineteenth century as indicative of an unbroken direct connection with that era. Dzhokhar Dudaev, the first president of secessionist Chechnya, placed a print of Mansur in his presidential office, but prior to the war he often wore a classic black felt Khrushchev-era trilby and suit, not traditional dress. Even when he wore military uniform it was of the Soviet type. Some Chechen leaders such as Dudaev's vice-president Zelimkhan Yandarbiev and his senior military commander Aslan Maskhadov, however, took to wearing the *papkha* (a traditional lambskin hat worn by Chechen elders). These were outward symbols of a sophisticated and nuanced phenomenon, and certainly at the outset in 1990–91 were attempts to build support and recognition in Chechnya by associating with traditional Chechen identity. As we shall discuss later, Dudaev's and Maskhadov's governments were initially driven by secular nationalism, and the Islamization which developed in Chechnya in the mid-1990s came about not by the design of Chechen leaders, but mainly as a result of the radicalizing experience of military conflict with Russia from 1994 on.

Conceptualizing the Meta-Conflict in Chechnya

Many conflicts are intractable because the protagonists contest the very basis and conceptualization of the issues at stake. Horowitz has termed this problem a "meta-conflict."[41] The issues are contested not only in politics or in the battlefield but also as a war of idioms. This is perhaps best encapsulated by the adage bequeathed by decades of colonial insurgencies that "one person's terrorist is another's freedom fighter." Comparative experience shows that management of the "information war" by controlling or influencing media output is widely employed by politicians to shape the conflict idiom and thus to frame mass perceptions. For an insurgency to be "criminalized" as a "terrorist" problem by one party will clearly have a formative effect on that actor's strategy, in particular on its military strategy. Idiomatic and ideological barriers are not insurmountable. Much greater complexity and difficulty arise, however, when a conflict involves disputed shared territory, or when some cleavages are reinforcing, for example religion-ethnicity-territory. In these cases the differing conceptualizations as to "what the conflict is about," and the perception that the conflict is "existential," compound the cost-benefit calculus of any exit from the conflict through negotiation and compromise, and thereby greatly narrow the parameters of any potential settlement. Similarly, what is perceived to constitute a "solution" may diverge across the parties to a conflict to such an extent that bridging through negotiations becomes almost impossible. A sensible compromise for some may be a "sell-out" to others, and a "just peace" may be derided as a "capitulation to terrorists."

There was no "meta-conflict" over Chechnya during the period leading up to the first war in 1991–94. There was a broad agreement among all the main parties to the conflict that the core issue was secession (generally referred to as "separatism" by successive Russian presidents and governments). This common conceptualization of the conflict should be distinguished from cleavages within and between the parties to the conflict. The use of the terms "Russians" and "Chechens" for the protagonists is an oversimplification. The "Russian" side of the conflict is best categorized by dividing it into pro- and anti-interventionist, or pro- and anti-militarist positions. These positions were a cross-cutting cleavage in Russian politics for much of the 1990s, as support for either was drawn from the elites to the right and left of the political spectrum.

On the "Chechen" side, the major elite cleavage was not only political (between anti- and pro-secessionists), but also regional and sociological. The lowland steppe regions of Nadterechny and Grozny were historically the most integrated into the Soviet regime, and the elites of the former area in particular were coopted into the Soviet nomenklatura and continued to exhibit a collaborationist tendency in relations with Russia after 1991. The rural highland region of the south of Chechnya is where anti-Russian sentiment has been historically strongest, but its inaccessible mountain-forest terrain is also where the retreat of state institutions as a result of the Soviet collapse was felt most. It is also ideal country for guerrillas to operate from and provides a natural heartland for insurgency.

For the Russian interventionists, the secession of Chechnya posed a threat to Russian statehood as it might undermine the territorial integrity and sovereignty of Russia, and thus it was to be prevented at all costs. To understand why the secession of Chechnya is such a problematical issue, it is important to locate it within the international norms that govern the recognition of new states, and we will discuss this aspect in detail in Chapter 6. For the Chechen secessionists, their right to self-determination and independence from the former USSR, the colonial power, and its successor state, the Russian Federation, is paramount and legitimate. The greatest test for international norms on secession arises in cases where there is no agreement between the parties and where the entity aspiring to self-determination falls outside the administrative category recognized under the legal principle of *uti posseditis juris*. Both factors apply in the case of the conflict in Chechnya. Much, then, hinges on whether the inclusion or incorporation of Chechnya into the new post-Soviet state, the Russian Federation, in January 1992 was legal, illegal, or of questionable legality. Indeed, we should distinguish between the economic, moral, and legal aspects of the right of Chechnya to self-determination.

The notion that economic self-sufficiency is an essential attribute of a state is spurious. Historically, not only have many of the states that have been accorded the right to self-determination not been self-sufficient, but they have remained heavily dependent economically on their former colonial rulers. Many states in the UN are wholly impoverished and dependent on external assistance. Moreover, in an increasingly interdependent world few states are truly economically self-sufficient. While Chechnya holds minor oil deposits and was an important oil-refining base in the Soviet era, the destruction of its economic infrastructure by almost a decade of war makes the issue of its economic attributes redundant for the medium term.

The morality of secession or self-determination for a "people" is generally determined by the strength of association between "people" and territory, whether this is an uncontested association (are there other groups residing on the territory with an equal claim?), and whether the demand is legitimated by an articulation of popular opinion, for example by elections or referendum. The morality of Chechnya's claim is contestable in two respects. Firstly, according to the 1989 USSR census, about one-quarter of the population of Chechnya were nonindigenous, mainly Russophone Slavs (see Table 1). The bulk of this substantial minority were in effect forcibly expelled between 1991 and 1993 by interethnic harassment and violence that was tolerated by the secessionist government in Chechnya. A strong case could be made that the secessionists in Chechnya attempted to strengthen their claim to self-determination by engaging in "ethnic cleansing" and that, consequently, it would be wrong of the international system to legitimize secession consolidated by such means.

Second, the idea that the current territory of Chechnya corresponds to a historical Chechen homeland is contestable because two regions of northern Chechnya bordering Russia, the Naurskii and Shelkovskii districts, were transferred from Russian jurisdiction to Chechnya under Khrushchev in 1957. Consequently, the use of a referendum by the Chechen secessionists in November 1992 to assert the moral legitimacy of the claim to secession must be qualified by the above factors.

The legal dimension of secession by Chechnya is best understood by analyzing it in the context of the collapse of the USSR. It is widely assumed that the recognition of post-Soviet states by the international system was based on the right of Union Republics to secede under Soviet law (a right established in the 1977 USSR Constitution), and on the fact that they were constituent "members" of the USSR, and thus that they were the only administrative tier that met the condition of *uti posseditis juris*. This ignores three crucial legal landmarks passed by the USSR Congress of People's Deputies during Gorbachev's *perestroika* that radically transformed the constitutional architecture of Soviet federalism: the law of 3 April 1990, "On the Procedure for Deciding Questions Concerning the Withdrawal of a Union Republic from the USSR"; the law of 10 April 1990 "On Principles of Economic Relations of the USSR, the Union and Autonomous Republics"; and the law of 26 April 1990 "On the Delimitation of Powers Between the USSR and the Subjects of Federation." These laws eradicated core features of the constitutional distinction between Union Republics and Autonomous Republics. The status of both was equalized as "subjects of the federation." At a time when some Union Republics were claiming "sovereignty" and demanding independence, including Russia under Yeltsin, and Gorbachev was desperately attempting to shore up the crumbling political order of the USSR, this law created a constitutional potential for a domino effect of secessionism as Article One of the Law of 26 April gave all subjects of the federation the right to "free self-determination."[42]

The combined effect of the laws was to make any secessionist Union Republic liable to a challenge of similar secessionist demands from its own Autonomous Republic(s). This was not a threat to the demands for independence from those republics which did not contain autonomous ethnic areas, but it was a serious potential danger for Russia, the Union Republic which contained most Autonomous Republics.[43] This kind of political maneuver is not unusual in state breakups, as the center attempts to constrain secessionism by arguing that peripheries within the secessionist unit should also have the right of secession. The constitutional changes legitimized a whole new political discourse in the USSR. The language of "delimiting powers," "power-sharing," "sovereignty," "independence," "secession," and "separatism" became widespread. The discourse of declaring "sovereignty," termed the "parade of sovereignties," was further legitimated within Russia by Yeltsin himself as means of provoking a total collapse of Gorbachev's Soviet regime. He led the RSFSR into a declaration of sovereignty from the USSR on 12 June 1990, which affirmed the "superiority" of the RSFSR constitution and RSFSR laws on the territory of the RSFSR. The declaration also framed the claim to sovereignty in language that was reminiscent of the UN Charter and international declarations on decolonization, notably by recalling the "right of all peoples" to sovereignty.[44] During the summer of 1990 Yeltsin conducted a series of lightning political tours across Russia. In the key ethnic republics he incited the leaderships to push for their sovereignty, even exhorting the leadership of Bashkortostan in August to "take as much power as you can swallow." It was soon evident, however, that there were different conceptions of what "sovereignty," "independence," and "self-determination" meant, whether for Yeltsin, the secessionist republics, or the international system.[45]

Whether or not Gorbachev deliberately reconfigured the nature of the federal bargain in the USSR through the new laws as a kind of doomsday weapon of mutual assured destruction for his confrontation with Yeltsin, he certainly envisaged that this would be the outcome of any attempt by Yeltsin to breakup the USSR. According to his memoirs, Gorbachev told Yeltsin at this time: "Remember, our state is held together by two rings. One is the USSR, the other is the Russian Federation. If the first is broken, problems for the other will follow."[46] It is evident that the tenor given by Gorbachev to the final efforts to refederalize the USSR during the first half of 1991 was characterized by a significant degree of ethnic Russian chauvinism that did not make his schemes to shore up the USSR any more attractive to the leaders of the non-Russian republics. His consistent theme was that "a strong Russian Federation is the foundation of a strong Union federation."[47] This emphasis within the Russian elite on the need for a "strong state" was carried over into the discussion about the nature of the Russian Federation after the collapse of the USSR. Yeltsin and his supporters were unwilling to assist Gorbachev to secure the strong Soviet state, but they were determined to retain the idea for the remaking of Russia.

A draft statement of principles on a new Union treaty to provide for a much looser confederation was agreed between Gorbachev and leaders of nine Union Republics in the so-called "nine plus one" meeting at the official Soviet leader's residence outside Moscow at Novo-Ogarevo on 23 April 1991.[48] The negotiations over the wording were immensely intricate, and the draft Union treaty was littered with ambiguities.[49] The constitutional framework, however, remained under discussion by Gorbachev, the leaders of the nine, and the leaders of the former autonomous republics (now all lumped together as the "republics"), until late July. The key question was how to regulate the relations among the three constituent units of the new Union: the Union government, the states that were former Union Republics, and the states which were former autonomous republics. Three main combinations or "trees" were debated as options: first, a treaty (agreement) plus the constitution of the republic in which the former autonomous republic was located; second, a treaty (agreement) plus the constitutions of both former Union republic and former autonomous republic plus the Union constitution; third, a treaty (agreement) plus the Union constitution. Gorbachev pushed for the third option as this would entrench the constitutional superiority of the Union level, while the Union republics (especially Russia) pushed for the first option, as this would subordinate the former autonomous republics to their constitutional order.[50]

A Nation-Building Conflict

The mobilization of an ethnic Chechen nationalism fell within a pattern of secular nationalist mobilization across the Soviet Union in response to Gorbachev's perestroika. When the policy of Glasnost' began to take hold in late 1986, thousands of so-called "informal groups" sprang up across the country, mobilized around a great diversity of political, economic, social and cultural issues. Intellectuals played a leading role in this movement. In Chechnya the membership of the academic association "Kavkaz" spawned dozens of such groups. In the aftermath of the Chernobyl' disaster, a pattern emerged for nationalist groups to mobilize under the cover of environmental issues. This so-called "eco-nationalism" became the battering ram for nationalists in Ukraine and the Baltic republics to attack the CPSU and demand democratization.[51] Similarly, in Chechnya the first significant political mobilization occurred around an environmental issue—protests against the proposed construction of a biochemical plant near the second main city of Chechnya, Gudermes, in 1987–88. As the politically charged atmosphere of impending revolution spread across the USSR in 1988–91, "informal groups" mutated and coalesced into "Popular Fronts," beginning with those of the Baltic republics which demanded "sovereignty." In Chechnya a secessionist movement began to assert itself through a Popular Front established in the summer of 1988.[52]

Pragmatic and cautious nomenklatura leaders came under increasing pressure from nationalist moderates and radicals, often led by intellectuals and academics, and bankrolled by local business leaders, to accelerate the drive for independence. Often the cleavage was generational as well as ideological. In Checheno-Ingushetia the nationalist pressure came from young radicals like Zelimkhan Yandarbiev, a teacher and poet who was a member of the Russian Writers' Union. Yandarbiev describes well how

students from different parts of the USSR mixed in the nationalist political ferment in Moscow's academic institutions in the late 1980s, forging
contacts that would later be drawn on when these young radical elites
were members of the new nationalist governments of independent states
after 1991. The influence of the democratic nationalism of the Popular
Fronts in the Baltic republics appears to have strongly influenced Yandarbiev, and, as we shall discuss later, Dudaev also.

Yandarbiev was known as an ideologist for the unity of Caucasian peoples and became the leader of the small radical nationalist Bart (Unity)
Party, which he and other young radical nationalists formed in July 1989.
The move came quickly in the wake of some history-making events in the
USSR, with Lithuania's declaration of state sovereignty in May 1989 and
the walk-out by most Baltic delegates at the session of the USSR Congress
of People's Deputies in June. These events started the rupture in Gorbachev's plans for a reformed USSR, and inspired the cause of national self-
determination across the USSR. The mutual support network of links
between these movements was such that the first three issues of Bart's
newspaper were printed in Riga by the Latvian Popular Front.[53] Contacts
were forged with nationalists across the Caucasus when Bart delegates
attended the first Congress of Mountain Peoples of the Caucasus in late
August 1989. Yandarbiev's activism and intellectually grounded form of
secular nationalism of this period would later mutate into a radical form
of Islamism as a result of the conflict with Russia—a personal development
that is quite evident from the content of the two collections of writings
that he published: the first mostly drawn from works written or published
in 1989–92, and the second from works written or published in 1994–
95.[54] In this early period, however, he was recognized as a leading intellectual figure among the secular nationalist movements in the Caucasus,
and as a key figure in the propagation of the idea of "Caucasian" solidarity against Russian imperialism.[55]

As in many other parts of Russia, the movement for "sovereignty" gathered pace in Chechnya around a confusion of motives and goals. On the
one hand, as the CPSU imploded, the ethnic Chechen section of the
Soviet nomenklatura in the republic attempted to redistribute power and
resources in their favor by falling in line behind calls for "sovereignty"
(*suverenitet*) or "self-rule" (*samostoiatel'nost'*), both Soviet and Russian constitutional terms that were ambiguous as to whether the final intent was
full independence. The nationalists, on the other hand, demanded "independence" (*nezavisimost'*), which was clearly understood as meaning secession and recognition as an independent state. The indigenous Soviet
leaders of Checheno-Ingushetia, under regional party secretary Doku
Zavgaev, were essentially unionists. Slav domination of the key authority
positions in Chechnya had been pervasive to the extent that no ethnic

Chechen had ever held the top position, the party secretary. Zavgaev, the first ethnic Chechen to hold the post of party secretary, was only appointed in June 1989, though he had been second secretary for fifteen years. Appointed in the early 1970s as the Brezhnev system of bureaucratic corporatism and corruption was consolidated, Zavgaev presided over the extensive interests of the Nadterechny network of Chechens. The fact that Checheno-Ingushetia was among the last areas in the USSR to join Yeltsin's "parade of sovereignties" and issue a declaration on "State Sovereignty" was a reflection of the conservatism of its nomenklatura and the deep divisions within Chechnya over how the declaration should be formulated. As we shall see, the final more radical form of the declaration was an indication of the weakness of the Zavgaev group.

Yandarbiev intensified the pressure on Zavgaev in early 1990. At that time the CPSU was officially the only legal party in the USSR (Gorbachev would only abandon the CPSU monopoly in March, after a massive public demonstration in Moscow). Yandarbiev challenged Zavgaev by establishing the Vainakh Democratic Party (VDP) in February 1990, with its primary goal of independence for Chechnya openly declared. At a time when democratization was accelerating in Soviet politics, the Zavgaev leadership was forced to respond to the VDP's radical nationalist agenda by moving in a nationalist direction. It was for this reason that the declaration on sovereignty was delayed, and ultimately assumed a more radical character.

In an attempt to subordinate the burgeoning nationalist movement in Chechnya, the Zavgaev leadership agreed to the convocation of the first Chechen National Congress (CNC) on 23–26 November 1990. About 1,000 Chechens, and several members of the Chechen diaspora in Turkey and Jordan attended the gathering in Grozny. The event marked the beginning of what became known as the "Chechen Revolution," for the CNC became the de facto umbrella movement for Chechen independence, combining mainstream secular nationalists and religious nationalist groups. Zavgaev hoped to steer the CNC indirectly and ensured that its organizing committee was led by a moderate, Lechi Umkaev. Yandarbiev and a number of close associates (including Movladi Udugov and Sait-Khassan Abumuslimov), with the financial support of Yaragi Mamodaev, a leading Chechen state manager and businessman with interests in construction and oil, quickly pushed the VDP to the front of a radical takeover of the CNC.[56]

The nationalist radicalization of the CNC culminated in pressure on the Supreme Soviet of the Chechen-Ingush Republic to adopt a declaration on "State Sovereignty," on 27 November 1990. This declaration was, in fact, one of the last in the so-called "parade of sovereignties," where most of Russia's autonomous republics declared their sovereignty, though nearly all did so with the proviso that they remained "within the RSFSR." Only Checheno-Ingushetia and Tatarstan omitted the proviso, though the use of the term "sovereign" or "self-rule" in Russian rather than the term "independent" still framed the declaration within a Soviet constitutional order and implied a negotiability over status.[57] The emphasis on "self-determination" (*samoopredeleniia*) in Article 1 of the declaration by the "Chechen Republic Nokhchi-cho," however, indicated a more assertive intent for true independence informed by international norms on anti-colonialism : "The Chechen-Ingush Republic is a sovereign state, created as a result of the self-determination of the Chechen and Ingush peoples." No mention was made of the RSFSR.[58]

The congress set out a number of grievances against Soviet (Russian) rule, including discrimination and under-representation in political, economic, and cultural authority structures. The resolution also addressed ethnoterritorial questions within Chechnya and between Chechnya and the neighboring republics. The bulk of Checheno-Ingushetia was declared to be the "Chechen Republic," while two western *raions* became the Republic of Ingushetia. An intention was stated to sign a new federal treaty with the USSR, but the declaration set out several conditions. The conditions included equal terms with the Union Republics, the return of disputed territories from North Ossetia (Prigorodny *raion*, and the right bank of Vladikavkaz), and the return of the territory of the Aukhov Chechens, termed Akkintsy in Russian, which were part of Dagestan—territories lost after the deportation in 1944. The dilution of the ethnic purity of the population of Chechnya was to be ended by controls on non-Chechen immigration. Provisions were made for protecting and promoting the Chechen language and culture and Islam. The USSR was cited for its "act of genocide" against the Chechen and Ingush, and other peoples, and the declaration demanded economic compensation and restitution for losses incurred during the Stalinist deportation.

The declaration of sovereignty and the resolution of the congress have been badly misread by previous analysts. Tishkov has described them as demonstrating the "aggressive nationalism" of the Chechens. Gall and de Waal underappreciate the importance of the declaration by simply noting that it was "fashionable" for the time and that the "local leadership had managed to keep the challenge to Moscow within official channels." In fact, the declaration set out a radical program for national independence, and moreover, like the declarations by the Baltic republics, focused on the historical injustice perpetrated by the Soviet Union and Russia as a foundation for the moral legitimacy of the claim to independence. On 1 December 1990 Chechnya's most famous Soviet military officer, Soviet air force Major-General Dzhokar Dudaev, was elected chairman of the executive committee of the congress, and hesitantly accepted. Although he was still a serving military officer, this was not an unusual occurrence in the USSR at this time. Dudaev was an outsider to both the local Soviet elite and the nationalist opposition networks in the republic, and faced an immense task of building unity among the nationalists.[59] Although he was born in Chechnya in 1944, just prior to the violent Soviet deportation, he was raised in Kazakhstan and never lived in Chechnya until 1990 at the age of forty-six. He retained a working knowledge of the Chechen language, but there is no evidence that he had a strong Chechen identity, and his primary language of communication was Russian. He married a Russian military officer's daughter, and was thoroughly Sovietized. As part of his military career he joined the CPSU in 1966. He had a distinguished military service, including bombing Islamic fundamentalists in Afghanistan in the 1980s, for which he was awarded the Order of the Red Star and the Order of the Red Banner. He appears to have experienced a belated but genuine conversion to nationalism and the idea of an independent Chechnya as a result of his observations of the rise of the Estonian nationalist Popular Front while he was based in Tartu. [60]

Tartu is Estonia's second largest city and one of Europe's oldest university towns, and was a center of the Estonian national revival in the mid-1980s. Estonian acquaintances of Dudaev report that his national consciousness as a Chechen seemed to be awakened by his experience of living amid the nationalist resurgence in Tartu. As the senior Soviet military commander in the district, he was ex officio a member of the city party executive committee (*gorkombiuro*), which would have brought him into close contact with local and national politics. It is significant to note that the Baltic Popular Fronts involved the mass mobilization of support around secular nationalism and a commitment to peaceful moral pressure on the Soviet authorities based on the legitimacy of the claim to national independence as an expression of democracy.

It has been argued that Dudaev was elected precisely because as an outsider he was a "good compromise candidate" who, it was hoped, would act to mediate and "balance interests" between the rival "clans" in Chechnya.[61] The rise of Dudaev, however, was Yandarbiev's master stroke and had nothing to do with "clans." Yandarbiev had visited Dudaev in Tartu to encourage him to accept the leadership of the nationalist movement for good logical reasons. Dudaev combined a number of remarkable qualities that made him an ideal choice as leader. Although small in physique, he had immense professional stature. With his military bearing and training, he would bring strong leadership, charisma, respectability, discipline and organizational skills to the nationalist movement. Most important, his speech at the congress had been inspirational and demonstrated his nationalist credentials. Dudaev would provide an authoritative and charismatic voice for the radical nationalist agenda of independence. Shortly afterward Dudaev's fame spread across the USSR, when in January 1991, as commander of the Soviet air force base at Tartu, he openly refused to cooperate with Gorbachev's attempt to deploy Soviet special forces for a crackdown on the Baltic Popular Front nationalists by closing off Estonian airspace, and assisted Yeltsin's security during the Russian president's visit to Tallinn.[62]

The growing chaos and weakness at the central government level in Moscow, as Gorbachev and Yeltsin battled for authority, encouraged the secessionists. Dudaev, however, did not retire from his commission and only returned permanently to Grozny to lead the executive committee of the CNC in March 1991. The struggle in Chechnya was by then polarized into an intra-Chechen competition for power between the unionist Chechen nomenklatura elite under Zavgaev and the nationalist secessionists.[63] This was a struggle about competing visions of Chechen nation-building. The unionist forces under Zavgaev favored the reintegration of Chechnya into either a reconstituted USSR or, failing that, a reformed Russian Federation. The nationalists aspired to self-determination and independence. The confrontation was dominated at the time by key aspects of constitutional legality. Zavgaev was pressured by the nationalists to keep Checheno-Ingushetia from participating in any constitutional acts that would undermine the assertion of secession. For example, he kept Checheno-Ingushetia from participating in the March 1991 all-union referendum on the existence of the USSR. Zavgaev, however, attempted to zigzag between the nationalists and Russian pressure.

Zavgaev betrayed his nomenklatura instincts for a reconstituted USSR by his willingness to sign on to the new Union treaty agreed at Novo-Ogarevo in July 1991 by Gorbachev and the leaders of the republics. This provoked outrage among the nationalists. Zavgaev's views are clear from his fawning statement to the leaders gathered at Novo-Ogarevo in late July 1991: "Now concerning the Russian Federation. We are all in favor, with both hands raised. We are committed Russian citizens and will never allow the collapse of the Russian Federation."[64] Zavgaev also compromised the claim to secession by allowing Checheno-Ingushetia to participate in the RSFSR presidential election of June 1991 (and ensuring a massive rigged vote for Yeltsin). Zavgaev came to be regarded widely in Chechnya as out of touch with the rapidly developing popular mood in the republic and as a Russian stooge. It was a common phenomenon in the rapidly changing political landscape of the period for conservative communists to be overwhelmed by the tide of nationalism that was sweeping away communism.

Dudaev accelerated the radicalization of the nationalist movement. In May 1991, on the basis of the declaration of sovereignty, he dissolved the Zavgaev-dominated Chechen-Ingush Supreme Soviet and declared the executive committee of the CNC to be the only legitimate provisional government in Chechnya until elections could be held. At the second congress of the CNC held in late June- early July 1991 Dudaev led a radical rout of the moderate nationalists. A new "Common National Congress of the Chechen People" (OKChN) was established, with Dudaev as chairman, supported by three deputy chairmen, two from the Vainakh Democratic Party (Yusup Soslambekov and Yandarbiev) and the third, professor Khusein Akhmadov, a moderate academic. With hindsight based on much later developments, some scholars have erroneously described Dudaev's leadership at this juncture as a "coterie of extremists" who advocated "the creation of an Islamic state."[65]

The evidence demonstrates that Dudaev, Yandarbiev, and other nationalist leaders were driven by a secular vision of nation-state building; beyond peripheral Islamic symbolism, such as the occasional cries of "Allah Akhbar!" there was no significant Islamic content to the nationalist drive for independence at this stage. In contrast, Dudaev inspired Chechen nationalism with a passionate rejection of the prospect of "colonial freedom" that loomed under Zavgaev, or any other "hybrid" version of sovereignty, and demanded a treaty with Russia that would legally recognize Chechnya's national independence. Whereas Chechnya's declaration of sovereignty of November 1990 had simply not included a proviso that its "sovereignty" was "within" the RSFSR, as was the norm at that time, the OKChN now approved a declaration that made the claim to independence from the USSR *and* the RSFSR explicit. The executive committee of the OKChN, headed by Dudaev, declared itself the only legal government of Chechnya (and named the new republic Nokhchi-cho). While Dudaev relied heavily at this time on the support of Beslan Gantemirov, a former Moscow Mafia boss turned leader of the "Islamic Path" party, whose militia formed a hard core of the new armed National Guard, this was far from being an Islamic party. In fact, of 46 political parties and movements identified by Muzaev at this time in Chechnya, only 3 were self-declared "Islamic" in orientation, and all of these had been dissolved by 1993, including Islamic Path.[66] Gantemirov was more of a freebooting criminal warlord interested in the opportunistic material gains that would come from overthrowing the Zavgaev regime.[67] Thereafter, demonstrations against the Zavgaev leadership became a daily occurrence in front of the main Soviet administration building that dominated the center of Grozny and was later to become Dudaev's presidential headquarters.

The opportunity to strike a terminal blow at Zavgaev's regime came during the failed coup by pro-Soviet conservative forces in Moscow in August 1991. The coup was timed to stop the ratification of the new Union treaty agreed at Novo-Ogarevo. Zavgaev, in Moscow at the time, like many Soviet apparatchiki, did not declare his support until the outcome was certain. His wavering in choosing sides irretrievably lost him the confidence of Yeltsin. The OKChN orchestrated demonstrations in Grozny and launched a nationalist uprising against the Zavgaev administration. The seizure of power by Dudaev and the OKChN occurred with the connivance of Yeltsin's "democrats," including his main ally at that time, the parliamentary speaker Ruslan Khasbulatov (also an ethnic Chechen). Yeltsin declared a state emergency in Chechnya and ordered local Russian military garrisons to arm and support the rebel forces.[68] Leading democrats from Yeltsin's administration, including Gennadii Burbulis and Khasbulatov, visited Chechnya to ensure that Zavgaev resigned and that there was a peaceful transfer of power from the Supreme Soviet to an OKChN-dominated Provisional Supreme Council.[69]

The Yeltsin administration that consolidated its power after the August coup was more concerned initially with reinforcing its authority internally over the Russian regions, and subsequently with economic reform, than with reasserting Russian sovereignty over secessionist republics such as Chechnya. Russia's historic involvement and perceptions of its immediate strategic security and economic interests in the North and South Caucasus region, however, made interference in Chechnya inevitable. In practice, the Autonomous Republic of Checheno-Ingushetia began to split into its two constituent parts in late 1991, as the elite in Ingushetia under General Ruslan Aushev preferred integration with the Russian Federation.

Reflecting the international zeitgeist of late 1991, as nationalist movements in the USSR and Yugoslavia sought to legitimize the assertion of independence through the ballot box, Dudaev and the OKChN called presidential and parliamentary elections in Chechnya in October 1991. They considered the elections to be a referendum on independence. The elections were far from being free and fair, and were disputed amid allegations of intimidation and vote-rigging; Dudaev and the OKChN triumphed. According to official Chechen sources Dudaev was elected president of Chechnya with 85 percent of the vote on a 77 percent turnout, and even allowing for vote-rigging, most observers accepted that Dudaev was the clear winner.[70] Dudaev's first decrees as president on 1 November 1991 were to formally declare independence for the "Chechen Republic of Ichkeria" (Ichkeria is an ancient Chechen name for the mountainous part of what is now Chechnya) and to give the Chechen and Russian languages equal status as official languages. In his public statements, Dudaev went beyond the normal rhetoric of the politics of the period and now stressed that he the Chechen people had expressed their "will for self-determination and freedom" and now sought "independence" (*nezavisimost'*), though he made this subject to a referendum.[71] He refused to negotiate with Russia unless it recognized him as president. The Russian parliament declared the elections illegal and void, and on 7 November

Yeltsin issued a decree to impose a "state of emergency" in Chechnya. Vice-President Aleksandr Rutskoi, Yeltsin's main emissary to Grozny in this period, helped turn Russian policy against Dudaev. One would think that Rutskoi, a former Soviet air force officer like Dudaev, would have been well positioned to reach an accommodation with Dudaev. On the contrary, it was he who first framed the Chechen "national revolution" as a power-grab by "criminals," warning that what was developing in Chechnya "was nothing else but banditism."[72] This idiom resonated easily in the Russian political elite and public opinion given their racist views of Chechens.

The "explosive" situation pushed the issue of Chechnya to the top of the political agenda. Gorbachev, who now saw his legislation on secession come to life, but whose power was now weakening, urged both sides to engage in dialogue.[73] Russia's leaders made the fatal mistake, at this stage, of seriously underestimating the capability of their own military to "restore order" in Chechnya, Dudaev's commitment to secession, even if it meant a military confrontation with Russia, and both the scale of Dudaev's popular support and the strength of Chechen military forces under his command. As former Soviet military commanders, Dudaev and his chief military advisor, former Soviet artillery colonel Aslan Maskhadov, were acutely aware of the need to quickly militarize Chechnya by arming and training a military force of volunteers which could resist any attempt by the Yeltsin government to use force to reclaim Russian sovereignty over Chechnya. If Chechnya's geographic location on the frontier with Georgia enhanced the capacity to assert independence, its defense required the speedy buildup of a military capability. The fact that Chechnya was a key regional base for Soviet military stockpiles made access to arms on a large scale a possibility.

As Tishkov has noted, "without arms, one cannot organize a war."[74] In particular, training in the use of weapons, and access to and the dispersion of small arms and explosives is critical for any conflict escalation. Paradoxically, the militarization of Chechnya was assisted by Russia. In September–October 1991, as the Soviet Union disintegrated into chaos, the small contingent of Soviet military forces in Chechnya was largely confined to barracks. During October 1991 the OKChN ordered the mobilization of all males of fighting age (between fifteen and fifty-five) into a National Guard. Over the next months military hardware and munitions stocks were formally transferred, illicitly sold, or simply seized from the Russian garrison by Chechen armed groups. According to later reports by officers, including the garrison commander and an emissary of Grachev's, when Dudaev ordered the garrison to withdraw "immediately" from Chechnya on 31 May, the orders from Moscow were for a speedy withdrawal leaving weapons stocks. It later transpired that what was handed over to the Chechens was sufficient for a small army. Some officers have claimed that Grachev (who was acquainted with Dudaev from the Afghanistan War) had a written agreement with Dudaev to split the weapons stocks on a 50:50 basis, though Grachev has denied this.[75] According to official sources the haul included 40,000 automatic weapons and machine guns, 153 pieces of heavy artillery and mortars, 42 tanks, 18 "Grad" vehicle-mounted rocket launchers, 55 armored personnel carriers, 130,000 hand grenades, 240 training aircraft, 5 fighter aircraft, and 2 military helicopters.[76] Significantly, the Chechen forces took possession of hundreds of infantry anti-tank weapons, including at least a hundred RPG-7 hand-held antitank launchers. These were to have a crucial impact on the military campaign.[77] Moreover, it is generally acknowledged that, although Russian governmental authority was removed from the republic, the secessionist government of Dudaev retained close contacts with corrupt elements in the Russian military command, which facilitated a range of illicit activities, including oil sales, trans-shipment of Western goods into Russia, drug trafficking, and, most important from the viewpoint of Dudaev, arms trading. Western journalists reported how Grozny developed an open arms bazaar at this time.[78]

The underestimation of Dudaev by Yeltsin was demonstrated on November 8–9, 1991 when there was the first of several botched attempts at military intervention in Chechnya by Russian forces. A small force (just over 600 men) of lightly armed interior ministry troops was flown into Khankala military airport outside Grozny. The force was surrounded, captured, disarmed and compelled to withdraw without a fight in humiliating fashion on buses escorted by the Chechen National Guard. The Russian parliament, under the leadership of Khasbulatov, blocked Yeltsin's decree on the intervention, and Gorbachev, in one of his last authoritative acts as Soviet president, declared it illegal and ordered the security forces not to cooperate. The Soviet ministry of internal affairs, ministry of defense, and KGB were in an administrative limbo between the rise of an independent Russia and the decline of the Soviet Union, and refused to comply with Yeltsin's orders. Meanwhile, the threat of invasion led to a mass demonstration of popular support for Dudaev on the "Freedom Square" in central Grozny. Dudaev was furious at Yeltsin's decree, calling it an "act of state terrorism." He declared a "state of war" and threatened that Moscow would be turned into a "disaster zone," and that he might resort to the use of "terrorist acts" against Russia, even against nuclear power stations.[79] His threat was almost immediately given effect by the hijacking of a Russian passenger airliner from the airport of Mineral'nye Vody in the neighboring Stavropol Krai by a group of Chechens led by Shamil Basaev. The plane was flown to Turkey, where Basaev and his men turned it over to the Turkish authorities and were later released to return to Chechnya as heroes. It was the first notable act of terrorism in the conflict.[80]

The embarrassment for Yeltsin was magnified by the fact that the botched intervention came immediately in the wake of his being given extraordinary decree powers to advance reform by the Russian parliament on 2 November. Not for the first time, Yeltsin's hubris may have led him to overestimate his power. The Russian and international media reported on much of the episode, and footage was shown not only on Russian television, but also internationally. In many circles within and outside Russia, the Chechnya question was being described as a "test of Russia's imperial will," with any hint of revanchism being criticized.[81] It was the first indication that propaganda would be a critical tool in the conflict, and the Chechens demonstrated that they were masters of the art of media manipulation. After the defeat of this first military intervention, Yeltsin escalated a campaign to undermine Dudaev's authority in Chechnya, which was characterized by a twin-track strategy alternating between coercion and isolation by blockade. Yeltsin, following Rutskoi, popularized the demonization of Dudaev and the Chechen government among the Russian political class generally, and the Russian mass media in particular. The labels "criminal" or "terrorist" were generally employed to refer to Dudaev, and Chechnya was branded a "bandit state." Dudaev and his ministers in turn increasingly embedded their anti-Russia rhetoric in a historical narrative of resistance to Russian "colonizers," though they too often succumbed to racist outbursts against Russians, often likening them to "Nazis."[82] Once he had removed Gorbachev from the scene in December 1991, Yeltsin turned to reorganizing the power ministries under his control. The strategy now was to organize and arm a proxy force of anti-Dudaev Chechens under former communist party leaders in the Nadterechny area, headed by Umar Avturkhanov. Military attempts to destabilize Dudaev's government from within, however, were unsuccessful.

Dudaev kept the nationalist leadership of Chechnya focused on the constitutional legality of secession. In numerous interviews to Russian and other foreign journalists at this time, Dudaev held that the USSR laws passed in April 1990 established the constitutional right of an Autonomous Republic to decide its own fate, whether it was to refuse to sign up to Gorbachev's draft new Union treaty of May 1991, or to secede from the USSR in circumstances when this state was already in the process of disintegration, as was the case after the August 1991 coup. In the absence of a constitutional ratification of the new Union treaty (which Zavgaev had signed, but the ratification of which was preempted by the August coup), Chechnya remained de jure outside the USSR within the terms of constitutional law. After his election as president, Dudaev pushed through a number of radical reforms to complete the repatriation of Chechnya's sovereignty. By the end of November 1991, all federal property in Chechnya had been nationalized, including the branch of the Central Bank, and all representatives of Chechnya in Russian Federation bodies were ordered to return home. The new parliament established its budgetary independence by stopping payments of taxes and revenues to the Russian federal budget, though state subsidies and state transfers of pensions and social payments were still accepted. Russia, for its part, was reluctant to terminate the transfers, since this would compromise its claim to sovereignty over Chechnya.

A political stand-off ensued that could be settled only by force or negotiation. The refusal of the international system to recognize Chechnya's secession meant ignoring the changes in the Soviet constitutional order adopted under Gorbachev. The collapse of the USSR was treated, in effect, as a case of decolonization that was to be informed by the innate conservatism of the principle of *uti posseditis*. The conservatism was reinforced by the predominance of Western interests in shoring up the Yeltsin regime to prevent instability in Russia, and policy caution in the wake of the Soviet collapse. In effect, the potential for international influences on the early negotiation of a peaceful resolution to the question of Chechnya were sacrificed to the national interests of Western governments in supporting the reformists under Yeltsin and demarcating Chechnya as an "internal" matter for Russia.

Chapter 2

Russia's Refederalization and Chechnya's Secession

The survival of the Russian Federation after the fall of communism is an exceptional case since all the other federal communist states failed to refederalize and collapsed. The Soviet Union dissolved suddenly and chaotically, Czechoslovakia had a peacefully negotiated disassociation, and Yugoslavia was ruptured by civil war. This pattern suggests that the combination of multiethnicity, federal state, and democratizing transition is a highly unstable compound. The Russian Federation exhibits many of the characteristics that contributed to the collapse of the Soviet Union: immense size, administrative and ethnic complexity, and a built-in territorialization and institutionalization of ethnicity in its federal structure. Theories of communist-type federations generally view them as not conducive to state stability, especially during political and economic crisis or transition.[1] In conditions of serious political instability or crisis at the center, the organization of the state system itself threatens a wholesale disintegration of the state along its own established administrative ethnoterritorial fissures. For these reasons there was much debate in the 1990s as to whether Russia could "survive" or would "go the way of the USSR."

Several scholarly accounts have described the Yeltsin-led "parade of sovereignties" that peaked in 1991 as a kind of "ethnic" revival, viewing it in similar terms to the mobilization of the nested-doll (*matreskha*) nationalism that led to the collapse of the USSR.[2] While it is certainly true that the demands for "sovereignty" from Russia's regions and republics were magnified by contagion effects from the revolutions in Eastern Europe and the "war of sovereignties" in the USSR in 1989–90, including Russia itself, obviously, time has revealed that the "ethnic" revival account of a trend to disintegration in Russia during the 1990s was overstated and flawed.

The refashioning of the Russian Federation beginning in early 1992 was founded on its administrative-territorial framework of "institutionalized multinationality" inherited from the RSFSR and USSR. At the beginning of 1992, of the eighty-eight constituent units (excluding Chechnya) in the Russian Federation, twenty were nominally ethnic "sovereign republics" and sixty-eight were overwhelmingly ethnic Russian populated regions.

While all the RSFSR's ethnic republics followed Yeltsin's lead in declaring their independence from the USSR in the so-called "parade of sovereignties" during the summer and autumn of 1990, all but two declared themselves sovereign "within the RSFSR." The two exceptions were the republics of Checheno-Ingushetia and Tatarstan, which viewed their status as independent states. Both of these republics persisted with their claims to sovereignty after the break-up of the Soviet Union in December 1991. Both republics refused to rejoin the Russian Federation. Neither republic participated in the negotiations or signed the Federal Treaty of March 1992, which refederalized Russia. Neither republic recognized the authority of the Russian president. Neither republic participated in the Russian parliament or other governing bodies, nor did they hold elections to the new Duma or conduct the constitutional referendum in December 1993.[3] In effect, these republics acted as if they were independent states outside the jurisdiction of Russia, akin to the other newly independent states that formerly had been Union republics. On the other hand, and somewhat undermining their claim to independence, both republics continued to operate within Russia's fiscal federal system by accepting subventions from the Russian budget, for example, to pay government salaries and pensions, though without transferring tax and other federal revenues to Moscow.

Within a few years Tatarstan was driven to negotiate a political compromise with Yeltsin, and in February 1994 it signed a bilateral power-sharing treaty that qualified its status as one of "association" with Russia, and gave it extensive exceptional powers compared with other units of the Russian Federation. Over the next three years there was a flood of bilateral treaties between Yeltsin and the leaders of the republics and regions, but only the handful of "early" treaties signed in 1994–5 devolved substantial political and economic powers. Yeltsin's policy compromised the symmetric federalism of the 1993 constitution, but by returning to a modified form of the asymmetric federalism of the Federal Treaty of 1992 he stabilized federal relations.[4] The question is why a similar political instrument was not successfully negotiated with Chechnya as the basis for an accommodation. Was this a result of particular conditions that favored secessionism in Chechnya and not elsewhere in the Russian Federation? Can it be explained by the historicists' focus on the zero-sum primordial calculations of ethnic conflict entrepreneurs in Russia and Chechnya?

Contrary to the assumptions of many political scientists, Russia's territorialized ethnofederal structure has not been generally politically destabilizing. The fundamental measure of political stability in any state is maintenance of its territorial integrity, and in a federal state this is generally understood as the management of "secession potential."[5] By this measure the Russian Federation has been very successful. The predicted break-up of Russia did not occur. A claim to secession was asserted in only two ethnic republics, Chechnya and Tatarstan. Only in Chechnya did the assertion of secession led to violent armed conflict. How can we explain the political stability of the Russian Federation and Chechnya's exceptionalism?

Obviously, to argue that the limited scale of secession potential was a factor in the noncollapse of Russia would be to present a circular logic. Nevertheless, the question remains why, in a state with thirty-nine significant ethnic minorities and twenty-one ethnically designated constituent units, has secession potential been vigorously asserted by just two, and violently by only one. Furthermore, why did the federal government take such a radically differentiated policy approach to the management of these two cases? In the case of Tatarstan, the federal government initiated a bargaining process, with negotiations proceeding for three years and including the direct involvement of the president, which led to an institutionalized settlement in a bilateral treaty that gave a wide level of autonomy to Tatarstan. In the case of Chechnya, Yeltsin refused to engage directly with the Chechen leadership, and presided over a disastrous policy of confrontation that led to war in 1994–96.

The exceptionalism of the conflict in Chechnya must be explained in the first instance by reference to structural and political characteristics that would make it the most extreme test case for ethnic conflict potential in the Russian Federation, while also these conditions acted generally to constrain ethnic nationalism elsewhere in the Russian Federation. The institutional engineering of a refederalization of Russia was also critical to its noncollapse and, moreover, this refederalization was flexibly arranged to allow for different degrees and forms of asymmetric federal power-sharing. Asymmetric federalism provided an institutional mechanism to defuse and manage some of the more assertive claims to power, such as in Tatarstan. Federal stability was also undoubtedly maintained by other institutional choices made as part of Russia's broader attempt at transition to democracy after 1991. In particular, refederalization was correlated with the rise of a strong presidency under Boris Yeltsin. Let us explore further how the informal and patrimonial character of the Yeltsin presidency assisted an accommodation with Tatarstan, but hindered one with Chechnya.

Structural Constraints on Secession

Secession potential in Russia has been softened by five types of constraints. Four of these were internal features of the Russian state: demographic composition, resource interdependencies, spatial location, and historical assimilation. The fifth was an external constraint: the nonrecognition of secession by the international system (this factor is discussed in Chapter 6).

DEMOGRAPHIC COMPOSITION

One of the most potent conditions for separatism is the presence of a territorially concentrated and dissatisfied minority group. Although Russia's titular ethnic republics account for 29 percent of the territory of the federation, this spatial significance is not matched by demographic presence. An important force for territorial cohesion in Russia is the high level and spatial spread of Russian ethnic homogeneity across almost all the federal units. At the time of the 1989 USSR census, Russians constituted a bare majority (50.8 percent) of the USSR's 286.7 million population. In contrast, in the RSFSR (renamed the Russian Federation on 1 January 1992) ethnic Russians were an overwhelming majority (81.5 percent) of a population of about 147 million. The multiethnic demographic complexity of Russia was evident from the 1989 USSR census, which identified 101 ethnic groups in the state, probably an underestimate. Although many ethnic groups numbered fewer than 5,000, the census revealed that there were 39 major ethnic groups numbering more than 100,000.[6]

According to the Soviet census of 1989, the then RSFSR contained thirty-one subjects with a titular ethnic designation (16 Autonomous Soviet Socialist Republics, 5 Autonomous Oblasts [regions], and 10 Autonomous Okrugs [districts]).[7] One would imagine that this significant number of diverse minorities would greatly complicate federal nationalities policy and constitute strong secession potential, particular given the standard accounts of the destabilizing effects of "institutionalized multinationality." This demographic structure, however, was subject to a crucial moderating factor. It is not simple numerical superiority as a proportion of the total demographic balance of the Russian Federation that makes ethnic Russian homogeneity a limiting constraint on secession potential, but the spread and strength of the ethnic Russian population throughout the vast majority of the eighty-nine federal subjects. The spatial spread of ethnic Russians is not a recent phenomenon but occurred as a historically gradual development linked to settler-colonialism during Russian imperial expansion from the mid-sixteenth century, and the Tsarist and Soviet modernization policies from the late nineteenth century onward. While the spread and strength of ethnic Russian homogeneity is an important factor, it is not a sufficient explanation. It is not unusual, after all, for cases of national and ethnic conflicts to arise where a titular homeland group feels threatened, discriminated against, or "swamped" by local majorities of settler-colonists.

Only four of these ethnically designated units (North Ossetia-Alania,

Tuva, Checheno-Ingushetia, and Chuvashia), all of them autonomous republics, had an absolute majority of the titular ethnic group. In three autonomous republics (Tatarstan, Kabardino-Balkaria, and Kalmykia) the titular ethnic group enjoyed a simple majority. In the remaining autonomous republics ethnic Russians were an absolute majority or the majority group.[8] In fact, the largest ethnic minority group in Russia, the Tatars (6.64 million), are a minority within their titular ethnic homeland of Tatarstan (Tatars are only 48 percent of the population, Russians 43 percent) and have a large diaspora population dispersed across the federation, but mainly concentrated in the large urban centers of European Russia. When Chechnya partitioned off Ingushetia, it became one of the smallest of the republics, approximately 160 kilometers long and 100 kilometers wide. According to the 1989 census the population of areas now in Chechnya was composed of just over one million persons, around 715,000 of whom declared themselves as Chechens, 269,000 as Russians, and about 25,000 as Ingush. Chechnya, therefore, had one of the largest absolute majorities of any titular ethnic group in its own territory.

RESOURCE INTERDEPENDENCIES

In the context of the early transition period of the early 1990s only four ethnic republics were among the most economically important units of the federation, enjoying significant natural resource endowments or being major industrial areas, while the others were heavily dependent on federal transfers from the center. In the early 1990s Tatarstan accounted for around one quarter of Russia's oil output and was a major industrial manufacturing region, Bashkortostan was a key oil refining and transit region, Sakha-Yakutia produced almost 100 percent of Russia's diamonds, while Chechnya's importance owed less to its small oil output and more to its refining capacity and strategic straddling of the main Baku-Novorossiisk oil pipeline linking one of Russia's major energy export hubs to the energy resources of the Caspian Basin. Outwardly, these resource endowments may indicate a capacity for economic independence from the center, or at least much less dependency on it. There were other constraining factors, however, on such capacity, principally the spatial location of these republics (discussed later). The question of "ethnic" separatism and secession potential, nevertheless, cannot be fully understood in isolation from the political economy of transition and how distributive issues and the intra-elite struggles to control economic assets affected secessionism and refederalization.

The demand for "sovereignty" was rhetorically salient in many republics and regions, but only those with significant economic assets had the leverage to bargain seriously for greater power-sharing with the federal government. Consequently, secession potential was propelled by political economy distributive issues (principally the extent to which a republic was dependent on federal budgetary transfers, and the scale of resentment at the lack of federal revenue sharing and the weakness of local control over local resources). The issue of decentralization and autonomy in economic matters was often coated with an "ethnic" veneer of political rhetoric about "sovereignty." The widespread use of the term "ethnic separatism" in studies of Russian federalism blurs many of the nuances of federal relations. Apart from Chechnya and Tatarstan, there is no evidence, beyond the overblown rhetoric of local leaders, for an "ethnic" mobilization against Russia from the "ethnic" republics, as there were no mass nationalist demonstrations and no significant events of inter-ethnic violence against Russian settler populations. The weakness of separatism among the autonomous republics of the RSFSR was also demonstrated, as noted earlier, by the fact that when they participated in the so-called "parade of sovereignties," beginning with North Ossetia-Alania in July 1990, all but Checheno-Ingushetia and Tatarstan affirmed their sovereignty with the proviso that it was "within the RSFSR."

The general trend in post-Soviet Russia was for a high degree of elite continuity. The former communist party nomenklatura adapted to the new conditions, colonized the new political institutions and businesses, thus largely retaining its grip on political-administrative power and influence on local economic development during the transition.[9] The ethnic elites in the key republics did not diverge from this trend, being deeply acculturated with Soviet values through the nomenklatura system. Not surprisingly, these elites were more concerned with the consolidation of their networks of local control, ownership, and distributive issues during the transition, than with the assertion of ethnic demands per se.[10] This is not to underestimate the accumulating anecdotal evidence for the "ethnification" of power vertically and horizontally in republics through nationalizing policies to promote, for example, "Tatarization," or "Bashkirization." Nationalizing policies in Tatarstan, for example, have a strong cultural dimension (mosque building, rewriting of textbooks, Latinization of the Tatar alphabet, censorship). We can reasonably assume that such discriminatory trends would over time accentuate the ethnonational cleavage within republics and lead to interethnic conflict. So far in Russia, outside the North Caucasus, they have not done so.

SPATIAL LOCATION

The secession potential inherent in Chechnya's demographic profile was compounded by Chechnya's geography. Geography has an immensely important impact on the capacity of a federal unit to assert secession potential. Generally, the more peripheral a unit the greater is the capacity for secession potential, and the more difficult it is to control. If the location of such a unit places it at or near an international frontier, this increases the likelihood that it will be influenced by external forces, or linked to other states, thus strengthening secession potential. Likewise, if the location of a unit places it close to the core of the federal state, and encircles it with loyalist units, then the capacity to achieve its secession potential is severely constrained.

Of the republics with strong secession potential, only the geography of Chechnya spatially favors its assertion of independence. Its location on the new international frontier of the Russian Federation bordering Georgia, on a border that was demarcated by the remote and poorly accessible Caucasus Mountains, was an immense advantage for the capacity to assert independence from Russia. This natural advantage is striking when one compares Chechnya with the only other ethnic republic to vigorously and consistently assert its independence, Tatarstan.

Tatarstan and Bashkortostan are blocked-in by ethnic Russian regions in the heart of European Russia, while Sakha (Yakutia) is peripheralized in a remote region of Siberia. The precedents are stacked against states with this kind of geography becoming independent, as the only other states wholly surrounded by the territory of another state are the Vatican and Lesotho.[11] Furthermore, the power advantages of significant natural resource endowments in such republics are counterbalanced by their geography, which renders them dependent on Russia for extraction, refining, processing and transshipment of their resources. In such conditions Russia has powerful economic leverage which it can apply to secure political compromise.

IDENTITY AND ASSIMILATION

When assessing the issue of secession potential in the Russian Federation, it is important to note the proviso that here we are contending with radically different historical traditions of statehood compared with secessionist cases in other post-communist states, or indeed in the USSR. Neither Tatarstan nor Chechnya, nor indeed any other Russian region or republic, has had recent historical experience of independent statehood for any significant period.[12] Secessionism is acutely weak in the only republic with prolonged experienced of independence, Tuva, which was an independent semiprotectorate of the USSR between 1921 and 1944, but which is currently virtually entirely dependent for its economic existence on federal transfers from the Russian Federation. The role of cross-cutting cleavages in republics is also much understated. For example, it is clear that a significant part of Tatarstan's large Russian minority supported its declaration of sovereignty in the April 1992 referendum and has consistently exhibited strong electoral support for its autonomy. This seems to indicate an embryonic "Tatarstani" identity.[13] The Bashkirs have been politically more hostile to the presence of the large Tatar population (around 30 percent) in Bashkortostan than they are interested in mobilizing against Russians. For example, Baskortostan's 1998 language law recognized only Bashkir and Russian as official languages, excluding Tatar.

While it is also true that many of the former Soviet republics, such as Ukraine, Moldova, Belarus, and the five Central Asian states, have weak or nonexistent state traditions, and many of them were opposed to the break-up of the USSR, these successor states have a combination of advantages that Russia's secessionist republics do not have. Most important, they have international recognition and an open geography, which gives them an effective capacity to communicate internationally and assert their independence. Moreover, in conditions of weak statehood tradition, nationalizing states are required to invest a great deal of institutional capacity in the construction of a new national identity. Recognition as part of the international community of states obviously helps to embed this, a factor that was absent in Chechnya and Tatarstan.

Historical mythologies are fundamental to the idea of statehood, and the weaker the provenance of a state, the stronger its nationalizing project tends to be. In stretching political mythologies to construct and solidify ethnic and regional identities into a new variant of nationalism, the Tatars mythologize the Kazan Khanate, which was annexed and destroyed by Ivan the Terrible in 1552. The Chechens, however, have been forced into a violent struggle to secede from Russia, and consequently have mobilized more around ethnoreligious myths of the nineteenth century and Islamist resistance to Russian imperial conquest.

Unlike many other empires, as the Russian state expanded beginning in the late sixteenth century, the distinction between the Russian *core* and its contiguous imperial *periphery* became blurred. The conflation of core and periphery in the making of Russian identity leads to a very distinctive problem of settler colonialism in Russia. Ethnic Russians perceive their "national" identity as being congruent with the current territorial boundaries of the *whole* Russian Federation, despite the fact that it is largely an administrative artifice of the Soviet era. The identification of core ethnic groups with peripheral territories is not so unusual. US identity was constructed through territorial expansion and settlement in the late eighteenth and nineteenth centuries. The Curragh Mutiny (1914) suggests that a large element of the British Imperial General Staff preferred the overthrow of parliamentary democracy to the loss of Ireland, and there is Mitterand's famous refusal to negotiate with Algerian rebels: "l'Algérie, c'est la France" (1954). When Yeltsin reflected on his decision to use military force against Chechnya he regarded his policy as one that was "saving the federation, saving the country."[14] Russian elite views of their own post-Soviet nation-building, consequently, became bound up with the ideas of refederalization for the whole territory of the RSFSR, including areas such as Chechnya where the overwhelming majority of the population supported independence.

Redesigning Asymmetric Federalism

Broadly, the political debate on refederalization in post-Soviet Russia is polarized into a hegemonic camp, which seeks to sustain ethnic Russian dominance of political and economic life, particularly at the federal level, and an assimilation camp, which promotes "civic" federalism, though this also acts as a cover for Russification. Hostility toward minorities is cloaked by arguments for federal symmetry and the equalization of status of federal units, a position often encouraged by Western propagators of the federal idea.[15] Western ideal types of "ethnic" and "civic" nationalism are used to associate asymmetric federalism with a dangerous "ethnification" of Russian politics that is counterposed to the cultivation of a harmonizing "civic" national identity. The asymmetric arrangements were seen by many as representative of "more the anarchy of the political market place than considerations of a coherent nationalities policy."[16] These are notions that, as we will discuss below, have persisted in debates on Russian federalism from the origins of the Russian Federation in 1990–91 to the recent changes to the federal structure made by Putin since 2000.

A persistent idea in the Russian debates has been that the forging of a "civic" identity requires that the federation be reconfigured into ten or twelve super-regions, largely defined by "economic" criteria (a dream of early Soviet-era planners), and eliminating the "ethnic" denomination of federal subjects altogether. The term "civic" also tends to imply the eradication of the constitutional recognition of citizens of the Russian Federation as a "multinational people" (*mnogonatsional'nyi narod*), and the inculcation of a new state identity of "civic Russian" (*rossiiskii* or *rossiianin*). For nonethnic Russians, however, these terms have an acquisitive "belonging to" or "demi-Russian" connotation. Thus, the mainstream proponents of a "civic" Russianess share a common trait with the radical Russian nationalists, whether it is Zhirinovsky's LDPR, Rodina, or communist groups. It is the view that multiethnic bargaining is somehow illegitimate, an appeasement, and a betrayal of the Russian "nation."

The fundamental issue in Russia's post-Soviet federal development, consequently, has been whether to break with seventy years of Soviet nationalities policy and the organization of state power by implementing an overtly symmetric federalism, or to endow the asymmetric ethnofederal institutions inherited from Soviet federalism with real powers. Symmetric federalism in Russia would inevitably unravel any meaningful form of "institutionalized multinationality." It would mean a concentrated Russian domination of minorities, not only in federal institutions, but also potentially in many "ethnic" republics where Russians are in a majority. As I argued some years ago, such a policy, if implemented, would require a strong authoritarian regime to impose it.[17] The tension between these alternate approaches to refederalization was most obvious in how Russia managed the secession of Tatarstan and Chechnya. Before considering the development of Russian federalism after 1991, let us examine how Russia's federal transition has been generally analyzed.

Despite his failure to refederalize the Soviet Union, many of the elements of Gorbachev's policy were retained by Yeltsin in the attempt to refederalize Russia. The Soviet federal system of the RSFSR was formally asymmetric to the extent that there was a territorial distinction between ethnically denominated "autonomous republics" and lower level autonomous areas and districts, and the mainly ethnic Russian populated "regions" (*oblasti* and *krai*). Real decisional and implementation power, however, lay with the CPSU bodies at all levels. One of the key challenges facing the democratizers and federal reformers in Russia in 1990–91 was whether to empower the existing inherited structure, or whether to devise a completely new institutional architecture.

The question of the status of the autonomous republics (mostly of which were not located on Russia's new international frontier) acquired great salience after Gorbachev equalized their status with that of the union republics in March 1990. In particular, the language of the new Union treaty process established a verbal currency for the political discourse of Russia's post-Soviet refederalization after 1991, with terms such as "treaties," "delimiting powers," "power-sharing" and "sovereignty" becoming all-pervasive.[18] The refederalization involved a difficult policy learning curve and a passage through three federal institutional designs.

ETHNIFIED ASYMMETRIC FEDERALISM

The first phase of refederalization in Russia began even while the Soviet Union still existed. In 1990–92 a Constitutional Commission of the Russian parliament worked under the guidance of its head Oleg Rumiantsev on proposals to abolish the asymmetric framework inherited from the Soviet Union, principally because of its "tribalism."[19] The distinction between republics and regions would be erased and about fifty new federal units called *zemli* (lands) would be created. The *zemli* would have equal status and powers and were modeled on the German *Länder*, though without the extensive powers of the latter and without transforming Russia into a decentralized federation of the German type. While this proposal was portrayed as contributing to a new "civic" Russia, in effect, it would have constructed a federal structure conducive to ethnic Russian hegemonic control as the ethnic areas would have been absorbed or merged into large territories where the ethnic demographic balance and power structures favored ethnic Russians.

The Rumiantsev plan was vigorously opposed by the leaderships of Russia's ethnic republics, who sought to reaffirm the ethnoterritorial basis of the federation and were able to apply their institutional power of control over the upper chamber of the RSFSR Supreme Soviet, the Council of Nationalities, to block change. Rumiantsev's proposals were also overshadowed by Gorbachev's own schemes to remake the USSR. As we noted earlier, Gorbachev had legislated at the USSR level to effectively give autonomous republics a veto over major constitutional change by their Union Republics, and he had agreed a new Union treaty to reform and confederate the Soviet Union at Novo-Ogarevo in April–July 1991. Equally, after his election as chairman of the RSFSR parliament in June 1990, Yeltsin used his great personal charisma to pragmatically build patrimonial relations with the leaders of the ethnic republics, whose support he needed to cultivate in the struggle against Gorbachev. This continued after his election as Russian president in June 1991, which was greatly assisted by the capacity of the leaders of the ethnic republics to deliver votes. The failure of the August 1991 putsch by conservative opponents of reform, however, created a revolutionary situation in Russia. As the Soviet Union collapsed, effective governing authority in Russia was seized by the RSFSR parliament that had been only recently elected in June 1991. In September, the parliament entrusted its chairman, now president, Boris Yeltsin, with emergency powers. Yeltsin appointed a government of young neo-liberals whose primary concern was the implementation of ready-made blueprints to dismantle the Soviet command economy and transform Russia rapidly into a market economy. The federal arrangement of the new Russia was a complex political question for which the neo-liberals had no blueprint and little interest.

In late 1991, however, Yeltsin needed the support of the Russian parliament for his economic reforms, and Russia's ethnic republics and areas used their representation in the parliament as leverage for concessions on federal reform. Consequently, when plans for the refederalization of Russia were formulated in late 1991, the negotiations led to an institutional arrangement that retained the inherited territorial structure but transferred significant powers from the central government to the republics. Neither Checheno-Ingushetia nor Tatarstan was attracted by the offer of new powers, preferring to remain legally insulated from the constitutional developments in Russia in order to preserve their claim to independence.

Consequently, the Federal Treaty, agreed between president, parliament, and the governments of the regions and republics and signed in March 1992, not only reaffirmed the ethnified asymmetric institutional architecture of the federation but empowered it in such a way as to make it the defining feature of the new federal system.[20] The Federal Treaty was a triadic agreement composed of three separate treaties: the first with titular "ethnic" republics, the second with overwhelmingly Russian-populated regions, and the third with the titular "ethnic" autonomous regions and districts. The treaty was a product of the honeymoon period of broad institutional consensus in Russian politics that followed the August putsch and the collapse of the USSR in late 1991. It also reflected the power of collective action in both chambers of the Russian parliament by the republics to defend and expand asymmetric federalism. The treaty was ratified at a time when there was an uneasy balance of power between president and parliament. Consequently, greater segmental autonomy for the titular ethnic republics was conceded in the context of a fragmentation of power at the center, where neither president nor parliament could afford to alienate the potential support of the leaderships of the ethnic republics. In sum, the Federal Treaty was a tactical grand political compromise by all sides. This is not to say that long-lasting constitutions are not often the product of tactical agreements, but in the case of Russia, the compromise came at the expense of the traditional hegemony of the ethnic Russian population and elites.[21]

The treaty empowered Russia's asymmetric federalism, not so much from the terminology, which recognized the twenty constituent republics existing at that time as "sovereign republics within the Russian Federation," in a replication of Soviet jargon, but from the effective and specific segmental autonomies that were granted to the republics compared with the sixty-eight regions. They were given the right to adopt their own constitutions, whereas regions could only have charters; they were conceded wide autonomy over their internal budgets and foreign trade; and, most important for budgetary independence, they were given powers of ownership and use of natural resources and land (Article 3, clause 3). In secret addenda three republics (Bashkortostan, Komi, and Karelia) were ceded even more power.[22] Four of the five titular ethnic autonomous *oblasti* were raised to the status of "republic," while the other ethnically denominated *okrugi* were given equal status with the *krai* and *oblasti*, thus ending their administrative subordination to overwhelmingly ethnic Russian regional governments. The *republics* were now treated as empowered autonomous units within the federation, while the *regions* were effectively dealt with as administrative units in the vertical power of a centralized and increasingly presidential state.

Only Tatarstan and Checheno-Ingushetia refused to sign the Federal

Treaty, and in so doing affirmed their bid for outright independence from Russia. In contrast, they developed their own state structures and adopted new constitutions (see Chapter 3). By mutual agreement of the respective political elites, the Checheno-Ingushetia republic was partitioned amicably in July 1992. The partition was motivated by the Ingush elite's interest in remaining within the Russian Federation, and it signed the Federal Treaty. The respective presidents, Dudaev for Chechnya and Ruslan Aushev (also a former Soviet military commander) for Ingushetia, agreed to retain the existing administrative boundary for five years.

Symmetric Federalism

The second phase of federal state-building lasted from March 1992 to the October crisis of 1993. In this period the elite consensus that had produced the Federal Treaty disintegrated. Some leaders in the ethnic Russian regions, incensed by the federal government's policy of "ethnic privileging" of the republics, reacted by intensifying a populist regionalism. For example, the eight so-called "inter-regional associations," or lobbying blocs of regions, formed in Russia in 1990–91 largely on the basis of planning regions, became an institutional platform for regionalism. The most politically significant challenges came from the regions with significant natural resource endowments, and in particular those regions from which Russia earns most of its export revenues: the Urals, Siberia, and the Far East.[23]

The disaffection of Russian society with the collapse of the socioeconomic system as a result of the shock therapy implemented by Yeltsin's governments, and the difficulty of adjusting to the speed of imperial retreat, rebounded on the discussions about federal reform and intensified Russian nationalism. During the conflict of "dual power" between the president and parliament in 1992–93, Yeltsin appears to have shifted his position on federal reform in Russia, for he began to promote the symmetric federalism option. The authority of the parliament was undermined by the Yeltsin camp, which increasingly played an "ethnic card" against the parliament by portraying it as being in the hands of ethnic minorities. The emblematic figure of hate for the Yeltsin camp was the speaker of parliament, Ruslan Khasbulatov, who, conveniently for them, was an ethnic Chechen. The increasing phobia about ethnic minority "privileging" was stoked by Yeltsin's key minister and advisor on nationality and regional affairs, the constitutional lawyer Sergei Shakhrai. It was he who orchestrated the Constitutional Assembly of July 1993, convened by Yeltsin to draw up a new constitutional allocation of powers between president and parliament, and between federal government and constituent units. Inevitably, given ethnic Russian hegemony in the state, the Constitutional Assembly was overwhelmingly dominated by ethnic Russians. The Assembly was a watershed for the outpouring of aggressive ethnic Russian nationalism among the Russian political elites, which was largely orchestrated by Shakhrai. Hostility toward the ethnic republics was evident in the agenda-setting and discussions, which focused on the symmetric federal option, under the heading of "equalization of status" of all federal units, to the exclusion of all other options. The republics saw this as an attempt to restore a de-ethnified "provincialization" (*gubernizatsiia*) of Russia.[24] Yeltsin also made a final attempt to win support for the symmetric federal option from regional and republic leaderships at the Petrozavodsk summit in August 1993.

Dudaev's government of Chechnya refused to participate in any of these gatherings. Tatarstan initially attended but withdrew its delegation early in the proceedings. The constitutional impasse over refederalization was only broken as a result of developments in the other major constitutional logjam in Russia's transition, the president versus parliament conflict. The latter conflict had intensified over Yeltsin's economic reform agenda during 1992, to reach a crisis point in late September–early October 1993, when Yeltsin used the military to forcibly dissolve parliament. Freed from political constraints and flushed with his success, Yeltsin imposed strong presidential rule on Russia and pushed through a new constitution ratified by a falsified referendum conducted in December 1993.[25]

The new constitution closely followed the proposal for an equalization of status, which had been advocated by Shakhrai at the Constitutional Assembly. Overriding the demands of the republics the Federal Treaty was unceremoniously abandoned. The referendum held in December 1993 to legitimate the new constitution polarized the Russian Federation along an ethnic cleavage as, according to the heavily falsified underestimations of the official reports, seven ethnic republics returned majority votes against the new constitution (unofficial estimates suggest even more). The leadership of Tatarstan advocated a boycott and, when only 13.4 percent of those eligible actually voted, declared the referendum invalid. The highest vote against was 79 percent in the Republic of Dagestan.

Article 5 of the constitution established a symmetric federation in which republics and regions were "equal (*ravnopravnykh*) subjects of the Russian Federation." The key segmental autonomies of the republics that were enshrined in the Federal Treaty, such as the ownership of land and natural resources on their territory, were replaced in the constitution by joint jurisdiction exercised by the federal government and the subjects (Article 72). Most pointedly, the references to the "sovereign" status of republics contained in the Federal Treaty were dropped and Russia became a single constitutional-legal space. All subjects had to ensure that their legal acts conformed to the federal constitution and to federal law (Articles

76–78). Despite the refusal of Chechnya to participate in either the constitutional discussions, or the referendum and election in December 1993, Russia included the "Chechen Republic" in the list of federal "subjects" in Article 65.[26] This in itself was a constitutional oddity, since Russia was thereby recognizing a partition of a territory that it claimed, yet it had not been involved in the partition negotiations.

PARTIAL ASYMMETRIC FEDERALISM

The irony is that Yeltsin's forced dissolution of parliament in October 1993 was a decisive step in the aversion of a parliamentary republic, which over time most likely would have eradicated completely the segmental autonomy of the republics and restored ethnic Russian hegemony over them. That outcome may well have led to an escalation of conflict with the most independent-minded republics, Chechnya and Tatarstan, and perhaps with Bashkortostan also. While enforcing the adoption of equality of status and joint competences in the new constitution, Yeltsin astutely moved to defuse the conflict potential with the key republics. Reflecting the nationalist resurgence in Russia, the new parliament elected in December 1993 was dominated by the nationalist and fascist extremists of Zhirinovsky's LDPR, and a communist bloc, both of which were in the grip of Soviet nostalgia and fantasies about restoring Russia as a great power (*derzhava*). Zhirinovsky's election campaign skillfully applied "Americanized" techniques in the mass media, using paid television commercials to target specific constituencies. His electoral success legitimized the public espousal of the rhetoric of Russian race-hatreds, particularly against minorities and specifically the peoples of the Caucasus.[27] Faced with a parliament that was as intransigent on reform issues as its predecessor, Yeltsin invoked the extensive presidential decree powers under the new constitution to bypass it. Article 90 of the constitution gave the president the power to issue decrees and orders that had force of law, with the only constraint being that they must conform to the constitution.[28] Having pragmatically pursued negotiations, often face-to-face, with the presidents of the key resource-rich republics of Tatarstan, Bashkortostan, and Sakha-Yakutia to end the constitutional stand-off, Yeltsin proceeded to use his powers to impose asymmetric federalism.[29]

Critics of Yeltsin's attempts to bilaterally negotiate, president-to-president, with the republics, and thus bypassing the Duma, stressed that his behavior was "extraconstitutional." Article 11 of the 1993 Russian Constitution, however, states that the division of powers between the federal government and the subjects "will be given effect by the present constitution, the Federal and other treaties."[30] Although Article 15 gave the constitution "supreme juridical force," and stated that it could not be contradicted by federal law, there was still an ambiguity as to the status of the Federal Treaty—was it a federal law or a kind of constitutional act? If the latter, how could the many conflicts between the constitution and the Federal Treaty be reconciled? It took four years for Russia's nascent process of judicial review to establish the precedence of the 1993 constitution over the Federal Treaty, in the February 1998 decision of the Russian Constitutional Court in a case brought by the Komi Republic. Thus, one of the paradoxes of Russia's federal development was that there was a relatively transparent judicial process about a nontransparent treaty process.

Significantly, Article 11 allowed for the further elaboration of federal relations through "other treaties." Negotiations between Yeltsin's administration and the leaderships of the key republics were already well under way *before* the constitution was adopted, and thus it was sensible for the Yeltsin team to insert such a provision in anticipation of a settlement with these republics. Discussions between Yeltsin and Tatarstan president Mintimer Shaimiev began even before the August 1991 putsch. By 1993 a number of power-sharing agreements in noncontroversial policy areas were signed by Yeltsin and Shaimiev.[31] Moreover, Article 11 did not specify any process or mechanism for treaty-making, thus giving Yeltsin carte blanche to enact them. Whatever the uncertainties of the 1993 constitution in this respect, the serious budgetary impact of an escalating tax war between Moscow and key republics during 1993, when federal revenues were withheld by Chechnya, Tatarstan, Bashkortostan, and Sakha, forced the presidential administration to act. To manage the problem of contested sovereignty between Russia and Tatarstan and other key republics, Yeltsin aimed to coopt the key republican leaders into his presidential patrimonial system through a highly selective system of partial asymmetric federalism, which would provide incentives for these leaders to cooperate.

Power-sharing treaties were signed with the key resource-rich republics, beginning in February 1994 with Tatarstan, and followed by Bashkortostan and Sakha (Yakutia). The treaties had a limited institutional basis of support within the Russian political system, since parliament was excluded from the process, and they were essentially executive agreements between the Yeltsin presidency and the presidents of the republics. The limited consensus of the bilateral treaties between the Russian president and the presidents of Tatarstan, Bashkortostan, and Sakha stood in sharp contrast to the Federal Treaty of 1992 which was agreed by Yeltsin, the speaker of parliament, Ruslan Khasbulatov (and was ratified by the Russian parliament), and involved all regions and republics of the federation (with the sole exception of Chechnya).

Tatarstan was by far the most economically important republic. It had significant oil reserves and accounted for about 6 percent of Russian oil output. It also was a key manufacturing center, and produced large volumes of Kamaz trucks, polyethylene, and automotive tires. Most important, key oil and gas pipelines and electricity supply grids traversed the republic. Shaimiev and his elite network were concerned to retain as much control as possible over the republic's wealth and assets, in particular the republic's oil monopoly Tatneft, in a period when Russia was in a state of "all out" insider privatization. The key autonomies and power-sharing arrangements for Tatarstan were detailed in a treaty codicil of twelve "cooperation agreements" on major policy areas (economic cooperation, production and transportation of oil, property, customs, environment, higher education, foreign trade, budget, defense, law and order, military organization). These were time-limited for a term of five years, after which they were to be reviewed and renegotiated if necessary. The cooperation agreements were initially secret but were published in 1997.[32] It is significant that the most prolonged negotiations involved policy domains that touched most on the sovereignty issue (law and order, budget, banking-credit-and foreign currency, foreign economic relations, and defense). Both presidents placed the treaty in the context of building a post-Soviet federation that guaranteed the republic's "sovereignty" while preserving the territorial integrity of the Russian Federation. Yeltsin was also determined that the preferential treatment of Tatarstan would not be a general "model" for an overhaul of federal relations, though Shakhrai and Shaimiev both publicly stated that it could be a model for negotiations with Chechnya.[33]

The selective asymmetric federalism was subsequently extended in a series of power-sharing treaties in 1994–95 with the other republics. The treaties, however, institutionalized a partial asymmetry that was exceptionally hierarchical. The core group of resource-rich republics on which the federal centre was economically heavily dependent, Tatarstan, Bashkortostan, and Sakha, were conceded an even deeper form of segmental autonomy than had been provided in the Federal Treaty. The treaties addressed five main policy areas (law, economy, culture, foreign economic relations, and security) in ways that institutionalized the special political and economic status of the republics. The language of these core treaties, in particular, the treaty with Tatarstan, was highly symbolic, as it resonated with references to "sovereignty" and the parity of status of the parties.[34]

The treaty between Russia and Tatarstan established a cosovereignty arrangement. The first sections declare that Tatarstan is a "State" that is "*united with* the Russian Federation" on the basis of *both* the Russian and Tatarstan constitutions and the treaty itself (author's italics). Differences of interpretation were to be resolved by a special conciliation commission. Consequently, the treaty was clearly viewed as having a paraconstitutional status in regulating Russia-Tatarstan relations. There are clauses in the

Constitution of Tatarstan of 30 November 1992 that declare its laws to be "supreme" (Article 59), proclaim it to be "a sovereign state, a subject of international law *associated to* the Russian Federation" (Article 61), reserve for itself the right to conduct foreign relations, hold exclusive ownership of natural resources, and restrict military service of its citizens to its own territorial jurisdiction.[35] Such constitutional provisions were obviously in flagrant disagreement with the 1993 Russian federal constitution, and were the focus of Putin's demands for amendments starting in 2000 (see Chapter 4). Under Yeltsin, however, these contradictions were considered to be intrinsic to the flexible arrangement of asymmetric federalism. Tatarstan's leaders also saw these ambiguities in a positive light, as the treaty formed an institutional buffer between the Russian and Tatarstan constitutions.[36]

By the autumn of 1995, all republics except Chechnya had signed bilateral treaties with the federal government. Only the key treaties with Tatarstan, Bashkortostan, and Sakha conceded significant economic privileges: ownership or use of natural resources and land, wide autonomy in budgetary and tax powers with enhanced revenue-sharing with the federal government, and the right to engage directly in foreign economic relations. As was the case with the Federal Treaty, the special political and economic arrangements in the new treaties provoked outrage among the Russian political elites, especially in the regions. In 1994–95 as Yeltsin allowed the shift to elected rather than appointed governors of the Russian regions, a major consideration was how to contain what was termed "separatism" from spreading to the regions, though in reality this term actually referred to the non-compliance of regional authorities with Yeltsin's policies or the contradiction of their legislative acts with the constitution and federal laws.

In the autumn of 1993 the regional governor who was among the most fervent advocates of regional "sovereignty," Eduard Rossel in Sverdlovsk (Yeltsin's home region), had made a mockery of the ethnic republics' special status under the Federal Treaty of 1992 by adopting a regional "constitution" and declaring a "republic."[37] Although dismissed from office by Yeltsin in October 1993, Rossel returned to power in August 1995 as one of the first democratically elected governors. His success was a further demonstration of the electoral power of Russian grievances against minorities and of localism at a time of societal upheaval. As with the republics, Yeltsin operated a policy of divide and rule in the pursuit of his presidential federalism. The first regional treaties were signed with Kaliningrad, Sverdlovsk, Orenburg, and Krasnodar in January 1996. As with the ethnic republics, the language of the regional treaties is indicative of a hierarchy of status and power-sharing. Sverdlovsk, in particular, achieved de facto "republic" status by winning substantial economic privileges, though time limited to five years as with the republics.[38] A further twenty-four treaties with regions were concluded in time for the first round of the presidential election in June 1996. If this was a calculated strategy by Yeltsin to woo the support of regional elites for his reelection campaign, it largely failed. In the first round of voting, only half the regions with treaties gave a majority vote for Yeltsin, illustrating the fact that for many regions the treaties were largely symbolic and politically irrelevant. The notable exception was Tatarstan, where Shaimiev ensured that the voting was heavily rigged in Yeltsin's favor.[39]

Partial asymmetric federalism was as deeply unpopular as was the ethnified asymmetric federalism of the Federal Treaty among the hegemonic ethnic Russian political class, across the whole political spectrum from communists, fascists and nationalists to social democrats and liberals. The key treaties clearly involved a massive loss of revenue for the federal government and were a source of considerable resentment among Russian elites, particularly as they hindered a common federal fiscal policy and regional strategy. For example, the 1994 treaty with Sakha institutionalized a prior informal agreement between Yeltsin and Sakha president Mikhail Nikolaev, which granted the republic the right to keep 25 per cent of the profits from its diamond sales.[40] The Yeltsin-Nikolaev agreement was an immense revenue-enhancing device for Sakha given that the republic accounts for over 80 percent of known diamond reserves and over 99 percent of Russia's diamond output, while Russia accounts for about one-quarter of global production. Russian parliamentarians were also incensed by the fact that the treaties created legislative no-go areas, while the representatives of the republics could vote on legislation that did not affect them.[41] This source of interethnic hostility is not uncommon in political systems with elements of asymmetric federalism. In the UK the problem is known as the "West Lothian" question and involves a jurisdictional problem when a Scottish parliament has exclusive spheres of policy competence independent of the Westminster parliament, yet Scottish representatives continue to legislate at Westminster in areas that will not affect Scotland.

The development of a post-Soviet federal institutional architecture in Russia was closely interlinked with the emergence of strong presidential rule under Yeltsin. The benefits and disadvantages of a strong presidency for a transition to democracy are widely debated. Juan Linz has argued that the tendency of a strong presidency to personalize power, among other factors, undercuts institutional development and makes it not conducive to advancing democratization.[42] Guillermo O'Donnell has developed the concept of "delegative democracy" to describe the informal politics of this kind of presidential rule during a transition to democracy.[43] In contrast, Donald Horowitz has observed that where ethnicity is territorialized and politicized, a strong presidency can promote stability by imposing mechanisms to cross-cut ethnic cleavages, and to accommodate and manage ethnic and regional challenges. Yeltsin's selective asymmetric federalism was a form of the latter.

The combination of multiethnic diversity, institutional debilitation, and rampant corruption in the Russian state has more parallels with the weak states in post-colonial Africa than with the overwhelmingly homogeneous states of Latin America. In such conditions, as Horowitz emphasizes, presidentialism may provide the only institutional bond to avert disintegration into ethnic conflict.[44] In the case of central politics and institutions there is much evidence of Yeltsin's reluctance to compromise with opponents and preference for unilateral action and confrontation. To a large degree, it was Yeltsin's uncompromising "winner takes all" approach to reform in Russia that led to the violence during the October 1993 crisis with parliament. This application of force created a precedent and changed the calculus as to what kind of coercive strategy could be pursued elsewhere in the country. Yeltsin did not shrink from using the Russian military to impose his will on parliament, but the strategy was repeated only in Chechnya.

Yeltsin's impact on the management of Russia's multiethnic diversity was on the whole a crucial stabilizing factor, with the notable exception of Chechnya. While Yeltsin's strong presidential rule undoubtedly disrupted the development of democratic institutions in Russia, it was critically important for managing the refederalization in a politically stable manner, and ensured the cooption of the leaders of almost all the ethnic republics into a new federal arrangement. In the absence of strong presidentialism, federal power-sharing would have been blocked and interethnic tensions exacerbated by a Russian chauvinist ethnocracy based on an ethnic Russian dominated parliament. Paradoxically, by destroying the parliament in 1993 and asserting presidential power over federal questions to marginalize the Duma elected in December 1993, Yeltsin probably prevented much wider scale confrontation between the federal centre and the ethnic republics. The integrative pull of the Yeltsin presidency drew its strength from the rejuvenation of the traditional elite patrimonial networks of the Soviet nomenklatura system. It was precisely the ability to coopt and integrate, however, that was absent from Yeltsin's management of the secession crisis in Chechnya, and the reasons for this will be discussed in Chapter 3.

Evaluating Yeltsin's Refederalization

Studies of transition, with the exception of Bunce's comparative study of the collapse of socialist federations, have tended to neglect the role of

federalism in the ethnic and territorial dimensions of democratization—
a neglect that is compounded significantly when both dimensions coincide in a federal transition, as they have done in Russia. Studies of post-
Soviet Russian federalism, particularly by scholars in the United States,
have been strongly influenced by those theories of federalism which draw
on the pessimism of liberal democratic theory about the prospects for
political stability in multiethnic societies, and advocate assimilation as the
solution. Consequently, a dominant consensus developed in the 1990s
among Russian and Western scholars that was generally dismissive of the
prospects for a stable refederalization in Russia.

Many scholars argued that any process of refederalization that institutionalized privileged arrangements on an "ethnic" basis would actually
strengthen separatist and secessionist threats to the territorial integrity
of the state. A branch of federal theory views the very principle of asymmetric federalism as inherently destabilizing because it creates "unequal"
levels of federalism, leads to discontent, and thus magnifies "secession-
potential."[45] More recently, it has been argued that the very institutionalization of autonomy for ethnic groups generates conflict.[46] Attempts to
construct a two-tier federation in Russia, with a few key "ethnic" republics
enjoying a privileged constitutional position and revenue-enhancing economic concessions compared with the majority of regions which are overwhelmingly Russian populated, consequently were almost universally seen
as destabilizing. Asymmetric federalism, it was argued, would create a
downward spiral of overlapping jurisdictions and legal-administrative in-
coherence and noncompliance that would fatally undermine the single
constitutional space. It would culminate with a deluge of ethnic "deviance"
that would lead to the break-up of Russia. Since the rebellious sub-state
elites that mobilized an "ethnic revival" were "rewarded," coopted and
bought off by the center through bilateral treaties, the rational choice
analysts argued that such demands would expand logically to the point of
a crisis of control and the disintegration of Russia.[47] Equally, World Bank
economists argued for the immediate adoption of "fiscal federalism," an
approach derived from the experience of advanced capitalist federal states
such as the U.S., Canada, and Germany, despite the absence of fiscal trans-
parency and a system of rule of law in Russia, and notwithstanding the
unreliability of published budgetary data.[48] Asymmetric federalism, it was
claimed, was fostering an anarchic "scramble for benefits," which by 1998
in Russia had fed into a logic for a "beggar-thy-neighbor race to the bot-
tom" that threatened its territorial integrity.[49]

The approach of many U.S.-based political scientists to Russian federalism was strongly influenced by the "federal bargaining" approach of
William Riker. Derived from a Madisonian understanding of federalism,
and based on the study of the U.S. federal system, this model stresses the

critical importance of political parties as agents for making federal institutions work and preventing "narrow" sectional interests, especially ethnic or territorially-based ones, from destabilizing the system. In the absence of the mediating presence of strong political parties, it was argued, the "bargaining game" of Russian federalism would be unworkable.[50] While it is true that the kind of federalism that emerged in Russia in the early 1990s cannot be equated with U.S. federalism, does this mean that we should dismiss it outright as a form of federalism?

There was a tendency to confuse Russia's asymmetric federalism based on power-sharing treaties with "foralistic federalism."[51] In particular, there is uncertainty as to whether "foralistic federalism" is stabilizing or destabilizing, and where appropriate comparative examples might be found. An influential Russian study demonstrates this erroneous tendency to interpret "foralistic federalism" as highly destabilizing, citing the Canada-Quebec, Germany-Bavaria (sic), and India-Punjab cases as evidence of the "damage" caused by this type of "treaty-federalism," claiming that it inevitably leads to the "break up of the federation."[52] Comparisons were also made with Spain, where the division of powers between center and "autonomies" was institutionalized by a series of bilateral agreements.[53] Again, this is an inappropriate comparison, as there are substantive differences. The creation of the Spanish "state of autonomies" through power-sharing agreements was a transparent process ratified by parliament and approved by regional referenda, and the texts were entrenched bodily as addenda to the 1978 constitution in the form of the Autonomy Statutes. This means that Spain is governed by a single constitution. While the territorial autonomies have asymmetric power-sharing arrangements, formally Spain is not a federal state.

Equally, some critics focused less on the "federalism" content and more on the weak "democratic" content of Russia's refederalization, which is, of course, a different perspective from one that focuses on the challenge of managing ethnopolitics and political stability.[54] As we noted earlier, political liberals tended to associate asymmetric federalism with a dangerous "ethnification" of Russian politics that was seen as an obstacle to assimilation and the building of a harmonious "civic" national identity.[55] Economic reformers tended to stress the negative impact that federal power-sharing had on the progression of economic reform. The treaties empowered ethnic elites who did not necessarily wish to cooperate with the implementation of neoliberal reforms, in particular insider-privatizations that benefited Moscow-based elites and the Yeltsin circle. Furthermore, the treaties diluted the federal government's control of economic management and fiscal policy, and contributed to disequilibria in tax and revenue collection, economic wealth distribution, and regional development. Such arguments underpinned a general scholarly consensus by the second half of the 1990s that Russian federalism was sui generis, unlike any form of federalism found in the West, and unlikely to be stable. In sum, the critique of asymmetric federalism contained moral (all citizens and constituent units should be equal) and practical components (without transparent "standard rules of the game" federal state capacity and coordination was impossible).

Russia's asymmetric federalism did selectively share power, and during the 1990s was characterized by the weak role of political parties in federal institutions, and yet the state did not disintegrate. The critiques were not confirmed by developments. This is partly because of an exaggeration of the threat posed by political negotiation and "bidding games" over power, authority, and status. In particular, those analysts who attempted to quantify "secession-potential" often relied heavily on constructing variables based on largely rhetorical devices that emphasized claims to "sovereignty," such as speeches of leaders and media content. The term "sovereignty" (*suverenitet*) in the Russian context of the early 1990s needs to be differentiated in a nuanced manner that is not easily captured by quantitative approaches. The claim to "sovereignty" almost always explicitly meant a claim for greater power-sharing and self-rule "within" the Russian Federation between the federal government and the federal units, and did not mean "secession." Inevitably, any undifferentiated focus on rhetoric exaggerates the threat of secession. Furthermore, authors who are discomfited by "asymmetry" tend to exaggerate the danger of centrifugal forces. As recently as 2000, for example, Shleifer and Treisman described Russia in a dismissive tone as "a crumbling peripheralized federalism, which the center has kept together mostly through a policy of fiscal appeasement and political accommodation."[56] As if fiscal trade-offs, nitty-gritty deals, and compromises are not the stuff of politics even in the most advanced democracies and gridlocked federal systems.

As Duchacek observed, all federations are asymmetric as regards the political influence and socioeconomic power of constituent units.[57] The issue is whether built-in constitutional or institutional asymmetries are exceptionally destabilizing. The critique that Russia's asymmetric federalism led to problems of weak federal control, difficulties with embedding democratic practice, and rule compliance, while also undermining constitutional order, economic reform, and state administrative coherence, is also not valid. These problems were not products of asymmetric federalism as they existed in Russia during the 1990s irrespective of the status of the subject, or whether it had a power-sharing treaty. Asymmetry may have led to some disparities in federal revenue distribution in favor of ethnic republics, but this pales into insignificance compared with the immense disparity of wealth concentrated in Moscow in the hands of a small number of oligarchs in a process characterized by large-scale defrauding of the state and the Russian people. Moreover, the "stealing" of the state in Russia was often done with the approval of and in consultation with Western advisors, including some of the same academics who are critical of asymmetric federalism.[58]

The critiques also overlooked the growing recognition of the role of institutionalizing "group-specific rights" for addressing ethnic concerns. Consociational arrangements and institutionalized power-sharing are credible foundations for stable democracy and federalism in multiethnic settings. The comparative experience of conflict regulation in multiethnic societies (as we discuss in Chapter 6) suggests that such institutional arrangements are vital for managing secession and conflict in a politically stable manner. Asymmetric federalism provided important institutional counterweights to the powerful residues of the centralizing unitarist state tradition in Russia, one that has historically practiced ethnic control, forced Russification, oppression, and genocide against its national minorities. In the 1990s Russia's asymmetric federalism also offered an alternative conflict resolution mechanism to the internationally sanctioned "Bosnian" model of segregation in "ethnic" enclaves. The Russian experience of federal transition has had beneficial contagion effects, for example, in the way the institutionalization of Crimean autonomy in the Ukrainian constitution of 1996 was influenced by the Tatarstan model.[59] In recent years, asymmetric federalism has been widely discussed by international mediators and the OSCE as a potential solution for the "frozen" conflicts in Abkhazia, South Ossetia, Transdnistria, and Nagorno-Karabagh.

The process by which asymmetric federalism was crafted is as important as the way it functioned. The negotiation, bargaining, and compromise that accompanied the institutional engineering of a treaty framework amounted to a federalizing process in politics itself. The negotiations for the treaties were lengthy and complex (lasting three years in the case of Tatarstan), and this bargaining continued over their operation and interpretation (even, as we shall discuss later, under Putin's federal reforms). Evaluating the impact of the treaties once adopted on federal relations is a more complicated task, given the nontransparency of the cooperation agreements covering key policy domains and the secrecy surrounding the reconciliation of differences. Consequently, asymmetric federalism institutionalized elite bargaining. Elite bargaining is generally recognized as a key precondition for a democratic transition, but per se it obviously does not presuppose a democratic outcome. It is a paradox that the absence of elite bargaining in central politics during the early 1990s hindered the consolidation of Russia's democratization, while its presence in the negotiation of federalism stabilized the country at the expense of entrenching thoroughly undemocratic elites in power in many of the republics. Secrecy may intensify bidding games but it also gives the center the flexibility to negotiate on a case by case basis, and is a useful instrument for breaking up potential regional and republican coalitions. Secrecy also serves the interests of those key republics (like Tatarstan, Bashkortostan, and Sakha) that have the most leverage and can extract the most concessions, and in the case of Russia, it was in these republics that resistance to federal control was greatest (except Chechnya).

Conclusion

Secession potential was extraordinarily weak in Russia in the early 1990s as it attempted to implement a post-Soviet refederalization. This was partly a result of significant structural limitations on secession. Sophisticated political bargaining, from the Yeltsin presidency in particular, also played a significant role in defusing and managing ethnic minority and ethnic Russian grievances in a delicate balancing act to craft forms of institutionalized power-sharing. The refederalization hinged on attempts to fully or partially recycle and empower the asymmetric federal architecture of "institutionalized multinationality" that was inherited from the Soviet Union. Rather than being a "subversive" flaw for federal state-building, this institutional legacy proved to be crucial for a successful refederalization and was quickly reconfigured into a system of selective asymmetry based on a hierarchy of bilateral treaties offering varying degrees of autonomy.

The main political problems with asymmetric federalism were, in fact twofold. Firstly, the treaties were a product of a relatively limited elite and institutional consensus, reflecting executive interests and based on executive agreements at the federal and republic or regional level, and excluding participation by or consultation with the Russian parliament. Their imprecise constitutional status took some years to be sorted out by the judicial review of the Constitutional Court. The asymmetric federalism, consequently, was principally an outcome of executive agreements (president-to-president in the case of republics, president-to-governor in the case of regions). Thus, the fundamentals of the federal arrangement were vulnerable to unraveling once there was a change of presidents, and primarily of the Russian presidency, or a challenge to presidential power. This is, in fact, what occurred under Putin's presidency from 2000.

Second, asymmetric federalism failed to resolve the question of Chechnya's secession. The strengths and limitations of the interaction of presidentialism and federalism during Russia's transition are evident in the contrast between the two most important cases of secession. The success of a negotiated power-sharing accommodation with Shaimiev in Tatarstan stands in sharp contrast to the failure of negotiation with Dudaev in Chechnya and the drift to armed conflict. Armed conflict between Russia and Chechnya began in late 1991, though it descended into all-out war only in late 1994. This conflict must be explained against a background of the attempts to refederalize Russia and build Russian "statehood." Only in Chechnya did this form of federal accommodation fail, and the reasons for this failure are explored in the next chapter.

Chapter 3

A Secular Nationalist Conflict

A period of over three years elapsed between Dudaev's seizure of power in Chechnya during the August 1991 coup in Moscow and the Russian military invasion in late December 1994. Because Chechnya was the most recalcitrant of the secessionist republics for the Russian Federation, one would have expected that it would be a priority to resolve this problem through President Yeltsin's policy of selective asymmetric federalism. From the Russian viewpoint, a power-sharing treaty offered the best prospect for a peaceful resolution to the conflict, as it would retain Russian sovereignty over Chechnya, and would have averted the drift toward war. The conventional wisdom is that Chechnya was excluded from the bilateral power-sharing treaty process principally because of a clash of leadership egos which prevented a compromise.

Previous studies of the conflict search for explanations in various compendia of political, economic, sectional, personal, and strategic factors. No single factor is advanced as an explanation. It is generally argued that Yeltsin and a "war party" within his administration preferred coercion against Chechnya to accommodation in order to defend Russia's strategic and economic interests in the Caucasus and Caspian. Moreover, the dynamics of Russia's politics had a profound impact on the course of Russian-Chechen relations after 1991. The question of Chechnya's secession became a useful political tool that was instrumentalized in the political infighting within the Russian elite as part of the "president versus parliament" struggle, and to advance or attack issues of political and economic reform during the post-Soviet transition. The Chechnya "problem" was to be similarly used by Putin in late 1999 (discussed in Chapter 4).

Academic studies of the conflict tend to focus on the dynamics of conflict from the Russian perspective and find significant differences about causation. While acknowledging the role of historical background and the catalyst of Soviet collapse, many scholars suggest that it was the broader problems of institutional debilitation in the post-Soviet political context that led to the conflict, in particular the struggle of "president versus parliament" in Russia's transition.[1] Lapidus explained that the conflict emerged from "a poorly institutionalized policy-making process, exacerbated by bitter intra-elite struggles and conflicts between the executive and legislative branches."[2] For Evangelista the conflict is driven by a sense of the "fragility" of Russia and fears in the Russian leadership under both Yeltsin and Putin that the independence of Chechnya could produce a general disintegration of Russia—though he demonstrates that such fears were unfounded.[3]

Tishkov's work, by far the most empirically rich and analytically sophisticated of the Russian studies of the conflict, denies that the conflict is about nationalism at all, for there is, he claims, no Chechen "nation." Rather, the conflict was the result of Russia's attempts to suppress a power grab or coup d'état by a small group of criminals under a deranged dictator. Moreover, Tishkov dismisses Western analyses that examine the question of secession and independence as "anti-Russian."[4] There is certainly some truth to the argument that much of the content of Western policy, media coverage, and scholarship on Chechnya is critical of Russian policy, and in some cases is motivated by the desire to criticize Russia per se. Equally, however, Tishkov's work is characterized by an implicit Soviet nostalgia, a distorted view of the harsh reality of Soviet dictatorship, a benign view of Soviet nationalities policy, and antipathy to the nationalist movement under Dudaev and Yandarbiev.

Personalizing the Conflict

A recurrent theme in the standard explanations of the conflict is that the failure to compromise was a result of a clash of presidential personalities. Yeltsin and Dudaev, it is argued, disliked each other, and were simply too dogmatic, with overly fragile egos, to negotiate a compromise. The "clash of personality" thesis for explaining the conflict is strongly influenced by the way that certain Russian politicians framed the conflict dynamics in the early 1990s. In particular, the thesis originated from some of the Russian academics who were considered to be "ethnic" policy specialists, such as Galina Starovoitova and Valerii Tishkov. Starovoitova was a leading member of Democratic Russia, the political movement which brought Yeltsin to power, and both scholars were recruited by the new Yeltsin administration as special advisors on nationality and ethnic issues. For a period in 1992 Tishkov served as Minister of Nationalities.[5] They quickly became disillusioned by their failure to make progress in the negotiations with Chechnya. They believed that the attempts to negotiate a solution through direct meetings were spoiled, and the conflict was escalated, by a trivial "personalization" of the issues between Yeltsin and Dudaev. The work of both scholars on nationality problems and Chechnya has been highly influential within and outside Russia. The evidence for the "clash of personality" thesis is, nevertheless, contradictory.

In a private conversation Shaimiev reported to Tishkov that Yeltsin had been ready to negotiate an agreement with Dudaev "on the Tatarstan model," but at the last moment, he was dissuaded because of reports of negative personal comments about him made by Dudaev. In one version, published in 1995, Tishkov suggests that the dissuaders were some of Yeltsin's ministers and advisers. In a later version, published in 1997, Tishkov reports that the conversation actually occurred in August 1996, and Yeltsin was dissuaded by negative comments from Dudaev reported in the press.[6] Tishkov believes that the personality clash was rooted in a status game, where Yeltsin would only negotiate face-to-face if Dudaev would show appropriate respect for Yeltsin's preeminence, while the latter would only negotiate if Russia first met a precondition of recognizing Chechnya's sovereignty. Furthermore, Tishkov's work faults the crude characterizations of the ethnic aspects of the conflict in other studies and in the mass media, yet his own work is highly personalized and based on crude stereotyping, as for example, in his one-sided contrasting of Dudaev's "arrogance and ambitiousness" and "cunning" with Yeltsin's "political morality" and "civic consciousness."[7]

Starovoitova, in contrast, avoids ethnic stereotypes but hints at an underlying racism on Yeltsin's part. She wrote diplomatically of Yeltsin's "psychological distance" from Chechens, which made it difficult for him to treat them as equal partners in negotiations. She also blamed Khasbulatov for playing a spoiling role, disrupting and blocking talks with Dudaev because, as she put it, of his "jealousy" of Dudaev.[8] It is not clear what kind of jealousy she was referring to: jealousy that Dudaev was a popularly elected leader? Jealousy of Dudaev's courage in standing up to Russia? Khasbulatov's motivations were more likely to have been fear and arrogance. He was an ideal type of the non-Russian "Soviet man" of the kind lauded in theory by Tishkov. He had been accepted into Moscow life as a student in 1962, almost directly from exile in Kazakhstan, and had made a career as a Komsomol apparatchik. As an upwardly mobile ethnic provincial who assimilated into the hegemonic colonial identity and was distant from his ethnic roots, Khasbulatov perhaps saw Dudaev as someone who raised Russians' racist hackles and realized their worst prejudices about Chechens and thus threatened Khasbultov's burgeoning career in central politics as speaker of the Russian parliament in 1991–93. Whatever his motivations, Khasbulatov certainly loathed Dudaev and regarded him as a "little Hitler."[9]

Other studies have also attributed the clash to a "deep-seated personal animus" between Yeltsin and Dudaev that was based on "ethnic" prejudice. The personal antagonism is sometimes extended into a collective phenomenon of mutual ethnic hatred between the respective leaderships. Again, the evidence for this is circumstantial rather than factual. For example, the ethnic and geographic origins of Yeltsin's key advisors, Minister for Nationality and Regional Affairs Sergei Shakhrai (a Terek Cossack), Ramazan Abdulatipov (a Dagestani Avar), and their successor, Nikolai Yegorov (a Russian apparatchik from Krasnodar), have been interpreted to mean that these advisors were predisposed by their origins to block a political accommodation with Chechnya.[10] Dunlop, for example, provides no evidence for the view attributed to Russian commentators that Shakhrai "as a Terek Cossack, appeared to share that group's corporate historical animosity toward the Chechens."[11]

The motif of the "evil Chechen" (*zloi chechen*) is deeply embedded in Russian culture.[12] Yeltsin's memoirs provide glimpses of racist prejudice against Caucasians, and Chechens in particular, that may have affected his judgment. Equally, it is now common knowledge that the Yeltsin of the 1990s was a deeply emotionally unstable alcoholic, a condition that undoubtedly also impaired his decision-making in domestic and foreign policy.[13] The conflict between Russia and Chechnya escalated during 1992–93 at the precise time when Yeltsin was absorbed by the struggle for power at the center with Khasbulatov and the Russian parliament. During this period Yeltsin met with Khasbulatov on numerous occasions to try to reach a political agreement on the division of power, and his memoirs offer reflections on Khasbulatov's character that give voice to stereotypical Russian suspicions about the duplicity of the "evil Chechen." Yeltsin wrote of Khasbulatov's "oriental nature," and reports how he told Khasbulatov, "you say one thing and do another."[14] Viacheslav Kostikov, Yeltsin's press secretary at this time, described Khasbulatov as being "just like Dzhokar Dudaev . . . using partisan methods, unrelated to any rules or decency."[15] The evidence suggests that in dealing with Dudaev, or any Chechens, Yeltsin reflected Russian racist ill-feeling toward this *ethnie*.

How plausible is it to attribute the political mistrust and the failure of negotiations to "ethnic" hatred? After all, Shakhrai was a shrewd constitutional lawyer and an extremely able and experienced negotiator. His handling of the complex negotiations with Tatarstan demonstrated that he could be party to carefully crafted political compromises with ethnic minority elites. The Russia-Tatarstan treaty of 1994 satisfied the Tatar elite's demands for "sovereignty," while conceding wide autonomy, and also preserved the territorial integrity of the Russian Federation. Dudaev told Russian journalists that he considered Shakhrai to be the most open and trustworthy of all the Russian politicians, and the one that he "liked best."[16]

Rather than assume that racist prejudice about "ethnic" origin, however distant, informs policy, it is more useful to examine other aspects of leadership character. When interviewed by a Russian journalist in March 1992 Dudaev said that he "sympathized" with Yeltsin in his struggle against the Russian parliament because he was "a democratically oriented person." Should Yeltsin recognize the right of the Chechen people to choose freedom, Dudaev avowed: "Russia will not have a more loyal and dependable ally than Chechnya."[17] A stumbling bloc to good personal relations may have been the fact that Dudaev, unlike Shaimiev and the leaders of the other republics, was not a former member of the party nomenklatura. Dudaev's life and career until 1989 demonstrate, nevertheless, that he was a loyal "Soviet man," schooled in the traditional ethos of the Soviet army. He made a career as an air force pilot and had risen through the ranks to one of the highest and most trusted levels of command in the Soviet military.[18] In 1988 he was promoted to major-general in command of a strategic nuclear bomber base near Tartu in Estonia, where he commanded a division of long-range nuclear-armed "Backfire" bombers. It was unprecedented for a Chechen to occupy such an important military post. Tishkov even claims that Dudaev's promotion to the rank of general was engineered as a political appointment after pressure on Gorbachev from the Zavgaev leadership of Chechnya, though there are no corroborating sources and Zavgaev never made such claims.[19]

The party nomenklatura of the late Soviet period was notoriously exclusive and snobbish in its attitudes to the rest of society—a hierarchy that was reinforced by ethnic prejudice. As a Soviet military officer, by career, temperament, and ethnicity, Dudaev was an outsider to the tightly closed patrimonial networks of the party nomenklatura. The military background is in itself an insufficient reason for the distance from Yeltsin, though it is not insignificant that Yeltsin did have a fractious relationship with the Russian military, and even imprisoned his Vice-President Aleksandr Rutskoi, a former general and Afghan war hero. Other former military commanders, notably, General Ruslan Aushev, who was elected president of Chechnya's kin republic of Ingushetia in February 1993, were amicably accommodated within Yeltsin's refederalization. Perhaps we need to focus more on the context in which Dudaev, as a senior military officer, worked in close proximity to party structures, as his most active period in this role coincided with Gorbachev's liberalization, when the conservatism of the party was on the defensive and its networks were disintegrating. Most important, Dudaev's experience of political work occurred in Estonia, where the party fractured on ethnic lines and Dudaev found himself aligned with nationalist elites who were pushing for independence. As his career was spent outside Chechnya, Dudaev was an outsider not only to the networks of the party nomenklatura, but also to the clientelist networks within Chechnya itself. The clash of personalities and egos, therefore, lay less in ethnic discordance between the main actors and more in the insider-outsider dynamic, and in ideological differences.

Shaimiev, the president of Tatarstan, and most of his ruling cadre were, like Yeltsin, former Soviet communist party *apparatchiki* who had rein-vented themselves as "democrats." During the transition they combined political power with economic interests, and the cynical manipulation of nationalism to protect both. The values, behavior, and thinking of the Tatar elite were very much aligned with their counterparts in the Yeltsin team, and they kow-towed and showed suitable deference to Yeltsin when it mattered. Military commanders like Dudaev were used to giving orders, not taking them, and tended, like the rest of society, to disrespect the nomenklatura for its cronyism and corruption. Consequently, the clash of personality owes much to the mismatch of personality-forming career backgrounds. Dudaev's personality was incompatible with the deferential ingratiation and cynicism required by Yeltsin's rejuvenated Soviet-style "command-administrative" patrimonialism. Moreover, Dudaev's deep attachment to the principle of national self-determination was perceived by Yeltsin as stubbornness and insolence. This dichotomy is not an un-usual state of affairs between a colonial power and the colonized, and it was a factor that may have fed Yeltsin's instinctive racial prejudice against Chechens.

Personal differences must also have been intensified by the harsh and uncompromising political rhetoric, and escalating violence, that increas-ingly framed the conflict on both sides beginning in late 1991. While Western journalists were quick to play up the "historic" aspects of the conflict in their reports, they found Dudaev's long speeches, when he attempted to contextualize the conflict for them, to be "histrionic" and boring. Some interpreted Dudaev's lengthy political monologues as a sign that he was "deeply unstable," others spoke of his "almost Satanic pride."[20] Yet embellishment and long-windedness in public speech-making is a clas-sic characteristic of the Soviet elite. Moreover, one wonders what Dudaev's reaction must have been to a Western journalist pack that fawned over Yeltsin's Russia and was dismissive of the immensely difficult task of build-ing an independent state in Chechnya against all the odds. In contrast to Western journalists, Russian journalists reported that they found Dudaev to be someone who was a "popular leader," and who always replied to questions in a "lively, concrete, and sensible" manner, but who appeared to be "tired and downcast" on the eve of war.[21] Though he is dismissive of Western interpretations of the conflict, Tishkov has absorbed the descrip-tions of Dudaev's character and behavior by Western journalists into his account to underline the idea of a personalized conflict. Accordingly, Dudaev's charismatic leadership was essentially flawed both politically (national independence was an "unrealizable" project), and personally (Dudaev was contradictory and "psychologically unstable").[22]

It is not necessarily irrational for politicians to be contradictory, nor is it uncommon. It is also not irrational for political rhetoric to harden when politicians are in negotiating mode—as Dudaev and Yeltsin were in 1992–94. The two presidents, however, never met in face-to-face negotiations, as Yeltsin left this task to advisors and ministers, such as Shakhrai. Consequently, any personal animus was felt second-hand. Consequently, the analysis that follows suggests that rather than look for the causes of conflict in slighted egos, or the "crazed dictator" (viz. Dudaev) thesis, we must examine how the issue at stake—secession—shaped the relations between Russia and Chechnya, and how the process of negotiation itself generated and escalated levels of mistrust, leading to a descent into war.

Nationalism and the Nature of the Dudaev Regime

Following the initial military embarrassment at the hands of Dudaev's forces in November 1991, and given that his own administration was immersed in the complex problems of dismantling the USSR and forging ahead with rapid economic reform in Russia, Yeltsin turned to a policy of blockade of Chechnya. The intention was to impose a *cordon sanitaire* around Chechnya to prevent any spillover effect in the other republics of the North Caucasus and economically strangle the Dudaev regime into submission.

Russia launched a sustained campaign of political, economic, and military subterfuge to undermine Dudaev by supporting Chechen proxies. The effectiveness of this strategy was undoubtedly greatly weakened by the chaos and systematic reorganization of the Russian state in this period, including the core "power ministries" of defense and interior responsible for such a strategy. Armed groups were organized by Russia in the Nadterechny area of northern Chechnya, the traditional center of pro-Russia loyalism. Russia's Chechenization strategy hinged on the alternative anti-Dudaev government established in December 1991 by Umar Avturkhanov, a former policeman, who was selected as chairman of the Provisional Council of Nadterechny district. These proxies were given support from the Russian military based in neighboring regions, but their writ barely extended beyond the Nadterechny town of Znamenskoe. By bolstering an internal opposition within Chechnya Russia hoped to undermine Dudaev's authority as the only legitimate Chechen partner for negotiations, as well as to disrupt his attempt to consolidate a state. The bankruptcy of this approach was demonstrated early in the conflict by the failure of Russia's Chechen proxies to win any significant popular support in Chechnya. It was further underlined by a succession of Russian political and military failures.

Dudaev in turn attempted autarchy by withholding federal taxes and other revenues, and by asserting his government's control over the Baku-Novorossiisk pipeline as it traversed Chechnya. The pipeline was a major part of the Russian state pipeline network, and carried significant volumes of oil. Grozny was the site of Russia's largest oil refinery, and a major petrochemicals industry. There were numerous oil fields scattered across Chechnya, though they were relatively small by Russian standards. The main railway line linking Russia to Dagestan and Azerbaijan also passed through Chechnya. Consequently, the economic assets available to Dudaev were significant and certainly made an independent Chechnya economically viable. In effect, Dudaev had control over major transport routes that were of immense strategic and economic importance to Russia.

Potentially, Dudaev's government had significant sources of income. Chechnya did not pay taxes or other revenues to the Russian budget, yet it received pension funds and other social subsidies. Anecdotal reports indicate that little of these funds were expended on the intended recipients. During 1992–93 the state service sector and state capacity of Chechnya began to collapse, due partly to non-payment of salaries and lack of funds, and partly to the expulsion or flight of ethnic Russians, who formed the backbone of the state sector (discussed later). An enormous amount of extortion and criminal activity around the oil industry is widely attributed to Dudaev's government. Russian sources, often FSB in origin, make wildly exaggerated claims about the nature of Dudaev's "criminal revolution" and "bandit regime" and are widely relied upon by Western journalists and academics.[23] According to the Russian sources, Grozny became a major center for organized crime, including counterfeiting, narcotics, and arms trading. Comparisons especially favored by Yeltsin and other Russian politicians were with Panama's former ruler General Noriega, Pablo Escobar and the Medellin drugs cartel in Colombia, against whom the United States deployed military forces, and the IRA's "racketeering" in Northern Ireland against whom the British waged war. In fact, Russia was largely to blame, both because the Russian blockade forced Chechnya to survive by any means, and because the Russian military exercised air and ground control around Chechnya. If criminal activity occurred, it required official cooperation at the highest military, if not political, levels in Russia.

The breakdown of civil order under Dudaev and the fact that his wider entourage included a few criminal figures gave some credence to the official Russian view, not only in Russia but also internationally. We should note, however, that some of the criminal figures (such as Beslan Gantemirov and Ruslan Labazanov) later went over to the Russian side. Dudaev's general arming of the male Chechen population in late 1991 and early 1992, at a time when command and control over Chechen forces was weak, led to an escalation of social disorder and abuses.[24] Many of those armed were unemployed highlanders who faced poverty as a result of the economic slump arising from the collapse of the USSR and the pursuit of shock therapy. Faced with difficulties of finding work in Chechnya or in Russia and the loss of their traditional seasonal work in other parts of the USSR, they readily joined the armed resistance. Armed Chechens, infused with a "Kalashnikov culture," turned against non-Chechens, mainly Russians, who did not have kin or clientelist protections. One consequence of the policy of blockade and nonintervention was that the ethnic Slav (overwhelmingly Russian) minority were left unprotected. A decade-long process of Slav emigration was suddenly accelerated as about 90,000, about one-third of the total number living in Chechnya, were physically expelled or otherwise forced to leave in 1991–92, and most of these were critical for the proper functioning of the state social sector, and oil and petrochemical industry (see Table 1 in Chapter 1).[25] The ethnic cleansing by direct and indirect methods of intimidation accelerated after Dudaev became president in October 1991.

Ethnic cleansing was not conducted under an official policy, but as relations between Russia and Chechnya broke down in late 1991, anti-Russian sentiment spilled out into uncontrolled violent attacks, routine humiliations and robbery of Russian residents by armed gangs of Chechens. Russia exploited the breakdown of civil order under Dudaev to "criminalize" the Chechnya question and foster the perception at home and abroad that Dudaev headed a "bandit" regime that fused traditional Chechen "clan" politics, transnational organized crime, and ethnic nationalism. The Russian viewpoint is summed up by Tishkov, who asserts: "The lack of federal control in Chechnya made it possible to transform this territory into a base of operations for the Russia-wide criminal community and into a place of refuge for criminals."[26]

Some works suggest that the conflict in Chechnya also had an economic subtext as a struggle over oil. It is not that Chechnya has significant extractable oil reserves, as these are a meager 50 million tons. In the late Soviet period Chechnya produced about four million tons of oil annually, and received another sixteen million tons from other parts of the Soviet Union for processing. Even after 1991, the Chechen republic produced about 90 percent of the aircraft oil consumed by CIS member countries.[27] In 1993 its production was some 1.25 million tons, less than 1 percent of Russia's total output, but together with the 120,000 tons annually pumped through the Russian pipeline from Azerbaijan it was sufficient for a lucrative and largely illicit oil trade with Russia from which Dudaev's government and other sections of the elite groups in Chechnya undoubtedly benefited.[28] It is claimed the Chechnya exported some twenty million tons of oil in 1991–94, and that Dudaev's government made hundreds of millions of dollars from the transactions.[29] The definition of "criminal" activity in this context is highly politicized. On taking power Dudaev's government nationalized the oil and infrastructure assets of

Chechnya, a move that was not recognized by Russia. Whereas Russian sources attempted to taint Dudaev with personally gaining from the illicit trade in oil, Yandarbiev blamed Salambek Khadzhiev (who later went over to the Russian side), who ran the state Grozneft oil company, for the losses of hundreds of millions of dollars to the budget of Chechnya. Moreover, Dudaev's reputation was undoubtedly tarnished by the activities of subordinates such as Gantemirov, who had plundered the mainly ethnic Russian-inhabited city of Grozny while acting as mayor in 1991–93.[30] The scale of criminal activity, on the other hand, is impossible to estimate, and the claims about Dudaev's involvement are not sufficiently substantiated with evidence. What we can say is that there was an ongoing "oil affair" under Dudaev which cost the state budget considerable losses and which he was either unwilling or unable to resolve.

Dudaev's chief concern after his election in October 1991 was with the difficult problem of building state institutions in conditions of socioeconomic collapse, internal disorder and external threat. He presided over the drafting of a new constitution for Chechnya, which was approved by the Chechen parliament in March 1992. Western and Russian commentators have exaggerated the role of Islam under Dudaev, based on a small number of seemingly iconic facts such as that he swore his presidential oath on the Qur'an, and on being sworn in as president declared: "By the will of Allah, and the people, I am the first president of the Chechen Republic."[31] The Chechen constitution, however, was a standard model of a secular nationalist parliamentary constitution.[32] The preamble states that the constitution is guided by the "idea of humanism." Article one states:

The Chechen Republic is a sovereign and independent democratic law-based state, founded as a result of the self-determination of the Chechen people. It exercises supreme rights over its territory and national wealth; independently determines its internal and foreign policies; the adopted constitution and laws have superiority on its territory. The state sovereignty of the Chechen Republic is indivisible.

Article two affirms: "The people of the Chechen Republic are the only source of all power in the state." Many aspects of the constitution would not look out of place in any other constitution informed by the ideals of secular republican nationalism. That the constitutional commitments to democracy and openness were not just a sham is suggested by the report of a fact-finding mission conducted by the well-respected London-based NGO International Alert, published in October 1992, which stated: "Chechen society is characterized by a remarkable degree of political openness and freedom of expression."[33]

It was difficult to tar Dudaev with the brush of Islamic radicalism in the face of such a secular nationalist constitution. The separation of the state and religion was affirmed in Article four, and the constitution provided for complete freedom of worship and opinions.[34] Dudaev wrote elsewhere that the "ideal" Chechen state would be one based on Islamic *shari'a* law, where a traditional council of Chechen elders would make decisions, but this was not the principle on which the constitution was formed.[35] His most explicit statement on the relationship between Islam and the state came in an interview with a Russian journalist in August 1992 and is worth citing in full:

Interviewer: What do you think can be the role played by Islam in the future republic of Chechnya? Which of the two models—that of Turkey or Iran—appeals to you?
Dudaev: I dislike both of them. The place for Islam in Chechnya will depend on the political situation in the republic and on the external pressure which will be exerted. That means exclusively on external factors. With the increase of negative external factors Islam is bound to grow. If we have an opportunity for the option of independence, independent development, a constitutional secular state will develop.
Interviewer: And what do you want? Do you want the influence of Islam to be limited?
Dudaev: Yes, of course. I would like Chechnya to become a constitutional secular state. We are seeking it, this is our ideal. Religion should play an exclusively important role in the spiritual development of people, in moral and humane attitudes. If religion gains an upper hand over constitutional structures, then the Spanish Inquisition and Islamic fundamentalism in their extreme manifestations appear. No religion, upon subordinating the state structures, coming to power, can maintain a purely religious course due its nature. Many will not obey such structures. A confrontation, rivalry are bound to come into being. And it leads to the Inquisition. It doesn't matter whether it is Islam, Christianity or any other religion.[36]

Some studies have pointed to Dudaev's supposed membership in the Qadiriia order and his Islamic rhetoric, especially when confronting the pro-Russian opposition attempts to unseat him in March 1992, as illustrative of his "adherence to Islam and piousness."[37] He called on the people to "rise in defense of their holy right to freedom, independence and national dignity" (a reflection, in fact, of his secular nationalism), but also condemned the opposition for violating Ramadan and the "holy norms of Islam." Moreover, Dudaev swore on the Qur'an before the Chechen parliament that he would not waver from the national independence struggle.[38] It is logical for a nationalist leader to mobilize forces around ideas that have popular legitimacy, and Dudaev's use of Islam was often correlated with moments of extreme urgency, when his leadership was seriously threatened. Moreover, there is no evidence that Islam played a major role in Dudaev's personal or political life until the conflict with Russia intensified in 1993–94, and it is uncertain even whether he was ever an active Muslim or Sufi adept. He would make similar calls infused with

Islamic rhetoric at the time of the Russian invasion in late 1994 and early 1995 (see below), but, as Lieven points out, these were more of an "expression of national feeling rather than a detailed program in its own right."[39] If the use of Islam was not instrumental, and if Dudaev had been intent on building any kind of Islamic state, one would have expected him to issue decrees and orders in this area. We would expect to see the infiltration of Islam into the state and society, and Islam as the basis for state-building.

In fact, there is no evidence for this. For example, when we examine the sixty presidential decrees, four acts, and forty-seven orders in this critical period of state-building in the second half of 1992, we find no attempt to Islamize Chechnya's state structures, or public life. Dudaev's only legal act in the matter of religion in this period was a presidential order calling for an ecumenical meeting of all the main heads of religious bodies to be held in Grozny to discuss ways of promoting religious cooperation in the Caucasus. When Dudaev elaborated his thinking on state-building in a long treatise published in April 1993, his vision was a secular one. The text began with a formal reference to the "will of Allah," but that is the only religious reference. His vision aspired to building a new state that would be of the same type as the developed capitalist countries, which would be free from Russia's "imperial diktat" and be "enlightened and civilized." While he recognized that the lack of experience of state administration was a problem for his government, he saw the main task as economic development. His vision would not have been out of place among the neoliberal "Harvard Boys" then advising the Yeltsin administration, for he stressed the need "to create the maximum possible conditions, by today's standards, for the intensive development of the entrepreneurial class." While the boom in small-scale so-called "shuttle traders" (traders who were buying or importing goods cheaply from abroad and then selling them on at a profit within the former USSR) in Chechnya during this period was part of a general trend throughout the ex-USSR, Dudaev saw it as a crucial part of the economic development of independence.[40]

That Dudaev's overriding concern was with the construction of a secular nation-state is reflected clearly in his presidential activities, which primarily dealt with the mundane issues of organizing an independent secular republic, such as appointments, the economy and budgetary matters, military affairs, social services, education, and culture.[41] Even the iconography of Dudaev's vision of the new Chechnya was largely non-Islamic. The new official symbol of the Republic, the wolf *couchant* under a full moon, was supposedly inspired by a drawing by Dudaev's Russian wife Alla, and drew on an ancient Chechen tradition of animism.

Dudaev did not build a governing or power network based on a kin notion of "clan", thus further demonstrating the weakness of this concept for understanding Chechen politics. Equally, Dudaev's distance from Chechen life and politics (he spoke Chechen poorly), and the remoteness of his own home area, the highland village of Yalkhoroi in southwest Chechnya, made it difficult for him to construct a territorial "clan"-based clientelist network even if he had so wanted. His approach was personalistic and ideological. He attempted to appoint persons who were loyal and competent, irrespective of their background. For example, he appointed an outsider, Jordanian-born Shamil Beno as head of the MVD, and an old classmate as Beno's deputy. He drew on territorial networks of support from areas such as Shali, which were traditional centers of the Qadiriia order but also a strong base of support for Yandarbiev's VDP. This simply reflected the politicized territorial cleavage within Chechnya, as the Naqshbandiia order was historically dominant in the pro-Russian Nadterechny region that was dominated by the old nomenklatura.

Russian political circles generally presented the conflict with the Dudaev government as a struggle not only against "criminality" but also against the "Islamic factor." Yeltsin, for example, explained the roots of the conflict in both Dudaev's attempt to secede from the Russian Federation *and* his goal of creating an "Islamic republic."[42] Huntington, in his by now classic polemic on the "Clash of Civilizations," framed the conflict in Chechnya as one of his so-called "fault line wars," though the empirical evidence given for this was insubstantial. For Huntington, Islam is the most conflictual and antagonistic of the eight "civilizations" that he identifies. In his references to Chechnya, he repeats either Russia's framing of the conflict or a few American studies which adhered to the Russian framing idiom. Moreover, he exaggerates the extent to which Muslims in the Russian Federation "rallied behind the Chechens."[43] Huntington's contribution was not insignificant, however, as it provided an important international academic confirmation, even if the route was circular, for Russian political paranoia about the "Islam factor" in the Caucasus. More recent Russian studies of Russia's involvement in the Caucasus recognize that "there was no 'Islamic national project' in Chechnya" and that at the beginning of the 1990s "the Islamic republic in Chechnya seemed to be a myth."[44] Much of the attention on the "Islamic factor," consequently, has fallen on how Islamic radicalism in Chechnya grew out of the war in 1994–96.

As discussed previously, Dudaev, Yandarbiev, and others often made symbolic references to Islam in the period 1991–94, though their focus was secular nationalism. While Dudaev engaged in secular state-building, and was determined to keep a separation between the state and religion, he was sensitive to the need for the development of Islamic religious life in Chechnya, which after all had been suppressed for decades under Soviet occupation, as part of a concern no doubt with social "values." His establishment of a Supreme Islamic Council in September 1991, almost immediately following the revolutionary overthrow of Soviet power, was an attempt to harness societal leaders and elders in the religious domain to his regime. The religious establishment, like the political establishment, in Chechnya was divided over Dudaev. The Supreme Islamic Council was regarded by the former religious establishment as being too dominated by the Qadiriia order, and a rival Naqshbandiia-dominated Spiritual Administration of Muslims was formed. As Dudaev became embroiled in his own president versus parliament struggle in late 1992 and early 1993, he attempted to create a unified "Muftiate" in August 1992. When the violent break with parliament came in June 1993 (discussed later), however, the Muftiate sided with the parliament against Dudaev.[45]

There was a growth in religiosity in Chechnya in the early 1990s, as there was across the whole of the former Soviet Union, in reaction to the decades of Soviet oppression of religion. The process in Chechnya was assisted by the increased contacts with the Chechen diaspora and the Islamic world, including not only the largely secular states such as Turkey and Jordan, but also Saudi Arabia and the Gulf States. Yandarbiev, for example, was part of a delegation that visited Mecca for the Hajj, which fell in June 1992. Performance of the Hajj, the fifth pillar of Islam, had been almost impossible for ordinary Muslims living in the Soviet Union. The fall of communism allowed many Muslims in the former USSR their first opportunity to fulfill this religious duty. It is therefore not unsurprising that some of Chechnya's leading politicians took the opportunity to perform the Hajj after 1991. Mecca was also the burial place of Imam Shamil, the singlemost important iconic historical figure in the resistance to Russian colonialism, and therefore had enormous political significance for Chechens. According to Yandarbiev, parliamentarians Iusup Soslambekov and Iusef Shamsuddin were received as official guests by the Saudi government and were given two gifts of religious significance—a large Qur'an, and a gold relic from the Ka'aba (almost certainly a piece of the holy covering of the Ka'aba, the Kiswa, which is replaced annually, and pieces of which are usually given by the Saudis to visiting delegations and dignitaries). Afterward, there was a dispute as to whether the gifts were personal or not, but it seems they were eventually handed over to Dudaev.[46] We will discuss Islamic radicalization in the latter 1990s in Chechnya in detail in Chapter 4, but at this stage it is important to recognize that while Dudaev's state-building was secular there was a steady development of Islamic religiosity in Chechnya prior to the military conflict with Russia, and over time this religious sentiment provided an important resource for mobilization against Russia once the military conflict was underway.

The Failure of Asymmetric Federalism, 1992–94

There were a number of attempts to negotiate during 1992–94. Some of the efforts to resolve the Chechnya "problem" from the Russian viewpoint were driven more by domestic political considerations than by authentic peacemaking. For example, Chechnya was instrumentalized by Yeltsin as a political tool in the president versus parliament conflict in Russia, which, given Khasbulatov's ethnicity, gave the struggle a Chechen dimension. Khasbulatov's policy of "bringing peace" to Chechnya in the summer and autumn of 1992 was an attempt to outflank both Yeltsin and Dudaev. Khasbulatov attempted to use his political connections in the Nadterechny nomenklatura elite to mobilize support for the forcible ousting of Dudaev. Solving the Chechnya "problem" by installing pro-Russian clients would enhance the authority of the Russian parliament against Yeltsin. Khasbulatov failed because he was out of touch with the growing nationalist popular mood in Chechnya. Yeltsin, however, also recognized the political need to engage with Chechnya beyond the policy of blockade.

As noted earlier, Yeltsin was not short of shrewd and knowledgeable advisors on nationality questions in 1992–93. His team of advisors included academic experts such as Starovoitova and Tishkov, whose views were sensitive to the political complexities of Russia's ethnopolitics, though they were opposed to self-determination for units of the USSR other than the Union Republics.[47] As we discussed earlier, they believed that their preferred "within-Russia" solution of autonomy for Chechnya, which exhibited a certain nostalgia for Soviet-style ethnofederalism, was sabotaged by "personal" differences between Yeltsin and Dudaev and hostility from Khasbulatov, though their main concerns were in any event to avoid a military escalation.

During 1992, as Dudaev consolidated power, there were at least four significant cases of Russian-Chechen cooperation. Russian and Chechen parliamentary delegations met and held talks on two occasions. The first meeting occurred on 28 May in Dagomys near Sochi, and there was a followup meeting in Moscow during the summer. The chairman of the Chechen Parliament, Khusein Akhmadov, told the members of an International Alert fact-finding mission in September 1992 that the meeting in Dagomys amounted to the "political recognition of an independent Chechnya" (see below). Moreover, the mission members were given copies of letters from Dudaev to Yeltsin, where he proposed negotiations and "civilized economic cooperation."[48] In fact, despite the Russian rhetoric about Dudaev's "criminality" there appear to have been some official intergovernmental agreements between Dudaev and the Russian government over oil export quotas and shipment of oil through Chechnya, since

Gaidar's government was reluctant to accept the disruption that would result from closing down the pipeline.[49]

A third form of cooperation occurred during the Abkhazia-Georgia conflict in the summer and autumn of 1992, when an "Abkhazian Battalion" of Chechen fighters under Shamil Basaev was transported in Russian military aircraft through Russian airspace, including a stopover in Russia, with the connivance of the Russian military and security services. Despite the fact that Basaev was wanted for his plane hijacking episode of November 1991, no attempt was made to arrest him or interfere. It seems improbable that Yeltsin did not sanction this operation. In this case there was an unholy alliance of interests, as on the one hand the Chechens were providing assistance to a Muslim brother people of the North Caucasus, while also serving Russian interests in shoring up the secessionist Abkhaz regime against Georgia's military intervention. The fourth episode of cooperation occurred shortly thereafter during the Ingush-Ossetian clashes in the Prigorodny district in autumn 1992, during which Russian troops had supported the Ossetians. In mid-November Russian Prime Minister Yegor Gaidar met with his counterpart Yaragi Mamodaev and negotiated a protocol to manage a deescalation of military deployment on both sides of the Chechen-Ingush border.[50]

Dudaev repeatedly blocked any outcome of negotiations that diluted Chechnya's independence. A series of meetings were held between Russian and Chechen officials, and between Russian officials and Chechen opposition figures, throughout 1992 and early 1993. In Russia, the process appears to have been managed from the Security Council, then headed by a consummate political negotiator Yurii Skokov, and was intended to sow divisions within Chechnya and isolate Dudaev.[51] Rather than assume a leading role, Dudaev left the negotiations to various subordinates, including Yandarbiev and prime minister Mamodaev, and other parliamentary leaders. The lack of president-to-president negotiations was a major flaw that ultimately brought the whole peace process to a standstill in 1994.

A major problem with the negotiations was the lack of consistency of positions on both sides. At the first high-level talks conducted by Yandarbiev and Viktor Zhigulin, the deputy chairman of the Russian Supreme Soviet, at Dagomys near Sochi in March 1992, an outline agreement on "recognizing the political independence (*nezavisimost'*) and state sovereignty (*suverenitet'*) of Chechnya" was included in the joint protocol. As we discussed in Chapter 2, this was a period when the Russian Federation was being reconstituted by the Federation Treaty (signed into law on 31 March 1992). Thus there was political momentum for a simultaneous agreement that would settle relations between Russia and Chechnya. The final discussions on the protocol were stalled by the Russian side, however, and by the time the next talks were held, in Moscow in May 1992, the Russians had retreated from the position of "political recognition" to one which talked merely of formalizing "relations" between the two sides.[52] Dudaev was enraged when the Gaidar-Mamodaev talks on Chechnya's status in December 1992 (following from the agreement after the Prigorodny conflict) appeared to lead to a "memorandum" on the principle of a future power-sharing treaty. Mamodaev even appeared on Russian television to confirm the success of the talks. When a delegation of senior representatives of the Russian government and parliament under Shakhrai and Abdulatipov, representing the Russian president and parliament, arrived in Grozny to finalize a power-sharing treaty with the Chechen parliament under its then chairman Khusein Akhmadov in January 1993, Dudaev moved to block it. The treaty was to be framed according to the model then being negotiated with Tatarstan, namely the "delimitation of powers" between the parties. This was a clear challenge to Dudaev's insistence that any treaty should be between equal states and recognize the independence of Chechnya. According to Tishkov, Dudaev was moved by the "arrogance of power," and his dissatisfaction with his subordinates brought him to sack Mamodaev, who had presided over the negotiations.[53] A more reasonable interpretation is that Dudaev had entrusted his prime minister with the dialogue but with absolute clarity that the core principle of Chechnya's independence was sacrosanct. When Mamodaev, for whatever reason failed to abide by this condition, he was sacked. The proposed treaty with Russia, however, was just one of several major disagreements between Dudaev and the Chechen parliament. As in Russia, where Yeltsin was bogged down in confrontation with the parliament over almost every aspect of policy-making, Dudaev was in almost constant battles with the Chechen parliamentary leaders.

The negotiations were consistently undermined by two other key elements. Firstly, the Russian and Chechen sides wavered between compromising and uncompromising positions, and the pattern of events was such that a propitious conjuncture when both sides were ready for compromise did not arise. Second, the constantly shifting negotiating positions were driven by rapidly changing political conditions in Russia and Chechnya, as both Yeltsin and Dudaev became absorbed in struggles with parliaments and constrained by growing nationalist popular constituencies. The dual power stasis between president and parliament in Russia led Yeltsin to turn his ethnic Chechen rival, Khasbulatov, into a bête noir. To reinforce his authority Yeltsin increasingly used harsh and uncompromising rhetoric toward Chechnya as a tool with which to strengthen his nationalist credentials and berate Khasbulatov, and thus by extension the Russian parliament. The results of the December 1993 parliamentary elections in Russia further limited the possibility for compromise with Chechnya.

The elections produced a massive surge in support for communists and the extreme Russian nationalist LDPR under Vladimir Zhirinovsky, and forced Yeltsin to stay in touch with popular opinion by taking a much more intransigent nationalist stance from early 1994.

Dudaev's authority was increasingly challenged by opposition groups in the Chechen parliament and warlords in the country, who wanted compromise with Russia. Having dismissed Mamodaev, he appointed the ideocrat Yandarbiev as his vice-president, while Mamodaev proceeded to form an opposition movement calling itself the "Government of National Trust." Like Yeltsin, Dudaev was confronted by an assertive parliament, which was theoretically constitutionally supreme, and thus entitled to negotiate with Russia, but was increasingly opposing his policies. He clashed with some of the Chechen leaders who had brought him to power, such as Gantemirov, Soslambekov, and Labazanov (all of whom eventually went over to the side of Russia). It was Dudaev who struck first to break the president-parliament standoff. He issued decrees on 17 April 1993 to dissolve the Chechen parliament, and on 18 April to dissolve the Grozny city council. His opponents resisted and during April, May, and June 1993, there were brief but bloody armed clashes from which Dudaev emerged triumphant. When the Constitutional Court ruled his decrees unconstitutional in late May 1993, Dudaev dissolved the court also. He was now in effect a dictator. His actions did not go unnoticed in Moscow, where Yeltsin was to apply the same methods a few months later. After the dissolution of the Chechen parliament, Dudaev's authority was increasingly restricted to south of the Terek, though the large pro-Dudaev demonstrations in Grozny in support of his actions in June 1993 suggest he retained a good measure of public support.

Dudaev's popularity appeared to decline during late 1993 and 1994, due to an acceleration of state breakdown, economic collapse, and increasing social disorder. The initial appeal of the nationalists that Chechnya could become a "second Kuwait" was proven hollow. The political divisions in Chechnya, however, encouraged the Yeltsin administration to increasingly stall an accommodation with Dudaev, in the expectation that he would be ousted by his domestic opponents, with or without some assistance from Russia. The pressures on Dudaev as a result of the blockade and the constant military threat of invasion and to his own security undoubtedly took a toll on his mental state, which now became increasingly erratic, dogmatic, and intolerant of criticism.[54]

Yeltsin's key constitutional advisor and negotiator with ethnic republics, Shakhrai, looked for a combination of "constructive ambiguity" in the wording of texts with real autonomy, and sought mutually profitable elite interactions to produce agreement.[55] During 1993 he was heavily engaged in negotiations with Tatarstan and Chechnya over their relations with the

Russian Federation. In the case of the treaty with Tatarstan, which involved the devolution of extensive powers of political, economic, and cultural self-rule (as discussed in Chapter 2), both Russia and Tatarstan had accepted a "constructive ambiguity" over the sovereignty question by employing the term "association" to describe Tatarstan's connection with the Russian Federation. The Russian government also agreed to co-sovereignty provisions in the Tatarstan constitution which declared the republic to be a "sovereign state" whose relations with Russia were regulated by *both* the Russian and the Tatarstan Constitutions. When the power-sharing treaty was signed in February 1994, Shakhrai stated that a similar treaty would be the basis for a solution to the Chechnya crisis, though Yeltsin warned that it would not be a "model" for federal relations in general.[56]

Views were polarized around irreconcilable differences over the acceptability of the principle of an internal solution, notwithstanding the details of power-sharing. Unlike Shaimiev, who had a pragmatic understanding of separatism and was prepared to accept the lawyer Shakhrai's clever wording of constitutional provisions, Dudaev was a charismatic nationalist leader who believed in the morality, legality, and necessity of independence for Chechnya. Dudaev made these values abundantly clear in his public speeches and interviews and in his private meetings with representatives of Yeltsin. It was not simply that he lacked the negotiating skills required for reaching a deal with Russia, but, as his dismissal of Mamodaev demonstrated, he refused to consider any compromise on full independence. Whether from a principled stance, lack of political skill, military-instilled decisiveness, or dictatorial hubris, Dudaev's refusal to compromise on the core issue of secession meant that there could be no internal settlement.

After the success with Tatarstan in February 1994, Shakhrai was appointed by prime minister Viktor Chernomyrdin to head a new negotiating team to resolve the conflict with Chechnya. By the summer of 1994, however, it seems that the Yeltsin presidential administration had determined to implement a military solution. Shakhrai was suddenly dismissed from the post of minister of nationalities. His replacement was Nikolai Yegorov, former governor of Krasnodar Krai, which bordered the Caucasus and had a strong Cossack lobby in its politics. Yegorov favored a hard line against Dudaev. Several direct appeals by Dudaev to Yeltsin for face-to-face negotiations were unsuccessful.[57] Russia's hostile intent was apparent from its escalation of attacks by its Chechen proxies in Znamenskoe under Avturkhanov, who had established a Provisional Council of the United Opposition as an alternative government to Dudaev's. The conditions were set for a civil war, or at least Russia now had a useful foil for its covert operations to destabilize Dudaev's government.

In late August Avturkhanov attempted to blockade Grozny, while Khasbulatov attempted to relaunch his political career by returning to

Chechnya in the autumn of 1994 on a "peace mission" to rally Chechen opposition to Dudaev. Avturkhanov's forces launched a new attack on Grozny in early November with the direct involvement of Russian military units. As in November 1991, Dudaev's forces easily subdued and captured the Russian troops who entered Grozny, and yet again, Dudaev paraded his prisoners before the Russian and international media. Direct negotiations between Russian minister of defense General Pavel Grachev and Dudaev led to the release of the prisoners and the temporary end to the crisis. The defeat was the final humiliation for Yeltsin, who was increasingly withdrawn and ill, and the hawks in the Russian government were decisively strengthened.

A high-powered coalition of key ministers representing sectional institutional and economic interests formed the so-called "Party of War," including the "power ministry" heads: minister of defense Grachev, minister of interior General Viktor Yerin, FSB chief Sergei Stepashin, but also First Deputy Prime Minister Oleg Soskovets, who was a patron of the military-industrial complex, minister of nationalities Yegorov, and perhaps most influential of all, Yeltsin's security chief and confidant Aleksandr Korzhakov, who controlled access to the president. Leading figures in the pro-Moscow Chechen opposition, especially Khasbulatov, were also clamoring for Yeltsin to destroy the "criminal regime" of Dudaev arguing that 99 percent of the people were against him.[58]

Tishkov has argued that Dudaev's regime would have collapsed due to intra-Chechen cleavages and opposition within Chechnya in late 1994, and it was only saved by Russian military intervention, which caused a reaction of "national unity."[59] The reality of developments in late 1994, however, was that the Chechen opponents of Dudaev were divided and incapable of organizing an independent concerted military effort against Dudaev. They were an odd rag-bag of former nomenklatura communists (Zavgaev, Avturkhanov, and Khadzhiev), new "democrats" (Khasbulatov), together with former Dudaev loyalists, both the respectable (former prime minister Mamodaev) and notorious and extremely violent gangsters (Gantemirov and Labazanov).

Even at this late stage, Dudaev appears to have made desperate attempts to avoid war. According to one Kremlin insider of this period, Yeltsin received many letters from Dudaev appealing for face-to-face talks, but they were destroyed by the president's press spokesman Viacheslav Kostikov. In his memoir Korzhakov reports that Dudaev phoned the Kremlin on eight occasions during 1994, in an attempt to speak personally with Yeltsin, but the president's chief of staff, Sergei Filatov, blocked Dudaev and did not inform Yeltsin.[60] Throughout this period Dudaev attempted to reach Yeltsin and Russian public opinion to demonstrate his willingness to compromise by giving many interviews to Russian journalists. Whereas in summer 1993 he had been completely intransigent, demanding "Independence and that's the end of it", during 1994 he became more conciliatory to Russia.[61] In May 1994 he expressed his sadness at the collapse of the USSR and interest in joining a new kind of "law-based union" with Russia.[62] In August 1994 he spoke of the need for "rational compromises" and negotiation, but still rejected the proposition that he was compromising Chechnya's independence.[63] In early December 1994, as the Russian invasion was starting, Dudaev told Russian journalists that Chechnya could remain part of Russia, but only a Russia that provides "law-based relations, secures the rights and freedoms of citizens, and rejects the use of force" and gives international guarantees to punish those who had engaged in the use of force. He declared that he had no preconditions for negotiations, and was willing for outside mediators to play a role.[64] It may be that Dudaev may have finally sought a compromise in late 1994, given the precariousness of his situation, but by then it was too late. It is equally plausible, however, that he already recognized that conflict was inevitable and sought to manipulate his legacy to ensure that the blame for the conflict lay at Yeltsin's door. The Yeltsin administration had passed the point of no return in the decision for war by this stage. The decision to invade Chechnya was taken on 29 November by the Russian Security Council, then headed by Oleg Lobov, a longstanding loyalist of Yeltsin's from his days in the Sverdlovsk party apparatus. The next day Yeltsin issued in secret decree No. 2137-c to give effect to the decision. Grachev later claimed that the military had vociferously opposed the use of force, but had been compelled by the civilian politicians. Moreover, when Grachev asked for at least a month to prepare the forces, Yeltsin ordered him to launch the operation within ten days. Grachev made a last attempt to avert war, and flew to Sleptsovsk in Ingushetia for a meeting with his old comrade Dudaev. In an atmosphere of great tension, with an armed crowd milling around the building, Dudaev reportedly told Grachev, "it's already too late. Do you see the crowd? If I concede to you, they will shoot both of us and put someone else in charge."[65] The government implementation decree, signed by Chernomyrdin, for the military operation was issued on 9 December and ordered the Russian security forces to "reestablish constitutional order in the Chechen Republic by all available means."[66]

Interests and the Instrumentalization of Conflict

So far, our analysis has concentrated on the fundamental issue at stake in the conflict between Russia and Chechnya—secession—which could not be resolved because it was nonnegotiable. However, important ideological, economic, and sectional interests also drove the process toward military conflict. The Russian decision to intervene militarily on a large scale against Chechnya in December 1994 came at a high point in Yeltsin's personalization of presidential power, but a low point in his popularity. After dissolving the Russian parliament by force in the "October events" of 1993, Rather than building democracy, Yeltsin had used his extensive decree powers under his tailor-made constitution of December 1993 to successfully reconstruct a vertical power structure based on a network of patron-client ties not unlike the Soviet nomenklatura system. The serious challenges to federal authority posed by separatist republics had been defused by his flexible approach to power-sharing treaties. Only Chechnya and Dudaev remained outstanding problems for a consolidation of the Russian state. The communist and nationalist Duma, however, blocked Yeltsin's domestic reform agenda. Consequently, the decision to invade Chechnya was partly impelled by the illusion that a "short victorious war" would boost Yeltsin's ratings and political authority in Russia.[67]

Within the Russian political and military elites, however, there were deep conceptual or ideological divisions over how to manage Chechen secessionism. These positions can be broadly categorized into liberal, pragmatist, and nationalist camps. It is equally important to note that positions on military intervention cross-cut the democratic-authoritarian spectrum in Russian politics.[68] Some leading Liberal reformers and "democrats" such as Sergei Stankevich, Andrei Kozyrev, Boris Nemtsov, and Anatolii Chubais supported military intervention, while others, such as Galina Starovoitova, Yegor Gaidar, Gavril Popov, and Yabloko leader Grigorii Yavlinskii, were opposed. Yeltsin's own special advisor on human rights issues, Sergei Kovalev, was a fervent critic of military force. Even the Liberal noninterventionist camp, however, struggled with the dilemma of reconciling Chechnya's demand for self-determination with their support for Russia's claim to "sovereignty" over Chechnya, as was evident from Kovalev's peace plan of early 1995:

We should recognize that the Chechens constitute a people, a nation. They, like other peoples, enjoy the right to self-determination, which should be exercised with due respect for the rights of other peoples and nations. We should at the same time acknowledge that the right of self-determination does not necessarily mean international recognition of every people as an independent, sovereign state.[69]

While the state-owned media followed the government line, the liberal non-state media of this period, especially the newspapers *Izvestiia* and *Nezavisimaia gazeta* and the independent television company NTV (the latter both owned by oligarch Vladimir Gusinskii, who was forced into exile in 2000), were strongly critical of military intervention. Their independent reporting finally broke the Soviet legacy of state-controlled media in Russia and would play a significant role in turning Russian public opinion against the war.[70]

One of the complications in evaluating the views of the Russian elites on Chechnya is that opinions changed over time as the conflict developed. It is perhaps more useful to analyze Russian elite positions as a dichotomy, between those who favored intervention and those who opposed it. These basic interventionist and noninterventionist positions were determined by the following arguments.

There was a strong security dimension to the interventionist argument. Dudaev's aggressive advocacy of Chechen independence, it was argued, threatened the integrity of the Russian Federation and had to be quashed, for if it was left unmanaged it might have a domino effect on other recalcitrant Russian ethnic republics, not only in the North Caucasus, but also in the Volga republics such as Tatarstan and Bashkortostan, where there were large Muslim populations. The liberal stream of thought in favor of intervention believed it was crucial to crush Chechnya's secession if Russia was to develop as a "normal" democratic constitutional polity and "civic" federation. This view predominated among Yeltsin's liberal ministers and advisors on nationality and federal questions, such as Shakhrai, Abdulatipov, Tishkov, Emil Pain, and Leonid Smirniagin, though these voices were marginalized from the center of decision-making by late 1994. There was also a strong nationalist impulse in the drive to crush the Chechens. Zhirinovsky struck a popular chord by portraying the secession of Chechnya and Dudaev's "arrogance" as humiliations for Russia's national prestige. It was critical to defeat the secession in order to restore Russian national pride as a great power (*derzhava*), and to reassert Russia's role as the hegemonic power in the Caucasus and Caspian region.

The noninterventionists argued that it was not only morally wrong to use coercion against Chechnya's exercise of its right to self-determination, but also hypocritical, given that Yeltsin himself had used the idea of national self-determination in his struggle against Gorbachev and the USSR. Furthermore, there was profound concern over the increasing authoritarian and nationalist drift by president and parliament, and war would likely accelerate this trend. Some democrats believed that in late 1994 the struggle was on to save Yeltsin "as a democrat."[71] According to Starovoitova, however, the battle for Yeltsin was lost even before the invasion of Chechnya as the president had lost "connection" with society and was increasingly motivated solely by power considerations. The Yeltsin circle, she believed, simply used the military intervention in Chechnya as "the most suitable object for demonstrating the leadership potential of the president."[72] Few of Russia's leading politicians openly supported independence for Chechnya, though some did so once the nature of the military quagmire became evident in the early months of 1995. They tended to be motivated more by racism than by concern with the morality of Chechnya's claim. Stanislav Govorukhin, head of the Duma investigation commission into the war, proposed that Russia should give Chechnya independence, cut off budget flows, annex Shelkovskii and Naurskii districts, and expel Chechen "criminal groups" from Russia.[73] The divisions in the military over the decision to invade were evident from the massive number of resignations, sackings, and the disciplining of more than five hundred officers before and during the war, including the commander and entire senior staff of the North Caucasus Military District on the eve of the invasion (a significant blow to Russian operational performance given that this cohort had most experience of the theater of operations).[74]

There was much debate in Russia as to the constitutional legality of Yeltsin's decree to launch the invasion, and whether the military should obey it. Yeltsin did not declare a state of emergency (arguably a constitutional requirement for the use of the military within the Russian Federation), since this needed the approval of the Federation Council (the upper chamber of the parliament). Yeltsin and the "party of war" were acutely aware that the senators, many of whom were the leaders of ethnic republics, would reject the use of force. Having issued the decree, Yeltsin retired to a hospital for treatment on his nose, and did not speak publicly about the invasion until he gave a television address on 28 December. Parliament appealed to the Russian Constitutional Court to clarify the legality of the decree. After seven months of war, the court decided in July 1995 that the integrity of Russia was a matter of state security that was within the powers allocated to the president by the constitution.[75]

An important motivation for intervention was Russian calculation about the potential threat to its strategic influence in the Caucasus and Caspian Basin from an independent and hostile Chechnya. Dudaev had a stranglehold on one of Russia's main oil pipelines and threatened Russia's eastern gateway to the South Caucasus. The Baku-Novorossiisk pipeline was crucial for Russia's access to the billions of tons of extractable reserves in the Caspian Basin, yet it traversed over 153 kilometers of Chechen territory (see Map 2). For many in the Russian elite, Chechnya had to be controlled or neutralized, for an independent Chechnya under an uncooperative leader such as Dudaev would pose a threat to Russian economic interests and strategic influence in the Caucasus and the Caspian oil business. The move to a coercive strategy against Chechnya occurred in an international context where the oil and gas resources of the Caucasus were becoming a salient issue of competition between the former Soviet states, and between Russia and Western states.

In September–October 1992 Dudaev went on a major foreign tour, visiting Turkey, Jordan, Saudi Arabia, United States, UK, and Germany. Part of the purpose of the trip was to snub Russian oil interests and search out partners for restoring oil production, and in particular refining, in Chechnya. He met with British parliamentarians in Westminster, and in Houston, Texas, he signed a two-year contract worth about $100 million with San Antonio-based EnForce Energy Corp., covering work, drilling, and other services in two oil fields north of the Chechen capital of Grozny. Dudaev also paid his respects to Chechnya's most famous political exile, the historian Abdurahman Avtorkhanov, in Olching (Bavaria), Germany.[76] The oil deals soon collapsed as a result of instability in Chechnya in 1993 and the increasing reputation of Chechnya abroad for "gangsterism."[77]

The shift to a military option by Russia followed quickly in the wake of the so-called "deal of the century" in September 1994, when a cluster of European and American oil companies (headed by BP and Chevron) formed the Azerbaijan International Operating Consortium (AIOC), in an $8 billion contract with Heidar Aliev's government in Azerbaijan for the development of three giant oil fields in the Caspian Sea. This was a challenge to the Russian-led Caspian Pipeline Consortium (CPC), established with Kazakhstan and Oman in 1992 to construct a 1,600-kilometer link between the Tengiz oil field in Kazakhstan and a terminal near Novorossiisk. The CPC, in which Russia's oil giant Lukoil was the major investor, was Russia's key lever to become the main route for Caspian oil, rather than the proposed construction of a Baku-Ceyhan pipeline route via Georgia and Turkey. The Russian pipeline monopoly Transneft was anxious to use its Baku-Novorossiisk route for "early" oil exports from three Azeri oil fields in the Caspian as the precursor to even larger shipments later. Sectional interests in the Russian "fuel-energy complex" exerted a strong influence on Yeltsin via emerging oligarchs such as Boris Berezovskii, who also had strong links to Chechen groups in Moscow and Chechnya.[78]

Another key sectional interest was the fnilitary-security elites. According to Grachev, Russian defense minister at the time of the December 1994 invasion of Chechnya, the General Staff had been reluctant to undertake the military operation and were pushed into it by the government of prime minister Viktor Chernomyrdin, himself an energy industry oligarch.[79] There is much speculation that in fact Grachev (nicknamed Pasha Mercedes) and his circle in the military hierarchy favored intervention as a way to cover up their role in organizing massive illicit sales of military equipment from the Western Group of forces to Serbia and Croatia, and in assisting Dudaev's government with the trade in oil and weapons. A war would allow much equipment to be written off. Reportedly, Chechnya was also used as a transshipment point for Russia to secretly arm its allies in other post-Soviet conflict zones in the Caucasus (Abkhazia, South Ossetia, and Nagorno-Karabakh). According to General

Aleksandr Lebed, Grachev and his aides were not the "party of war" but the "party of business."[80] Furthermore, the fiscal austerity of the economic liberals threatened the military with reforms and significant budget cuts during the spring of 1994. The military commanders around Grachev, it is suggested, shifted in support of intervention in Chechnya to cover the traces of their corrupt activities, avert reform and pursue budget maximization.[81] Dudaev himself believed that a decision for a military move against Chechnya was related more to the internal politics of Russia and attempts to create a dictatorship there than to the state of Russia's relations with Chechnya. This "force," he claimed, wanted to "cut the Chechen knot with one blow."[82]

The First War, 1994–96

The relentlessly brutalizing nature of the first Russo-Chechen War has been well described and documented by other studies. As with other conflicts, there is by now an extensive literature of military studies, narrative accounts, and personal testimonies of the conflict in Chechnya written by Russian and Western journalists. Despite an emphasis on the "Chechnya syndrome" of murder, rape, looting, and other abuses by Russian troops, the cultural distance between reporter and soldier means that the *mentalité* of the troops is not well captured, and none of these works compare favorably to such journalistic and memoir classics of U.S. military involvement in Vietnam as those of Michael Herr and Mark Baker.[83] There are few memoirs from the Chechen side.[84] The war of 1994–96 was extremely costly in human, economic, and political terms. It resulted in the wholesale physical destruction of Grozny and widespread damage to many other towns and villages in Chechnya, despite claims by the Russian government that its military employed "pinpoint" targetting. The devastation was such that the respected Russian newspaper *Literaturnaia gazeta* published a photograph of the ruins of Grozny with the headline: "This is not Stalingrad in '42, It's Grozny in '95."[85] The lower estimates of casualties suggest about 4,379 military deaths and more than 20,000 civilian deaths, with no accounting of wounded.[86] Recent Russian General Staff statistics state that 5,835 Russian soldiers died in the war, but unofficial estimates are much higher.[87] Estimates of the full scale of Chechen military casualties are almost impossible to calculate. General Aleksandr Lebed, who negotiated the truce that brought the war to an end (see below), estimated that the war cost about 80,000 dead and 240,000 wounded.[88] John Dunlop has provided the most comprehensive analysis of the sources on casualty figures for the first war. He conservatively assessed Russian and Chechen estimates and concluded that about 11,500 combatants died (7,500 Russians and up to 4,000 Chechens), 25,000–29,000 civilians (mostly ethnic Russians) were killed in the bombing of Grozny, and perhaps as many as 35,000 civilians were killed overall. His conservative estimate for total dead is 46,500.[89]

A large part of the Russian population left in 1991–92, but those who remained mainly resided in Grozny, and consequently suffered disproportionally higher casualties from the indiscriminate bombing and shelling of the city by the Russian military. The modern infrastructure of Chechnya (housing, industry, communications, social services) was almost completely destroyed by the conflict. Several hundred thousand Chechens became internally displaced persons (IDPs), and lived as refugees in camps in the relative safety of neighboring Ingushetia.

Much of the credit for the initial success of the Chechen resistance was due to Dudaev's military commander, Maskhadov. Like Dudaev, Maskhadov had been a career officer in the Soviet army, rising to the rank of anti-aircraft and artillery division chief-of-staff at the Baltic Military District in Vilnius, Lithuania. Like Dudaev, he had lived through the "Baltic revolution." He had resigned his commission and returned to Chechnya in December 1992 to take up the post of first deputy-chief of staff of the Chechen armed forces. In July 1994, as Russian aggression against Chechnya escalated, Maskhadov was appointed to the post of chief of staff. Dudaev had devoted a great deal of his time in office to military affairs, and the building of an army. The Chechens were well-supplied with weaponry but lacked a trained officer corps. Of twenty officers in the general staff, only three had been through Soviet military academies. According to Russian intelligence sources in 1992 the Chechen armed forces existed only "formally" and were fragmented into more than eighteen different units.[90] There was undoubtedly a large element of criminality in the operations of many of these groups, and some were "private armies," a trend associated in comparative experience with weak states that are unable to pay salaries to armed state functionaries. Even the Chechen leadership recognized this: Yandarbiev, for example, admitted that the so-called Shali Tank Regiment (composed of tanks seized from the departing Russian garrison in early 1992) was under the command of "local thieves" who refused to submit to Dudaev's authority.[91]

We must be careful not to apply loosely the Russian government's idiom of the conflict, nor to rely uncritically on dubious material that originates from intelligence services. According to official Russian sources, any Chechen armed force is "criminal," "a bandit formation" (*bandformirovaniia*), or "terrorists." (The more neutral term "fighter" (*boevik*) was also in wide use during the first war among the more independent media.) As we shall discuss in Chapter 5, the issue of "terrorism" is often conflated with national resistance, in particular by colonial rulers and occupiers. Armies of national resistance are often unprofessionalized in their organization and guerrillas often do not wear uniforms, factors that allow state armies to give them no quarter. In fact, there was no shortage of uniforms, in the sense of military fatigues, in Chechnya, and they were widely worn by the Chechen armed forces and fighters. By the summer of 1994, a more disciplined and trained regular army some four or five thousand strong had been forged. Between Dudaev's decree on a general military mobilization on 11 August 1994 and February 1995 Russian sources estimated that the Chechen armed forces swelled to some 15,000 regular full-time soldiers. The Chechens had dozens of tanks and armored vehicles, and were an exceedingly well-equipped infantry fighting force, but the main problems remained command and control.[92] The only battle-hardened and well-disciplined force in 1992–93 was Basaev's Abkhazia Battalion, no more than two hundred strong. Of course, there were also many armed civilian volunteers (*opolchentsy*), perhaps as many as 30,000–40,000, formed into a loosely coordinated "Home Guard" local militia, but who wore either only civilian or mixed civilian-military dress.

The experience of the Bosnian war has led to an incongruous association between the activity of civilian militia, war crimes, and genocide—as if state militaries are incapable of war crimes.[93] Some studies question the military efficacy of such civilian formations, though naturally distinguishing them from the exemplary historical civilian militias of the American Revolution.[94] Let us then see how the Chechen fighters performed against Russian armored units in late 1994.

After Russian armored convoys crossed the Chechen border on 11 December 1994, the war quickly became a catalogue of military disasters for the Russians, which laid bare the poor state of Russian military readiness. Snow and fog, together with uncertainty among the commanders over how to deal with civil protests against their presence, slowed the advance of the three Russian armored columns approaching from the north, east, and west. The poor weather conditions also grounded air support for the columns as Russia lacked an all-weather air capability. It was only around 22 December that the weather cleared sufficiently for a massive air bombardment of Grozny, initially focusing on Dudaev's presidential palace and the main "Lenin" oil refinery.

As an armored column approached Grozny there was a part spontaneous and part organized mobilization of Chechen fighters to defend the city. Dudaev's presidential television service broadcast video instructions on how to load and fire anti-tank rockets, and where to target the weak points of T80 and T82 tanks and other armored vehicles. Fighters with military experience were dispersed among the Chechen units.[95] The Chechens attacked when Russian armored columns moved into the city center toward Freedom Square and Dudaev's palace. The Chechen units in the central defense ring were led by Basaev, with the Abkhazia Battalion playing a leading role. The Chechens employed textbook military tactics by surprise attacks at close range, destroying the first and last armored vehicles in the Russian columns, and then systematically attacking the others from close range. The Russian 131st Motorized Infantry Brigade was annihilated. About 200 of the 350 armored vehicles participating in the assault were destroyed or captured, and officially over 500 soldiers were declared killed. In the heat of battle few prisoners were taken.[96] These were the heaviest losses incurred by the Russian military in a single battle since the end of the Second World War.

The defeat in the battle for Grozny and other early military setbacks inflicted heavy damage not only to Russian military capacity but, more important, to the morale of its soldiers. It established a pattern from which there was no recovery. The "Afghan war syndrome" recurred, as the poorly officered and largely conscript army was reduced to drunkenness and drug-taking that impaired military performance, and fueled indiscipline that led to routine atrocities against Chechen civilians. Selling weaponry to Chechens was an endemic problem. The use of professional contract soldiers (*kontraktniki*), better paid and better equipped but generally more brutal, rapacious, and undisciplined, contributed to the rampant demoralization. The Russian war effort also suffered from institutional incompetence, as the command of Russian forces was divided between the army and ministry of interior, who competed against each other, refused to coordinate their operational activities, and on occasion even shot at each other.

Yeltsin and the Russian elite had seriously underestimated Dudaev and his armed forces. Grachev had earlier promised Yeltsin that he would take Grozny within "a couple of hours." From the beginning of 1995, Russia found itself bogged down in a guerrilla war of attrition that suited the Chechens, who were highly motivated, well organized and well armed for this type of conflict, and were fighting in their own terrain with local support. The Chechen volunteers fought sporadically, moving in and out of the armed conflict from day to day depending on their circumstances and commitment. This often made it difficult for Russian forces to identify the enemy combatants, and led them to adopt many of the brutal tactics of classical counter-insurgency, such as collective punishments on civilian communities where fighters operated and on the relatives of fighters (discussed further in Chapter 5).

Russian training and equipment were badly matched against the hit-and-run guerrilla tactics of the Chechens, whether in the urban warfare in Grozny and other towns or in the poorly accessible mountain terrain. Russia lacked all-weather aircraft, night-fighting aircraft and equipment, electronic intelligence gathering and other essentials necessary to conduct such warfare. Incapable of countering the Chechens militarily, Russian troops, in echoes of Soviet military conduct in Afghanistan and U.S. military conduct in Vietnam, turned to the reckless use of airpower and artillery and the abuse of prisoners and civilians. One of the most widely reported massacres of civilians by Russian soldiers occurred in the village of Samashki in April 1995, when over one hundred civilians were killed in one operation.[97]

From the outset of the war, a trend toward radicalization became apparent among Chechens. The brutal experience of war and Russian occupation, and the exhilaration of the victory against the odds in Grozny in December 1994, intensified a shift from secular nationalism to greater religious and cultural sensibility about the nature of the conflict. It is important to stress that this religious-cultural framing of the conflict by Chechens became more widespread only as a result of the escalation of Russian military activity against Chechnya in late 1994. In January 1995, in the immediate aftermath of the Russian bombing of Grozny, and the victory of his forces in the intense battle for the center of the city, Dudaev himself epitomized this change when making a televised address to the Chechen people by declaring in Russian "rise Chechnya, rise for the *ghazavat*" and ended with "Allahu akbar!"[98] Chechen fighters from Islamic militant groups took to wearing the green headband of martyrdom, a marker of *ghazavat*. For some undoubtedly this was a religious-cultural statement, but for others it was simply part uniform and part iconic cultural marker, devoid of deep religious significance.

That Yeltsin personally was central to the decision for a military intervention is suggested by the fact that he pursued the war through to summer 1996, even after the removal from office of the key ministers associated with the "party of war." In a later defense of his actions, Yeltsin observed, "The mistake I made was to share faith in the common might of our army," and he made no other apologies for his "war against terrorists." It was the presidential electoral cycle in Russia that eventually turned the policy on Chechnya from coercion to political accommodation. The approach of the presidential election of June 1996 concentrated the minds of the Yeltsin administration on finding an alternative solution to the unwinnable and bankrupt military strategy.

Losing wars is never likely to be a vote-getting strategy for politicians. In the case of Chechnya, Yeltsin was faced with a "dirty war" which was being lost not only in situ but also in the mass media, as independent media in Russia, along with foreign mass media, undermined official Russian propaganda and helped make the war deeply unpopular in the country and abroad. Moreover, Dudaev had long threatened to spread any armed conflict beyond the territory of Chechnya, warning a Russian journalist in 1992 that "any armed intervention of Russia in Chechnya's affairs will mean a new Caucasian war."[99] There were episodes of terrorism in neighboring Russian regions and republics by some elements of the Chechen forces, notably those operating under Basaev, now a "field commander." Two incidents in particular, the maternity hospital siege at Budennovsk, and the bus hostage-taking at Kizliar, shocked Russian public opinion into the reality that the war in Chechnya could not be contained within Chechnya itself, but was increasingly likely to spill over into terrorist acts within Russian proper (see Chapter 5). The Budennovsk incident led to a truce agreement between General Romanov for Russia and General Maskhadov, then head of Chechnya's armed forces, in July 1995, but neither side was able to secure compliance from its forces and the truce broke down.

In early 1996 a number of peace plans and proposals were produced by prominent Russian politicians. A staged peace plan for talks, a ceasefire, Organization for Security and Cooperation in Europe (OSCE) mediation, and an agreed formula for a referendum in Chechnya on the status of the republic, was proposed in February 1996 by a group of prominent pro-democracy Duma deputies: Ramazan Abdulatipov, Yegor Gaidar (both former ministers under Yeltsin); Sergei Kovalev, Valerii Borshchev, Mikhail Molostvov, Iuli Rybakov, and Lev Ponomarev (human rights activists); and Grigorii Yavlinskii, Vladimir Lukin, and Viktor Sheinis (leading Yabloko deputies).[100] At this stage Tatarstan's president Shaimiev also played a vital mediating role. He submitted a seven-point peace plan to Yeltsin and Dudaev in February 1996, which also called for a staged process of talks on status, ceasefire, OSCE mediation, withdrawal of federal forces, and new elections, reconstruction, and demilitarization in Chechnya.[101] The most influential proposal for peace in Chechnya emerged from the "Hague Initiative," a series of informal roundtable talks on post-Soviet conflicts conducted in 1995–97 between government officials and politicians from various protagonists in the region and experts on conflict regulation. The talks were hosted by the Carnegie Foundation in the Carnegie-built Hague Peace Palace. The second round of these talks was held on 25–27 March 1996 and brought together Russian and Chechen officials (including Shaimiev, Russia's minister of nationalities Viacheslav Mikhailov, presidential advisor on ethnic issues Emil Pain, and Dudaev's representative in Moscow Vagap Tutakov, among others) and academic experts to discuss the prospects for "bridge-building" in Chechnya and other post-Soviet conflict situations. The "Hague Initiative" produced a ten-point plan for Chechnya, which essentially replicated the proposals discussed above but with one innovative and important addition. Point Seven called for the resolution of the political status of Chechnya "on the basis of the principle of a delayed decision." The suggestion drew on the international management of the Saar question in 1919–20. The Treaty of Versailles (1919) made Saarland (a major coal-producing region of

Germany adjacent to France) an autonomous territory, administered by France under League of Nations supervision. A plebiscite to determine its final status was postponed for fifteen years, and in 1935 the Saarlanders voted overwhelmingly to restore German sovereignty. In the case of Chechnya the Hague dialogue appears to have settled on a ten-year delay.[102]

Political pressures in the run-up to the Russian presidential election of June 1996 forced Yeltsin to return to a negotiation strategy to find a face-saving exit from the conflict. The policy change was made more palatable for Yeltsin when Dudaev was killed by a Russian air strike in April 1996, possibly after being deceived by Russian promises of negotiations into revealing his location.[103] The removal of Dudaev, also allowed the Russian leadership to spin the peace process in a more positive manner. Equally, Dudaev's death appeared to remove a major obstacle to negotiations. Yandarbiev assumed the presidency, and although his shift from ideologue for Chechen nationalism to radical Islamism had been accelerated by the war, he was de facto subordinate to Maskhadov, the military leader of the resistance who was regarded as a moderate and known more for his technocratic military professional competence. Yeltsin did not personally take a leading public role in the process. He instructed key subordinates, with Prime Minister Viktor Chernomyrdin taking the lead, to negotiate a settlement.

Progress on negotiations was made only as a result of the impending presidential election. Yeltsin himself concluded a truce in face-to-face negotiations with Yandarbiev on 27 May 1996, followed by a tense and fleeting visit to Grozny under Yandarbiev's "protection," where Yeltsin told a gathering of what must have been incredulous Russian soldiers: "The war is over. Victory is ours. We have defeated the rebellion of the Dudaev regime."[104] Yeltsin dusted off the power-sharing treaty option and a version of a Draft Treaty between the Russian Federation and Chechnya was circulated to the media, which included similar textual ambiguities to those in the treaty with Tatarstan.[105] For example, relations were to be governed by both the Russian and the Chechen constitutions and the treaty (an obvious contradiction), and suggestions of a more confederative "special status" for Chechnya and wide-ranging self-governing powers (Articles 1–3). Subsequently, two protocols were signed at Nazran, Ingushetia, by Maskhadov and Russian Nationalities Minister, Viacheslav Mikhailov, on 10 June 1996, which provided for the withdrawal of most Russian troops (not all—two brigades would remain) and free elections in Chechnya.

The Russian presidential election in late June and early July was a nerve-wracking experience for the corrupt circle (known as the "Family") of political, security, and oligarchic figures in Yeltsin's entourage. Yeltsin had suffered a heart attack during the campaign, and there was panic in the "Family" that his removal from power, death, or incapacitation would destroy their political and economic control of the country, possibly with the choice for many of them being arrest or exile. Yeltsin's election victory was secured by the massive use of the financial power of the oligarchs, often illegally, to assist Yeltsin's campaign and by a pact of convenience with the former Soviet army general, Aleksandr Lebed, who had performed well in the first round of voting. Lebed's votes secured Yeltsin's victory over the communist party candidate, Gennadii Ziuganov, in the second round. Lebed, however, had strong views on the need for peace with Chechnya and for a Russian military withdrawal, among other matters, that disrupted the patrimonial harmony of the Yeltsin "Family."

After the election Yeltsin appointed Lebed head of the Security Council and gave him the task of leading the negotiations with Maskhadov to secure a final settlement. The summer of 1996 presented a small window of opportunity when Lebed's authority was sufficiently strong within the administration, the government, and the country at large to push through a peace settlement, though the political class was deeply divided and significant forces in the communist and nationalist-dominated Duma, the power ministries and military command, and Yeltsin's circle were vehemently opposed to concessions.[106] The Yeltsin administration found it difficult to abandon one key aspect of the Chechen strategy—reliance on pro-Moscow Chechen elites. Already in February 1995, after Russian forces occupied Grozny, a pro-Moscow government was set up under Khadzhiev. In July 1996 Zavgaev was brought back to Chechnya from Moscow and installed as Chechnya's new president. He acquired the epithet Doku Aeroportovich, since he rarely traveled outside the heavily fortified Russian base at Grozny's Khankala airport.

The peace process was accelerated by the prospect of a major Russian military defeat. The Russian military stepped up operations in Chechnya even before the election was over, thus sabotaging the agreements of May and June. Lebed was even prepared to face down open revolt among some of the Russian military commanders in Chechnya. General Troshev recalled that the commanders felt that they had been denied a total victory over the "bandits" by the way Chechnya had become a political issue in the presidential election. They wanted to "decisively resolve the problem" and were outraged by the "time-out" that allowed the Chechens to regroup.[107] In August 1996 Lebed entered a battle of wills with the military commanders in Chechnya, generals Viacheslav Tikhomirov and Konstantin Pulikovskii who, supported by Minister of Internal Affairs General Anatolii Kulikov, wanted to continue the war. The move to a truce and peace talks, however, came only in August 1996, after Maskhadov organized a surprise Chechen assault—"Operation jihad"—on the Russian garrison in Grozny that led to a disintegration and encirclement of the major part of the Russian forces in their fortified outposts within city. The final straw for Yeltsin seems to have come on 19–20 August, when Pulikovskii issued an ultimatum for all civilians to leave Grozny "within 48 hours" so that he could flatten what was left of the city with Maskhadov's rebels in it. There was a massive public backlash within Russia and internationally that forced Yeltsin to publicly endorse Lebed's bid for peace and countermand his generals. For Yeltsin and Lebed, action was needed as much to save Russia from a humiliating military defeat in Grozny as to advance the agenda of securing an exit from Chechnya, but for the Russian military this was the moment when "complete dilettantes in military questions" decided the fate of the campaign in Chechnya.[108]

Lebed had developed a reputation for inconsistency and flippancy. On the status of Chechnya, on some occasions he argued that a referendum should be held in Chechnya, and if the vote was in favor then Chechnya should be allowed its independence. On other occasions he declared that Chechnya was an integral part of Russia.[109] This ambivalence was ultimately reflected in the agreement he negotiated with Maskhadov in talks held in late August in the village of Khasaviurt in Dagestan, close to the border with Chechnya. In contrast to the Yeltsin-Dudaev relationship, Lebed and his Chechen adversaries, Maskhadov and Basaev, negotiated face-to-face. Senior officials from neighboring republics to the conflict, including the president of Ingushetia, Ruslan Aushev, also attended and played a mediating role.

Significantly, for the first time in Russian-Chechen negotiations, talks were conducted in the "presence" of an international mediator, the head of the OSCE Assistance Group in Chechnya, Tim Guldimann, an experienced Swiss diplomat.[110] Guldimann, who was in regular contact with both sides of the conflict and was a recognized intermediary, had been called to Moscow by Lebed for discussions. Lebed presented Guldimann a text which provided for a delayed decision on Chechnya's final status, and which he hoped would be a basis for negotiation with the Chechens. He had worked it out with Vadim Lukov, then head of the Foreign Planning Policy Unit of the Ministry of Foreign Affairs, on the basis of France's "New Caledonia model."[111] It seems that Lebed and Lukov had revived the "Hague Initiative" idea of a delayed decision, but did not wish to attribute it directly to the influence of a dialogue that had been funded and developed by American experts. Guldimann returned to Chechnya and presented it to Yandarbiev in Novye Atagi to see if it would "fly" with the Chechens, and Yandarbiev agreed that it would. After some hours, during which time Lebed and his team arrived in Khasaviurt, and Guldimann was provided with a Russian helicopter to track down Maskhadov in the Chechen highlands, all sides finally met together at Khasaviurt on 30–31 August 1996.

The negotiations lasted from around 7:00 p.m. until 2:00 a.m., with five or six persons from each side plus Guldimann seated at a table. The discussions centered on the Lebed-Lukov text and a package of documents that Lebed's team had worked out, and which he claimed had been drafted "not by bosses, but by lawyers."[112] According to Lebed, the Russian team had the initiative, since they read out their own drafts and the Chechens responded. As was to be expected in such negotiations, much of the discussion focused on the textual nuances of meaning, particular words, and certain formulations. According to Guldimann, Lebed "did very well," was open to any changes suggested by the Chechens, and prevented the talks becoming aggressive. The negotiations were eased by an atmosphere of good will and rapport between the key actors, with time even for games of football, chess, and cards in the breaks between talks. The mutual respect of Lebed and Maskhadov was obviously also conducive to the negotiations.[113]

The Chechens believed that they now had a Russian negotiating partner who was prepared to compromise on the issue of sovereignty and self-rule, and who at that time appeared to have the necessary political collateral to ensure implementation by the Russian side. But there was no Russian intention to allow independence, for they wanted a delay, a limbo in the conflict. Lebed seems to have shrewdly played on divisions within the Chechen team between the more pragmatic leaders, such as Maskhadov, and the more ideologically driven, such as the formal head of the Chechen delegation Dr. Sait-Khassan Abumuslimov, Yandarbiev's vice-president. Abumuslimov had been professor of history at the State University in Grozny in the early 1990s, and had been involved in underground Chechen nationalist organizations during his student days at Lomonosov University in Moscow, from which he had graduated in 1981. He had been one of the drafters of the 1992 Constitution of Chechnya and was an intellectual secular nationalist.[114]

In a later account of the talks Lebed reported how Abumuslimov demanded outright recognition of independence, including Russian acknowledgment of Chechnya's right to join the UN, and questioned many of the formulations in the Russian documents. For Lebed, this represented fastidious nit-picking, though we can assume that Abumuslimov mistrusted the Russians, and suspected that Lebed's bonhomie approach to the Chechen military delegates was a deliberate ploy to weaken their resolve. Lebed relates the following:

I will give you one example: "The legal system of the Chechen Republic will be built . . . (*stroitsia*)"—Stop!—cried the relentless Abumuslimov.—What does "will be built" mean? It is already built (*postroeno*), fixed, and you propose that some kind of construction is only to begin!" Eventually they agreed on the formulation "will be based" (*osnovyvaetsia*).[115]

The Khasaviurt Agreement between Russia and Chechnya of 31 August 1996 (see Appendix 1) "internationalized" the conflict, in the sense that the Joint Statement accepted that certain international norms such as the right of nations to self-determination, the 1949 Universal Declaration of Human Rights, and the 1996 International Covenant on Civil and Political Rights would inform the process for determining the relations between Russia and Chechnya. Guldimann was also a signatory, at his own request, but this was used by both sides as an international endorsement. A masterstroke to secure the agreement was the ambiguity whereby the final decision on the status of Chechnya was postponed. As Guldimann explained to the author, he was skeptical that the agreement meant anything other than that Chechnya remained under Russian sovereignty: "There was no Russian intention to allow for independence. They wanted a limbo."[116] The date 31 December 2001 was set as the deadline for a final resolution of the status question. The time delay on the status of Chechnya would have been familiar to the Chechens since the Chechen-Ingush agreement of June 1992 included a five-year moratorium on the status of their boundaries.[117]

The "internationalization" of the conflict was reiterated in the "Principles" for determining the future relations between Russia and Chechnya that were appended to the Joint Statement. The Principles also established a Joint Commission to decide on the Russian military withdrawal, measures to combat crime, terrorism and ethnic violence (aimed at protecting Russians still living in Chechnya), future economic relations, reconstruction and emergency aid. It was far from the treaty of recognition of Chechnya's independence that Dudaev had insisted upon. Nevertheless, the wording was sufficient for the Chechen leaders to accept. These leaders were bargaining from a position of strength on the military front, and thus a main priority for them was to secure a Russian military withdrawal. It was clear to them that they had achieved de facto independence, but they also believed that they had locked Russia into a process of negotiation that would be determined by international norms and ultimately lead to secession. Equally, Lebed could claim to have averted the de jure secession of Chechnya, while saving the Russian army from certain defeat.

Chechen suspicions of Russia's bad faith appeared to be confirmed when on 17 October 1996 Yeltsin sacked Lebed from the government, just two weeks after Chernomyrdin and Yandarbiev had signed a 12-point Joint Declaration, consolidating agreements reached between Lebed and the Chechen leadership. Yeltsin and his entourage were reluctant peacemakers, and feared that Lebed's growing authority made him a potential "Bonaparte." The agreement was increasingly presented in Russian political circles as a "sell-out" that offered too many concessions to the Chechens and had humiliated the army through its withdrawal. The views of recalcitrant military and security officials gave the "sell-out" thesis substance. Along with other generals, Kulikov regarded Lebed's activity as tantamount to the "surrender of Grozny, and the surrender of Chechnya." The Chechens, according to this thesis, were "made a present of victory" by Lebed.[118]

The Joint Commission established under the agreement soon ran into difficulties when Lebed's replacement as head of the Security Council, Ivan Rybkin, insisted on a coalition government in Chechnya that would include Russia's Chechen loyalists. The Yeltsin administration was in effect attempting to backpedal the peace process to the leadup to the war in late 1994 by bolstering its Chechen proxies at the expense of the authority of Maskhadov. The Russians had conducted a charade of "free elections" in Nadterechny in June 1996, which had resulted unsurprisingly in a landslide for the old communist party boss Zavgaev. During the Khasaviurt negotiations the Russian team had tried to leave open the possibility of a coalition government in Chechnya that would include some of their proxies, such as Zavgaev. This was one aspect that Maskhadov, now acting prime minister of Chechnya, decisively rejected. Consequently, Russia was forced to secure the "voluntary resignation" of its proxy Chechen government on 20 November 1996. In the meantime, on 12 November, Rybkin and Maskhadov agreed to establish a special commission to draw up a final status agreement. These developments opened the way for Yeltsin's decree on a complete Russian military withdrawal and a Maskhadov-Chernomyrdin interim agreement on provisional political and economic relations prior to elections, both signed on 23 November 1996.[119]

Presidential and legislative elections were held in Chechnya in January 1997 under OSCE and international monitors who declared them "democratic and free." Maskhadov achieved a decisive victory over Basaev, polling 60% of the vote (see chapter four). The election established the legitimacy of his government not only internally within Chechnya, and for the Russian leadership, but also internationally. Full recognition of the independence of Chechnya, however, required an agreement with Russia. Yeltsin stalled the process of negotiation on the most difficult issue, as was permitted under the agreement. He hardly inspired trust from the Chechens by insisting that a power-sharing treaty could be signed with Chechnya which, while being "somewhat broader" (*neskol'ko shire*) than other treaties (a kind of Tatarstan model *plus*) would retain Chechnya as a "subject" of the Russian Federation.[120]

A formal peace treaty titled "Peace Treaty and Principles of Interrelation Between the Russian Federation and the Chechen Republic of Ichkeria" (see Appendix 2) was signed at a televised ceremony in the Kremlin on 12 May 1997. The treaty was significant for its symbolic rather than substantive importance. Yeltsin looked particularly stern as he grudgingly shook hands with Maskhadov. The stress on international norms in the treaty made it unlike any of the power-sharing treaties that Yeltsin had signed with Tatarstan and other republics of the Russian Federation. It locked the Yeltsin leadership into the peace process, since the Khasavi-urt agreement had been made with and signed by Lebed. Maskhadov, previously denounced as a "bandit" and "terrorist" by the Yeltsin leader-ship, was now hosted as the legitimate president of Chechnya. It was far from being the first time in history that the leader of an anticolonial rebel insurgency was entertained as a respected statesman by the leadership of the imperial power. The treaty lacked, however, the detailed agreements on policy issues that accompanied the power-sharing treaty with Tatar-stan, and did little more than restate the basic principle of internation-alization that was agreed at Khasaviurt, as both sides agreed that their mutual relations were to be regulated by "standards of international law," and both renounced "forever" the "use or the threat of force in the res-olution of any disputes between them." Two further agreements, on the integration of Chechnya into Russia's economic space and a common cur-rency, were signed (by prime minister Chernomyrdin for Russia) at the same time.

The treaty emerged from a period of intense negotiations conducted over several months, but its ambiguity reflected the impasse over the sta-tus of Chechnya. The special Joint Commission on final status rarely met. The essential ingredients for a process of negotiation to work, trust and goodwill, were missing. Russia failed to deliver the economic and recon-struction aid promised and returned to its pre-invasion policy of blockade and subversion in Chechnya, and of securing its international isolation. Maskhadov's government had the immense task of rebuilding a devastated country in conditions of Russian blockade and international isolation. Although Russian government officials portrayed Chechnya's indepen-dence as no different from the "independence" of Tatarstan, Bashkorto-stan, or other republics with high levels of autonomy, de facto Russia had relinquished its control over Chechnya, which now operated outside Rus-sia's legal, political, security, and economic space. Russia had not, how-ever, relinquished its sovereignty over Chechnya—a factor that allowed it to keep Chechnya isolated in a regional and international vacuum until the final status talks were completed. As we discuss in the next chapter, it was this Russian policy of blockade that helped to undermine Maskha-dov's attempt to build state capacity and impose peace in Chechnya.

Chapter 4

Dual Radicalization: The Making of Jihad

Conflicts that become protracted are generally associated with the polarization of opinions and radicalization of protagonists. Prolonged conflicts create openings and opportunities for new actors, new forces, and new ideas to come to the fore in the struggle. The renewal of conflict between Russia and Chechnya in late 1999 is often attributed, especially by Russia, to the failure of the agreements of 1996–97, and to the failure of nation-state building and the breakdown of order under President Maskhadov. While the political differences over the unresolved status of Chechnya remained strong, the erosion of the political space for negotiation and compromise and the drift to a renewal of armed conflict in late 1999 was caused more by a dual radicalization that enveloped politics in Russia and Chechnya. This radicalization was both part of the conflict process and a cause of the second war. It was not an issue of Chechnya becoming a "failed state." It was simply that no effective postwar state-building and reconstruction occurred in Chechnya due to lack of funds and weak governmental capacity in a highly militarized, impoverished, and traumatized society. Russia's blockade and international isolation left Maskhadov with an impossible task.

The radicalization in Chechnya was a direct product of the experience and practice of violence in the first war, and the emergence of a new "meta-cleavage" within the Chechen national movement along a religious fault line. The radicalization in Russia was largely unrelated to Chechnya and was driven principally by domestic political developments around the succession to President Yeltsin. Nevertheless, the momentum of the radicalization accelerated through mutual interaction, culminating in the armed clashes of August 1999. Consequently, by the summer of 1999, the nature of the "meta-conflict" over Chechnya had altered. Leading protagonists on the two sides no longer had a common conceptualization of the conflict as one of secular nationalist aspirations for secession, but rather saw it as one where the "Islamic factor" was now predominant.[1]

Radicalization and Islamization in Chechnya

If a national revolution is concerned with state power, jihad is its antithesis, given its "absence of a vision of the state" and its concern with the a-national community of believers.[2] An intra-elite struggle for power within the Chechen national movement was already apparent by the time Russian forces withdrew from Chechnya at the end of 1996. Maskhadov had the difficult challenge of asserting his authority over recalcitrant field commanders such as Basaev and Raduev, and over Khattab's internationalist Islamist groups. The murder of six Red Cross medical staff in Novye Atagi, near Grozny, on 17 December focused international repulsion on the disorder in Chechnya, even before elections were held. Maskhadov was faced with restoring order in a society whose infrastructure, economy, and social fabric had been devastated and traumatized by two years of intense armed conflict. It was widely recognized that urgent demilitarization was required, and Maskhadov was under enormous Russian and international pressure to secure it, but in conditions of massive unemployment and the ubiquitous ownership of small arms, it was difficult to see how this could be achieved. The expectations on all sides of what was achievable in Chechnya were simply unrealistic.

The first open signs of a major political schism occurred during the presidential and legislative elections held simultaneously in Chechnya in January 1997 under international monitors. There were 16 candidates for the presidency, and the 63 parliamentary seats attracted 766 candidates. About half a million people voted after a vibrant campaign. Maskhadov ran with his former deputy chief of staff, Vakha Arsanov, as his vice-president, and gained an outright victory with 59.3 percent of the votes. Basaev, who attracted much support from young radicals, came second, with 23.5 percent, and Yandarbiev third, with 10.1 percent.[3] These were the first and last elections held in Chechnya that approximated to OSCE norms of democratic criteria. Tim Guldimann, coordinator of the OSCE mission in Chechnya, said that the vote "reflected the freely expressed will of the voters" and "established a legitimate foundation for the new system of authority."[4] Nevertheless, there were significant shortcomings. Some potential candidates, such as Khasbulatov, were blocked from running. Former residents of Chechnya who should have been entitled to vote, notably ethnic Slav residents who would have accounted for about 25 percent of the vote, but also Chechen refugees, were denied participation. Armed fighters saturated the republic and created an atmosphere of intimidation at polling stations in some areas. Moreover, the campaign saw bitter personal exchanges between the candidates.

After the election Maskhadov attempted to create a broad-based government that incorporated all the major factions. Two leading field commanders, however, Basaev and Raduev, were excluded as a concession to Russian sensibilities. Basaev, unlike Raduev, had committed himself to the peace process and accepted the broad consensus with Maskhadov that relations with Russia should be based on the concept of being "politically separate, economically together."[5] During the election he told Russian journalists, "it is beneficial for both Russia and Chechnya to have a common economic and energy space, a unified monetary system and a unified defense system. . . . [But] we need political freedom—that is, we want to live in the same house but in our own apartment."[6] Raduev, in contrast, regarded the peace process as tantamount to treason, declared the elections a farce, and promised to continue the war against Russia. In particular, as leader of the so-called "Caucasus Home" movement he intended to spread the conflict to the 100,000 Chechen-Akkins who live in the Khasaviurt region of Dagestan.

Isolated and blockaded, Maskhadov's government simply did not have the capacity to manage these challenges. The most obvious forms of disorder were twofold. First, the peace with Russia led to a sharp rise in criminality in Chechnya, in particular through systematic fund-raising through hostage-taking. Second, Maskhadov was unable to achieve Weber's principal condition of statehood—the monopoly of the legitimate use of force in a territory. He was unable (Russians claimed he was unwilling) to disarm the many armed groups in Chechnya, and in particular to counter the growing power of the Islamists around Basaev. Hostage-taking had been a phenomenon of Chechen attacks on Russian targets, and had expanded during the armed conflict, partly as a means of fund-raising, but also in retaliation and exchange for the many hundreds of Chechens who were detained by Russia in "filtration" camps, and often subjected to torture and rape. The notoriety of these camps would grow internationally only after the start of the second war in late 1999 (discussed later).[7]

After the Russian withdrawal in 1996 armed gangs in Chechnya stepped up a lucrative trade in hostage-taking and assassination. What had been a minor embarrassment to Dudaev, now became a serious problem for his successor Maskhadov, with some 506 cases, including high profile cases involving Westerners, such as the four British telecommunications workers who were beheaded by Arbi Baraev's group in December 1998. A final straw for the Russian government was the kidnapping of the Russian deputy interior minister, General Gennadii Shpigun, who was forced off a plane at Grozny airport at gunpoint in March 1999 following talks with Maskhadov (and was later killed). The situation was described in the 1998 and 1999 annual reports of the OSCE Assistance Group in Chechnya as one where "crime, unrest and acts of terrorism have acquired endemic proportions, adding to a volatile political situation and a general breakdown of law and order," and where the deprivation of rights had become "a norm of life," with routine abductions, murders, robberies, and provocative attacks on neighboring North Caucasian Republics. According to the OSCE officials, Chechnya was a "hotbed of crime and terror."[8] Ministers in Maskhadov's government, notably the Chechen media spin doctor Movladi Udugov, who at that time was also head of the Chechen State Commission for negotiations with the Russian government, were inevitably drawn into brokering the negotiations over ransom payments and releases, the murky nature of which tainted the government as a whole.[9]

The growth of crime and hostage-taking led to the withdrawal of many international organizations from Chechnya, including the removal of the OSCE Assistance Group from Grozny to Moscow in December 1998. While Russia allocated funds for reconstruction and economic aid to Chechnya, little of this reached Chechnya—most apparently being siphoned off by bureaucratic corruption in Moscow. The most serious obstacle to improved Russian-Chechen relations, however, was the lack of progress on final status. Maskhadov repeatedly called for a final status treaty, but Yeltsin and his government stalled. As late as December 1997, at an international conference of experts on Chechnya held in Kazan under the "Hague initiative," and even while disorder was intensifying in Chechnya, Rybkin was insisting that there was no urgency for a final status agreement.[10] In the absence of significant external support, Maskhadov's attempt to consolidate his authority and establish an effective system of governance was severely weakened and proved incapable of preventing further destabilization by the armed Islamists and other discontents opposed to the peace process. From this period the word "dead-end" (*tupik*) became generally employed by both sides to describe the state of the negotiations, and Chechnya became another "frozen conflict" in the Caucasus where secession could not be reconciled peacefully with competing nationalisms.

ISLAMIZATION

The rise of a radicalized "political Islam" may evolve over decades and exist as a subversive counterculture to official corruption, as a reaction to Westernization and the decline of "authentic" Islamic values. Alternatively, it may be the product of a speedy radicalization that is associated with a profound societal crisis, usually arising from rapid socioeconomic transformation or a social breakdown caused by conflict or war. Olivier Roy has observed that one of the major contradictions and weaknesses of "political Islam" is an identity that is torn between the universal community of believers, the *ummah*, on the one hand, and the local clan, tribe, and ethnic community, on the other. In the case of Afghanistan under Soviet occupation in the 1980s, he noted that "true politicization has arisen through militarization."[11] The rise of "political Islam" in Chechnya illustrates well the difficulties of reconciling localist (territorialized) and universalist (deterritorialized) ideologies within Islamist movements. Whereas Islamic radicalism has sometimes fused with nationalism (perhaps best exemplified by Hamas in Palestine), and has done so with some tension, the Islamic religious Wahhabi reformism that inspires Al-Qaida aspires to a global *ummah*.[12]

There is by now a conventional wisdom in much of the writing on the conflict in Chechnya that the rise of the "Islamic factor" was a product of the experience of the first war in 1994–96. In fact, there are several layers to the growth of Islamic radicalism within the Chechen resistance. The radicalization was endogenous to the extent that the experience of military conflict inevitably led to the instrumentalization of Islam as a resource for mobilization and for inspiring the struggle. Chechen leaders framed the conflict by historical iconic references to anti-colonial and religious wars of the past. There were also, however, exogenous proselytizing influences. For the conflict in Chechnya beginning in the early 1990s occurred in a context of a growth in the influence of Al-Qaida. Chechnya, along with the conflicts in Bosnia, Kashmir, and others, was seen by Al-Qaida as one of the fronts in its global jihad against the "West." Arab volunteers and funds were sent to support the resistance in Chechnya from Osama Bin Laden's Khost base.[13] The emergence of Islamic radicalism in Chechnya is also seen as the result of a paradox: the Chechen leadership employed Islamic slogans instrumentally to radicalize the population and inspire them to military victory against Russia, but the victory itself empowered the radicals and created a situation where they attempted to impose a form of Islam (Wahhabism) that was alien to the vast majority of the population.[14] This view oversimplifies the complexity of the "Islamic factor" by not differentiating between the different forms of Islamic radicalism that were mobilized for the conflict. As we observed in Chapter 3, there was a trend for growing religiosity in the post-Soviet states, including among the Chechens. Therefore it was not unexpected that this would fuse with the traumatic experience of war to produce a more intense religiosity. The spread of Islamic radicalism was also uneven within Chechnya. Wahhabism took a foothold in the highland region, the heartland of Basaev's forces. One could argue that its success here had sociological explanations. Traditional Sufist Islamic communities were more embedded in the highlands, and social marginalization and a deeper sense of historical enmity with Russia were more engrained there. The key factor, however, as we shall discuss below, was Basaev's personal connection to the Wahhabis. Once victory was achieved and the Russians were expelled, and Chechnya's leaders were faced with the task of rebuilding the state, the divergence between the different forms of Islamic radicalism and the different layers in the "Islamic factor" became more apparent.

The turn to religion in some parts of society, however, does not equate per se to a transformation of the Chechen national revolution into a jihad.

It is important to note that the drift to Islamic radicalism is of political rather than social significance in Chechnya, where most religious communities still adhere to Sufism. We must distinguish, therefore, between the contingent factors in the radicalization, such as the experience of conflict, clientelism, financial support, and especially political developments that provided conditions in which radical political Islamism could take root among certain elements of the Chechen resistance. Moreover, we must assess the extent to which these elements of the Chechen national resistance were truly interested in jihad.

The descent into lawlessness and the fragmentation of authority that enveloped Chechnya in 1997–98 evoked a moral vacuum under Maskhadov's presidency that brought increased tensions between the traditional Sufist religious establishment and the social discipline and doctrinal purism of the Wahhabists.[15] Given the breakdown in state structures, and the reluctance to collaborate with Russian structures, the use of *sharīʿa* courts, already promoted by Yandarbiev in 1995, provided one of the few useful mechanisms for social regulation. Within postwar Chechnya, there was a social milieu of poverty, disease, trauma and disorientation. The physical infrastructure and social fabric of whole communities had been badly damaged by the war and by repeated flight as Internally Displaced Persons (IDPs).

The key political development was the growth of Wahhabi influence over Basaev and his fighters, and its transformation into a jihadist formation. How did this occur? As we discussed earlier, when Dudaev seized power in 1991 he saw himself as the leader of a secular anti-colonial nationalist movement, ideals that were reflected in the new Chechen constitution of March 1992 and his lack of interest in promoting Islamization of the state. A creeping radicalization unfolded in reaction to the struggle with Russia. Dudaev, as we shall discuss in Chapter 5, promoted the fanatical militant forces under Basaev as an elite force within the Chechen armed forces that would spearhead the use of "shock" tactics, including terrorism and suicide attacks. This move together with his use of Islamist rhetoric about *ghazavat* could be seen as "last resort" actions to fuse Islam with nationalism to defend the national revolution from Russian aggression. There is also some evidence that Dudaev's own identity was undergoing a transformation toward increased Islamic religiosity. Grachev, for example, recounts how at a meeting with his old comrade in arms from the Afghanistan war in December 1994, in a last attempt to stop the momentum for war, Dudaev astonished Grachev by initially refusing alcohol on the grounds that he was a Muslim.[16] During the war Dudaev revived the traditional Councils of Elders and promoted the role of mosques in the organization of the resistance. After his death, Yandarbiev (another secular nationalist who was transformed into a religious zealot by the experience of conflict) promoted the Islamization of the judicial system through s*hari'a* courts. Again, one could argue that such tactics were instrumental and a rational use of those resources which could assist with the mobilization of society for the independence struggle.

Above all, it was the success of Basaev's units in the battle for Grozny, and subsequently during the war, together with the foreign Islamists' reputation for discipline and courage, that gave politicized Islam great respect and made it attractive to the younger fighters. Moreover, the dynamics of the radicalization were not merely internally driven. While the first Gulf War in 1990–91 is generally seen as the catalyst for the growth of Al-Qaida, it had its origins in the Mujahidin resistance to the Soviet invasion of Afghanistan and the war of 1980–1988. By the middle of the 1990s the conflict in Chechnya became part of the ensemble of cases that involved Muslim communities who were perceived by Islamists to be under attack from Christendom and the "West." The globalization of Islamic radicalism was also assisted by new information technologies, such as the video, mobile phone and later the internet, which allowed the speedy transmission of graphic battlefield propaganda.

There can be little doubt that the apparent conversion of Basaev, from a secular nationalist in the early 1990s to the concept of jihad in the mid-1990s, was a profound turning point for the conflict in Chechnya. Basaev's native village, Vedeno, had political iconic significance in the history of Chechen resistance to Russia. It had been a mountain citadel-capital for Imam Shamil, and was the meeting place for the Congress of the Peoples of the North Caucasus in 1917. Basaev was named after the imam and no doubt grew up in an environment permeated by political and religious tradition. He spent formative years in his late teens and early twenties doing military service in Russia, and then lived in Moscow at the time of perestroika, making a living from a mix of shuttle-trading and racketeering. He claims to have participated in the defense of the White House when Yeltsin was besieged in August 1991. Basaev's turn to radical Islam evolved gradually from the political ferment of the Chechen national revolution in 1990–91 and the direct military experience of leading his Abkhaz Battalion in the war in Abkhazia in 1992–93, during which about 150 Chechen volunteers were killed and many more wounded.[17]

Basaev declared that he was not "a nationalist," and supported Dudaev only because of the latter's "sense of purpose."[18] There was bombast in Basaev's adoption of the Mujahidin label for his forces, especially when dealing with Russians. During the first war he often emphasized his Islamist credentials to the Russian media. In November 1995 an *Izvestiia* journalist reported that "the whole highland area of Chechnya lives under Islamic law," supposedly largely thanks to Basaev's actions. Basaev told the journalist that his fighters regarded themselves as "warriors for Islam" against a "godless" Russia, and that he promoted the use of *sharia* courts.[19] When he dealt with Western journalists at this time, however, Basaev appears to have played down his "Islamic" credentials. Anatol Lieven, for example, who reports four encounters with Basaev between August 1994 and December 1995, observes that, while he was "looking more and more like a Mujahid" (because of his beard), Basaev gave no indication that he was interested in political Islam or an Islamic state. Lieven surmised that his later support for this project appeared "to have come out of the war."[20]

Since 9/11 some Chechen leaders have become sensitive to the association of their resistance struggle with Al-Qaida. For example, in November 2004 Movladi Udugov, head of the information service of the State Defense Council of the Chechen resistance, responded to the leaking of a U.S. Defense Intelligence Agency (DIA) report of 1998 by a conservative foundation by claiming that such reports about Bin Laden's ties with Chechnya were "nothing but a pack of lies."[21] But Udogov's complaint seems to be motivated more by a reluctance to accept that jihad was foreign-inspired rather than an endogenous movement in Chechnya.[22] The DIA report revealed very superficial intelligence about the links between the Chechen resistance and Al-Qaida, and linked these to the arrival of Al-Khattab, one of Bin Laden's senior commanders, in early 1995. There is clear evidence, however, that Shamil Basaev's interest in radical Islam predated the first war with Russia. Yandarbiev already referred to Basaev with the Islamic military title "amir" in 1994, before the arrival of Khattab, and in one of his books included a photograph of Basaev in military uniform crowned with the green headband of martyrdom and jihad, bearing the *shahada*—the first pillar of Islam: "there is no God except Allah."[23] In an extraodinary admission to the Russian press, Basaev stated that he, together with thirty of his fighters, visited Khost (Al-Qaida's main base) in Afghanistan to undergo military training between April-July 1994. By that time he envisaged that war with Russia was inevitable. The decision was a reflective and rational one in conditions of relative peace with Russia, not a product of the extreme trauma of war.[24] It is odd that no mention of this visit is made in the DIA report or in much of the writing on the Chechnya conflict. The choice of Khost is a clear indication of the political direction in which Basaev had moved. Like Chechnya, Afghanistan is a society where the Hanafi School of Islam and Sufism predominates. In contrast to Chechnya, Afhganistan was a pre-modern clan-based society, which had been radicalized by thirteen years of resistance to Soviet occupation and civil war. It must have struck a chord with Basaev. By choosing to visit Khost, Basaev was also overtly identifying and allying himself with the new wave of Islamic radicalism—Saudi Islamist Osama Bin Laden's Al-Qaida.

The Khost tunnel complex, close to the Pakistan border, had been

constructed by Bin Laden with CIA assistance in 1986 as a munitions storage and training area for the Mujahidin. In the late 1980s Khost became
a center for Bin Laden's operations and the location for several camps
for training international, in particular Arab, volunteers. It was here that
Bin Laden formed Al-Qaida (literally "The Base" or "Database") to foment
a Wahhabi-inspired form of Islamic jihad not only in Afghanistan, but
globally. Wahhabism was generally not welcomed by the Sufist Afghanis,
though Bin Laden forged a close alliance with the purist Taliban movement, which was gathering strength in the mid-1990s with support of
Pakistan and the United States.[25] Given that Basaev spent several months
in Khost in 1994, we must assume that he became part of the Wahhabi
jihad at this time and that the initiative for this was taken by the Chechens.
In early 1995 he was joined in Chechnya by the Al-Qaida amir operating
under the nom-de-guerre Al-Khattab, in homage to one of Islam's greatest historical military leaders, the second Caliph Umar ibn Al-Khattab.
He was a Saudi follower of Abdullah Azzam and Bin Laden, a veteran of
the Mujahidin war against the Soviets, and brought financial support and
a small group of well trained fighters called the "Islamic International
Brigade" from Afghanistan.[26] Khattab was certainly welcomed by the Chechen resistance, and given his military expertise and probably also his links
to Islamic funding, he was appointed to important military command
and training posts by Dudaev. Khattab's principal connection, however,
was with Basaev. He became Basaev's deputy commander and chief advisor and remained in Chechnya until his assassination by poison letter by
the FSB in March 2002.

Maskhadov did not confront his former comrades-in-arms, such as
Basaev, for fear of provoking civil war. Given the de facto Russian blockade and international isolation, Maskhadov was also dependent on financial support from the Arab world, the bulk of which appears to have been
channeled through Wahhabi organizations operating in Afghanistan,
Saudi Arabia, and Qatar.[27] Consequently, what should have been a successful legitimating device—his clear triumph in the presidential election—became a source of weakness for Maskhadov as he was unable to
assert his political or military authority over the radicals. His failure to
assert his authority was reflected in an erosion of his stature as a viable
negotiating partner for Russia and the international community who
could deliver peace and stability in Chechnya.

Dudaev had popularized the idea of the confederation, even unity,
of the peoples of the North Caucasus but had not seriously acted upon
it; the Islamic radicals, however, did not feel constrained by territorial
boundaries. They made no secret of their intention to take the war beyond Chechnya into the neighboring Caucasian republics. They aspired
to create an Islamic caliphate in the North Caucasus. Dagestan was a

primary target. It was in geographical proximity to the most radicalized parts of Chechnya (Basaev's native area of Vedeno was close to the border) and the topography of the area—heavily wooded highland areas, with few roads, almost inaccessible to vehicles, and difficult to guard—provided cover for the fighters to move almost unimpeded. There was also a large Chechen ethnic minority living close to the border in the Khasav-iurt lowland region, and there were historic Chechen ethnoterritorial claims on the Akinntsy mountain area, from where Chechen communities had been deported in 1944.

There had been sporadic raids and low-level interethnic riots and disorder in the region during the first war. A major escalation occurred in December 1997, when a combined force of Chechen, Dagestani, and foreign fighters from Basaev's and Raduev's forces, led by Khattab, attacked a federal garrison in Buinaksk, about 50 miles into northwest Dagestan.[28] The attack intensified fears in Russia about the destabilization of the wider North Caucasus. Thereafter the Russian political class, the elites in neighboring republics, and the mass media became obsessed by the supposed threat of Wahhabi pan-Caucasus movement.[29] The idea of an Islamic state in the North Caucasus was not limited to the Wahhabi-influenced groups. Udugov, First Deputy Prime Minister in Maskhadov's government, became head of the "Islamic Order" in February, and then the "Islamic Nation" movement, founded in Grozny in August 1997 at a congress of Chechen and other North Caucasian delegates. Its goal was the recreation of an "Imamate" approximating to that claimed by Shamil in the mid-nineteenth century. The call for an "Imamate" cloaked a potential land grab of historic Chechen lands under the guise of religious duty. While the Islamic ideas persisted, such movements tended to be short-lived.

By late 1997, it is important to note, Chechnya and Russia had already reached a "dead end" in the talks over final status. The core issue of the conflict—secession—could not be resolved. By then it was also clear that there would be no reconstruction aid from Russia or elsewhere. This political failure provided an opportunity for the Islamists under Basaev and other radicals to return to war. There was a downward spiral of failure, as lack of progress on the political front stalled progress on economic aid, boosting the radicals while undermining Maskhadov. During late 1997 and early 1998 the radical challenge to Maskhadov intensified and became evident through numerous public gatherings, conferences, and meetings of veterans and fighters. At a rally of his supporters in Grozny in November 1997, Raduev called for Maskhadov's removal and gave Yeltsin an excuse not to proceed with a planned visit to Grozny by threatening to execute the Russian president for "war crimes."[30] In an attempt to coopt and control the radicals, Maskhadov appointed Basaev acting prime minister. Basaev in turn found it difficult to manage the radical momentum. His attempt to bring Raduev to account for unsanctioned military activities (including the assassination attempt on Georgian president Eduard Shevardnadze) proved to be politically untenable after a congress of 10,000 veterans in the Grozny sports stadium spontaneously acclaimed Raduev.

Basaev chose instead to channel his new institutional power into the preparations for a jihad and the undermining of Maskhadov. His creation of the Congress of Peoples of Chechnya and Dagestan in April 1998, the aim of which was to unite the two republics in an independent North Caucasus state, made his intentions clear and brought him into open conflict with Maskhadov. The crisis peaked in June–July 1998, when brief armed clashes between Maskhadov's forces and those of Raduev over control of the television station in Grozny, and with Islamists near Gudermes, left dozens dead and injured and forced Maskhadov to declare a state of emergency. Basaev resigned from the government, and the radicals increasingly demanded the resignation of Maskhadov on the grounds that he was too conciliatory toward Moscow and had "sold out." Maskhadov, consequently, was squeezed from two sides, internally from the radical opposition, whose ranks were swelling from veterans and new recruits of disgruntled young unemployed Chechens, and externally from Russia, whose blockade stunted economic growth and exacerbated social collapse in Chechnya. Both internal and external enemies of Maskhadov despised his government for being too soft in dealing with the other. The choice for Maskhadov was between civil war and concessions. Despite viewing Wahhabism as an "alien" and destructive presence in Chechnya, he chose to make concessions to avert the slide into civil war.[31]

Maskhadov had earlier delivered a major blow to Dudaev's secular constitution of 1992 by amending Article 4 to make Islam the official religion of the state.[32] The weakness of his hold on power in 1998–99 was revealed in two key developments. First, in July 1998 he brought Basaev back into the government as deputy commander-in-chief of the armed forces. Then, on 4 February 1999, he decreed the transition to the introduction of *shari'a* in Chechnya, established a state committee to prepare an Islamic constitution, and suspended the parliament as a prelude to the adoption of a fully Islamic constitution. The sight on Russian television of public executions in Chechnya under *shari'a* created a hysterical reaction against the "Islamic threat" in the Caucasus from the political elite and public opinion alike across the Russian Federation. The move could be interpreted as a desperate effort by the moderate nationalists to counter the growing power of the Wahhabi-influenced groups. Maskhadov backed traditional Sufi Islam by forging a closer working relationship with Chechen mufti Akhmed Kadyrov, an outspoken critic of Wahhabi influence, but even this relationship broke down by August due to Maskhadov's conciliatory approach. The factionalism that had split the Chechen national movement in 1998–99, together with the spread of cynicism and disillusionment at the lack of progress after independence, considerably weakened the prospects for a coordinated fighting capability of Chechnya as a new Russian assault loomed.

Radicals require a radicalized context in which to thrive. The culmination of the radicalization came in August 1999, when a force of Islamists several thousand strong, led by Basaev and Khattab, crossed from Chechnya into the Botlikh highland area of Dagestan as the start of the jihad to "liberate" the North Caucasus from the Russian "infidels" and establish a Caliphate. The attractiveness of these "Che Guevaras in Turbans," according to Derlugian, was that they appeared to be "the only force capable of replacing the old certainties and clear social order which was previously provided by the Soviet system."[33] Basaev may well have intended to precipitate an all-out Russian military attack on Chechnya, not only to initiate the jihad but also to preempt any further consolidation of Maskhadov's government. The invasion of Dagestan provided Russia's new prime minister, Vladimir Putin, who was a former head of the FSB, with just cause to intervene militarily against Chechnya (discussed below).

The second period of military conflict, from late 1999 to the present, has revealed the religious divide between Wahhabi radicals led by Basaev and moderate forces led by Maskhadov to be the salient cleavage within the Chechen side. It is a cleavage, furthermore, that has been reinforced by tactical divisions. Maskhadov's forces generally have conducted guerrilla operations against the Russian military within Chechnya similar to that which brought victory in the first war. In contrast, Basaev favored spectacular, headline-grabbing terrorist acts against civilians in the Russian Federation proper, such as the Moscow metro bombings, Tushino concert bombings, Vnukovo airline bombings, and Dubrovka theater and Beslan school attacks. These tactical differences in the second war will be analyzed further in Chapter 5.

The final act of Islamization in the shift from secular nationalism came after the renewal of war with Russia. The Chechen Madjlis-Shura (War Council), presided over by Maskhadov, reached a consensus in the summer of 2002 to formally Islamize the 1992 constitution. Article 1 of the constitution was amended to: "the Chechen Republic of Ichkeria is a sovereign, independent Islamic law-based state, founded by the self-determination of the Chechen people. The source of all adopted decisions is the Qur'an and Sunna."[34] When Maskhadov declared that he would put Basaev on trial for war crimes over the Beslan massacre, Basaev himself retorted that he was prepared to face only a *shari'a* court. The killing of Maskhadov in March 2005 opened the way for the completion of the Islamization process. Maskhadov's replacement was a religious leader, Sheikh Abdul Khalim

Sadulaev, approved by Maskhadov himself at the Madjlis-Shura meeting in summer 2002.

Sadulaev's rhetoric initially was cautious with regard to Islamization. He framed the struggle against Russia in much the same nationalist terms that Maskhadov had done, though with a somewhat more Islamic flourish. He spoke of continuing the Chechen's "centuries-long national liberation struggle against Russian colonial aggression" and of his aim to defend "state sovereignty, freedom and independence."[35] A radical departure from Maskhadov's line came in the summer of 2005, when Sadulaev made changes to his cabinet and brought Basaev back into the government as deputy prime minister. Such a move would have been unthinkable under Maskhadov after Basaev's involvement in the Beslan attack. Furthermore, in the first move against the Westernized and exiled moderates in the leadership, he sacked U.S.-based Ilias Akhmadov from the post of foreign minister.[36] A year later, in February 2006, Sadulaev decreed additional moves toward Islamic norms. He reshuffled the Chechen government and removed the moderate ministers, focusing in particular on exiled Sovietized and Westernized intelligentsia such as Umar Khambiev and Akhmed Zakaev. Sadulaev justified the changes on the grounds that the exigencies of war required all Chechen ministers to operate within Chechnya. In a subsequent decision, Sadulaev decreed the end of presidential and parliamentary democracy (associated with the West), and the establishment of the Madjlis-Shura as the highest state authority and its leader, the amir, as the head of state.[37] While Sadulaev advanced Islamization of the political structures of the resistance, he ordered a shift away from some of the terrorist tactics employed by Basaev's forces, such as hostage-taking. He had insufficient time to oversee the implementation of any of these policies, however, as just three months after his appointment, in June 2006, he was killed by pro-Russia Chechen forces loyal to Ramzan Kadyrov.

The extent of the Islamization has become obvious from changes in what Geertz termed "parapolitical warfare"—forms of language and dress or appearance.[38] The conflict idiom of the Chechen resistance has been Islamized. The appeals of Sovietized moderates to Western anti-Russian constituencies, typified by leaders such as Zakaev and Akhmadov in exile, have been made peripheral to the resistance by the Islamists. In the 1990s, the struggle for a secular nationalist vision of an independent Chechnya was reflected in the idiom of the conflict, whereby the Russian forces were generally termed by ethnic criteria or by the even more secular designation "the federals" and "occupiers," and Chechen collaborators were termed "puppets." From 2000 the Islamists steadily framed the war as a jihad by Mujahidin and martyrs (*shahids*) against "infidels" (*kafirs*) and their Chechen "traitors to the faith" (*munafiqs*).[39] By 2005 Basaev, crippled by the loss of a leg in the withdrawal from Grozny in late 1999, and with his dead comrade Khattab now replaced by a new Saudi militant, Abu Whalid, assumed the stature of a legendary amir leading the jihad. For Russia he was the "most wanted terrorist", while he and his fighters grew their beards long and shaved their heads in Mujahidin style, and during military operations usually sported the green headband of martyrdom. Basaev had even assumed an Islamic name, Abdallah Shamil Abu-Idris, and written a book outlining his philosophy as a Mujahid.[40] We should, however, remain cautious about the fundamental motivations of leaders such as Basaev. When pushed to define his philosophy of struggle as recently as June 2005, Basaev emphasized the predominance of the statist content of his ideology over the religious, imparting the sense that taking power in the state was his political and military objective: "For me, it's first and foremost a struggle for freedom. If I'm not a free man, I can't live in my faith. I need to be a free man. Freedom is primary. That's how I see it. *Shari'a* comes second."[41] Basaev was finally killed in an explosion in unclear circumstances, though claimed by the FSB, in July 2006.[42]

Radicalization in Russia

PUTIN'S WAR

Putin's policy toward the Chechnya question is typical of the leaders of the security establishment, the so-called *siloviki*, in Russia. As a former FSB officer and head of the FSB in 1998–99, Putin would have been party to the argument of the "power ministries," best exemplified publicly by former minister of defense Kulikov, which repeated the mantra-like formula that Chechnya was ungovernable, a "bandit" and "terrorist" state, increasingly dominated by fanatical Wahhabis and intent on wider destabilization in the North Caucasus. The only solution was force—to reconquer Chechnya by military means and "reimpose order." According to this script, Russia's de facto recognition of independence for Chechnya only served to promote further chaos and the growth of "terrorism." The strategic fears about Chechnya were not confined to the *siloviki*, but were broadly held in the energy sector elites. The attack on Botlikh by Basaev and Khattab threatened to destabilize Dagestan, which given the anarchy in Chechnya provided Russia with its only land corridor for the newly constructed Transneft pipeline linking the Caspian and Novorossiisk.

A lack of scruples and preference for coercion rather than negotiation was also very much acculturated by Putin's training and experience as a "Chekist," which must have given him a low threshold for the use of violence as a policy instrument. The attraction to the use of force also tends to be rational when negotiation has obviously failed, as was the case in the

Russian-Chechen talks over final status and cooperation during 1998–99, and when it seems likely to produce a successful result. Moreover, even if Putin had wished to enter negotiations with Maskhadov after the invasion of Dagestan (and there is no evidence that he did) his room for compromise was severely constrained by nationalist sentiment in the "power ministries." In particular, the Russian military high command still smarted from its humiliation in 1996 and sense of political betrayal by Yeltsin. The military view was that Chechnya was unfinished business—"neither war, nor peace," as Troshev put it.[43] A new war might not only help restore morale, but also replenish military power, which had been significantly depleted by the 1994–96 war and further run down by budget cuts in its aftermath.[44] Indeed, whereas Yeltsin and Grachev had been faced with divisions and resignations over the invasion of Chechnya in 1994, Putin was faced with the complete opposite situation, when in November 1999 leading Russian generals threatened to resign if he started negotiations before they had completed their military campaign. Attempts to mediate by president Aushev of Ingushetia and president Shaimiev of Tatarstan were brushed aside by Putin.[45]

The radicalized military-security interests had been vocal in Russian politics since 1996, and even had widespread political support in the Duma, as was demonstrated by its opposition to Khasaviurt and the peace agreements with Chechnya. They only came to dominate Russian governmental policy, however, in the summer of 1999. There were two contingent reasons for this development. First, in response to the attack on Dagestan, Yeltsin sacked prime minister Sergei Stepashin, who was associated with the failure of the first war, and replaced him with Putin, his chosen successor. The appointment projected *siloviki* interests into the heart of government at a time when Yeltsin was weakening and preparing his succession. Yeltsin's main concern was the protection of his family security and interests by a hand-picked successor, who would have to win the presidential election that would follow his resignation, if Yeltsin's future was to be ensured. This element of political expediency combined with sectional interests created momentum in the Kremlin for a new military intervention in Chechnya.

Second, Putin may have been Yeltsin's chosen successor, but his public profile in the country was low. It seemed unlikely from the viewpoint of August 1999 that Putin could emerge as winner from the highly personalized politics of a presidential election that was due in early March 2000. Public opinion polls conducted in August showed a zero-rating for Yeltsin and just 2 percent for Putin (see Figure 1). The "Family" and the *siloviki* had six months to build Putin's authority. It is a paradox that Russia's democrats naively considered that the first war with Chechnya was brought to an end by Russian democracy—according to Sergei Kovalev, it was "the first serious battle for democracy in Russia," and it was "won by freedom of speech"—whereas the *siloviki* found it expedient to launch a new war in order to boost their candidate's credentials in a democratic election.[46] The political cycle in Russia once again drove the government's policy toward Chechnya. The phenomenon of the "khaki election" was not new in Russian politics. After all, Yeltsin had hoped that a "small victorious war" in Chechnya in 1994 would help boost his popularity at a low point in his presidency, and the peace process launched in April 1996 was driven by the presidential campaign. Berezovskii (acting on behalf of the key Family members: Valentin Yumashev, Tatiana Diachenko, Aleksandr Voloshin and Roman Abramovich) claims to have met with Putin on several occasions in France and Spain during the summer of 1999 to discuss the succession to Yeltsin and the looming election.[47] Clearly an event of some kind was required to bolster Putin's authority and maximize his electoral prospects. There is much speculation that Berezovskii and Putin made an arrangement to purchase Basaev's assistance through the intermediary of his brother Shirvani, an acquaintance of Berezovskii.

The Chechen radicals had provided a *causus bellum* by attacking Dagestan, but the mass of the Russian public, despite or because of their overt racism against Chechens and other Caucasian peoples, were not likely to be mobilized by Chechen acts of "terrorism," as government propaganda portrayed it, against Dagestanis. In fact, the constituency for Islamic radicalism in Dagestan was marginal, and in early September 1999 the Russian military, with the support of Dagestan's police and local militia units,

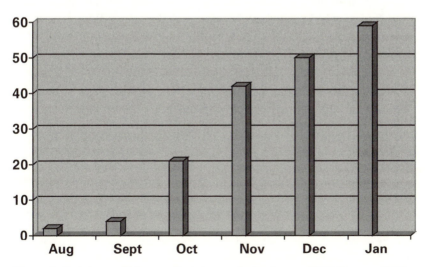

Figure 1. Opinion poll data on Putin's popularity, August 1999–January 2000. Data accessed February 2000 at the Levada Center, http://www.levada.ru

repelled the Basaev-Khattab force through massive use of firepower, including air-fuel bombs.[48]

Chechnya was to be the anvil on which Putin hammered out a public position as an ideologue for a new kind of Russian nationalism. The reconquest of Chechnya would not only undo the national humiliation of the defeat in 1996, but also serve as the vehicle for a recentralization and strengthening of state power in Russia, and for the consolidation of a new Putin regime. Putin's manifesto, later published as a long policy statement on the eve of his appointment as acting president on 31 December, equated the "renewal" of Russia with restoring Russia's pride in itself and "strong state power."[49] The resumption of war with Chechnya was now instrumentalized as the means to boost Putin's popularity in advance of a presidential campaign. The bombings of apartment buildings in Moscow, Volgodonsk, and Buinaksk in September 1999, which killed or maimed over three hundred civilians, allowed Putin and Russia's political elites generally to demonize the disorderly regime of Maskhadov as a front for "international terrorism." It justified Putin's framing of the war as a "counterterrorist operation," and mobilized the support of the Duma, mass media and public opinion.[50] The apartment bombings seemed to fit a pattern of Chechen "terrorism" set by the hostage taking and deaths in the episodes in Budennovsk in June 1995 and Pervomaisk-Kizliar in January 1996. The fact that Basaev, whom Russians regarded as "terrorist No. 1," had led the assault into Botlikh, seemed to offer reasonable grounds for the assumption that he was behind the bombings. Suspicions that the bombings were actually conducted as a provocation by the FSB to legitimize and increase support for the war were roused when security forces were caught in the act of planting explosives in an apartment building in the Russian city of Riazan, though the government later claimed this was an "exercise."[51] Another variant is that the apartment bombings were perpetrated by Wahhabis from Dagestan under the command of Khattab and Basaev, while the Riazan incident was part of an attempt by Putin to opportunistically assist the mobilizing effect of the bombings on radicalizing Russian opinion.[52] Maskhadov and Basaev denied responsibility to Western media and claimed that the bombings were part of an FSB plot to justify the war and boost Putin's popularity. Basaev told the BBC, "Again they want to sacrifice our people for the sake of elections."[53] After the apartment bombs, Putin's stance received strong cross-party support from all the parties in the Duma and his popularity in the country began to surge.[54]

A new military adventure in Chechnya was far from being a risk-free strategy, given the abysmal performance of the Russian military in 1994–96. Yeltsin himself thought that Putin had thrown "his entire stock of political capital into the war," as if he was a "political kamikaze."[55] Putin,

however, appears to have shared the view widespread in the higher ech-
elons of the Russian military and security apparatus that the defeat in
1996 had been due less to military shortcomings and more to a "stab in
the back" by Russia's weak political leaders and, in particular, its Western-
influenced critical news media. Putin's justification for the return to a
war policy stressed not the only the necessity of the "counterterrorist operation," but also the political spin that an independent Chechnya was a
failed state in the hands of Islamic fundamentalists which threatened a
wider destabilization in the North Caucasus. As he explained in an interview shortly after 9/11: "it is not an issue of Chechnya's membership, or
nonmembership, of the Russian Federation"; rather, Chechnya was an
"irresponsible quasi-state" that became "a gangster enclave while the ideological vacuum was quickly filled by fundamentalist organizations."[56]

Polls conducted by the independent VTsIOM, then headed by the respected pollster Yuri Levada, demonstrated that between August 1999
and January 2000 there was a trend for a surge in Putin's popularity (see
Figure 1). Levada himself later made no connection between Putin's rise
and the success of the war against Chechnya, but many other commentators have remarked upon the correlation.[57] Russia's invasion of Chechnya on 1 October 1999 involved the overwhelming use of military power
and secured a collapse of Maskhadov's government by the New Year as
Chechen forces dispersed to fight a guerrilla war. The quick military successes (and the fall of Grozny by Christmas 1999) turned public opinion
in favor of Putin, but views on the war remained divided and uncertain.
By February 2000 only 46 percent supported the war, while 43 percent
favored sealing the frontier. Not surprisingly, few of those polled were prepared to volunteer personally or see their relatives go to Chechnya (only
17 percent), though public perceptions of the success of the campaign
were extremely high (69–70 percent in December 1999–February 2000).[58]

The success of the early stage of the war was a key factor in the strong
showing in the Duma elections of December 1999 for the pro-Kremlin
Unity party and the poor showing of Yabloko, whose leader Yavlinskii
was one of the few Russian politicians consistently to criticize the return
to a strategy of coercion.[59] Putin's narrow success in the first round of
the presidential election of March 2000, passing the 50 percent threshold and winning by 52.9 percent, was largely due to his image as the vic-
tor in the war against Chechnya.[60]

THE "COUNTERTERRORISM OPERATION"

Unlike Yeltsin, Putin did not use the constitutional power to declare a
"state of emergency," which had been controversial in 1994–95, to justify
the intervention in Chechnya; rather he relied on Russia's 1998 law "On

the Struggle Against Terrorism" (discussed in Chapter 5), which allowed the deployment of the army in counterterrorist operations. Moreover, he personally framed the intervention in an idiom that took the conflict in Chechnya to a new low level of dehumanization. Putin declared his aim was to destroy Chechnya as a "terrorist state," "an outpost of international terrorism," and a "bandit enclave" for foreign-funded "Islamic fundamentalists." He also, however, used slang to remark on television during a visit to Kazakhstan in September 1999, that he wanted to "waste them in the shithouse (*mol'chit v sortire*). The question is closed once and for all. And we have to do this today, quickly, decisively, with clenched teeth, strangle the vermin at the root." The crude rhetoric was mirrored by Russia's leading judge, Constitutional Court chair Marat Baglai, who declared that "The problem of terrorism has created an extraordinary situation. We cannot use the same methods as in the fight against common crime when all complicated procedures should be observed . . . the liquidation of bandits is acceptable in this situation."[61] To cement his reputation as a war-winning "hawk" Putin went to Grozny during the New Year holiday in early 2000 to personally award hunting knives to Russian troops serving in Chechnya—a scene that was broadcast on Russian television.

The crude, dehumanizing idiom persisted as the conflict dragged on after the initial military successes. For example in November 2002, shortly after the Dubrovka theater attack, when questioned at an EU-Russia summit in Brussels by a journalist from *Le Monde* about Russian abuses in Chechnya, Putin angrily retorted: "If you want to become a real radical Islamist and are prepared to be circumcised, then I invite you to Moscow. We have many religions. We have many specialists in this area. I will recommend that they do the operation in such a way that you will have nothing left to grow back." The Kremlin protocol chief termed it an "emotional outburst," but as one Russian journalist put it, the language was more like that used by Putin "in the bania with Patrushev" (the FSB chief).[62] When speaking more rationally, Putin stressed that Chechnya was part of the "global war on terrorism." He declared that Chechnya was "a platform for the expansion of terrorism into Russia," "hotbeds of terrorism," "an outpost of international terrorism," a "bandit enclave" for foreign-funded "Islamic fundamentalists," a "medieval world."[63]

The success of the Russian military was due to several factors. Lessons were drawn from recent successful Western military operations. From the Falklands and the Gulf Wars, the propaganda lesson learned was to control media access and manage the "information war." From NATO's war against Serbia over Kosovo, the military lesson learnt was to apply massive airpower, distance bombing, and accept extensive "collateral damage," rather than risk troops. Russia's military performance was transformed also by the use of larger professional forces rather than conscripts, who were better trained, well led, and well equipped.[64] Rather than engage the Chechen forces, Russia relied on massive bombardment. What remained of Grozny from the first war was turned into a wasteland by a sustained aerial and artillery bombardment in December 1999. Maskhadov ordered Chechen forces to disperse and retreat into the highland hinterland. Later, some fighters were forced to retreat over the border with Georgia into the remote Pankisi Gorge. The Russian tactics confirmed to some elements of the Chechen forces the futility of further resistance, and the risk of a genocidal collapse of the Chechen population. If the first war had the characteristics of a guerrilla war, with regular engagements between military forces, the second war soon settled into a pattern that had more of the characteristics of a military insurgency and counterinsurgency, with terrorism and counterterrorism focused more on the civilian population. The question of terrorism on the part of the Chechen resistance will be assessed in Chapter 5, here we focus on the question of Russia's military and security strategy.

History demonstrates that in counterinsurgency even the best trained and equipped military forces, such as those of the United States and Britain, suffer from a mismatch between the strategy and tactics required and the capacity of the military to implement them in the field. The ongoing war in Chechnya, together with the more recent insurgencies involving U.S., British and other forces in Afghanistan and Iraq, suggest a collective colonial and post-colonial experience of counterinsurgency that reveals that professional state military and security establishments are ill-equipped to manage it, thus confirming T. E. Lawrence's aphorism that for professional armies "to make war on rebellion is messy and slow, like eating soup with a knife."[65] Lawrence, although a British intelligence officer, and by his own admission untrained in command and self-taught in military theory, was astonished by his successful leadership of a rebellion by untrained and poorly equipped Arab "irregulars" against the Turkish Army, one of the most competent of the First World War. From this experience he identified many of the enduring advantages of the irregular fighter over the professional soldier; greater flexibility, initiative, motivation, mobility and doctrinal influence over civilian populations.[66] It is ironic that the global experience of counterinsurgency has drawn on the classic models provided by British and French generals who presided over strategic defeats and the retreat from empire.[67] Both models emphasize the importance of controlling the communities in which insurgents operate to secure a cumulative build-up of human intelligence or "humint" in defeating the insurgency, but differ as to how this might be achieved. The British approach, epitomized in Kitson's work, emphasizes the lack of "easy answers," "quick fixes," and the impossibility of a military "victory." He argues for a long-term commitment of military force in support of the civil power, a pragmatic use of the "rule of law," cooption of elites, sensitive treatment of local communities, and the need for a combination of political and military strategies. Trinquier, drawing on the disastrous French experience in Algeria in 1956–62, emphasized the role of torture and reprisals in the field and strict political control and commitment by the government to override domestic political opposition. In practice, colonial militaries employed a mixture of both models and the classic characteristics of counterinsurgency were to control territory from fixed positions in military blockhouses, and apply collective punishments in order to deprive insurgents of the support and cover provided by civilians. The obvious conclusion, given that the British and French empires are no longer with us, is that colonial counterinsurgency was a failure.

The implementation of counterinsurgency policy itself often plays into the hands of the insurgents, as it becomes contaminated by poor discipline and frustration among military and security forces that suffer routine attrition from the insurgents and are dissatisfied with the long haul approach. The paradox of the state's use of "counterterror" is that its success depends on a solution to the fundamental problem identified by Kitson and Trinquier—accurate intelligence on the enemy—yet the use of state terror tactics alienate and antagonize the local population from which the intelligence must be gathered. States will often resort to the policy of "terrorizing the terrorists." This operates along a spectrum from the very specific: for example, targeted assassination whether by state agents or locally recruited state sponsored "death squads" to "take out" key enemy figures; to the generic: as in area bombardment of villages or towns considered to be supporting insurgents. According to Grachev, it was Dudaev himself, then a Soviet air force colonel, who initiated the concept of aerial bombardment of "enemy" villages during the Afghan war.[68] This tactic was used by Russia during the first war, but it was reemployed on a colossal scale during the second war. There is some debate as to whether democracies can ever win such wars, given the moral conflict between human rights and the intrinsically "dirty" and "uncomfortable" nature of counterinsurgency.[69] This is particularly the case when the military is unable to control the propaganda war by denying media access to the zone of conflict. Negative images of brutality and failure have a severely corroding effect on popular and political support for counterinsurgency. A high degree of brutality in counterinsurgency, however, is no guarantee of success, and much depends on the international context of support. If we compare, say, the German experience in Yugoslavia during the Second World War and the Soviet experience in Central Asia in the 1920s and in the Baltic States and Western Ukraine after the Second World War, we may conclude that a successful counterinsurgency requires not only a high degree of brutality against the insurgents and their civilian populations, but also the isolation of the insurgency from internal and external sources of support and sustenance. Of course, such tactics are more easily implemented by authoritarian states than the militaries of democracies operating in the glare of publicity and under political accountability.

Lawrence observed that "Rebellions can be made by 2 per cent active in a striking force, and 98 per cent passively sympathetic."[70] One of the most prominent metaphors in the debates about counterinsurgency practices is "the battle for hearts and minds", which is often an erroneously over-used term. The metaphor originated in British General Gerald Templer's so-called "hearts and minds" strategy during the war in Malaya in the 1950s, when, it is claimed, a series of political and economic reforms and propaganda campaigns won over the support of the local ethnic Chinese population from the communist insurgents. Something akin to a folklore has developed in British circles surrounding the claimed success of the strategy. A brief exposition of this case is important for understanding the viability of the strategy, and to see parallels with Russian tactics in Chechnya. The conflict in Malaya was an ethnic civil war compounded by Cold War ideology between a communist-leaning ethnic Chinese community, largely excluded from power, and the indigenous Malay. As in Chechnya economic resources were a major issue, as Malaya was hugely important for the economy of the British empire, and during the Korean war economic boom its rubber and tin earned Britain annually more dollars than the sum of UK exports. Strategic interest, therefore, induced a major British effort to quash the communist insurgency at all costs. The Malaya "Emergency" was the first major colonial counterinsurgency since the Boer War where the British Army was given wide strategic and tactical latitude by its home political leadership to apply all necessary means to secure victory. Templer was a colonial plenipotentiary, commanding the military and security forces and political administration. The "hearts and minds" metaphor was a later cover employed in the propaganda war for a pre-existing brutal coercive counterinsurgency strategy designed to break the link between an active insurgent cadre and its mass base of support, supply and recruits.[71] Success lay, in fact, in the rigorous application of security measures and tactics that the British had adopted prior to Templer's arrival in Malaya in 1952, and which were devised from their costly experiences in previous counterinsurgencies against the Boers, and in Ireland and Palestine. The Boer War witnessed the British use of barbed wire to invent the modern concentration camp for civilians, but the controversy over the neglect in the camps that resulted in the deaths of tens of thousands of Boer women and children was such that the instrument was abandoned as a counterinsurgency tactic. It was revived in the late 1940s in Malaya and under the Brigg's Plan of 1950 the British systematically, area by area, forcibly deported and concentrated in camps secured by barbed wire, searchlights, and guards (termed by the British "resettlement" in "protected villages") most of the rural ethnic Chinese population (about 600,000 people by 1954), applied collective punishments, curfews, and imposed food deprivation and subsistence level food rationing. Areas cleared of the local population became freefire zones. A major effort was put into psychological warfare ("psywar") and intelligence gathering, focusing on a "carrot and stick" approach by expanding the role of intelligence services (especially the colonial police "Special Branch") and persuading insurgents to surrender through amnesties and monetary rewards, offering bounties for the heads (literally) of insurgent leaders, and employing former insurgents in the front line of the intelligence war. Propaganda was not only rigorously employed in the zone of conflict but also in the manipulation of British media reporting. The only significant breach of the government line on the conflict came from the communist Daily Worker.[72] Templer's value to the British was to provide a determined and inspirational leadership in the implementation of the overall strategy. When it was evident that the insurgency was in decline, Templer ensured that the British colonial administration developed political, social and economic reforms, and some basic development projects (schools, health, piped water) which, the British claimed, lessened the alienation felt by the imprisoned ethnic Chinese community. Most important, Templer promoted a divide and rule approach towards the two main ethnic groups by promises of independence and consolidating Malay political supremacy. What Hack terms "population control" was the key to the British success, and the insurgency subsided rapidly after 1952.[73] This counterinsurgency model was transplanted and applied by the British during the contemporaneous Mau Mau revolt in Kenya, where during the mid-1950s between 160,000 and 320,000 persons were interned in what has been appropriately termed "Britain's Gulag".[74] The "hearts and minds" metaphor, consequently, is a misunderstanding, deliberate or not, of what produced a successful counterinsurgency for Britain.

Some recent studies of counterinsurgency highlight how tactical mistakes by low-level abuses perpetrated by military and security forces against civilians during a counterinsurgency can have major negative strategic consequences through undermining the legitimacy of the state's forces, and strengthening popular support for the insurgency. Yet, these same studies are enraptured by the mythology surrounding the British "hearts and minds" strategy in Malaya.[75] When the "hearts and minds" metaphor is shorn of its mythology, it is clear that the strategy of denying the active insurgents a mass base of support by putting the mass of the civilian population into secured camps is highly exceptional, and is not one that has much currency for a modern democracy. Racism undoubtedly played a large role in the British use of this method in these colonies, for after the decolonization of the late 1950s and early 1960s the "gulag" for civilians was never again employed as a tool of counterinsurgency. Many of the operational tactics of the British military in Malaya, however, were subsequently adapted into the global experience of counterinsurgency. Let us examine how some of these elements were employed by the Russian counterinsurgency in Chechnya since 1999.

Prior to the conflict in Chechnya, the Russian military's recent experience of counterinsurgency—the war in Afghanistan, 1980–88—had been a failure. Given the poor state of the Russian military it is not surprising that we find major problems developing in the military operation in Chechnya. The war generated a major debate within the Russian Armed Forces over the question of professionalization and the allocation of resources, particularly in the light of the strategic dominance of NATO and the USA.[76] Estimates of the costs of the war are difficult to evaluate because of lack of data, and the nature of military accounting, but it clearly runs into billions of dollars.[77] While professional special forces (*spetsnaz*) have been deployed to search and destroy Chechen insurgents (following the Soviet Afghan War model), the main body of the Russian military forces in Chechnya was made up from special paramilitary police units (OMON), quasiprofessional contract soldiers (*kontraktniki*), and a large conscripted element, generally serving for a year in the field. It is generally recognized that the nonprofessional soldiers are poorly trained, poorly commanded, frequently drunk or drugged, and engage in some of the worst abuses. The decision by the Russian military to use overwhelming and disproportionate force, with a gross disregard for civilian casualties (the "collateral damage" of military jargon), inevitably further alienated the Chechen population. In organizational terms Russia's military strategy of disproportionate force in the war of 1994–96, which was replicated even more vigorously in the early part of the campaign in late 1999—early 2000 had major consequences for its capacity to gather intelligence and to isolate the insurgents from the civilian support base. As we shall discuss later in an examination of the international reactions to the conflict, the complaint that Russia's war policy in Chechnya lacked "proportionality" and employed "excessive use of force" became widespread among governments and human rights organization domestically and internationally. Judging the Russian campaign for its "excess" does not help us understand why this strategy has been pursued. The reality is that Russia recognized that it could not win "hearts and minds" in the sense of ideologically winning over the civilian population of Chechnya from support for national self-determination. Negotiations had been tried and failed. Consequently, the logical strategy for Russia to pursue in the second war was one of *coercion and control* of territory.[78] As with the British in Malaya, the Russian strategy had two dimensions: military force plus a major political effort from Putin to win over elements of the resistance who could be used as local collaborators—Chechenization.

CHECHENIZATION

Proxy rule by a reliance on a collaborationist indigenous stratum to manage rebellious territories is an essential instrument in the imperialist's toolkit. Chechenization was an attempt by Russia to divide and rule the resistance by sowing a form of covert, and often not so covert, civil war. In examining the logic of violence in civil war, Kalyvas has suggested that "a major reason why wars of occupation turn into civil wars is that indiscriminate violence is counterproductive. The need for selective violence forces occupiers to rely on local agents, thus driving a wedge within the native population."[79] This is not a new wisdom but a restating of the professional counterinsurgents' axiom that one needs "humint" to kill off the insurgents, and that it is best obtained from local proxies. The experience of counterinsurgency in Malaya and elsewhere suggests that incentives (such as amnesty and rewards) can be an effective way to win over ex-insurgents, who can then be employed to help crush the insurgency. The need for a coopted local ruler or elite is often magnified in conflict by war weariness and the increasing political costs of the attrition of occupation, especially where this extends to attacks by insurgents on targets in the occupier's homeland. Local proxies, consequently, can be a useful tool for containing an insurgency. It is naïve to think, however, that the use of local proxies promotes "selective violence" by more exact targeting of insurgents. They are often at least as indiscriminate as the regular forces of occupiers, especially once a cycle of revenge attacks and killings is launched against them and their relatives by the resistance.

The policy of Chechenization is an enduring feature of Russia's strategy since 1991. The policy was driven by the paramount importance for Russia of achieving a peace settlement that retains Chechnya under Russian sovereignty—decolonization is not an option. The list of proxies in the 1990s was extensive—Zavgaev, Avturkhanov, Khadzhiev, Gantemirov, and others. Of these only Gantemirov, former Grozny mayor and Dudaev loyalist, played a role in the second war. Released from a Russian prison, he was appointed leader of a new paramilitary force under Russian control, the Gantemirovtsy. With the coming to power of Putin, the strategy of Chechenization was given a major emphasis and the elements of an incentive structure for fracturing the insurgency were put in place. An amnesty for fighters who surrendered to Russian forces and turned in their weapons was passed by the Duma in December 1999. Already by late 1999 two pro-Russian Chechen paramilitary units had been formed with recruits from former resistance fighters who had been amnestied and rewarded, the "Vostok" (East) Battalion (headed by the Yamadaev brothers), and the "Zapad" (West) Battalion. It was rational for Putin to seek to vigorously pursue the policy of Chechenization as a substitute for a real peace process once the immediate war aims of removing Maskhadov from power had been attained. Finding a high profile collaborator was crucial if Russia was to further develop its new policy of refusing to recognize Maskhadov's presidency. The major problem for Putin was to find a credible partner, a "civilized" leader as he put it, on the Chechen side. The policy of Chechenization only became viable when Akhmed Kadyrov decided to abandon the insurgency and help Putin. Kadyrov may have been motivated partly by personal ambition and Putin's lure of some form of power in Chechnya, but he was also tired of war and pragmatically recognized that Putin's overwhelming use of force made resistance futile. He was also concerned with the desperate condition of the Chechen population, again subjected to arbitrary Russian military occupation. Moreover, Kadyrov had been increasingly alienated from the resistance by a sectarian fear of the Wahhabi influence over the radical Islamists that had come to dominate Chechen politics under Maskhadov's rule.[80] Kadyrov's increasingly vocal criticism of this influence led to a rift with Maskhadov, who had removed him as mufti in August 1999. When in October 1999 Kadyrov surrendered and declared that he was ready to support Russia, he proclaimed the city of Gudermes as well as the Gudermes and Kurchaloi districts "Wahhabi-free territory." He was appointed by Putin to head the pro-Moscow Chechen civil administration on 12 June 2000. The pro-Moscow Chechen administration was effectively a triumvirate composed of head and mufti Akhmed Kadyrov, prime minister Stanislav Il'iasov, and Duma deputy for Chechnya, former police colonel Aslanbek Aslakhanov, a Moscow-based Chechen who had been long-standing loyal supporter of Russian policy on Chechnya from the early 1990s.

Russia's policy of Chechenization and the empowerment of the Kadyrovtsy demonstrates the flaws in the notion that local proxies and "turned" insurgents promote "selective violence". War crimes by poorly disciplined and brutalized troops on both sides had been a characteristic of the first war. This pattern of "dirty war" quickly resumed in the second war. Some aspects of a classic colonial counterinsurgency strategy that were developed in the first war became a permanent feature of Russia's strategy in the Caucasus. In the absence of support from the civilian population, Russian forces employed torture systematically in an attempt to extract intelligence. Thousands of suspects were held in "filtration" or internment camps or "torture pits" (*zindany*), and each security branch (army, MVD, FSB, Kadyrovtsy etc.) had its own secret prisons, all of which are unregulated and operate outside the Russian judicial system (the most notorious being Chernokozovo, a camp operated by the Russian military in Northern Chechnya, and "ORB-2" a secret detention center in Grozny operated by the MVD). Accurate data on detainees is not available and even Memorial estimates that Russia's Chechen "gulag" contained no more than 3,000 persons in 2003–04.[81] This is a fraction of the numbers detained in Malaya and Kenya. Many detainees were rounded up, often arbitrarily, at road checkpoints and in "cleansing sweeps" (*zachistki*) of towns and villages—classic tools of military counterinsurgency designed to gather intelligence and clean out rebels "sector by sector," but which were applied in a disorganized and sporadic manner by the Russian military. From early in the campaign, late 1999, the Russian military used overwhelming force recklessly against armed resistance in civilian areas. As in August 1996, so in December 1999 civilians were given an ultimatum to leave Grozny prior to a massive aerial and artillery bombardment. Chechen civilians were coerced into acting as human shields for Russian troops. Russian forces meted out collective punishments on communities were there was armed resistance or noncooperation, including exemplary shootings and massacres. There were well-documented cases of massacres of civilians by Russian forces in late 1999 in the village of Alkhan-Yurt and in Aldi, a suburb of Grozny, among others. Putin subsequently awarded the medal "Hero of Russia" to the commander of the forces involved, General Shamanov. A tactic which became much more generally applied in the second war from 2001 on, however, was the blatant criminal kidnapping of civilians by Russian forces (and their Chechen proxies) in exchange for ransom payments. There was also an escalation in the use of what were in effect state "death squads" of hooded armed groups, which "disappeared" those suspected of being in the resistance.[82] Even more insidiously, the family members of those suspected of being fighters, or of Chechen government representatives in exile, were targeted, including relatives of Dudaev, Maskhadov, Basaev, Umarov, and other leaders. An illustrative case is that of Magomed Khambiev, minister of defense in Maskhadov's government and a Chechen military commander, who was compelled to surrender in March 2004 after more than eighty members of his extended family were detained and tortured by the Russian and pro-Russian Chechen militia.[83] Historically, the targeting of family members of insurgents is standard military practice. In the case of Russia, the rational was made explicit to Politkovskaia by senior Ministry of Justice officials responsible for the "special" prisons in Chechnya; "Brother must answer for brother and if someone in the family has been fighting for Basaev, then all of his relatives are accomplices and deserve extermination."[84]

If successful Chechenization was one key pillar of the Russian counterinsurgency, another was the management of the civilian population. As in any insurgency the number of active fighters was small but their passive support base in the Chechen population was immense. It was not Russia's intention, however, to replicate a British-style "population control" strategy through wholesale detention of civilians. It is difficult not to draw the conclusion that from late 1999 Russian military strategy was to depopulate Chechnya of the bulk of the civilian population and thus create freefire zones. The homes, property, and livelihoods of several hundred thousand people were destroyed, and they were forced to become IDPs (over 90 percent more than once). According to international agencies, about one-third of the population, more than 350,000 persons, were forced to flee from their homes in the early phases of the second war, mostly to camps in Ingushetia, but also to other neighboring regions, such as Stavropol-skii Krai, Krasnodarskii Krai, Dagestan, and inside Chechnya itself.[85] The Russian strategy was recognized by Politkovskaia, who titled one of her reports "Ingushlag. A New Concentration Camp." Understandably, there was an "accumulation of hatred" among the refugees.[86] Boris Nemtsov, one of Russia's leading Democratic politicians and critic of the second war, spoke of the "appalling conditions" in camps that "stretch as far as the eye can see."[87] The IDP figure does not include the 100,000 Russians and other non-Chechens who outmigrated or were expelled from 1991, and as many as 100,000 Chechens who outmigrated to other parts of Russia after the first war ended in 1996.[88]

There was an inherent contradiction in the use of the Chechenization policy by Putin, in that its success depended on a level of mutual trust between Russia and the collaborationist administration that could not be realized. Attempts by Russia to build Kadyrov's authority barely moved beyond the rhetorical level, as Chechnya remained under de facto Russian military occupation and emergency rule. As with Zavgaev in 1996, Russia resorted to electoral fraud to secure a victory for Kadyrov in the referendum on a new "constitution" held in March 2003, which affirmed Russian sovereignty over Chechnya, and the presidential election of October 2003, which confirmed Kadyrov in the position. Putin offered to give Chechnya, under Kadyrov's leadership, "autonomy in the broadest sense of the word" within the Russian constitution.[89] The new power-sharing treaty, however, has been repeatedly postponed. Russia continues to build a façade of local political structures in Chechnya, however, and conducted new parliamentary elections in November 2005, which were widely declared internationally to be a sham. The lack of discipline of Russian forces and the counterinsurgency operations, which involve systematic murder, torture, and mass human rights abuses, could not but highlight the puppet nature of the collaborationist administration and prevent it from accumulating popular credibility. Putin's Chechenization policy was finally given the coup de grace by the assassination of Kadyrov in Grozny stadium in May 2004, which seemed to demonstrate the fragility of a policy founded on one Chechen leader.

As with British policy in Malaya, Russia was not seeking to win "hearts and minds" in the sense of achieving doctrinal or ideological dominance over the Chechen population; the purpose of its strategy was to secure control and reduce the insurgency to what is classically known as an "acceptable level of violence." If acts of terrorism can be contained within Chechnya proper, Putin and the Russian political class and public opinion more broadly would consider this a success. As we shall discuss in Chapter 6, when we examine "terrorism," it is precisely when the war spills over outside Chechnya into the Russian Federation, as in the attacks at Dubrovka theater in October 2002, on Nazran, the capital of Ingushetia, in June 2004, and the Beslan school siege in North Ossetia in September 2004, that Putin's Chechen policy is questioned within Russia. The large-scale assault on Nalchik, a major Russian military base and the capital of Kabardino-Balkaria, in October 2005 by a mostly locally recruited force of fighters, several hundred strong, commanded by Chechen subordinates of Basaev, demonstrated that the military campaign now extended across a large swath of the North Caucasus. Basaev claimed that "jihad, by the grace of Allah, is spreading."[90] These and other attacks made a mockery of Putin's claim in April 2002 that the "military stage of the conflict can be considered to be completed."[91] Putin's popularity, however, has remained consistently high despite setbacks in Chechnya, and he was overwhelmingly reelected president in March 2004. His popularity only dipped significantly after Beslan, though recovered within some months in 2005 (see Figure 2). The Russian democrats talk of Chechnya as "Putin's War."[92] The support for Putin in elections and polls show that it is also very much a "people's war."

Q. On the whole do you approve or disapprove of the performance of: ?

Source: Levada Center (formerly VCIOM) surveys, 1999–2006

Figure 2. Putin's performance in office trends, 2000–2006, http://www.russiavotes.org/

Russian policy in Chechnya has been manipulated to justify authoritarian aspects of "Putinization" in Russia, employing what Baev terms a "counterterrorist mobilization" to recentralize and consolidate his hold on power in Russia.[93] Putin institutionalized what he termed a "dictatorship of law" and unraveled the asymmetric federalism that had developed under Yeltsin in order.[94] In May 2000, he divided the whole country into seven new federal districts, each headed by a presidential plenipotentiary representative (commonly compared with Tsarist-era "governor-generals") (see Map 3).[95] The control factor was evident from the strong military-security bias in the appointments; two of the new presidential representatives were former commanders in the first war and two others were former senior officials in the internal security apparatus. It was a simplistic military-bureaucratic solution to the complex problems of center-regional and federal relations in Russia.

Putin also radically restructured the upper house of parliament, the Federation Council, in August 2000, replacing the governors with representatives nominated by the governors and approved by a republic's or region's legislative assembly for a four year term. After Beslan, he introduced presidential selection of the governor nominees. He forced Tatarstan, Bashkortostan, and other republics to become fully integrated within the Russian federal constitutional and economic space, undoing the privileged status they had won from Yeltsin in 1994. He curbed the political ambitions and power of the oligarchs, as demonstrated by the exile of Berezovskii in early 2000 and the "Yukos affair," which resulted in the imprisonment of Mikhail Khodorkovskii in May 2005. Most significantly, he imposed state control of the mass media, less through direct renationalization and more by managing compliance through key aides in the Kremlin, such as Deputy Head of the Presidential Administration Vladislav Surkov. Pressure for self-censorship was applied to Oligarch owners of the media and journalists, critical media organizations were closed down, and the circulation of critical print media was obstructed. The coverage of the war in Chechnya was transformed by Putin's media clampdown. For the Kremlin not only employed police action and judicial measures to strictly control the media's access to Chechnya, in particular foreign media, to prevent the kind of negative images that had undermined public support for the first war, but also engineered a revolution in media ownership and control in Russia. The main focus of the Kremlin attack on media freedom was Gusinskii's NTV media organization, which had played such a crucial role in criticizing Russian policy during the first war. In April 2001 it was effectively renationalized through the use of the state's control of Gazprom (NTV's main shareholder). Gazprom sacked Gusinskii and the main television news anchor, Yevgenii Kiselev, one of the Russian media's leading critics of the government. While Gusinskii fled into exile, Kiselev attempted to set up a new independent television company, TV6 (later TVS), but they too were closed down by the Kremlin in 2002–03. The Kremlin's thinking was summed up by Kiselev: "This country under this regime does not want any real democratic, independent, free electronic media at all."[96] In 2000 Sergei Kovalev, one of Russia's leading human rights campaigners, argued that the relationship between the second war and the authoritarian drift in Russia under Putin marked the "twilight of Russian freedom."[97] By 2006 this prediction has come to fruition, for Putin has molded a de facto one-party state centered on the presidential party "Unity," which has delivered to the *siloviki* the control of the federal parliament, local governments, the election process, judiciary, and mass media.

In Chechnya, the control strategy pivoted on the so-called Kadyrovtsy, a paramilitary group about three thousand strong, under the command of Akhmed Kadyrov's son Ramzan. It was formed as a bodyguard detachment, but after Akhmed Kadyrov's assassination it expanded into a full-fledged paramilitary formation operating under the guidance of the FSB. The Kadyrovtsy force is responsible for many of the acts of kidnapping and "disappearances" from 2001 to the present.[98] The Kadyrovtsy partly fit the classic definition of "death squad," derived from global experience, as a semi-autonomous state agent using extreme "extrajudicial" violence against defined targets to achieve political goals. A key difference, however, is that death squads are generally small and clandestine organizations interested in "deniability" for their "targeted killings," which is partly tactical but also reflects moral shame at the illegal nature of the activity.[99] The Kadyrovtsy, in contrast, are a large military formation that operates openly, even brazenly in Chechnya, concerned with "claimability" rather than "deniability," as a key element of Russia's counterinsurgency policy of "terrorizing the terrorists." Ramzan Kadyrov's approach of mixing brutality toward fighters who persist with the resistance, and especially against their relatives, with leniency for those who surrender (often rewarding and reemploying them in his own forces) has been an effective instrument for demoralizing and containing the insurgency. The empowerment of the Kadyrovtsy under Putin's protection, however, has allowed this force to operate with impunity in terrorizing the civilian population of Chechnya. That Putin regards Kadyrov as central to Russia's policy in Chechnya is confirmed by his numerous meetings with Kadyrov, and effusive praise, as for example during a meeting held in Sochi on 21 August 2005:

I would like to thank you for this—good lad—I would like to thank you not only for the effective way Chechnya's law enforcement agencies have worked, which has been absolutely evident, especially over the last year. The results, how shall we say, have been clear to see, but they have been confirmed by the Interior Ministry's leadership in their reports also. The minister is happy with your work. You have selected good people for this very important and responsible sphere of work.[100]

Kadyrov's appointment as prime minister in February 2006, and his confirmation as acting president in February 2007, demonstrate that the brutality of the Kadyrovtsy approach is now the central plank not only of the security strategy, but also of Putin's political strategy for Chechnya.

One of the most serious obstacles to the stabilization of Chechnya is the lack of reconstruction and socioeconomic recovery. Obviously, the reconstruction of Chechnya will take immensely longer than its destruction. The wholesale demodernizing consequences of the conflict on Chechnya are rarely analyzed, but it is clear from the scale of the devastation and the number of displaced persons (IDPs) that modern urban society in the capital Grozny and the bigger towns, such as Gudermes, was essentially obliterated as a result of the conflict. If Russia seeks a longer-term political stabilization in Chechnya, it needs to restore the socioeconomic fabric of the country, including such basic essentials as housing, health, education, and employment. The scale of the task is colossal. After Putin declared victory over the insurgents in 2002, Russia began to close down the IDP camps in neighboring republics and regions and forcing the IDPs to return to Chechnya as part of its attempt to portray the "normalization" of Chechnya. No preparations were made for the return of the IDPs. For example, not one of Grozny's 4,664 apartment blocks was intact, and 32,000 private houses were categorized as badly damaged or destroyed.[101] At the current rate of reconstruction it will take decades to rebuild Chechnya. Health and ecological problems, in particular, mental health, TB, and industrial-chemical pollution of the water supply, have simply overwhelmed local and international humanitarian aid agencies. Simply supplying food aid on a daily basis to the IDPs is a major challenge. If calculating conflict-related deaths and injuries is problematical (see Chapter 5), the question of how many have been mentally traumatized is even more so. A Médicins sans Frontières survey conducted among IDPs in August 2004 attempted to quantify the trauma of war-related violence, and indicated high levels of trauma in the population. The report found that almost all people interviewed had been exposed to crossfire, air bombardment, and mortar fire. More than one in five had seen killings, and nearly half had seen maltreatment of family. About two-thirds had experienced the death of a neighbor, while about half the IDPs in Chechnya and one-third in Ingushetia had experienced the death of a close family member. Most had suffered starvation, and all had lost their homes and possessions.[102]

While reconstruction assistance has been consistently included in the Russian budget, even under Yeltsin in 1997–98, and a federal Program for Reconstruction in Chechnya was established in 2001, only a trickle of the funds is spent effectively. The immensity of the task of reconstruction is indicated by the Putin-Kadyrov meeting of 9 August 2006, after which Kadyrov claimed that they had already restored or built "500 thousand square meters of municipal housing, 103 kilometers of intercity roads, 54 kilometers of water pipes, 14 schools, 11 medical facilities, 10 sports facilities, more than 200 kilometers of gas pipes, more than 100 kilometers of electricity gridlines and 150 kilometers of rural roads."[103] The problem lies less in the languid pace of Russian bureaucracy and chronic funding delays than in systematic corruption. Even the Federal Audit Chamber accepts that most of the funds either remain in Moscow ministries, where they are allocated elsewhere or embezzled, or are lost in "illegal payments" by the administration in Chechnya. Interviewed in 2005, the chief accountant of the Audit Chamber, Sergei Riabukhin, found that almost $700 million dollars in 2003 and about $600 million in 2004 were lost in "financial violations," on a scale that "could simply make one cry."[104] At the same time Russia is extracting profits from the restoration of oil production in Chechnya which significantly exceed federal budgetary allocations for reconstruction. In November 2000 a new state-owned company, Grozneftegaz, was established as a subsidiary of the Russian state oil company Rosneft (with Rosneft holding a controlling 51 percent stake; and Kadyrov's Chechen government 49%). By 2005 oil production reached about 2.2 million tons and, given the surge in oil prices in 2005–06, profits have been estimated at over $900 million—only a fraction of which is kept by Chechnya. The retention of oil profits is now a major issue of contention between the Russian and pro-Russian Chechen administration of Ramzan Kadyrov.[105]

While the ultimate success of the Russian counterinsurgency depends on reconstruction, its major effort concentrated on the marginalization of Maskhadov internally and internationally. The defection of Kadyrov gave Russia a key lever with which Maskhadov could be made irrelevant. Putin rebuffed all attempts at serious negotiation and set impossible preconditions (such as the complete disarmament of Chechen forces, the surrender of "terrorists" such as Basaev, and the abandonment of the aspiration for independence). This was the uncompromising agenda set by Putin after the Al-Qaida 9/11attacks on the U.S., which allowed him to frame the conflict in Chechnya as part of the "global war on terror." The preconditions mentioned above formed the basis for the talks held near Sheremetievo airport between the Russian presidential envoy for the Southern Russia Federal District, General Viktor Kazantsev, and Maskhadov's envoy, Akhmed Zakaev on 18 November 2001. When a kind of "track two" (informal) negotiation process appeared to be developing in August 2002 from a broad-based Russian and Chechen dialogue sponsored by the Duchy of Liechtenstein, Putin seized the opportunity presented by the Dubrovka theater attack to step up the international pursuit of the most moderate Chechen leaders in exile. Russia sought the extradition of Maskhadov's deputy Zakaev from the UK and Foreign Minister Akhmadov from the U.S. (discussed in Chapter 5).

Putin's intransigent opposition to negotiation persisted even when

Maskhadov seemed to soften his position by favoring the so-called "Akhmadov Plan." Akhmadov, based in the U.S., devised his plan in consultation with Western experts. Formulated around the concept of an internationally supervised "conditional independence," it proposed a three-sided framework at the level of the United Nations, consisting of the U.S./EU, Russia, and Chechnya, to resolve the conflict. Chechnya would be placed in the United Nations Trusteeship system under Chapters XII and XIII of the UN Charter or by a resolution of the Security Council. The latter would be preferable since Russia's veto would give it confidence to shape the process. The models of East Timor and Kosovo (this was prior to the international push for secession in Kosovo) informed the plan. It was envisaged that there would be a transitional international administration the aim of which was to guarantee the establishment of democracy and the rule of law, and assure reconstruction. Akhmadov's plan was, in essence, a road map for independence, as it declared:

The real distinction here is that in the case of Chechnya, granting *de jure* statehood on completion of the international trusteeship terms should be explicitly defined as a purpose of the trusteeship system, conditional on Chechnya's transformation into a viable democratic state.[106]

The Akhmadov plan called for the U.S., the EU, and its member states to "assign the Russian-Chechen conflict a top priority in their relations with Russia." Intriguingly, Umar Khambiev, one of Maskhadov's representatives living in exile in Western Europe, told journalists in early February 2005, in the wake of Beslan and at a time when Maskhadov's truce and calls to Putin for negotiations were receiving much international attention, that "influential European politicians" would soon launch a major peace drive and pressurize Russia.[107] Maskhadov's proposal for talks "without preconditions" was somewhat disingenuous given that the fundamental issue of independence was already predetermined in the Akhmadov plan.[108] The killing of Maskhadov in early March 2005 could have been a fortunate opportunistic event for Russia, or it could have been the outcome of a decision by the Kremlin to remove from the scene the only Chechen leader with international respect, and thus would have been the focus of any internationally brokered peace process. Russian military tactics during the second war initially generated severe international criticism from Western governments and international organizations. The criticism from Western governments tended to speak diplomatically of "excessive" use and "lack of proportionality" in the use of force by Russia and called for a negotiated settlement. The calls for negotiations became a consistent feature of the Western response, and by itself implicitly underscored Western recognition of the legitimacy of Maskhadov as a "partner" in a peace process. Putin was resolute, however, that "there will be no second Khasaviurt."[109]

Chapter 5

Chechnya and the Meaning of Terrorism

Previous studies of the international aspects of the wars in Chechnya have tended to focus on how Russian foreign policy has managed the conflict internationally.[1] The determinants of the foreign policies of other states and the decisions of international organizations on the question of Chechnya are a much-neglected field of study. It is not the case that there were no opportunities for international leverage or even international conditionality, which if applied, might have changed the course of events in Chechnya. The international politics of the conflict in Chechnya is illustrative of how the relations of states and international organizations and businesses to Russia are heavily loaded with pragmatic calculations about the costs and benefits of cooperation in political, military and trade issues. On the issue of Chechnya, the self-interest of states and international organizations in preserving good relations with Russia, and protecting the material dimension of the relations, has consistently trumped concerns over other more value-based issues such as democratization and human rights.

The expectations of moderate Chechen leaders for international pressure on Russia were naive. The pragmatism in the relations between the United States, EU, and Russia from the beginning of the conflict in the early 1990s to the present has become more pronounced over time. Furthermore, since 2003 the relationship has become increasingly characterized by an asymmetric interdependency that favors Russia due to the surging costs of oil and gas, Russia's regional and international importance as an energy supplier, and the high degree of European dependency on Russian energy exports.[2] Thus, the reluctance of Western governments to make Chechnya an issue in their relations with Russia has grown over time, and not only because 9/11 helped to frame Chechnya as a "terrorism" problem.

U.S. Policy

In terms of scale and abandonment of international laws on rules of engagement, Chechnya was comparable to the war in Bosnia-Herzegovina.

Unlike Milosevic, however, Yeltsin was a reformer considered to be sympathetic, compliant even, to Western interests. Moreover, Russia was a nuclear and strong military power, with a Security Council veto. It simply could not be forced to comply with Western demands over Chechnya, even if Western governments had been proactive. It is generally accepted, however, that Western governments did not pressurize Yeltsin over the first war because they feared it would damage their much more important strategic interest in keeping Yeltsin in power. In the period 1993–96 Yeltsin's popularity plummeted and the popularity of the communists and nationalist extremists surged. The elections of 1993, which resulted in a communist and nationalist majority in the Duma, demonstrated that there was a real chance Yeltsin would lose the 1996 presidential election. The Clinton administration struck a blow against the credibility of the IMF when in early 1996 it pressurized it into releasing billions of dollars of loans to Russia irrespective of the usual economic conditionality. The overriding aim for the U.S. was to shore up the Russian budget and assist Yeltsin's political chances of survival.[3] Chechnya was simply a peripheral issue for the Clinton administration—and merits only two brief mentions in Clinton's memoirs.[4] There is an immense gulf between Clinton's activism on a whole range of protracted and recent conflicts—South Africa, Israel-Palestine, Northern Ireland, Bosnia—and his inaction over Chechnya. During Yeltsin's presidency U.S. policy retreated into subdued references to "excesses" and "lack of proportionality," in the Russian response to Chechnya. U.S. foreign policy was in tow to Russia's framing of Chechnya as an "internal matter" that was concerned with the territorial integrity of the country. In the absence of U.S. support, attempts by international organizations such as the OSCE or UN to challenge Russia's policy faltered.[5] According to Strobe Talbott, Clinton's thinking on Russia in the summer of 1994 in the run-up to the Naples G-7 Summit was "We get the Russian's into the G-7 and they get out of the Baltics. If they're part of the bog boy's club, they've got less reason to beat up on the little guys."[6] However, Russia was about to beat up a "little guy"—Chechnya—though this "little guy" had no significant ethnic electoral constituency in the U.S., nor was it considered useful for NATO enlargement. Clinton was also unrepentant about his most infamous public remark on Chechnya, delivered at a press meeting following a summit with Yeltsin in the Kremlin in April 1996 (the day Dudaev was killed): "I would remind you that we once had a civil war in our country . . . over the proposition that Abraham Lincoln gave his life for, that no state had a right to withdrawal from our union."[7] To be fair to Clinton, it seems to have dawned on him very late in his second term that the question of Chechnya had serious consequences for democratic development in Russia itself. At the Istanbul OSCE Summit in November 1999, Talbott states, Clinton was goaded by one of Yeltsin's wild outbursts to extemporize and declare that "Russia's brute force in Chechnya was unworthy of Yeltsin's own legacy as a champion of democracy."[8]

Western governments in the pre-Kosovo era were also constrained by the international norms unfavorable to secession. With the exception of Estonia, no foreign state considered normalizing relations with Chechnya, and only the internationally isolated Taliban regime in Afghanistan extended formal recognition. While Chechen officials were allowed to travel internationally, none were received with the formal diplomatic protocol of recognition. Many countries did, however, hold talks with Chechen officials and even with Dudaev and Maskhadov during their foreign travels in 1992 and 1998 respectively. Ichkerian passports were issued in January 1998 but they were not internationally recognized.[9] Unlike the situation in the Balkan wars, there were no calls from Western governments for international involvement, or for Russian military or political leaders to be brought to an International Tribunal in Le Hague for war crimes or acts of genocide perpetrated in Chechnya. In any event, if such proposals had been made Russia would have used its Security Council veto to block them. Russia's violation in Chechnya of the 1990 Conventional Forces Europe 1 Treaty, which established ceilings in the geographic deployment of conventional weaponry, was equally muted, and in fact Clinton initiated a change which allowed Russia "additional flexibility" to pursue the war in Chechnya.[10]

The second war occurred in an international environment characterized by Western hubris at the success of NATO's "humanitarian intervention" against Serbia over Kosovo. While there are comparisons to be drawn between Chechnya and Kosovo as cases of ethnic secessionism, the key difference, as noted earlier, is the severe limitation on outside intervention in Chechnya due to Russia's nuclear and Great Power status.[11] Some Russian foreign policy experts have even argued that the war over Kosovo provided a model for Russia's war against Chechnya in late 1999, and legitimated the use of force irrespective of international law.[12] The fundamental questions of comparison between Kosovo and Chechnya, however, hinge on two principles. First, the issue of when international intervention (what Prime Minister Blair termed "conditional noninterference") is legitimate.[13] By the standards set by NATO for its intervention in Kosovo (preventing infringements of international humanitarian law), there was an obvious double standard with Chechnya. Second, there is the issue of when secession may be justified or allowed by the international system. We will return to this question in Chapter 6. U.S. criticism of Russian policy in Chechnya intensified in the first six months of the Bush presidency, but was sidelined after the Slovenia summit in June 2001 as the U.S. prioritized its national interests in securing concessions from Russia over the ABM Treaty. The 9/11 attacks led to a complete reversal of U.S. policy on Chechnya. This was partly moral revulsion against the associations between some Chechen radicals and Al-Qaida, and partly a concession by the U.S. to secure Russian support for its campaign against the Taliban regime in Afghanistan in 2002 and for the war in Iraq in 2003. Consequently, the U.S. has returned to the pragmatic Clinton policy of viewing Chechnya as an "internal" matter but with a post 9/11 stress on the "terrorism" dimension. After 9/11 Putin's framing of Chechnya as part of the "global war on terror" has been incorporated into Western foreign policy approaches to Chechnya, and Chechen groups and leaders have been placed on the U.S. and UN lists of "terrorist" organizations (see below).[14]

EU Policy

If U.S. policy under Clinton was essentially one of muted and occasional formulaic criticism of Russian policy in Chechnya for its "excessive force," there was more debate within the Europe over the issue of human rights abuses during the conflict. There were two prominent opportunities for the use of some form of influence or conditionality. The first arose with Russia's application to join the Council of Europe, an organization where EU member states usually coordinated their foreign policy. Russia's application had been suspended in February 1995 because of concerns over its actions in Chechnya.[15] Membership was eventually approved in January 1996 on condition that Russia would ensure compatibility between its actions in Chechnya and its international obligations and the ambiguous concept "European values." Russia also had to allow the operation of an OSCE "Assistance Group" to monitor its compliance.[16] A second opportunity occurred when the EU and Russia negotiated a primarily economic Partnership and Cooperation Agreement (PCA) in 1995. A few member states delayed the ratification, but this was more a symbolic protest at Russia's policy on Chechnya than a serious attempt to block the PCA, for the ratification process was complete by the end of 1997.[17]

The leading European powers consistently deflected any attempt to seriously sanction Russia for its policy in Chechnya, even at the height of the military campaign in late 1999. The EU summit in Helsinki in December 1999 made a fanfare about its essentially hollow decisions to "review" its strategic relations with Russia, and to implement the PCA "strictly."[18] European leaders, interested in improving their relations with Russia and securing economic opportunities, frequently expressed their solidarity with Putin in his struggle against "terrorism" even before 9/11. As Blair explained in a visit to Moscow just prior to the 2000 presidential election, "We have always made clear our concerns over Chechnya and any question of human rights abuses there, though it is important to realize that Chechnya isn't Kosovo . . . the Russians have been subjected to really severe terrorist attacks."[19] At the EU-Russia summit and the European Council summit at Goteborg in June 2001, the Swedish presidency, unprecedented before or since, made EU-Russia relations a separate heading in its work plan. Sweden placed a high priority on restoring cooperation with Russia and refocused the EU agenda on the core issues of mutual interest with Russia—EU enlargement, the Kyoto Protocol, the EU "Northern Dimension," and trade.[20] By late September 2001, when Putin addressed the German Bundestag and held one of five bilateral summits in this period with Chancellor Gerhardt Schroeder, the latter spoke of the need for "world opinion" to take a more understanding and "differentiated approach" to Russia's conflict in Chechnya.[21] The attacks of 9/11 led to an even more obvious divergence in the EU "common strategy" toward Russia, marked by stronger bilateral approaches, with states such as Germany, France, Italy, and UK openly accepting Putin's framing of the Chechnya conflict as a problem of "terrorism," whereas the historically rooted suspicions of Russia in the candidate countries of Central and Eastern Europe made them much more sympathetic to the cause of Chechnya.[22] This divergence was also partly a product of a prolonged diplomatic strategy by Putin to fracture the common EU position by targeting these leaders. For example, at the EU-Russia summit in Rome in November 2003, Italy's Prime Minister Silvio Berlusconi brusquely intervened against journalists' questions and defended Putin's policy against "terrorists" in Chechnya, and at a trilateral summit between Putin, Chirac, and Schroeder in Sochi in August 2004, Chirac defended Putin's Chechnya policy and supported the Russian-supervised presidential elections in the region which affirmed the presidency of Akhmed Kadyrov.

Even at the level of aid, despite the humanitarian catastrophe in Chechnya, EU assistance has been paltry. Virtually no assistance was provided to the Maskhadov government. In 1999, before the outbreak of the second war, the EU provided aid assistance of just €2.4million, a fraction of EU aid to the Palestinian administration. Since the start of the current crisis in 1999, total EU aid for the whole of the Northern Caucasus amounts to almost €150 million, but again this is a small fraction of the billions of euros the EU spends through its TACIS program in the CIS, the bulk of it on improving economic opportunities with Russia.[23]

By the 14th EU-Russia Summit in The Hague in November 2004, there was mutual agreement to sideline such controversial issues to a new and separate round of EU-Russia "consultations" on human rights, and in this way prevent them from spoiling the spectacle and business of the main summit forum. Rather than confront Russia directly over Chechnya, the EU has tended to operate through the coordination of its member states' presence in other international organizations. In particular, its dominating presence (including candidate states until May 2004) in the OSCE and Council of Europe, where the EU presidency presented the common positions of the member states.

The Role of the OSCE and Council of Europe

Perhaps the single most important international influence on the conflict in Chechnya during the first war came from the OSCE Assistance Mission under Tim Guldimann in 1996–97. Guldimann, by all accounts, played a crucial mediating role during the Khasaviurt negiotiations, and then provided much needed financial assistance and monitors for the elections of early 1997, which were critical for securing the initial international legitimacy accorded to Maskhadov's government. After the agreements of 1996 and 1997, Russia and the international system consigned Chechnya to a limbo status, effectively acknowledging Russia's blockade. The increasing disorder and hostage-taking even deterred international humanitarian organizations from operating in the republic.

At the start of the second war, there was a new intensity in Western governments' positions on Chechnya. The criticism peaked with the rare joint statement by OSCE High Commissioner on National Minorities Max van der Stoel, Secretary-General of the Council of Europe Walter Schwimmer, and United Nations High Commissioner for Human Rights Mary Robinson, on 8 December 1999 expressing concern about human rights in Chechnya, and in particular the Russian ultimatum for civilians to leave Grozny.[24] A sign of the increased pressure on Russia was its agreement to allow the OSCE to reestablish its mission in Grozny in June 2001 (which had been withdrawn to Moscow at the height of the hostage taking in 1998, and had moved to Znamenskoe in December 2000).

What is striking, however, about the role of the OSCE and Council of Europe throughout the period from 1996 to the present is their lack of leverage over Russia and weak capacity to influence Russian policy in Chechnya. Annually throughout this period, reports from PACE, for example, revealed details of human rights abuses and noncompliance with the conditions of Russia's membership in the Council of Europe. The Committee of Ministers (i.e., member states) did suspend Russia's voting rights in April 2000 in response to concerns about the second war, but the suspension was lifted just nine months later in January 2001. Thus, the pattern whereby the issue of Chechnya was subordinated to national interests was consolidated in the second war. Moreover, from 2002 on Russia has been more proactive in European organizations such as the OSCE in highlighting "double standards" and condemning what it regards as the imbalance towards human rights issues over security. This is another factor which has made Western governments cautious about raising the question of Chechnya.[25]

Lord Frank Judd, the PACE Rapporteur on Chechnya from 1998 to 2003, made strenuous and ultimately futile efforts in this period to initiate a peace process. It was not simply a case of Russian intransigence, where Putin would not negotiate with Maskhadov. Judd's efforts were also hampered by his reliance on moral persuasion and reluctance to apply sanctions to Russia, for example, by recommending the suspension of its voting rights in the Council of Europe. Furthermore, governments refused to pressurize Russia over Chechnya, according to Judd, because they had "bigger agendas" and did not want to disrupt their broader strategic and economic relations.[26] Putin's ability to deflect criticisms of his Chechnya policy has been helped by the growing tension in EU foreign policy between attempts to secure a "common strategy" towards Russia, and the material interests of those member states who are the biggest trading partners with Russia, notably Germany, whose national interests are best served by bilateralism.[27]

The bankruptcy of the PACE activity on Chechnya was demonstrated again in January 2006 when the head of its Legal Affairs and Human Rights Committee, German socialist Rudolf Bindig, announced by far the lengthiest, most detailed, most critical, and most up-to-date report on Russia's abuses in Chechnya, including the disappearances and extra-judicial killings. The subsequent PACE resolution revealed the exasperation at the policy of the member states on Chechnya: "The Assembly fears that the lack of effective reaction by the Council's executive body in the face of the most serious human rights issue in any of the Council of Europe's member states undermines the credibility of the Organization."[28]

Putin's Foreign Policy

The decline of Chechnya as a salient issue in EU-Russia relations is not a product of any change of Russian policy with regard to human rights abuses; in fact as we discussed earlier the activities of the Kadyrovtsy are well documented and continue. The decline rather can be attributed to two main developments. First, Putin is an astute foreign policy navigator. He made a major investment in diplomacy to forge personal relationships with the key Western leaders, Bush, Schroeder, Chirac, Blair, and Berlusconi (in contrast with Yeltsin, who tended to focus more on the relationship with Clinton). Second, the West's policy on Chechnya is given a normative declaratory dressing, but its substance is informed by pragmatic priorities. This has meant a focus on major economic issues such as energy and major international issues such as Iraq, Afghanistan, Iran, and Middle East. Western leaders have become desensitized to criticisms

of their approach to Russia. Chechnya is rarely even raised during bilateral summit meetings. Putin's imposition of stringent controls on the
media's "battlefield access" greatly reduced accurate coverage of the conflict, and enhanced the capacity of the Russian government to manage
the propaganda war domestically and internationally. 9/11 and the horrifying images from Beslan allowed Russia to internationalize its idiom
of the conflict as one that matched Western concerns about Islamic terrorism. The associations between the Chechen radicals under Basaev and
Al-Qaida were spotlighted, and as we discussed earlier Putin was force-
ful in presenting the Russian position in international affairs.

Information about systematic human rights abuses and atrocities perpetrated by Russian forces became more widely known largely through
the activities of independent human rights organizations such as Memorial, Human Rights Watch, and Amnesty International. It is ironic that
as the volume of their reporting has grown during the second war, international criticism from governments has become somewhat formulaic.
Moreover, as such organizations have become critical of Western governments' counterinsurgency practices in the "war on terror" in Iraq and
Afghanistan, and over the erosion of democracy, their influence over
policy-makers and the media has declined. The inaction at the level of
governments is only recently being counterbalanced by judicial activism
at the European level. In January 2003, the European Court of Human
Rights (ECHR) established a precedent by declaring admissible six peti-
tions from Chechens alleging human rights abuses by Russian forces in
Chechnya. The court decided in favor of the six petitioners, mostly unan-
imously, on 24 February 2005.[29] By 2006, the number of cases being considered by the ECHR reached 120. The ECHR can only award financial
compensation for material and moral damages and legal costs to be paid
by the Russian government, and even then its decisions are difficult to
enforce. Complainants also leave themselves open to harm in Chechnya.
Nevertheless, it opens a new front in the political war over Chechnya, as
it brings Russia into disrepute among international public opinion, if
not among governments.

Putin has been an extremely effective operator on the international
scene. He has largely succeeded in tarnishing the whole Chechen insurgency and covering his policy of coercion under the idiom of the "war
on terror." The success of his foreign policy was clearly demonstrated by
the decision of the G8 summit in June 2002 to hold its summer 2006
summit in Russia, thus signaling that Russia was a full member. The combined effect of coopting the Kadyrovs and the Chechenization strategy,
the easing of international pressure as a result of an accumulation of revulsion over attacks by Islamists, not just at Beslan but also in Madrid (March
2004), London (July 2005), and elsewhere, was to give Putin no incentive

to negotiate with Maskhadov, or any leader from the side of the resistance, and indeed to create the conditions where Maskhadov could be "taken out" without any significant repercussions. It is also simply the case that international interest in Chechnya has become jaded by the protracted nature of the conflict, and concerns about "Islamic terrorism" more generally.[30] To what extent, then, can the Chechen resistance be located within the "terrorism" paradigm?

The Meaning of Terrorism

When in early 2004, more than four years into the second Russo-Chechen war, President Putin was asked by a journalist about the potential for a peace process in Chechnya, he retorted combatively, "Russia does not negotiate with terrorists, we destroy them."[31] Putin's public nihilism toward negotiations with the leaders of the Chechen resistance is reminiscent of the assertions by past leaders of colonialist regimes, and even of more recent democratic leaders. The ranks of leaders who publicly took an uncompromising political stance toward opponents that they denounced as "terrorists," while they secretly negotiated through back channels or eventually entered overt negotiations, include President Reagan, Prime Minister Thatcher, Prime Minister Rabin, and President Yeltsin. Even the Bush administration has negotiated with insurgents in Iraq.[32] Russian policy toward Chechnya from the early 1990s forward had consistently framed the conflict against the Chechen resistance in the idiom of a struggle against "terrorism." The National Security Concept of the Russian Federation (2000), for example, listed eighteen separate mentions of terrorism.[33]

The conflict between Russia and Chechnya has seen a number of the most atrocious and spectacular acts of terrorism of recent decades. The most notorious incidents involved large-scale hostage-taking of civilian noncombatants: the hijacking of civilian airplanes in November 1991 and August 2004, the seizure of the Budennovsk maternity hospital in June 1995, the Kizliar hospital in January 1996, the Dubrovka theater in October 2002, and the Beslan school in September 2004. Similarly, international organizations such as the OSCE, PACE, and UN, as well as internationally respected human rights organizations and humanitarian groups, have reported on the systematic use of excessive force and human rights abuses perpetrated by the Russian military and their Chechen collaborators, including area-bombing of urban areas, large-scale "disappearances," extrajudicial killings, torture, collective punishments, use of civilians as human shields, and targeting of relatives of insurgents. Incidents of mass killing of civilian noncombatants by Russian forces include the area-bombing of Grozny in late 1994-early 1995, and late 1999, and the massacre at Samashki in April 1995. The Russian and Chechen protagonists have consistently classified each other as "bandits," "terrorists," and "criminals."[34] Given the charges and countercharges, is the term terrorism useful for understanding the conflict in Chechnya?

Irregular warfare is as old as warfare itself. It has many synonyms—guerrilla war, insurgency, partisan war, special operations, commando raids, and so on. Over the last decade this form of warfare has been given a new label by Western security policy-makers—"asymmetric warfare." As a concept, it embraces the notion of low cost military actions, whether by state or nonstate actors, which extract high costs from the enemy in terms of damage inflicted or ongoing defense costs. The use of terrorism fits within this concept well, and indeed it has been increasingly incorporated into Western national security and defense concepts as a form of "asymmetric warfare."

The term "terrorism" is one of the most politicized and contested concepts in the modern era. The suffix *-ism* is a noun suffix. When it is added to words or word roots, *-ism* forms nouns and imparts the meaning of "act," "state," "theory," or "ideology" relating to the noun. Thus, terrorism should refer to the act, state, theory, or ideology of terror. Logically, the term captures two main notions: action, or what may be better termed "method," and a set of ideas or values, or what may be better termed "principles." Consequently, for the term terrorism to be conceptually useful, its meaning in terms of actions and principles must be generally understood and widely accepted.

To understand why the term terrorism is so politicized and contested requires us to examine more closely the method and principles with which it is associated. For the multiplicity of meanings arise because there is no agreement as to what actions or principles should be covered by the term. The adage "one person's terrorist is another person's freedom fighter" is often today presented as a rather tired, hackneyed cliché. In fact, the adage captures succinctly the essential problem of politicized usage inherent in the use of the term terrorism. We must also ask whether it is possible to devise a meaningfully useful definition of terrorism that might win a wider consensus. An examination of the question of terrorism in the conflict in Chechnya will contribute to this goal.

Modern conceptions of terrorism are based on interpretations of three interrelated core issues regarding the use of political violence: first, what is legitimate in the use of political violence, second, what is moral in the use of political violence, and third, what constraints should there be on the use of political violence? The absence of a consensus on the meaning of the term terrorism derives from the absence of a consensus over these fundamental questions. Furthermore, the whole issue has a dynamic nature, as opinions on these fundamental questions are also politicized, changing over time and depending on the context.

Criminalization and the List Approach

In the period prior to 9/11 states tended to attempt to manage terrorism by criminalizing it. This involved specifying certain types of criminal activity associated with terrorism, such as assassination (murder), hijacking, kidnapping, racketeering, bombing, and weapons-related offenses. It also often involved specifying or designating certain organizations as "terrorist." The compilation of "lists" of illegal activities and organizations, and in some cases persons, is central to this approach. The philosophy underpinning the approach was encapsulated in UK prime minister Thatcher's statement in 1981, during the hunger strike by IRA prisoners demanding political status: "There is no such thing as political murder, political bombing or political violence. There is only criminal murder, criminal bombing and criminal violence. We will not compromise on this."[35] This uncompromising rhetoric came shortly before the British government made concessions to the IRA, illustrating the difficulty of criminalizing nationalist political violence that has widespread popular support.

The crudeness of the list approach, however, is best illustrated by the U.S. example, mainly because the nature of open government in the U.S. allows us to explore the contradictions more openly than in more closed systems. Since 1976 the U.S. has collated reports on terrorism and designated terrorist organizations, principally as part of its Cold War policy. After the end of the Cold War, in the mid-1990s, the State Department began to produce Congressionally mandated annual reports entitled *Patterns of Global Terrorism*, and lists of "Foreign Terrorist Organizations" (FTOs). The reports are presented as a full and complete record for those countries and groups involved in what the U.S. State Department designates as "international terrorism."[36] In fact, they are little more than a list of those groups that are required by U.S. foreign policy interests to be designated FTOs. That this approach is driven by U.S. national interests, rather than by any attempt at designation by objective criteria, is clear from the official procedure for drawing up the lists, as it states, "the Secretary of State may at any time revoke a designation upon a finding that the circumstances forming the basis for the designation have changed in such a manner as to warrant revocation, or that the national security of the United States warrants a revocation."[37]

The overt politicization is reflected in the fact that many of the FTOs designated in the 1970s and 1980s were Palestinian groups and groups supported by Soviet Union. The politicization of the list continued after the end of the Cold War and was evident before and, especially after, 9/11.

For example, Secretary of State Madeleine Albright justified the removal of the Provisional IRA from the list in October 1997 primarily because of the absence of "terrorist activity" and not on the basis of the inherent nature of the organization per se.[38] In the build-up to the Iraq War in 2002–3, the Bush administration manipulated the FTO list to win support for its policies at the UN and as a kind of "wish list" to reward members of its international coalition. For example, in late August 2002, during a visit to Beijing, Deputy Secretary of State Richard L. Armitage announced the designation of the East Turkestan Islamic Movement, a little-known group of Muslim separatists active in western China. In May 2003 three Basque nationalist groups (Batasuna, Euskal Herritarrok, and Herri Bata-suna) were added to the list, following the support of Spain's right-wing government under People's Party prime minister José-Maria Aznar for the war in Iraq, and as a means of influencing the outcome of the Spanish elections. There was a significant increase overall in the number of FTO's listed between 2000 and 2004, from 44 to 76 groups. Included in this increase were the first Chechen groups to be designated as FTOs by the U.S.

It was in the context of the post-9/11 "global war on terror," and just over nine years after the violent conflict in Chechnya began, that the U.S. added three Chechen groups to the FTO list in February 2003.[39] The three groups listed had claimed responsibility for some of the worst terrorist atrocities perpetrated in Russia. The Special Purpose Islamic Regiment (SPIR), led by Movsar Baraev, carried out the October 2002 Dubrovka theater attack. Two other groups linked to Shamil Basaev were also added: the Riyadus-Salikhin Reconnaissance and Sabotage Battalion of Chechen Martyrs had been founded by Basaev, and the Islamic International Peacekeeping Brigade (IIPB) was under the command of Khattab and Basaev. The designations came at the height of U.S. attempts to win UN Security Council approval for the invasion of Iraq, and was part of the effort to persuade Russia not to use its veto. Subsequently, in August 2003, the U.S. designated Basaev a "threat" to national security under the executive orders issued after 9/11. The U.S. partly justified the inclusion of Chechen groups by linking them to Al-Qaida, however, it gave an immense boost to Putin's attempt to win international credibility for Russia's claim that the war in Chechnya was part of the global war on terrorism, and for his refusal to negotiate with the "terrorist" Maskhadov.

The criminalization of terrorism tended to adhere to a proximate definition across countries. The definition of terrorism in Russia's law "On the fight against terrorism" passed in July 1998 was broadly in line with previous "catch-all" Western legal definitions, though it was more tightly defined than the even broader definitions that were introduced under U.S. and British law in 2000–2001. The 1998 Russian law defined terrorism as follows:

terrorism is violence or the threat of violence against individuals or organizations, and also the destruction (damaging) of or threat to destroy (damage) property and other material objects, that threaten to cause loss of life, significant damage to property, or other socially dangerous consequences and are implemented with a view to violating public security, intimidating the population, or influencing the adoption of decisions advantageous to terrorists by governing authorities, or satisfying their unlawful material and (or) other interests; attempts on the lives of statesmen or public figures perpetrated with a view to ending their state or other political activity or out of revenge for such activity; attacks on representatives of foreign states or employees of international organizations enjoying international protection, and also on the official premises or vehicles of persons enjoying international protection if these actions are committed with a view to provoking war or complicating international relations.[40]

There was one feature of the law, however, that did not replicate Western practice. The 1998 Russian law gave legal "protection" (immunity) to state officials, military and security personnel engaged in counterterrorism.[41]

The new Prevention of Terrorism law passed by the Russian parliament on 1 March 2006 provides an even more generic definition. Article 3 states that "Terrorism is the ideology and practice of violence for the influencing of decision-making by government authorities, local authorities and international organizations, involving the frightening of the population and (or) other forms of illegal violent actions." The Russian law-makers followed closely the debates in Western democracies about legal measures, in particular the debate over the criminalizing of the concept of "glorifying terrorism" which is ongoing in the UK. The Russian law not only criminalizes all the usual forms of activity associated with the preparation and carrying out of "terrorist" acts, but also "inciting," and "the propaganda of the idea of terrorism, spreading materials or information promoting terrorist activity or justifying and approving of the necessity for such activity." The hard-line approach of the law was strongly influenced not only by Putin and the *siloviki*, but also by politicians representing regions and republics in the North Caucasus, which have borne the brunt of Chechen cross-border attacks over the last decade.[42] Prior to the new law, anyone who sympathetically reported the case for Chechnya was likely to be charged with "inciting racial hatred."[43]

After 9/11 there was intense pressure applied to key international organizations to broaden the definition of terrorism. The EU followed the Anglo-American model by adopting a very imprecise definition to include any act that "may seriously damage a country or international organization" if designed to seriously intimidate a population, "unduly compel" a government or international organization to act, or that may be "seriously destabilizing" for a country's "fundamental political, constitutional, economic or social structures."[44] In contrast, the UN retained a common sense perspective when addressing the issue of terrorism that reflected sensibility to the profound politicization of the term. Security Council Resolution 1373 (2001), passed in the immediate aftermath of 9/11, made no attempt to define terrorism, while it restated "terrorist" type activities that were already banned under international law in the twelve international conventions that are deemed to cover "terrorist" type activity.[45] Most of the international conventions were adopted in the 1960s and 1970s in an attempt to deter the hijacking of aircraft and ships, and nuclear terrorism.

The problem of identifying "what is" and "when is" an "armed conflict" remains central to the question of identifying terrorism. In effect, the UN has moved to a position where terrorism is regarded as a political act but equally is essentially a kind of war crime—deliberate attacks on civilians and noncombatants—that is not covered by other international law regulating armed conflict.[46] The UN Working Group on terrorism observed that, historically, "terror" was also an instrument employed by "rulers" (carefully avoiding the use of the word state). It noted also that, while terrorism is often related to armed conflict, the prevention and resolution of armed conflict should not primarily be conceived of as "anti-terrorist activities." Putin, after all, had framed the second war in Chechnya as a "counterterrorism operation." The Working Group warned that

Labelling opponents or adversaries as terrorists offers a time-tested technique to de-legitimize and demonize them. The United Nations should beware of offering, or be perceived to be offering, a blanket or automatic endorsement of all measures taken in the name of counter-terrorism.[47]

The contradictions and different interpretations of the criminalization and list approaches and the flaws in the international conventions on terrorism may also be illustrated by the operation of the UN's own list as compiled on the basis of Security Council Resolution 1267 (1999), and by how Chechen leaders were treated by foreign countries. The most notable cases involved three leading political figures in the Chechen resistance: Akhmed Zakaev, deputy prime minister of Chechnya and a spokesman for Chechen president Maskhadov, Ilias Akhmadov, foreign minister of Chechnya, and Yandarbiev, the former president of Chechnya and leading ideologist of the Chechen national movement.

In the wake of the Dubrovka theater incident, and on the basis of an Interpol warrant, Russia charged Zakaev with murder and leading an "illegal armed formation." Russia applied to the Danish Ministry of Justice to extradite Zakaev from Denmark when he attended the World Chechen Congress in Copenhagen in October 2002. Denmark rejected the application for lack of evidence and "imprecision" in the Russian case.[48] Zakaev then sought refuge in the UK, and Russia applied to the UK courts for his extradition. Zakaev's case became a cause célèbre in the UK. The campaign for his defense was headed by the actress Vanessa Redgrave and he was defended by some of the UK's leading lawyers. The case was thrown out of court in November 2003. Senior district judge Timothy Workman, who heard the case, reasoned that the "scale of the conflict" in Chechnya meant it could not be defined as a case of terrorism but "amounted in law to an internal armed conflict" that fell under the Geneva Conventions. Indeed, he argued that many observers would have regarded it as a "civil war." Moreover, he judged that the case was "politically motivated," and that Zakaev was likely to be tortured if returned to Russia.[49]

While most reasonable persons would accept that it would have been wrong to extradite Zakaev to Russia, the reasoning provided by Judge Workman was extremely vague. It seems odd to classify an internal armed conflict on the basis of scale. The Protocol to the Geneva Conventions dealing with non-international "armed conflict" provides specific conditions under which an "armed conflict" is deemed to exist, namely, when it takes place "in the territory of a High Contracting Party between its armed forces and dissident armed forces or other organized armed groups which, under responsible command, exercise such control over a part of its territory as to enable them to carry out sustained and concerted military operations and to implement this Protocol." The Protocol also specifically bans "acts of terrorism" and attacks on civilians.[50] These are the conditions that should have been applied to the case of Chechnya.

In the case of Akhmadov, the host country was the United States, the self-declared leader in the "global war on terrorism." Akhmadov had applied for political asylum in the U.S. in 2002. Russia applied for his extradition on the grounds that Akhmadov was involved in terrorism and had links to the armed incursion from Chechnya into Dagestan in the autumn of 1999. An immigration court in Boston declared the charges of terrorism against Akhmadov "baseless" and granted him asylum in April 2004. The immigration judge pointed out that if Akhmadov were returned to Russia, the Chechen leader would be "shot without being afforded the opportunity to defend himself in a trial, as has happened to other members of the Chechen government." The U.S. Department of Homeland Security challenged the decision on the basis that Akhmadov was involved in "acts of terrorism," but in August 2004, following pressure from Congress, the State Department, and the mass media, it withdrew its objections and confirmed that the charges were "baseless."[51] Unsurprisingly, Russia saw the U.S. decision as "a clear display of double standards in the struggle against terrorism."[52] Russian sensibilities on the issue were further trampled on when Akhmadov was awarded a Reagan-Fascell Democracy Fellowship by the National Endowment for Democracy, a U.S. political foundation funded by an annual congressional appropriation.

In Yandarbiev's case, the host country was Qatar, a Muslim state closely allied to the United States. Security Council Resolution 1267 (1999) imposed sanctions on a list of persons and organizations that were determined to be members of or "associated with" the Taliban regime and Al-Qaida because it was determined that they constituted "a threat to international peace and security." Basaev and Yandarbiev had been placed on the UN "consolidated list" of individuals "belonging to or associated with the Al-Qaida organisation" in June 2003.[53] The Security Council resolutions that framed the operation of the list obliged all states, among other things, to freeze the assets, and prevent the entry into or the transit through their territories, of the individuals and organizations on the list. Yet Yandarbiev had lived "temporarily" as a "guest" in Qatar since November 2002. According to the Russian Foreign Ministry, Qatar refused to "fulfil its international obligations, and in practice took Yandarbiev under its guardianship," providing him with a haven from which he could prepare new acts of terrorism.[54] Russian presidential aide Sergei Yastrzhembskii claimed that Russia had requested Yandarbiev's extradition, but that Qatar had not complied.[55] In this case, Russia decided to resolve the matter by its own act of "international terrorism." Yandarbiev was assassinated by a car bomb, which also killed two bodyguards and mutilated his young son. A Qatari court convicted two Russian FSB agents of the murders, and in December 2004 under a bilateral agreement Qatar agreed to transfer the agents back to Russia to serve out their sentences.

These cases demonstrate that there was a reluctance internationally to deal with Chechnya on Russia's terms, that is, that the conflict be treated as a case of terrorism, even after 9/11. The reluctance of countries to cooperate with Russia on Chechnya was despite the fact that Russia increasingly framed its policy on international terrorism along Western lines, by compiling lists and focusing on "Islamic" terrorism supposedly related to Al-Qaida.[56] Equally, Russia applied its own concept of national interest in the designation of "terrorist" groups. This was most clearly illustrated in February and March 2006 following the Hamas victory in the Palestinian elections. Although Hamas has for many years been on the U.S. FTO list, President Putin invited Hamas leaders to come to Moscow, pointing out that Russia had never regarded Hamas as a "terrorist" organization. A Hamas delegation was duly received in Moscow in early March and met with Russian foreign minister Sergei Lavrov.[57] Putin's reasoning for this decision, at least in public, again illustrates the politicization of designations:

burning bridges, especially in politics, is the easiest but not a very constructive approach. So, taking this into consideration, and after analyzing the behavior of each side engaged in the conflict, we did not rush into declaring this or that organization a terrorist organization, rather we are trying to work with all the organizations taking part in the process of bringing a peaceful life to this very volatile region of the world.

For this reason we did not recognize Hamas as a terrorist organization. Today we need to recognize that Hamas came to power in the Palestinian Autonomy as a result of democratic and legitimate elections, and we must respect the choice of the Palestinian people.[58]

A similar position was taken with Hizballah in Lebanon, which is considered a "terrorist" organization by the U.S., during the Israel-Hizballah conflict of August 2006. When Russia published its own official list of seventeen "terrorist" organizations in July 2006, all of those groups included were Islamist, mainly Chechen, but Hamas and Hizballah were not listed.[59]

Old and New Definitions of Terrorism

We may further assess the basis for the ambiguities of the international politics of terrorism by examining how the term terrorism has been traditionally defined and conceptualized internationally in a variety of fields—not only by states, but also by social scientists, lawyers, historians, and philosophers. There are multiple meanings of terrorism within and across academic disciplines. In the first edition of his magisterial survey, *Political Terrorism: A Research Guide*, published in 1988, Alex Schmid devoted more than a hundred pages to examining more than a hundred different definitions of the term terrorism in a futile effort to devise a definition that would have a broad consensus. By the time of the second edition of the book, four years later, Schmid had conceded that he was no nearer to reaching an "adequate definition."[60] The multiple meanings of the term terrorism arise because of the imprecision in the way it is employed in four key areas: first, in the variety of the acts of violence covered by it; second, in the variety of motivations attributed to it (political, economic, social, national, ethnic, religious, criminal, or issue specific); third, in the variety of actors employing it (states and non-state actors); and fourth, in the variety of contexts or arenas in which it is employed (local, national, regional, international, global). The single most contentious definitional problem with the term terrorism is how it should be distinguished from war crimes perpetrated by states, and certain forms of unconventional warfare, such as insurgency and guerrilla and partisan war, which are often associated with nationalist resistance and revolutionary movements aimed at overthrowing "bad" regimes.

Nationalist and revolutionary political violence, and the state's violent repression of such resistance, in the late nineteenth and early twentieth centuries, laid down a pattern that has largely remained unchanged into the contemporary period, though the technological aspects of this type of conflict have become more sophisticated. This type of violence is characterized by an expanded struggle that incorporates not only the internal but also the international dimension, with regard to both the enlargement of what was considered to be the legitimate theater for violent acts, and "internationalization" in terms of drawing on international opinion, émigré communities, and foreign states and international organizations for support. This kind of struggle is also, as mentioned above, marked by periodic "spectacular" attacks, for example, bombings of important regime targets and assassination of key regime figures.

The use of political violence and the varying response of states to it have been characterized by demonstration effects in techniques and methods. Forms of organization, such as the cell structure, and types of action (in particular assassination), spread among groups committed to the use of political violence, while there was a concomitant expansion of the apparatus of the modern security police and military structures to deal with it. States have traditionally denied the political motivations and aspirations of nationalist resistance, and defined such prisoners as "criminals," "gangs" "bandits" and "terrorists" though generally not employing ordinary criminal procedure but special legal or security regimes to repress such resistance.

Traditionally, "partisan" warfare and related activities were treated harshly by the customs of war, as defined by states and interpreted by their militaries. The goal was to deter such activity by treating anything regarded as terrorism or unconventional resistance by nonprofessional state armed forces as falling outside the laws and customs of war. Generally, this meant giving no quarter and conducting mass reprisals against the civilian communities from which partisans operated. There were understandable reasons for this kind of harsh response. The unconventional character of such resistance centered on secret organizations that were the antithesis of the traditional state military order. Often, partisans wore no uniforms, had poor command and control and were poorly disciplined, and preferred surprise attacks against "soft" targets. Partisan attacks were also often characterized by no quarter and by iconic acts of brutal revenge against occupying forces.[61] The absence of an international consensus as to the difference between freedom fighters and "terrorists" and the patterns of engagement in this type of violence is, therefore, more than a century old. By the beginning of the twentieth century the meaning of terrorism had assumed more or less its modern confused, ambivalent, and relativist connotations.

The common strand in most modern academic definitions of terrorism is that it must involve political violence against civilians or "noncombatants."[62] In the international laws and customs of war (notably, the Geneva Conventions), "noncombatant" is generally a synonym for "civilian."[63] The greatest controversy arises over whether the act or method should be applied to state as well as non-state actors and groups. Hoffman, for example, following U.S. policy, is confused as to whether terrorism directed or "sponsored" by states, let us say in the form of "death squads," is best characterized as just "terror" or is in fact terrorism.[64] Schmid et al. (1988) found that the most common elements in the existing definitions were that terrorism involved *the use of violence or the threat of violence* to achieve *political goals* by instilling *fear in a wider targeted audience.* In a later work Schmid made the following attempt at a comprehensive definition:

Terrorism is an anxiety-inspiring method of repeated violent action, employed by (semi) clandestine individual, group, or state actors, for idiosyncratic, criminal, or political reasons, whereby—in contrast to assassination—the direct targets of violence are not the main targets. The immediate human targets of violence are generally chosen randomly (targets of opportunity) or selectively (representative or symbolic targets) from a target population, and serve as message generators.[65]

Perhaps the key element in this definition is the notion that the immediate target of a "terrorist" attack is secondary and is a proxy for communicating a threat to a primary target that is elsewhere—the "wider" political community or government. For this reason, the modern conception of terrorism is almost synonymous with the manipulation of modern mass communication through the mass media, especially the visual medium of television. It is also for this reason that a key feature of government counterterrorist policies is to deny the "oxygen of publicity" to "terrorists," often through stringent forms of censorship and media manipulation. The "framing" of a conflict as terrorism is also a classic state tool employed to denigrate legitimate resistance. However, "terrorist" attacks may involve a mix of personal and political motives, and may have no ulterior strategic goal other than "revenge," or "hitting back." Attacks on property and other assets, that is straightforward attempts to do damage, do not easily fit within this paradigm. Most important, the above definitions do not sufficiently capture the dynamic nature of terrorism and its role as an instrument within a broader repertoire of armed struggle. A soldier or fighter can be a legitimate killer or a "terrorist" almost simultaneously, depending on the conditions of combat and the nature of the target.

Prior to 9/11 the scholarly literature on terrorism was dominated by one case: the Provisional IRA which emerged from the civil conflict in Northern Ireland in 1969–70. The interest in the IRA and Northern Ireland has been difficult to shift, for while this was a rather small-scale conflict the IRA was a formidable organization which engaged British security forces in a twenty-five year long struggle. The lack of anticipation within the study of terrorism is revealed by the fact that there was very little research conducted into Al-Qaida before 9/11.[66] The lop-sided focus of research was compounded by imbalance and lack of distance in scholarly analyses, given the high degree of politicization in the study of the I.R.A. in the U.K. The work of Wilkinson, for example, an influential academic policy advisor to British and American governments, usefully distinguishes between "acts of terror," which may be incidental and epiphenomenal, and political terrorism, which is "coercive intimidation" designed:

usually to service political ends. It is used to create and exploit a climate of fear among a wider target group . . . and to publicize a cause. . . . Terrorism may be used on its own or as part of a wider unconventional war. It can be employed by desperate and weak minorities, by states as a tool of domestic and foreign policy, or by belligerents as an accompaniment in all types and stages of warfare.[67]

There is less consensus over the rationality and efficacy of terrorism, and whether it can ever be justified. According to Wilkinson the defining characteristic of terrorists is their "rejection of all moral constraints" in the use of violence. He regards this method of armed struggle as lacking a "strategic rationale," "remarkably unsuccessful in gaining strategic objectives," and without moral justification, irrespective of the nature of the regime against which it is employed.[68] Others argue that new technological developments in communications and weaponry have increased the power of terrorism compared with the past, and thus groups that use "directed terror . . . can achieve effects on a target community which are out of all proportion to their numerical or political power," by causing governments to make concessions.[69] Some have delegitimized terrorism as a form of political violence not so much because of the nature of the method, but because it is claimed to lack popular support. According to Wievorka, terrorism is a "spin-off" product, an "anti-movement" of "radical disengagement" formed out of the "disintegration of some collective action": "The truly terrorist actor has become cut off from the sole ground on which he might have legitimated his action. This is the legitimacy conferred by a population group that recognizes itself in his action."[70] This may be a valid understanding of the marginalized left- and right-wing extremist terrorism in Europe in the 1960s and 1970s, but is less plausible for explaining the political violence of popular nationalist resistance movements, such as the IRA in Northern Ireland, ETA in Spain, the Tamil Tigers in Sri Lanka, or the Chechen resistance.

As Silke has noted, the motivation or "psychology" of terrorism is a much-neglected area of study.[71] The established "security expert" approach tends to pathologize terrorism as a form of "madness" that is driven by fanaticism, delusions, and paranoia.[72] Psychologists are drawn in by governments to provide a scientific basis for pathologies and to "profile" the "terrorist personality," to advise on siege situations, and to assist the traumatized (not only the victims, but also those engaged in acts or countering acts of terrorism). The empirical evidence for a "terrorist personality" is dubious, though governments and opponents use the notion as part of the armory for demonizing terrorism.[73] Recent academic studies by psychologists, however, have grappled with the question of motivation for terrorists. Such studies reveal the "normality" of terrorists, and conclude that "terrorist psychology is just like that of everyone else . . . in the wrong circumstances most people could either come to support a terrorist group or possibly even consider joining one."[74] Studies of the lives of suicide-bombers, one of the most radical forms of terrorism, demonstrate how "commonplace" they are. The motivation for such attacks is almost always political.[75] It is the ordinariness of those who commit acts of terrorism that is remarkable, not their "deviance." The question that is almost never posed is what turns law-abiding citizens into terrorists.

Philosophers tend to agree that terrorism is a form of violence that may be justified under certain "emergency" conditions. At one end of the spectrum, Honderich argues that what he terms "terrorism for humanity" may be justified as "a means to which there is no alternative," that indeed there may be, under certain conditions, a "moral right" to terrorism. The conditions envisaged are those which involve state oppression, which itself may be widely recognized as falling outside international law.[76] Walzer also accepts that under certain exceptional conditions (what he terms "supreme emergency") there is a moral case for "overriding the rules," and thus terrorism may be justified as a "last resort," though he is ambivalent as to whether the fear of extinction as a political community is sufficient or whether the existential threat must be physical also.[77]

We discussed the human rights abuses and policy of state "terror" by Russia in Chapter 4. Two key questions arise at this point. First, do the explanations and attributes of terrorism in the policy and academic literature justify the conceptualization of the conflict in Chechnya as "terrorism"? Second, are the conditions in Chechnya sufficient to meet a test of "last resort" that would legitimize such violence? To categorize the conflict in Chechnya as a struggle against terrorism we must demonstrate that the Chechen resistance to Russia is characterized by *systematic* and *indiscriminate* violence against civilians/noncombatants. Although the literature on terrorism identifies these core attributes, there is an absence of rigorous empirical testing of how and when they might apply to particular cases and organizations. Often the mention or claim of specific atrocities is deemed sufficient to demonstrate the terrorists' rejection of moral constraints.[78] There is little to guide us on the fundamental question of how we can properly measure *systematic* and *indiscriminate* violence by terrorists against civilians/noncombatants and how stringent the tests should be. Does this mean that *all* the violence, *most* of the violence, or just *some* of the violence should be organized as systematic and indiscriminate attacks on civilians/noncombatants for the definition of terrorism to be satisfied? Under this definition I am excluding any attacks on combatants from falling within the category of terrorism unless they constitute a war crime.

Terrorism in Chechnya

We can assess the meaningfulness of the term terrorism in the conflict in Chechnya by examining how it is employed in the conflict idiom to frame perceptions, and by studying how the protagonists recognize each other. Much of the conflict narrative and analysis of this book demonstrates that the idiom and process of recognition oscillated over time. The periods when the conflict idiom was dominated by derogatory terms and charge and countercharge of terrorism were followed by periods of negotiation, when the conflict idiom had of necessity to be amended. In this way, the "terrorist" Maskhadov was received by President Yeltsin in the Kremlin in May 1997 as the legitimate democratically elected president of Chechnya. This kind of idiomatic, if not cognitive, shift is quite common in conflicts. The number of anti-colonial resistance leaders denounced as terrorists by colonial powers but later entertained as statesmen is legion. We also noted earlier that a UK court decided in the Zakaev case that the conflict in Chechnya is a case of internal "armed conflict" and not one that can be categorized as an "anti-terrorist operation." The judgment did not provide a thorough reasoning for the decision, although it certainly bolstered the claims of the Chechen resistance to legitimacy. The politicization and inconsistencies of the idiom of the conflict mean that we should obviously be cautious about the way we treat labels employed by one side or the other.

There are two more directly relevant ways to test for the prevalence of terrorism on the part of the Chechen resistance. First, we can analyze the violence itself and compose a balance sheet of casualties inflicted during the conflict to assess the balance between civilians/noncombatants versus "combatants" (soldiers/police/ and other combatants for the Russian side). Second, we can examine whether the intentional targeting of civilians/noncombatants was an essential or peripheral part of the Chechen strategy of resistance to Russia.

Targets

The most well-founded, though perhaps still conservative estimate for total dead in the 1994–96 war is 46,500, of which 11,500 (over 8,000 Russian) were combatants and as many as 35,000 were civilians.[79] The data on casualties for the second war beginning in 1999 to the present are much less reliable. The respected Moscow-based human rights foundation Memorial estimates that from 5,000 to 10,000 civilians have died, and its lowest estimates are that 2,000–2,800 civilians have been abducted and "disappeared."[80] Estimates of Russian combatant casualties vary immensely. Valentina Melnikova, head of the NGO Soldiers' Mothers of Russia, based on her own group's sources, estimated that as many as 11,000 soldiers were killed and up to 30,000 wounded. The Russian ministry of defense estimated that just under 3,500 soldiers were killed, excluding Ministry of Interior, FSB, and other federal agencies between the start of the second war in October 1999 and August 2005, while respected journalists estimated the figure to be closer to 8,000, including all branches of the military and security services.[81] None of these figures take into account the many thousands of troops on both sides who were mutilated or otherwise disabled. In the period from 1995 to November 2005, there were 3,033 registered cases of civilians being injured by landmines and unexploded shells in Chechnya, of whom 692 people were killed.[82] The perception among Chechens is that the human costs of the conflict have been vast, though some have attributed this to an unquestioning acceptance of exaggerated casualty figures provided by Lebed in late 1996.[83] On two occasions in recent years, pro-Moscow Chechen officials have claimed that either 150,000–160,000 or up to 300,000 have died.[84]

When we compare the above figures with the casualty figures caused by indiscriminate attacks by Chechen groups on targets that can be clearly defined as "civilian/noncombatants," we find that such attacks account for a small proportion of the overall casualties during the conflict. Any calculation of the number of casualties caused by Chechen terrorism between 1993 and 2006 is an order of magnitude, given that the reported numbers of killed and injured are not always reliable, and that some acts of terrorism attributed to the main Chechen resistance groups may have been perpetrated by marginal or criminal groups, or by Russian state forces or pro-Russian Chechen forces. For example, much controversy surrounds the apartment bombings of September 1999, which caused hundreds of dead and injured. If we attribute all the disputed attacks to Chechen groups and thus take the highest likely number of civilian casualties that could be attributed to attacks by these groups, the total is 1,544 killed and 3,463 injured in the period from July 1993 to September 2004.[85] If we accept the conservative estimates of deaths in the wars from 1994 to the present discussed above, then the number of deaths from "terrorism" by Chechen groups is likely to be less than 3% of the total number. This is not a conflict that can be characterized as "terrorism."

It could also be argued that the high death toll in some of the "spectacular" incidents—Budennovsk, Kizliar, Dubrovka, and Beslan—was as much a result of the poor tactical response by Russian forces, and their use of excessive and indiscriminate force, as of action by the Chechen groups involved. Indeed, in two of these incidents—Budennovsk and Kizliar—it is questionable whether there was any initial intention by the Chechen forces to target "civilians/noncombatants," although they were certainly reckless and indiscriminate in their subsequent use of violence in these cases.[86] In the case of the attacks on the Dubrovka Theater and Beslan School, the excessive and incompetent use of force by Russian authorities contributed significantly to the high casualty rate. In the former, a disabling gas injected into the theater prior to the rescue assault by Russian Special Forces caused most of the civilian deaths. In Beslan, by far the most shocking and costly terrorist incident so far, with 317 hostages killed, including 186 children, Russian forces used rocket-propelled incendiaries and tank fire, almost certainly contributing to the collapse of the school gymnasium and fire, which caused many of the casualties.[87]

Reuter's study of Chechen "terrorist" attacks from June 2000 to June 2004 revealed that most attacks (23 of a total of 36) and most casualties (361 killed and 1518 injured of a total of 498 killed and 1923 injured) involved suicide bombings, in what the Russians term "suicide-shahid" (*smertnitz-shakhidok*), and the Chechens "shahid" (religious martyr) attacks. The study confusingly conflates attacks on military and civilian targets under the generic heading "terrorist act." Nevertheless, it indirectly provides us with evidence of a strong correlation between an escalation of Russian abuses against civilians in Chechnya, which surged in 2002 (when there were more than 700 "civilian killings" and over 500 "disappearances" attributed to Russian forces and their local militias) and the trend for suicide bombings (which jumped from 2 incidents in 2002 to 12 in 2003).[88] Most suicide attacks involved participation by women (15 of 23). The Russian government is keen to attribute the motivation of Chechen suicide bombers to Islamists. The sobriquet "black widow" (*chernye vdovy*) was employed in the Russian media to describe the black hijab-wearing women who wore belts of explosives at the Dubrovka theater siege. The sobriquet, in fact, is a pointer to what Russians and many others perceive to be the principal motivation—most of these women have been direct or indirect victims of Russian abuses during the "counterterrorist" operation in Chechnya and have lost husbands or close relatives. Studies of the Chechen suicide attacker phenomenon have focused on the personal motives and also have genderized the issue in a manner that stresses that women are acting out of despair and are seeking revenge for the loss of *male* relatives, whether husbands, fathers, brothers, or sons, either as combatants in the conflict or through extrajudicial killings by state forces or state-organized "death squads." In fact, there is no evidence, and it seems odd to assume, that it is necessarily only because of the loss of male relatives, given that women have been targets of attacks and humiliations such as rape, and may just as readily be ideologically motivated. Though the numbers are small, an estimated 60 percent of female suicide bombers lost husbands in the conflict, while others lost close family members. Any explanation for suicide bombing which stresses the personal motivations oversimplifies the complex mix of the personal, political and religious elements involved in such acts of resistance.[89]

The latest Russian and comparative research into suicide attacks reveals a wide variety of motives. Mia Bloom sees female involvement in political violence, in particular suicide attacks, as a misconstrued form of "empowerment," for those "who choose the role of martyrs do not enhance their status, but give up their sense of self as they contribute to this ultimate, albeit twisted, fulfillment of patriarchal values."[90] Iuliia Iuzik attempted to analyze the motives of the women suicide-shahids who were involved in attacks in Russia by interviewing their close relatives. She found that there was no common denominator. Some were acting from overt political stances, some from personal motives, some from loyalty to husbands, and some from abuse and coercion.[91] Psychologists suggest that the scale and intensity of the conflict, high casualties, desperation, and a historical context where values of self-sacrifice are prominent are common though not universal denominators.[92] More recent research stresses altruistic political motivations and the fact that such attacks bring major gains to the groups that organize them (though usually not strategic victory).[93]

This mix of personal and political motivations is illustrated in the case of Chechnya by the Baraev family. The first female suicide bombing occurred in June 2000, when Khava Baraeva , the twenty-two-year old cousin of Chechen field commander and notorious hostage-taker Arbi Baraev, drove a truck laden with explosives into the OMON base in Alkan-Yurt and destroyed it. Her example is used by the radicals in the Chechen resistance to recruit others, and the mythology is reinforced in popular culture by a "Khava's song." After the killing of Arbi Baraev by Russian forces in June 2001, his nephew and close associate of the national movement's chief ideologist, Yandarbiev, Movsar Baraev led the attack on the Dubrovka Theater. This attack also included several female suicide bombers, including the widow of Arbi, Zura Baraeva.[94]

Datasets on Chechen "terrorist" attacks illustrate some of the inherent difficulties of this form of measurement.[95] It is not only a question of what should count as a "terrorist" attack. Such datasets record attacks that result in deaths and injuries, and we generally have no systematic record of other attacks that do not result in any deaths or injuries or were preempted. The datasets also tend to record attacks mostly *outside* Chechnya. Furthermore, the datasets do not record forms of terrorism such as kidnapping or hostage-taking. This is a particular flaw, given the systematic use of kidnapping and hostage-taking for both criminal and political purposes in Chechnya from the outset of the independence struggle.

Basaev's airline hijacking of November 1991 was a hostage-taking episode that inspired the extension of the method to other kinds of civilian spheres beginning in March 1992 with the hijacking of a bus by armed Chechens in Lermontov in Stavropolskii Krai.[96]

STRATEGY

It is argued that terrorism, in the sense of the intentional targeting of "civilians/noncombatants," was an inherent part of the Chechen strategy of resistance to Russia from an early stage in the conflict and was unrelated to the peaks and troughs of Russian military aggression.[97] While the former claim may well be plausible, the latter is clearly not. An acceptance of the use of terrorism as part of the armed conflict with Russia has been consistent under successive Chechen leaderships, but it has been reactive to Russian aggression against Chechen independence. From the outset of the independence struggle, Dudaev repeatedly made it publicly clear that his policy was to use "terrorist" methods if Russia attacked Chechnya. As tensions with Yeltsin intensified in October–November 1991, Dudaev claimed that Russia was planning to use "terrorist" agents provocateurs to tarnish the image of the "national revolution" and thus provide an excuse for militarily intervening in Chechnya. Yet, enraged by Yeltsin's decree for an intervention in early November, Dudaev threatened to retaliate by using "terrorist acts" against Russia, even raising the possibility of attacks on Russian nuclear power stations.[98] Interviewed by a Russian journalist in March 1992 he promised: "We will resort to any extreme measures when it comes to the defense of our sovereignty. Any . . . "[99] Dudaev predicted that should an armed conflict with Russia erupt, his policy would be to take the war into Russia:

It will be a war without rules. It's impossible to find the necessary rules. I may say that we are not going to fight in our territory. Three hundred years of bloodshed are quite enough. We have been well taught to transfer those wars to the place they have come from. This will be a war without rules.[100]

Dudaev's embrace of terrorism as a tactic in the overall strategic struggle against Russia is most clearly demonstrated in his treatment of Shamil Basaev, who, until his death in an explosion in Ingushetia in July 2006, was wanted by Russia as "terrorist number 1" and was synonymous with "Chechen terrorism." As the Chechen "national revolution" developed in August 1991, twenty-six year-old Basaev lived in Moscow, where he worked in a "Chechen cooperative" (probably in racketeering and trading in computers). In normal times Basaev would probably have become a small time crook or small entrepreneur. He was politically radicalized by the liberalization under Gorbachev and assisted with the defense of Yeltsin's White

House against the putsch. On returning to Chechnya, he formed an armed detachment, the core of which was composed of relatives and associates from his native highland village of Vedeno, from which the detachment received its name. Basaev's "Vedeno" force acted as bodyguards for the CNC and worked closely with the nationalist forces under Dudaev and Yandarbiev to crush opposition. In response to the Russian intervention in November 1991, Basaev and two accomplices, seemingly at their own initiative, hijacked a Russian domestic airliner with 178 passengers on board at the airport in Mineral'nye Vody in neighboring Stavropolskii Krai. They took the aircraft to Ankara in Turkey, where there was a large Chechen diaspora and they could expect sympathetic treatment. Negotiations resulted in the release of some Chechen prisoners from Russian prisons. Although Turkey was then engaged in its own "dirty war" against Kurdish separatists, the Chechen hijackers were allowed to take the plane back to Grozny, where the passengers and crew were freed.

The incident was the first clear case of terrorism, even by international law (since it contravened international conventions), yet Basaev was treated as a conquering hero by Dudaev, who awarded him the rank of colonel in charge of a regiment of Special Forces in the newly formed Chechen army. Under Dudaev's government, Basaev became a leading figure in military affairs, and in particular, in the volunteer forces of the Caucasian People's Confederation, which aimed to unite all the Caucasian Muslim peoples under Chechen leadership. At a time when the conflicts in the wider Caucasus region were hot, he led a 300-strong Chechen detachment to fight for Azerbaijan against Armenia in the struggle over Nagorno-Karabagh, and the Chechen "Abkhazia Battalion" in the successful offensive against Georgia in the summer of 1993. His leadership skills and prowess were such that he was even made a deputy defense minister by the Abkhazian government. His force worked closely with, and was trained, equipped and transported by the Russian military and military intelligence, which was supporting Abkhazia against Georgia. Basaev and a core group of followers used Russian military textbooks to train in irregular warfare, recognizing from an early stage that to win independence for Chechnya required a sacrifice "paid in blood."[101] In Abkhazia his force earned a reputation for battle-hardened aggression and ruthless excess, including the torture and murder of prisoners and other war crimes. As we discussed previously, Basaev by his own admission made several trips in 1992–94 with some of his Abkhazia Battalion to Khost province in Afghanistan, to train in Mujahidin camps.[102]

On the fiftieth anniversary of the Chechen deportation on 23 February 1994, Dudaev organized a mass display of his armed forces in Grozny. At a press conference after the event, Dudaev threatened to detonate a nuclear bomb in Moscow if it attempted to crush Chechnya's independence. Most journalists interpreted the warning as a bluff from someone many of them perceived as a deranged "real-life Dr Strangelove" character.[103] Rumors abounded in the Russian media that Dudaev did have a nuclear device, possibly from a nuclear-tipped missile left by the Russian garrison, but the only incident of "eco-terrorism" occurred in November 1995, when Basaev claimed responsibility for placing a container with a small amount of radioactive cesium-137 in Izmailovo Park in Moscow. It was a classic case of a relatively low-cost and low-threat "terrorist" act, which had an enormous impact in "terrorizing" the population of Moscow.[104]

The role of suicide or martyrdom as a tactic in warfare and armed struggle had gained global attention from the use of suicidal waves of headband-wearing young volunteer soldiers (*basij Mostazafan* or "mobilization of the oppressed") by the Iranian Revolutionary Guards during the 1980–88 Iran-Iraq War, by the Mujahidin against Soviet forces in Afghanistan beginning in 1980, by the IRA hunger strikers in 1981, and by the "suicide-bombings" of the Tamil Tigers beginning 1987. By the 1990s suicide attacks were widely seen as an effective form of "asymmetric warfare" against conventional armed forces and had become a regular feature of nationalist resistance struggles. Dudaev, Maskhadov, and other Chechens would have been familiar with the challenge posed by such attacks from their experience of the war in Afghanistan. The concept of suicide attacks was encouraged by Dudaev from the beginning of the armed conflict in late 1994. It seems that there were spontaneous instances of "death or glory" suicide attacks by Chechens on Russian tanks and armored vehicles during the brief armed conflict of November 1994. Dudaev spoke of the "amazing heroism" of those involved, and warned that "suicide battalions" (*smertnye batal'ony*) would be formed because, he stated, "we do not have armaments, military vehicles, military equipment, a military-industrial complex. We were left naked, and therefore we have been forced to establish suicide battalions."[105] These suicide-fighters were recognizable by their black headbands—a marker of Apocalyptic warriors in the Islamic tradition. The black headband was employed by participants in the Dubrovka and Beslan attacks—whereas regular Islamist fighters wore the green headbands of jihad. Just a few months later, at a meeting of the Congress of the Chechen People in the mosque at Shali on 9–10 March 1995, Dudaev chaired sessions that not only discussed a general mobilization of the population against Russia, but also approved a list of volunteers for Chechnya's first "kamikaze battalion."[106] The move led to Dudaev being labeled a "kamikaze leader."[107] This was the first time the concept of "suicide" attacks within an Islamic framework of martyrdom was used in the conflict with Russia.

The infamous raids on Budennovsk by Basaev's forces in June 1995, and Kizliar and Pervomaisk by Raduev in January 1996, have been discussed earlier as attacks designed as military raids (in the former case, on government and police buildings, and in the latter, on a military airport), but which degenerated into hostage-taking and terrorist attacks on civilians. The Budennovsk raid, in particular, was designed with a strategic purpose. A Russian military offensive in the spring and summer of 1995 had seriously weakened and disrupted Chechen forces. The Budennovsk raid, deep into Stavropolskii Krai in Russia, was a massive psychological blow to Yeltsin's claims to be winning the war. The media publicity and nature of the incident—the seizure of a maternity hospital and hostages including hundreds of women and children, a bloodily botched attempt at rescue by Russian forces—forced Russia to negotiate. Basaev himself may have been further motivated by the fact that Russian military operations were being conducted in his highland native area, and apparently his wife and children were killed in Russian bombing. The incident led directly to a positive strategic result for the Chechens—Russian prime minister Chernomyrdin came to Budennovsk personally to conduct the negotiations with Basaev, and a delegation of political and cultural dignitaries acted as human shields to allow his forces safe passage back to Chechnya in return for releasing the hostages. Moreover, it prepared the way for the military truce agreement of 30 July 1995. The truce stopped the Russian offensive and allowed Dudaev's forces to regroup and disperse across Chechnya. Dudaev's approval of the Budennovsk attack was obvious from the award of the title "Hero of Chechnya" to Basaev's detachment, and three of Basaev's men were decorated.[108]

The airline hijacking of 1991 and the Budennovsk raid of 1995 demonstrate some of the rational criteria under which Basaev operated in the first phase of the armed conflict. These were mass hostage-taking incidents, where in return for political concessions (release of prisoners, Chernomyrdin's "truce") and safe passage back to Chechnya, Basaev released the hostages. Old research (from 1981) indicates that "terrorist" hostage-takers are rarely suicidal (less than 1 percent of cases) and that the publicity generated for their cause by the event coupled with safe passage is often sufficient to terminate the event.[109] The rise of jihad in the 1990s, however, and the commitment to demonstrative "spectacular" attacks and revenge (see below), as Dubrovka and Beslan indicate, suggest that we must change the calculation over such events.

The strategic use of terrorism continued under Maskhadov's presidency, though Maskhadov was much more cautious in his public statements than Dudaev. There were several reasons for this. Maskhadov was a democratically elected president and was protective of his democratic legitimacy, and was keen to maintain the respect of international actors in

Europe and the U.S.. His caution also was required given the still tense relations with Russia after Khasaviurt. He could not afford to antagonize Russia given that he was engaged in protracted negotiations from August 1997 through 1999 in the Joint Commission for working out a "comprehensive" agreement on Chechnya's status, and, moreover, his government depended on the paltry Russian and international financial support and humanitarian assistance. He was also faced with a profound schism in the Chechen resistance movement. Chechen authority was increasingly split between Maskhadov's largely secular nationalist "governmental" forces, and the radical Islamic forces under Basaev and other commanders, assisted by a small number of Arab Islamists under Khattab, who were loosely united under the Military Madjlisul'-Shura, and which functioned as a "parallel" authority.[110] During the period of peace with Russia in his presidency (January 1997-autumn 1999) he was critical of "terrorist" attacks on Russia, within Chechnya (including at least two attempts on his own life), and especially of the hostage-taking which became an embarrassing and endemic problem that corroded the authority of his presidency at home and abroad.

With the renewal of armed conflict with Russia in late 1999, however, and confronted by Putin's intransigence on negotiations, Maskhadov, like Dudaev, tolerated Basaev's methods and occasionally justified them. Ultimately, Maskhadov could not control Basaev. The shift to a greater use of terrorism was brought about by the renewal of armed conflict and the increasing Islamization of the whole resistance movement. Basaev was appointed deputy commander in chief of Chechnya's armed forces (under Maskhadov) in July 1998, and subsequently became chairman of the Military Committee. He was only removed from this post after the particularly horrifying Dubrovka theater attack in September-October 2002. The Dubrovka attack was immensely damaging to the international support for the Maskhadov government. The removal of Basaev from his official command could be seen as a clever device by Maskhadov to create political distance from Basaev, who Maskhadov could now claim was operating "independently," while retaining military and political coordination.[111]

By May 2003, Basaev's announcement of "Operation Boomerang" abandoned any pretence that terrorism was not central to his strategy of "hitting back" at Russia. He defended his methods by claiming that Russia was engaged in "genocide" against the Chechen people, and that he was the "antiterrorist":

The leaders of the shahid brigade Riyadus-Salihiin adopted the following decision at their enlarged meeting: since the Russian invaders and their hangers-on apply the principle of collective responsibility to all Chechens, we can call to account all relatives of the invaders who are committing atrocities on our land. For this reason we have decided to conduct Operation Boomerang in the native towns of those who commit outrages in Chechnya on the behalf of the Russian people. May the great Allah help us in this cause.[112]

Basaev's sentiments already informed the modus operandi of Russian forces in Chechnya whereby family members of "terrorists" were targeted and civilians who were caught up in firefights were considered to be legitimate targets.[113] The increase in suicide attacks in 2003 led more moderate elements in the Maskhadov government to become more critical of Basaev in their public statements. Zakaev, for example, in exile in the UK, denounced Basaev's methods as "unacceptable," and claimed that there was no political cooperation between Maskhadov and Basaev.[114] Maskhadov, however, became increasingly ambivalent *in public* about the role of Basaev. Perhaps disillusioned by the failure of the West and international organizations to apply pressure to Russia, Maskhadov no longer even offered convincing opposition to Basaev's methods. When Maskhadov provided a taped interview for *Le Monde* in October 2003, he strenuously denied any association with Al-Qaida, affirming that "We have nothing in common with international terrorism. What is going on here is a national liberation struggle. We do not recognize Bin Ladin. He represents nothing for us." He was more circumspect, in contrast, on the issue of Basaev. Asked whether he considered Basaev to be an "international terrorist," Maskhadov replied:

Basaev has no links with international terrorism. He has no contact either with al Qaida or with bin Laden. . . . Basaev is a warrior. He is someone who is taking revenge. He is using the same methods as the enemy, who uses those methods against Chechen civilians. It is an eye for an eye. His primary target is the principal structure of the Russian state, the FSB—the secret service or ex-KGB. . . . If it were possible to subordinate Basaev and to direct all his energy against the enemy, with the use of acceptable methods, then he would achieve much more. Unfortunately, we disagree about this. I say that it is necessary to fight Russia in an organized way, with a combination of diplomatic policy and military strategy and tactics. I condemn methods and forms of action which lead to the suffering of innocent civilians. Basaev has his own methods. But he has nothing to do with international terrorism.[115]

Even at this time of increased suicide attacks, when Maskhadov commented on Basaev's methods he went out of his way to speak of how close he was to Basaev, and how "sincere" Basaev was in his belief that "all methods" were legitimate in the struggle against Russia.[116] Moreover, there is evidence of political cooperation between Maskhadov and Basaev. During the Kremlin organized presidential election campaign in Chechnya in August 2004, both men made simultaneous local television broadcasts denouncing the election and urging a boycott. The main website of the Chechen resistance posted photographs of the two leaders working closely together, possibly taken in late 2004.[117]

Basaev's concept of "total war" against Russia was fully elaborated by the time of Beslan. His thinking was that in order to "stop the genocide," "the more brutal I could make it, the quicker they'd get the message."[118] Yet the Beslan tragedy appears to have shocked even Basaev by its brutality, as he was not expecting such a bloody outcome. Maskhadov called it a "terrorist act," but contextualized it, noting: "such acts are a consequence of and reaction to the genocidal war of the Russian government against the Chechen nation, during which the Russian army has killed 250,000 people, including 42,000 children."[119] In what was to be in effect a last testament, Maskhadov wrote to Javier Solana, the EU High Representative for Foreign Affairs and Security, in February 2005, in the wake of the EU activism over Ukraine's "Orange Revolution." He reiterated his support for the Akhmadov "peace plan," and pleaded for a more proactive EU policy on Chechnya, but also observed on the issue of terrorism:

It is the action of desperate people, most of whom have lost loved ones in atrocious circumstances, and believe they can respond to the aggressor and the occupier by using the same methods. This is not my point of view, nor will it ever be. In fact, I have been doing everything within my power to keep actions of the Chechen resistance within the internationally recognized rules of war. When I fail to prevent terrorism, I fail only in the circumstances where no one could have succeeded. The terrorism at work in Chechnya, whether it is the action of the occupying forces or of isolated elements of the resistance, is born and prospers out of war, abject abuse and the daily violation of the most fundamental rights. The truth is that only peace and democracy can bring it to an end.[120]

There was a period of reflection and a consensus among all sections of the Chechen resistance, including Basaev, to support Maskhadov's call for a ceasefire and negotiations in January 2005, which was rejected by Putin. The killing of Maskhadov in March 2005 removed the only authoritative voice preventing the Basaev strategy from becoming a more pronounced philosophy of the Chechen resistance, reflecting the new dominance of the Islamists over the national movement. In interviews with Western journalists conducted in February and July 2005, however, Basaev promised more attacks "like Beslan," declaring that his legitimate target options included *all* Russian citizens because rather than seeing them as "blameless," he considered them to be "accomplices" (*posobniki*) in Putin's war against Chechnya. This was presented by the media as a startling new development.[121] In fact, Basaev had told a Russian journalist as early as November 1995, in response to a question about the suffering of "innocents" at Budennovsk, that "there are no innocent Russians."[122]

Conclusion: Terrorists or Freedom Fighters?

The attempt to define terrorism suffers from inherent flaws that can be demonstrated by examining the case of the conflict in Chechnya. The use of the term is not only highly politicized but is, in practice, suffused with ambiguity over what is a "noncombatant," "target group," "soft target," and so on. It is often difficult to disentangle a symbolic target from an important state asset. As with the state definitions of terrorism, academic work is often politicized and suffers from selective labeling, in particular where "security experts" and "terrorism experts" have become coopted into working in support of state security agencies. The historical evidence employed in most works on terrorism is fairly shallow, and datasets are constructed poorly and subject to manipulation. Setting out the philosophical conditions that would satisfy Walzer's "last resort" hypothesis is as contentious and problematic as defining the term itself. At what point is the existence of a "political community" threatened with extinction? Is terrorism legitimate to preempt genocide?

Certainly, the Chechens had good historical grounds to fear a threat of genocide from Russia, notwithstanding the potency of the more direct threat to destroy their political community. In theory such threats would justify the use of terrorism as a "last resort." Perhaps the single most important flaw in the conventional wisdom about the nature of terrorism, however, lies in the core element of the generally accepted definition—that is, the claims that "terrorism" is systematically organized, and that its motivations and goals are to spread terror in a wider community in order to extract government policy changes.

"Terrorist" attacks, as the case of Chechnya demonstrates, are rarely systematic. More often, such attacks on civilians/noncombatants are peripheral to the main use of political violence, which is directed against a state's military, security, political and economic assets. There are cases of conflict in other parts of the world where "terrorist" attacks are the norm (in the sense of systematic and indiscriminate attacks on civilians), notably the Israeli/Palestinian conflict, loyalist paramilitaries in Northern Ireland, the Sunni/Shia conflict in Iraq, but Chechnya is not such a case. Civilians and noncombatants are more often killed by reckless disregard, akin to the collateral damage caused and tolerated by conventional military forces. Walzer, in fact, observes that the spread of terrorism during the nationalist and anticolonial struggles after World War II emerged as a method of violence learned from the poor example set by state militaries in their failure to adhere to the laws and customs of war: "after it had become a feature of conventional war."[123] Within the broadly accepted canon of contemporary philosophy on the ethics of political violence, and despite the ambiguities of that philosophy, there is a case to be made for the legitimacy of terrorist acts carried out by the Chechen resistance to Russia. Both Walzer's fairly rigid test, that terrorism may be a legitimate "last resort" defense against a threat of genocide and/or the destruction of the "political community," and Honderich's much looser test, that terrorism is justified when there is "no alternative," could be applied to the conflict in Chechnya. It is very clear from the perceptions of Chechen leaders as publicly expressed over time that they consider Russian actions in Chechnya as tantamount to a policy of genocide. By any balanced reckoning, Russia's reckless and disproportionate use of force against civilians in Chechnya at times has been genocidal, in particular its reliance on indiscriminate bombardment of civilian areas and the well-documented cases of massacres. If we apply the test of systematic indiscriminate attacks on non-combatants to the conflict in Chechnya we find that it is Russia that is the most guilty party and its policy amounts to "state terrorism." The use of terrorism by some elements of the Chechen resistance is broadly justified within the national movement as a whole, for being reactive to Russia's strategy of excesses, whether to deter it, or to exact revenge.

Chapter 6

Chechnya and the Study of Conflict

Are the post-communist states particularly prone to national and ethnic conflict? Is there something specifically structural or cultural about the bloody conflicts that have followed the collapse of communism? Comparative studies of conflict by Gurr and others have identified a global resurgence of nationalism and ethnic conflict in the second half of the twentieth century, which is correlated with the spread of decolonization and democratization.[1] For many scholars the post-communist conflicts are prime examples of such national and ethnic conflicts, but the rare context of immense and rapid changes after the collapse of communism tends also to be identified as a significant part of the explanation. The momentous changes have involved the collapse of communism as an authoritarian political system of single-party dictatorship and its replacement by multiparty democracies and new forms of authoritarianism; the collapse of an empire in Eastern Europe and Eurasia and its succession by numerous new nation-states and nationalizing states along a spectrum from consolidated democracies to failed states; and the death of a state socialist economy and the restoration or attempted introduction of modern capitalism. But do Sovietologists and regional specialists overemphasize these remarkable local transformations to the detriment of locating post-Soviet conflicts within broader comparative trends?

When we examine the regions and successor states which have been most prone to violent conflict—the North Caucasus in the Russian Federation, Georgia, Moldova, Azerbaijan, and the Ferghana Valley in Central Asia—the outcome is attributed not to any single cause but rather to a combination of structural (presence of significant levels of multiethnicity, territorially concentrated ethnic groups, or territorially mixed areas); systemic (the Soviet system of institutionalized multiethnicity); and historical and contingent factors. These latter include past grievances, such as contested boundaries and historical interethnic rivalries; recent grievances, such as antipathy to the policies of nationalizing states, competing claims to state power and economic assets, leaders who were nationalist and ethnic "entrepreneurs" fomenting conflict; and other forms of ethnic tension and competition which were heightened by the central state collapse and the economic downturn and impoverishment of the initial transition phase. Even where multiethnicity did not result in violent territorialized challenges to the state, as with the management of the Russophone minority in the Baltic States, it still exercised an enormous influence on the character of nation- and state-building, the nature of assimilation, democratization and interethnic relations. The notable exception to this pattern of national and ethnic explanatory factors is the civil war in Tajikistan, which was driven by specifically nonethnic local competition between elites for control of the state and by ideological factors (secular elites versus radical Islamists). One cannot understand the construction of the new political orders in successor states such as the Russian Federation, Georgia, Tajikistan, Azerbaijan, and Armenia without taking account of the impact of war and conflict in their making, irrespective of whether the conflicts remain "hot" as in Chechnya, or "frozen" as Abkhazia, South Ossetia, Transdnistria, and Nagorno-Karabagh, or stabilized by a peace agreement as in Tajikistan.[2]

Nevertheless, the sheer diversity of factors in play makes any attempt to generalize about post-Soviet conflicts a daunting enterprise. Some of the new successor states have employed different strategies for managing conflict potential in different areas. Russia, for example, as we have seen, employed asymmetric federalism, but was also prepared to go to war against a recalcitrant, secessionist Chechnya. The post-Soviet conflicts would fall within the thesis developed by Fearon and Laitin, that it is not the presence of national and ethnic diversity per se that makes for ethnic conflict, civil war, or insurgency, but rather the presence of "conditions that favor insurgency," such as weak central governments, poverty, mountainous terrain, and brutal and indiscriminate counterinsurgency strategies.[3] By themselves, however, such correlates of violence do not offer a complete explanation as to why and when violence occurs, or how conflicts may change over time. Moreover, they do not explain why many other equally mountainous, peripheral, and poverty-stricken areas remained relatively peaceful until very recently, most notably other parts of the North Caucasus near Chechnya, including its kin-republic of Ingushetia. In Chechnya, for example, it is not only the mountainous terrain (and it should also be said, forest cover) or poor communications per se that favored the guerrilla war, but also the shortage of Russian military equipment, such as all-weather aircraft, night-fighting capacity, and good intelligence.

After several decades of extensive research, social scientists not only lack a theoretical consensus on the causes of "ethnic conflict" or "ethnic violence," but also cannot agree on what is meant by these terms. In other words, disagreement extends from the unit of analysis (groups, events, forms) to the conceptualization of the problem itself. This has led

Brubaker and Laitin to question whether the diverse phenomena lumped together and studied under the label "ethnic violence" can be explained by a single theoretical lens, and to propose a research agenda that accepts "disaggregation," in the sense of a pluralism of approaches.[4] In the spirit of this pluralism, let us try to disaggregate the by now enormous body of literature on post-Soviet conflicts. Four macro-level themes can be identified in the literature, reflecting those that are paramount in the comparative study of conflict, and each is informed by a fundamental thesis. These themes are

- The role of *nationalism*: stressing how nationalist mobilization causes conflict.
- The significance of *ethnicity*: developing an "ethnic hatred"/ "ethnic belligerence" account of the causes of conflict.
- The collapse of *empire*: associating the end of empire with disorder and conflict.
- The impact of *democratization*: observing the tendency for newly democratizing states to be "war-prone."

While there are studies which prioritize one or other of these themes, most tend to take the inter-relationship of these key elements as a given. What then does the study of the conflict in Chechnya tell us about the assumptions and claims of these approaches?

Nationalist Conflict: From Construct to Contingency

Following the work of Gellner and Anderson, the "modernist" understanding of nationalism is now dominant in political science, and its theoretical assumptions underpin the study of the role of nationalism in Soviet and post-Soviet politics. By tracing the roots of nationalism to the "structural requirements of industrial society," modernists view nationalism as an "unavoidable" political manifestation of the functional requirements of the social transition from traditional to modern society.[5] Gellner famously originally denied any ethnic core of a nation and suggested that "nationalism invents nations where they do not exist," not the other way round.[6] Nationalism emerges from the functional and rational need for cultural homogeneity in industrial society and the modern centralizing state, which necessitates the imposition and spread of a "high" or dominant culture within the state's territory. Thus, according to Gellner, "nation-states" become "culturally homogeneous, internally undifferentiated, cultural polities."[7] The importance of Anderson's work is that it elaborates many of the ways the state employs modern literary and organizational forms to engage in the social construction of identity. The state, according to Anderson, reforges "imagined" communities, substituting nationalism for religion in giving meaning and structure to society.[8] In his later writings Gellner to some extent incorporated the idea of *ethnie* associated with Antony Smith: "some nations possess genuine ancient navels, some have navels invented for them by their own nationalist propaganda, and some are altogether navel-less."[9] Much of the controversy between modernists and essentialists has been resolved by a consensus about the civic-ethnic mix of modern nationalisms, for, as Smith observed, "In fact, every nationalism contains civic and ethnic elements in varying degrees and different forms."[10] What the dominant modernist approaches share, however, is a common material emphasis—that assimilation to the dominant culture is critical for life-chances and social mobility in modern society.[11]

Most Sovietologists analyzed the question of nationalism in the USSR through the prism of constructivism and regarded the Soviet Union as a classic case of a multiethnic society that was being inevitably homogenized as a result of the development of socialist industrial society and its key hallmarks: urbanization, the spread of mass communications, literacy, and social mobility. This is not to overlook the fact that the contradictions in Soviet nationalities policy at both cultural and systemic levels were well recognized: the homogenizing effects of "drawing together" (*sblizhenie*) through Sovietization (essentially "Russification") versus "nativization" (*korenizatsiia*); the repression and elimination of the "residues of bourgeois nationalism" versus the state's development and mobilization of national cultures; the centralization of power in the CPSU versus the institutionalization of national autonomies in the organization of the state. With a few notable exceptions, however, most Sovietologists were stressing the success of the Soviet Union as an alternative form of modern society, the effectiveness of Soviet nationalities policy in managing, if not surmounting, ethnic differences, and the inherent stability of the Soviet system—even as it stumbled toward collapse in the early 1980s. Many of those who predicted that ethnonationalism would undermine the state approached the subject using the term "Soviet empire" as a rhetorical, even ideological metaphor for oppressive communist rule, rather than as a conceptual and analytical device to explain the corrosion of the authority of the regime. Arguably, the only study that analyzed in depth the Soviet ideological contradictions and systemic weaknesses from a theoretical perspective, and which predicted the key role of nationalism in the fall of the Soviet Union, was that by Walker Connor.[12]

It would be fair to say that the underestimation of the appeal of nationalism was not confined to Sovietology but was evident in the social sciences more generally. Horowitz has suggested persuasively that there were two principal reasons for underrating the potential for national and ethnic conflict in the Soviet Union: the tendency to see social conflict in class terms, and the antipathy of Western liberal individualism to ethnic affiliations.[13] In other words the Left-Right ideological cleavage among Western intellectuals created a bias against understanding the political pulling power of nationalism and ethnicity. Belatedly, as the Soviet system collapsed, these ideological prejudices became untenable when posed against the realities on the ground of a rise of national and ethnic conflicts.

How, then, do modernists account for the role of nationalist mobilization in the collapse of the Soviet Union? Gellner delineated two principles of political legitimacy in *Thought and Change*: the relationship between the success of industrial society (the GNP measure of economic growth as the crucial indicator of performance) and national homogenization.[14] When economic growth falters, there is a crisis in the mode of legitimacy of the regime, and destabilization follows as homogenization breaks down under pressure from the rise of alternative nationalisms. The tensions that arise from the processes of modernization, homogenization, and assimilation make the identity politics of nationalism more salient during these periods of great social transition and instability, when a so-called "identity-crisis" or "clash" of competing identities may become more transparent. Elites, intellectuals in particular, tend to be seen as the key purposeful agents, organizing the political mobilization of nationalism and propagating and manipulating the growth of political myths and symbols to construct a nationalist ideology and identity.

When modernists have addressed the collapse of the Soviet Union substantively, they have invariably emphasized the role of contingent factors such as leadership, rather than structure per se. Broadly speaking, all the pro-democracy movements in Eastern Europe and the former Soviet Union that emerged during Gorbachev's liberalization of the late 1980s and early 1990s were nationalist movements. It is an irony that those most familiar with the work of Lenin were aware that the struggle for democracy would be, in the first instance, a struggle also for national self-determination against imperialism, though, in this case, Soviet imperialism. The transition in the Soviet Union and its successor states generally passed through two overlapping phases. The first was a phase of liberalization "from above" pursued under Gorbachev's perestroika. We can debate the extent to which Gorbachev was a "democratizer" or was intent on a revitalization of the communist system, but certainly the initial goal of his limited economic and political reforms was to manage the problem of "stagnation," that is, the systemic authority leakage arising from a poorly performing economic system. The second was a phase of "revolution from below," characterized by a simultaneous nationalist political mobilization for national self-determination and widespread struggle for democracy at the grassroots, leading to the end of the communist monopoly of power.

For leading modernists, it was primarily the context of liberalization and Gorbachev's failure to control it, rather than systemic faults, policy contradictions, or the organizing principles of the state (whether multiethnic institutions or empire), that was critical for the rise of these nationalisms. Gellner argued that Gorbachev's reforms had created a "double vacuum," where "there is no serious rival ideology, and there are no serious rival institutions" to contain nationalism.[15] Few would disagree with Horowitz's restatement of the "old proposition in the sociology of ethnic relations that times of transition frequently provide occasions for serious ethnic conflict."[16] Moreover, Eisenstadt first voiced an idea that was developed later in more substantive studies by Brubaker (1995) and Bunce (1998), and that became a generally accepted explanation for the collapse of the Soviet regime: "The crux of the change lay in the fact that the revolutionary center mobilized and activated the periphery to a very high degree, but at the same time attempted to control it tightly. . . . Once the totalitarian grid was weakened or loosened—as happened under Gorbachev—these contradictions exploded, threatening the very existence of the system."[17] It is odd, nevertheless, that the focus of leading modernists is on the role of agency (Gorbachev's leadership) and contingency (the liberalization), rather than on more systemic features of the collapse.

Certainly, the chaos produced by Gorbachev's reforms, combined with his inconsistent and uninformed policy responses to nationalist and social protest, swinging wildly from over-tolerance of disorder to often brutal crackdowns, fueled a nationalist revival. It was not that Gorbachev was personally repelled by the use of coercion to reestablish order, as the repeated deployment of Soviet troops to crush popular protests in Tbilisi in 1989, Baku 1990, and Vilnius and Riga in 1991 demonstrated, but rather that Gorbachev was incapable or unwilling to resort to the large-scale application of force that would have been required to restore his authority in the country.[18] The decline in the authority of the center opened opportunities for other forms of politics and was followed by a flight of the pragmatic elites from the Soviet communist party into nationalist movements. Moreover, while the episodic use of military force by Gorbachev was intended to bludgeon recalcitrant nationalities into submission to the center, it had the reverse effect. Nationalist sentiment in Georgia, Azerbaijan, the Baltic States, and elsewhere surged in response. How this "tide" of nationalism swept through the system in a mobilization cycle of demonstration and "domino" effects in the years leading up to the collapse in 1991 has been comprehensively analyzed by Beissinger.[19] Even areas of the USSR that were relatively nonviolent and calm in this period, such as Chechnya, were not unaffected by the "tide" of nationalist sentiment.

As we discussed earlier, Dudaev was deeply marked by his experiences in the Baltic states, and had something akin to a conversion to nationalism. Leading intellectual ideologues of the Chechen national movement, such as Yandarbiev, were in the forefront of the new political pluralism and activism that emerged under perestroika.

Common explanations for the collapse of the Soviet Union and the rise of nationalism concentrate on two dimensions: the breakdown of the economy and the destabilizing effects of perestroika on the institutional fabric of the state, particularly as regards the institutionalized autonomies for managing multinationality. That Gorbachev's perestroika turned economic stagnation into a crash that speedily eroded the political legitimacy of Soviet communism is now widely accepted.[20] There is less consensus on why the Soviet federal structure imploded. Modernists offer two principal explanations for this rapid institutional debilitation: the "deep freeze" thesis and the "subversive institutions" thesis (discussed later).

The "deep freeze" thesis attributes the conflicts that emerged as the Soviet Union was in terminal collapse to causes that lay dormant or suppressed under the political controls of communist authoritarianism. The notion originated in the modernist response to the period of collapse and conflict in 1989–91. Suny's comparative study of the nationalist revivals and conflicts in the Transcaucasus region framed them as the "revenge of the past," rooted in decades of antagonisms.[21] Gellner and Sovietologists took up this theme. Gellner was uncertain about the implications of the Soviet collapse and held a pessimistic view of the possibilities for conflict regulation, aside from assimilation: "It must always be borne in mind that, generally speaking, there are *no* solutions or answers in ethnic confrontations" (my italics).[22] The "deep freeze" thesis was derived from two core assumptions about the relationship between political stability and Soviet nationalities policies: first, that coercion had sustained Soviet communism and controlled national and ethnic tensions from degenerating into intercommunal violence, and second, that nationalist elites had been successfully integrated into a Soviet elite by their cooption into the ruling party apparatus.

The "deep freeze" thesis rests on a correlation between the rise of post-communist conflict and the end of communist "controls" on conflict, in the sense of a breakdown in the communist system of power and coercion. It assumes that there were historical and recent grievances that were readymade for elite mobilization once the communist system began to liberalize. The question is, however, to what extent post-communist conflicts are rooted in historical "ancient" or modern hatreds, and to what extent they are derived more from the context of mobilization during the collapse phase, or indeed the post-communist transition. How nationalist mobilizations unfold in a particular contingency, and are managed or mismanaged, significantly affects how they develop and their prospects for success.

Diffusion and escalation in national and ethnic conflicts are not unusual, particularly at the transnational level.[23] Beissinger has persuasively applied these notions to the rise of nationalism during the collapse of the Soviet Union to demonstrate that when mobilization occurs in a temporally contiguous sequence, diffusion and spillover effects are likely, as the example and precedent of one form of nationalism inform the perceptions of success or failure of other similar movements.[24] His study, however, is concerned with how mobilization and diffusion occurred *within* the communist system. To explain why national and ethnic conflicts occurred during and after the collapse of the USSR requires more than this. It requires an examination not only of domestic changes but also of the interplay between the domestic and international levels. The constraints on conflict are generally understood to be those generated by the system of controls of the communist apparatus itself (whether coercive or other more subtle forms of control), but the regional stabilization in Europe that had been established during the Cold War was an additional constraint on nationalism. The success of nationalist movements is determined not only by what is achievable domestically but also by what is realizable internationally. It is important to consider, therefore, the various forms of "external" constraints on certain types of domestic change, and we shall return to this issue later when we examine the question of secession.

The "Belligerent" *Ethnie*

The main reason why national and ethnic conflict remains a politically significant issue in the contemporary world is that many ethnic groups persist as politicized minorities. Although the terms "national" and "ethnic" are often used interchangeably in discussing conflict, the idea of *ethnie* entails a broader set of kin and cultural ties than the core idea of nationalism, which is focused on the idea of remaking or building a state in a particular territory for a particular group. But the political mobilization of ethnicity, however authentic or imagined, is a potent ingredient of nationalism. There is a dialectical relationship between old and new in the way awareness and the mobilization of cultural or ethnic identity relates to state-building. As Geertz and others have demonstrated, tradition and identity often provide the impulse for the aspiration to modern statehood, and for state-building once statehood is achieved, while the actual process of modern state building and the establishment of statehood often rely on enlivening traditional identity. The linkage between ethnicity, culture, and territory is also one of the most important driving forces behind national and ethnic conflict. Historical experience demonstrates that conflict is as probable in states where a minority ethnicity is territorialized, as it is where ethnicity and boundaries are not synchronized, thus creating irredenta.

The debate over the role of ethnicity in conflict hinges on whether one sees it as a fixed or malleable form of identity. The instrumentalist approach to ethnic conflict is that ethnic identities per se are not inherently fixed or conflictual. Rather, they are manipulated to become so as a result of a rational strategy by actors (individuals, groups, or elites) who mobilize ethnic identities for self-interested purposes, often during periods of great economic crisis and social change.[25] While both instrumentalists and modernists recognize the malleability of ethnic identity, the former are concerned with the political uses of ethnicity, whereas the latter focus on the social contexts which shape ethnicity. For the modernists, ethnic identity is manufactured by organizational and institutional modernity based on four pillars—the state, capitalism, technology, and the dense networks of social interactions of civil society (which is another way of describing class structure). Whereas instrumentalists focus on the values, behavior, and collective action of individuals and elites in explaining ethnic conflict, modernists explore the relationship between social structures and social behavior, and often focus on ethnic symbolism.

The *primordialist* approach, in contrast, rests on the assumption that ethnicity is rooted in what are considered essentialist and stable markers such as the biological (race, color), and the historically conditioned (language and culture).[26] Primordially defined ethnicity is seen as exercising an enduring power over group psychology that constrains individual calculations of rational self-interest and the modes by which this is instrumentalized.[27] Ethnic conflicts are understood by primordialists to be a logical consequence of incompatible preexisting *ethnic* differences, and thus the scope for finding different explanations of the causes of conflict in political, social, or economic structures, and the potential for remedies are greatly reduced. These accounts, emphasizing fixed ethnocultural markers, are essentially historicist, focusing on the unique historical provenance of conflict in "ancient hatreds" and "blood feuds," and employing crude "ethnic" stereotypes to illustrate the positions of protagonists.[28] Today, few social scientists share the fundamental assumptions of primordialism, but as they have developed new theories about nationalism and the state, they have explored the role of ethnicity as a mobilizing resource in nationalist conflict. These studies tend, however, not to overtly analyze the complex interaction between the primordial and the modern elements in state-building—the dialectical process Geertz termed the "integrative revolution." Geertz may have popularized the term "primordialism," but he was no primordialist. He viewed the modern state-building process as an "adjustment" and "clash" between "primordial" and "civil" sentiments, which were not in "evolutionary opposition." Rather, the stability of modern states depended on how the "integration" was managed.[29]

When trying to understand the causes and dynamics of conflicts or, when trying to devise a strategy for conflict resolution, it is useful to distinguish between different types of conflicts. The most obvious distinction would be the one between national and ethnic conflicts and other types. For analytical purposes, the definition of a conflict as "national" or "ethnic " can only plausibly be understood as meaning that in the case of the former, the ideas of secession, self-determination, and nation-state building are the main driving forces of the conflict; in the latter case ethnic identity, rivalry, and competition for power are the most prominent features of a conflict.

These are conflicts that involve contested issues of identity and the rights accruing from it. The issues can be complex, including nationality, language, religion and culture, rival claims to territory, economic and social rights and discrimination, class, the distributive role of the state, and so on. It is not that these issues may be equally salient temporally, but that they tend to overlap and reinforce each other. Ethnic conflicts are inevitably about power: specifically, access to and use of power by ethnic groups. The build-up of contested issues eventually reaches a tipping point when it crashes into violent conflict. Distinguishing the existing or emerging cleavage structures (societal divisions or fault lines) underpinning a conflict is critical for understanding its causes and trajectory. We must also take account of the capacity and roles of the state, social hierarchies, and group leaders in the management of conflict potential.

This distinction, however, is problematic, as the concept of identity often represents an extremely malleable and nebulous category that is not easily measurable and therefore cannot be rigidly tested by hypotheses. We see this very clearly in the misuse of the term "clan" to describe the organization and operation of particular clientelist groups in Chechnya. Properly understood, "clan" requires blood ties and a shared understanding of the inheritance of actual genealogies, usually patrilineal. It is also difficult to trace identity formation because it oscillates psychologically between the conscious and unconscious, between the rational and irrational. Its nature is difficult to capture because it changes over time and varies according to the context. In some contexts, for example, "ethnic" identity may be a matter of choice and be "politically negotiable," while in others, particular in violent conflicts, it is made into a fixed and nontradable category, in particular by a hostile *ethnie*.

Moreover, there is a practical dimension to the role of identity, which is common in conflicts but is well illustrated by the case of Chechnya. For example, in the implementation of a military response to contain the insurgency, how do Russian troops distinguish between hostile and loyal Chechens? This is a critical policy issue, for as we discussed previously in relation to the counterinsurgency strategy, low-level tactical errors of nondiscrimination can have strategic consequences by widening the support base of the insurgency. To constrain cruder forms of ethnic belligerence in a conflict requires a solid system of command and control, something that the comparative history of conflicts indicates is not easily achieved by state militaries.

Nevertheless, primordialism remains of practical importance because it implicitly informs a great deal of the international journalism on conflicts. Journalists play a leading role in the framing and dissemination of perceptions. The development of modern political communications means that primordialism gains currency from the incestuous relationship between policy-makers interested in agenda-setting on a particular conflict and journalists who either are constrained by the views of their employers, prefer a pack-like drive for a particular line, or pursue an individualist mobilization of public opinion around a particular cause. The so-called "CNN effect" of continuous and instantaneous television coverage on shaping foreign policy, in particular on international interventions and withdrawals, is widely misunderstood. In the advanced democracies there is an intense and selective focus on a small number of violent conflicts and emergencies, which serves to distort international responses, often in ways that are irrational or serve the interests of foreign policymakers.[30] In the case of ethnic conflicts, the relationship operates at two main levels: the domestic networks between government and national media and the international networks between governments, international organizations, and media. The policy-maker and media nexus plays a critical role in shaping three key aspects of ethnic conflict. First, it determines the idiom by which a conflict is framed and understood. In particular, negative labeling and stereotypes can be instrumentally employed to denigrate opponents as part of the propaganda war. Equally, confusingly erratic ascriptions are often applied to the non-state protagonists, depending on the media organization and politician commenting, and even the same organization/politician may be inconsistent and change the use of terms over time: they may be terrorists, freedom fighters, insurgents, guerrillas, militants, radicals, hardliners, criminals, and so on.

Second, it is often the case that the dominant or hegemonic idiom in a conflict is fed by and reinforces the stereotypical images the conflicting parties have of themselves and the other protagonists. While the variation in the timing and scale of conflicts, and the reasons why ethnicity becomes salient in a given context and time period and not in others, are not easily explained by reference solely to the ethnic factor, ethnic differences provide some of the most colorful and potent language of description, mobilization, reification, and demonization. The primordialist stereotyping is well illustrated by an example of coverage on post-communist conflicts in the Caucasus published in the internationally influential magazine the *Economist* in 2000. The article presented a crudely composed table of stereotypical characteristics of the parties to the various conflicts in the region under the ironic heading "Such a Lovely Place." According to this particularly trite Economist table the Abkhaz are viewed by Georgians as "Murderous, idiotic Russian stooges"; the Armenians see themselves as being surrounded by "genocidal maniacs" (Azerbaijan, Turkey); the Azeris are "primitive, murderous American lackeys" to their neighbors; and so on. The *Economist* described the UN, UNCHR, and OSCE as "do-gooders."[31] Scholars too can resort to stereotyping when confronted by the challenge of evaluating ethnicity against a range of other causes of conflict, such as nationalism, class struggle, economic interests, and intra-elite competition. The post-communist conflicts in the Caucasus region, for example, have been attributed by Snyder to the "belligerent ethnic nationalism in all the states of the Caucasus."[32]

Third, the policy-maker-media nexus plays an important role in the way the conflict is addressed on the international stage. The nexus was a core feature of the rise of a new international interventionism to manage ethnic conflict, particularly in the Balkans. The substantial output of journalistic work, Russian and Western, including numerous books and documentary films, about the conflict in Chechnya was in a similar vein—mainly intended to inform, mobilize opinion, and change policy by governments. These motives are what we should expect of good journalism, but if the underlying assumptions of this work are mainly primordialist, and if it is focused on the personality traits of leaders as a key explanation for why the conflict occurs, then clearly misperceptions will be disseminated.

The notion of class conflict has gone out of fashion among academics, however, and often the term "status conflict" or something similar is employed as a proxy to capture the importance of the element of social hierarchy and socioeconomic competition. Such approaches risk reducing the authentically ethnic element in a mobilization for conflict to a form of false consciousness. The political mobilization of identity is usually articulated most obviously in exchanges between elites, and between elites and other social groups. By focusing on the actual demands at the center of a particular conflict we can better understand what forces are driving a mobilization and what it is intended to achieve. In practice, in certain cases, the "national" and the "ethnic" factors may be overlapping and reinforcing. Thus rather than look for explanations in "ethnic belligerence" or think in terms of *the* cause of *the* conflict, we must examine the plurality of causes and sub-conflicts and how they change over time.

Ultimately, the question what motivates a person to participate in political violence, from low-scale riots to full-scale war, from petty humiliation or discrimination to torture, terrorism, and genocide, remains both the most basic and most difficult question to answer. Obviously, all conflicts involve a clash of interests, mutual fears, hatred, and envy, but in a recent study of post-communist ethnic conflicts Petersen has placed emotions, in particular *resentment*, at the center of his analysis. In essence, Petersen uses the idea of resentment as a synonym for envy. Resentment and fear can take many different forms, for example, loss of status, labor market and other kinds of economic competition, discrimination, threats to cultural distinctiveness, resistance to territorial encroachment at the local level, feelings of "being swamped," "losing out," and generally being poorly served compared to the "other." He also argues that the motivation to participate in or support ethnic violence and discrimination is an inherent feature of human nature.[33] It is common sense that social uncertainty can intensify resentment and fear, which can be mobilized into politically salient cleavages, including the depersonalization of the defined "other" group (ethnic, religious, or other), and lead to a resort to violence. Competition over economic resources is obviously an important factor in many conflicts, including ethnic conflicts. Control over distribution of resources and welfare is closely linked to conceptions of political legitimacy. Economic crises and scarcity can heighten the sense of win-lose calculations. Sudden changes in the state's capacity to provide security and resources to individuals and groups, or sudden alterations in previous patterns of state allocation, especially if these were ethnified, can undermine the political legitimacy of the state. The result can be a "market of violence": a social system in a weak state where violence itself is a commodity and is highly profitable to the predominant warlords.[34]

If Petersen is right, then ethnic conflicts are a result of rational calculations by ethnic actors about the use of violence as a corrective instrument to redress the resentment (or envy) caused by abrupt status reversals and social uncertainties. Arguably this is a satisfactory descriptive and prescriptive model for understanding the "ethnic riot," that is, low-level and localized interethnic violent conflict. It is certainly questionable whether emotions per se can operate independently and become politically salient without the intervention and manipulation of political leadership or "ethnic conflict entrepreneurs," at least not as a durable basis for sustained mobilization, whether peaceful or violent. While such studies are useful for understanding micro-level, local, or sub-state ethnic competition and violence, they do not elucidate the macro-level relationship between ethnic mobilization, nationalist movements, sentiments about the state and the aspiration to statehood, and resort to violence. Resentment is not simply motivated by envy, but is also a symptom of perceived injustice(s) that is (are) usually objectively well-founded. Historically, nationalist movements have been impelled by policies of violent repression and subjugation by foreign governments. Let us turn to the question of nationalist mobilization for statehood by examining the third major theme where resentment at the injustice of oppression is best illustrated: empire.

End of Empire

Theories of the end of empire are largely derived from the experience of British and French decolonization. Generally, they fall into two main categories: "metropolitan" and "peripheral."[35] Metropolitan theories search for the causes of imperial collapse by focusing on the domestic politics of the imperial core, and the implications for its international role. A realist explanation emphasizes the way significant changes in the power and orientation of the imperial core, for example, by defeat in war, economic decline, loss of ideological motivation, loss of will, or redefinition of strategic interests, accelerate the disengagement from the "burden" of empire. The peripheral theory, as its name suggests, attaches great weight to the subversive effect of political mobilization in the colonies themselves. Most usually, it is an anticolonial struggle of national liberation that undermines the political will and military capacity of the imperial power to retain its grip on empire. Sometimes international intervention in support of liberation is required (one thinks, for example, of French intervention against the British to liberate the U.S.). Both theories recognize that the management of empire is a delicate balance between forms of control (from sustained military rule to milder forms of temporary repression) and methods of cooption, patronage, and clientelism.

The kind of crisis of the state that followed the collapse of communism had been matched only during rare tumultuous phases in the international order, accompanying the collapse of empires—the Spanish empire in America during the Napoleonic era, the Habsburg, Hohenzollern, and Romanov empires during and after the First World War, and the wave of decolonization of the remaining European empires in Africa and Asia after the Second World War, from the 1940s until the 1970s. While the study of post-communist nationalist conflicts is increasingly informed by notions of empire and post-imperialism, it is important to remember that the contemporary study of nationalism is, in fact, a product of the end of the European empires in the post-Second World War era. The critique of nationalism as a "bad idea" contrived by European (mainly German) intellectuals in contravention of the liberal principles of civil society originated with the debate sparked by Elie Kedourie's *Nationalism* (1960). Kedourie's book was an essay of despair at the "failure of nerve" by imperialists (specifically the British). It was an ideological proclamation of the benefits of imperial "order" and the "civilizing mission" of the great

European empires—notably the Habsburg, Ottoman, and British. For Kedourie, "good government" was based not simply on democracy per se, but rather on an idealization of the specific form of liberal institutionalism exemplified in the systems of government of Britain and the United States. It was an idealization which failed not only to recognize the sectarian and racial genesis of these systems, but also to admit the contribution of discriminatory and brutal imperialist misgovernment in the rise of nationalism. The work has been rightly and critically dissected for its poor history and "unconvincing account" of the origins of nationalism, and moreover for its reluctance to address the issue of the political management of nationalism.[36]

The collapse of the Soviet Union has come to be seen as a significant testing ground for understanding the relationship of empire, nationalism, democratization, and conflict. There is, however, a fundamental paradox in how the term "empire" is applied to the USSR. As Beissinger has noted: "The general consensus now appears to be that the Soviet Union was an empire and therefore it broke up. However, it is also routinely referred to as an empire precisely because it did break up."[37] Post-Soviet Russia is sometimes referred to as an empire as much because of Western suspicions as to the intent underlying Yeltsin's and Putin's use of the Tsarist term *derzhava* (Great Power), as because of Russia's problematical refederalization, its bloody repression of recalcitrant republics such as Chechnya, and its interference in the Soviet successor states. The lack of legitimacy, repression, the tendency to nationalist disintegration, and a disposition to expansionism continue to be essential ingredients in the use of the metaphor of empire in relation to Russia. Elsewhere, however, empire is seen in more glowing terms.

Kedourie asserted "with certainty," but without any evidence, that "the nation-states who inherited the position of the empires were not an improvement."[38] Kedourie concluded that it was a "fallacy" that "good government" can be developed elsewhere through national self-determination because of the "limits imposed by nature and history." That is to say, the national, ethnic, and racial character and political traditions of many regions of the world meant that their best interests lay in "European domination." Kedourie's apologia for the British empire and antipathy to the spread of the nation-state are now embedded in the repertoire of contemporary Anglo-American conservative ideas about global politics and their critiques of nationalism.[39]

Empires are by definition systems of power and control. The extent to which historically they have attached policy sensitivity to managing the combination of ethnic groups with territory and self-administration is a matter of great debate. If we compare Doyle's definition of empire as "a relationship, formal or informal, in which one state controls the effective political sovereignty of another political society," with Gellner's classic formulation of nationalism as the politics of reaction that occurs when the political unit and the national unit are not "congruent," we are guided to perhaps the single most important source of end of empire—the desire for national self-determination and statehood.[40]

The comparative history of empire demonstrates that there is often as much violence in the exit from empire as there is in empire-building. One of the great myths about the end of empire, fostered by the British in particular, is that it involved generally voluntary and peaceful "transfers of power" to the new states.[41] The use of the relatively benign term "transfer" in this notion of end of empire is almost certainly designed to frame the process as a voluntary act and to blank out the nationalist side of the story. The reality is that the great European empires that disintegrated during the twentieth century ended with bloodshed wherever the imperial power considered it had a significant strategic or economic interest, or a settler population was present, and whenever the imperial power miscalculated that military coercion ("counterinsurgency") might successfully crush nationalist resistance and sustain control.[42] Moreover, several of these end of empire conflicts dramatically revolutionized the domestic politics of the imperial power (De Gaulle's coup d'état over Algeria in 1961 and the Portuguese military-led revolution of 1974 are among the most important post-Second World War cases).[43] Other imperial disengagements have steadily affected regime change, as in the erosion of constitutional liberties in Britain in response to the conflict in Northern Ireland, with which the conflict in Chechnya is often compared by Russian politicians and media commentators.[44]

The conditions exhibited by the collapse of the Soviet system—the implosion of a multiethnic empire[45]—differed from that of preceding empires in four key respects. First was its speed: little more than two years in 1990–91. A dominant section of the metropolitan Russian elite, under Yeltsin's leadership, largely initiated and forced the process whereby the empire was dismantled. This rapid and chaotic disintegration, however, allowed virtually no time for an adjustment to a post-imperial role on the part of Russia's elites or society, or indeed among the decolonized peoples. Moreover, many Russians saw themselves as the greatest victim of the Soviet empire and an integral part of the process of decolonization. The speed of disengagement left little time for Russia to plan for the management of conflict potential, whether internally or externally. Strategic thinking on how to manage the end of empire was, in any event, far from the priorities of the economic liberals (or their foreign advisors) whom Yeltsin gathered into his first government after the failure of the August Putsch of 1991. Much as they applied "shock therapy" to the Soviet economic legacy in 1991–92, Gaidar's government of late 1991 operated a "quit and run" strategy toward the governments of the former Soviet republics, but was determined to consolidate Russian "statehood" on the whole of the former RSFSR.[46]

Second, territorial proximity, blurred identities, cultural familiarity, and economic interdependencies made for a much more complex and destabilizing disengagement. One of the distinctive features of Russia's imperial expansion across the Eurasian plain from the middle of the sixteenth century on was that as a contiguous land empire, as opposed to the European maritime empires, it was characterized by a much closer connection between metropolis and periphery and a blurring of identities and territory. Third, the sheer scale of the disintegration, the Soviet Union being one of history's greatest land empires, contributed to the surge of demonstration and contagion effects among the new states, from which the colonial territories of the Russian Federation were not immune. Chechnya's location on Russia's new international frontier enhanced its capacity to achieve secession, particularly given that its immediate neighbor to the south, Georgia, was friendly to its aspirations and hostile to Russian hegemony.

Fourth, the Soviet Union collapsed inward and downward on to its own ethnofederal structure. The policy of "institutionalized multinationality" created nation-states in embryo, for although most of them had no provenance as states, they became the default political-administrative template for the post-Soviet space. International norms of recognition for end of empire scenarios are determined by the principle of *uti posseditis juris* (discussed below), which holds that states can only be formed on the basis of the existing administrative boundaries constructed by the colonizers, and at the next lower administrative level after the imperial authority. Adherence to this norm has contributed to a problem of frozen conflicts, with many post-Soviet secessionist entities, such as Chechnya, Abkhazia, South Ossetia, and Transdnistria existing temporarily or permanently as de facto independent territories, while de jure unable to assert their statehood because of nonrecognition by the international system.

Russia's imperial retreat up to 1990 was primarily impelled by the liberalizing and erratic impulses of Gorbachev, which drove the Soviet disengagement first from Eastern Europe, and then from the periphery of the Soviet Union itself. In 1990–91 the retreat was transformed into a rout by the Yeltsin administration in the RSFSR, which popularized a self-interested "Russia-first" reform program and speedily abandoned the system of economic interdependencies and cross-subsidies that had been built up within the Soviet economy. The changed economic calculus of Russia under Yeltsin accelerated Russia's auto-decolonization from the Soviet empire. The dismantling of empire was stopped, however, at the boundaries of the Russian Federation. The conflict in Chechnya developed as a result of this shift within the Yeltsin administration, from a position which rejected the burden of empire and favored speedy imperial disengagement in the period to August 1991, to the rediscovery of imperial nerve to preserve the territorial integrity of the RSFSR in late 1991. There was nothing intrinsically definitive about the RSFSR boundary, since it was as much of an administrative artifice as were the borders of the other Soviet republics. Yet, in the decade after signing the formal end of the Soviet Empire in the Belovezha Accord of December 1991, the Yeltsin presidency led Russia into two costly wars to prevent the secession of the small Caucasian Republic of Chechnya.

It is important to appreciate that Russia's involvement in military conflict in Chechnya is not unique in the former Soviet Union after 1991. Russia has been directly militarily involved in several of post-Soviet conflicts, irrespective of their geographical proximity or distance. Russia's involvement in the conflicts in Abkhazia and South Ossetia, for example, was in territories that are adjacent to Russia's Caucasian borders. As we have discussed, Russia played a vital role in the creation of a militarily proficient Chechen insurgent army by assisting Shamil Basaev's "international brigade" in Abkhazia. Russian military intervention has also occurred in Tajikistan, Transdnistria, and Nagorno-Karabakh, territories well beyond Russia's post-Soviet borders, though within Russia's self-declared zone of strategic interest. There are several explanations for this continuing military engagement.

Security and strategic interests created a logic for continued Russian *droit de regard*, interference and, when its national interests were perceived to be at stake, direct intervention in the affairs of successor states in the "near abroad." Russia may have renounced its Soviet global role, but it aspired to a hegemonic role over the successor states. Russian involvement in some areas was logistically straightforward because some structural elements of empire remained—critically the military elements, such as the presence of Russian military bases in Transdnistria, Georgia and Abkhazia, Armenia, the Baltic states, Crimea, and Tajikistan. There were also a major military base and weapons storage facilities near Grozny in Chechnya. The gradual assertion of Russian hegemony over its "near abroad," in its own form of "Munrovskii" doctrine, was eventually embodied in the new Russian Foreign Policy Concept of April 1993.[47]

Certainly, the origins of the conflict in Chechnya lie in the end of the Soviet Empire, but we must recognize the two faces of this end of empire: the view from the former colonizers and that from the formerly colonized. As we have seen in our earlier discussion, a significant turning point in thinking occurred in the wake of the August 1991 coup. The Chechen "national revolution" of late 1991 sought to share in the opportunities for nation-state building presented by the end of empire. The retention of Chechnya as part of the Russian Federation, however, was internalized within the Russian elite as essential for the preservation of Russian "statehood" and for the credibility of its self-image as a *derzhava*. As was the case at the end of other empires, however, national self-determination at the end of the Soviet Empire was not open to all. As we shall discuss later, it was a highly selective process, because of the constraints of the international system.

War-Prone Democracies

The theories of nationalism and democratization that are widely employed to understand the fall of communism and the rise of post-communist conflicts broadly share two fundamental axioms. First, it is assumed that conflict potential will increase exponentially the greater the dissonance between nation, demos and the state. Second, the theories distinguish between the advanced and politically stable democracies and the inherently unstable newly democratizing states.

The belief that democracy must be promoted internationally because democracies do not go to war against each other (the "democratic peace theory") has become a cornerstone of Western thinking on international relations, in particular in the United States. Making the world "safe for democracy" has been a core element in U.S. declaratory foreign policy since Wilson's decision to take the U.S. into the First World War on the Allied side in 1917. Wilson's infusion of this doctrine with the messianism of American Presbyterian religiosity has persisted. Even in the secular Clinton administration of the 1990s, effusive rhetoric of democracy promotion toward the post-communist states was often endowed with messianic hyperbole, although the funding for it was a fraction of the foreign aid budget.[48] The latest incarnation of the democracy-building project is the Bush administration's mission to spread democracy in the Middle East. Under Bush the contradictions in the mission are more obvious, as is evident not only in the attempts to reconcile support for Israel and the use of American military force with winning "hearts and minds" in Iraq, Afghanistan, and the Middle East generally, but also in the administration's policy toward the successor states to the Soviet Union.[49] There are clear parallels between the *mission civilisatrice* of empire and the mission of "spreading democracy."

The essence of democratic peace theory is that the established democracies have, over time, developed the capacity to coexist peacefully, have stable trade relations, and do not go to war with each other. Implied also is that they have more stable mechanisms and policies of internally managing ethnic and other diversities through institutional engineering or policies of assimilation, integration or multiculturalism. Cases of national, ethnic, racial, and religious conflicts within these democracies, however, demonstrate that such capacity is not always effectively implemented. The numerous conflicts in newly democratizing states in the 1990s, including those in the former Soviet Union, renewed debates about the validity of the theory and provided the data for the critique by Mansfield and Snyder. They argue that in the "transitional phase of democratization, countries become more aggressive and war-prone, not less, and they do fight wars with democratic states."[50] The susceptibility of these states to conflict arises, apparently, from the relationship between democratization and nationalism.

This thesis was elaborated in a later work by Snyder, who observes: "a country's first steps toward democracy spur the development of nationalism and heighten the risk of international war and internal ethnic conflict."[51] The probability of conflict increases, he argues, because "elites use nationalist appeals to compete for popular support" and then entrench a "partial form of democracy" that protects their interests.[52] Snyder claims that post-communist conflicts, in particular those in the Caucasus region, have arisen because of the "interaction of mass nationalism and weak democratic institutions with corrupt, clannish, patronage politics."[53] This view may well be descriptively correct, but it is not empirically grounded, for Snyder tells us very little about the nature of the "elite" interests at stake or how they operated in the making of conflict, or why the idea of national self-determination has had universal appeal in the region.

The complex array of post-communist conflicts from the Balkans to the Caucasus has also helped to popularize the thesis that they are subsets of "new wars." In this view, "old wars" were fought between formally organized militaries of nation-states in the historical era when the concept of national sovereignty was paramount. The "new wars" are seen as a consequence of state failure in an era of globalization, where loosely organized and poorly disciplined armed groups and militias, frequently driven by criminal gain and genocidal intent, are the prevalent combatants, and where international intervention is regarded as the only effective means of bringing order (stability).[54] But this study of Chechnya, one of the most violent post-Soviet conflicts, reveals that there is little that is historically substantively "new" in regard to the nature of the nationalist conflict. Nation-state building, democratization, and decolonization in previous eras of history were often preceded by and progressed from bloody national, ethnic, and sectarian conflicts. It is not unusual for loosely organized bands of ethnic militia and paramilitaries operating out of weak states and declining empires to be the foundation around which formal militaries and effective nation-states are constructed. What is new about this conflict is the transformation from secular nationalism to religious jihad, and we will return to this important question later.

How, then, should we understand the reasons for the existence of "war-prone" democratization? First let us note that many theories of nationalism, democratization, and ethnic conflict are not properly reversible: they do not adequately explain why conflict potential does not turn violent. Nor do they attach much importance to the analysis of the nature of violence per se in a conflict. Yet the questions of how violence is used, by whom, when, and on what scale are all important factors in shaping a conflict. Once initiated, violence exerts its own dynamics, as we have seen from this study of the conflict in Chechnya, and has transformative effects on protagonists, events, and identities. Beissinger's study of the disintegration of the USSR showed that violence was concentrated during the latter phases of the mobilization cycle, at the apogee where the empire was in collapse and nationalism was nearing its peak of mobilization. It is not surprising, nor unusual, for the end of one regime and birth pangs of its replacement to be marked by violence. But what happens when violence becomes a sustained phenomenon? Sustained violence requires a high degree of organizational resources.[55] Violence is costly not just in its effects but in its making. Success, of course, brings the reward of attractiveness, and can popularize the use of violence.

The idea that a defining attribute of the state is "to monopolize the legitimate use of physical force as a means of domination within a territory" is now an axiom, originating from Max Weber's 1918 lecture "Politics as a Vocation."[56] But Weber was building on Trotsky's declaration at the Brest-Litovsk negotiations (also in 1918) that "every state is founded on force."[57] Trotsky's words have a double meaning: force is required to carve out a state, and every state is consolidated by the establishment of control over the use of force within its territory. Logically, new states are more likely to have weaker capacity than existing consolidated states. One of the features of post-communist transition is that conflicts do not occur in every case where the state itself is contested (for example, there have been no violent conflicts in the Baltic States, Kazakhstan, Ukraine/Crimea), but only where the successor state is weak and the state's capacity to concentrate and control violence collapses.

Conflicts also require the means of armed force. One critically important aspect of the disintegration of the state in the post-communist context was the disruption of central control of military supplies. In some states control of small arms, in particular, was weakened, and these weapons became dispersed, exchanged, and seized, thus becoming readily available for use or sale cheaply.[58] Moreover, it was not simply the dispersion that was significant, but also the fact that, given the practice of general military service in communist states, small arms were dispersed among populations that were militarily trained and knew how to use them. This was an immensely important "risk-increasing factor" for conflict in this group of states, from the Balkans to the Caucasus and Central Asia. As we have seen in the case of Chechnya, a huge stockpile of light and heavy weapons and war materials was transferred by the Russian military to the Chechen nationalists at an early stage of the conflict. If Yeltsin created Chechen nationalism, the Russian military armed its insurgency.

The conflict in Chechnya confirms the thesis that the "production of violence" has an economic as well as political logic.[59] Various forms of criminal activity (protection rackets, robbery, hostage taking, trafficking in human beings, drugs and arms) were common revenue-raising activities in Chechnya. Chechnya was a weak state, despite Dudaev's attempts to build state capacity. The basic functions of the state (law and order, tax collection, service provision) were very limited in Chechnya. Neither Dudaev nor Maskhadov monopolized the legitimate use of force. Industrial production and agriculture failed to generate sufficient income, thereby pushing employees from these sectors toward employment in the violent market sector and the black economy.

For some scholars, however, violence per se cannot be a rational pursuit of goals, and therefore it is explained as a product of information failures, or the inability of political elites to credibly deliver on a commitment, or the "security dilemma" whereby preemptive strikes are employed to avert violence from an enemy. Violence is also widely understood as being strongly influenced by diffusion and escalation principles that operate both internationally and domestically. Thus, the international spread of ethnic conflict from one state may increase the likelihood of conflict in another state.[60] Contentious events, Beissinger observed, "can act as part of their own causal structure" because they alter expectations about future action, thereby facilitating further agency.[61]

The idea that violence breeds violence is not new. Political violence tends to reproduce itself in a process of exchange through the so-called "cycle of violence." The spillover and demonstration effects of violence are, of course, important, but we must also analyze how violence changes the nature of the conflict itself. Feldman's innovative study of conflict in Northern Ireland argues that we should not treat the practice of violence as a derivative symptom of the causes of the conflict, as conventionally understood by social scientists: perceptions of social deprivation and injustice, and competing ideologies. Rather, he argues, because the status of violence in Northern Ireland is embedded as a "residual cultural and political institution" it acts as an autonomous "determining force" in causation and is a "developing ideological formation in itself."[62] Feldman undoubtedly overestimates the embeddedness of violence in Northern Irish society and its autonomy in the conflict, and fails to sufficiently distinguish between symbolic and actual violence. For while Northern Ireland was a deeply divided society, it was also one of the least violent parts of the UK prior to the eruption of the conflict in 1969, and for several years in the 1960s political contestation centered on a civil rights movement that practiced non-violent direct action. The transformation of Northern Ireland into a violent society was a product of the practice of violence that became a protracted war driven by political differences that were not easily reconcilable. Nevertheless, Feldman rightly draws our attention to the importance of violence in a conflict process and its key role in mutating the causative factors in play. What this study of the conflict in Chechnya has attempted to show is how the extreme and sustained violent conflict in Chechnya was the product of a particular context of politicization, and the radicalization of Chechnya arose from militarization and the practice of violence. Chechnya was one of the most peaceful and stable parts of the former USSR on the eve of the USSR's dissolution in the late 1980s. It was the context of the rise of nationalism in the Soviet Union under Gorbachev's liberalization, followed by systemic collapse and a selective application of the principle of national self-determination, that provided the conditions for the conflict. Some successor states are formed peacefully and consensually from the detritus of empire, while others are disallowed. International recognition tends also to be selectively applied. Nationalist conflict, first and foremost, is a response to the perceived injustice of the denial of rights, and in particular the denial of statehood.

Conflict may also be a consequence of the problems of sovereign state formation during the post-communist transition, which are heightened by communist-era legacies of covert ethnic privileging and territorial boundaries that generally were only partially sensitive to ethnic factors. These features of the communist system were shared with colonial empires, notably in Africa and the Middle East. While such common features are observed, they have yet to be systematically compared, and it is not the function of this book to do so.[63] It is generally accepted that the macro-level issues of redefining the sovereign territory and the demos, building state capacity, and securing international recognition tend to accentuate nationalism and, where multiethnicity is present, the ethnification of politics and exclusionary policies of ethnic privileging. How plausible is this linkage between democratization, nationalism and the role of the state as an explanation of the causes of post-communist conflict more generally, and in particular what does it tell us about the conflict in Chechnya?

There is an observable trend for many post-communist states in the "new" Europe to be "nationalizing," in Rogers Brubaker's sense of pursuing a project to "realize" a "nation-state" by adopting policies designed to recast the newly sovereign state in a form which privileges the dominant ethnic group by securing its political, economic and cultural hegemony.[64] The scale and intensity of this trend varies immensely across the post-communist region, from policy preferences for assimilation to exclusivist strategies of discrimination against minorities, and, at worst, policies of war and ethnic violence through what is now commonly termed "ethnic cleansing."[65] Furthermore, the time frame or temporal sequence of the strategies and policies followed differs markedly across the region. What is most evident is that while the "nationalizing" of the state or "ethnification" of politics may intensify conflict potential, where such policies have been applied it has not consistently resulted in actual violent conflict.[66] How the Soviet legacy of "institutionalized multiethnicity" is managed in the post-Soviet setting may be a significant factor in determining whether there is an accommodation or conflict, but it does not explain all the variance.[67]

Historical theories of development have stressed the relationship between the context under which nation-states emerge, what forms they take, and what determines their effectiveness.[68] Nation-building requires a strategic understanding among elites of the importance of the abstract notion of "nation." State-building, in contrast, is a technocratic exercise of modernity that is concerned with the establishment of a modern state administration, coercive apparatus (police and military), a public education system, a coherent and integrated system of tax collection, a particular social and economic organization, and mediating political structures (parliament, parties, and organized interests). The cumulative effect of all these institutions is expected to be the formation of the "homogenized citizenry" which modernists refer to as the "nation" (in a civic sense). As we have seen, for Gellner nationalism was about making territory and identity functional, and it first arose in Western Europe, he argued, in places where the notion of an existing state "is already very much taken for granted."[69] The state may have been a prior logic at the genesis of nationalism, but it is clear from Gellner's later work that he recognized the conflict potential inherent in the proposition that some nations without states wanted them, though he believed most to be "slumberers" that would never "bark."[70]

Perhaps it is because their work arrived relatively late on the scene and was concerned with recent transitions that late twentieth-century theorists of democratization, such as Linz and Stepan, eschewed the more functional arguments of the modernist theory of nationalism and the state. Democratizing states are building the state and nation in conditions where they exhibit weak capacity and are transforming the social and economic foundations of the state, often in multiethnic settings, and where there may be nationalist and ethnic challenges to the successor state itself from secessionist groups. Linz and Stepan emphasized that state-building

and nation-building are "two overlapping, but conceptually and historically different processes." While state-building focuses on the establishment of state institutions in newly defined boundaries (including defining
constitutional and institutional choices such as presidential or parliamentary systems, type of electoral system, and so on), nation-building emphasizes the promotion, if not construction in some cases, of a national
identity, generally by laws and policies which privilege a dominant ethnic group or groups with regard to language, citizenship, education, state
employment, and participation in privatization of the economy. The sense
of intention and proactivity in the actors' motivations is captured by the
word "building." Thus, there appears to be a temporal simultaneity to
state-building and nation-building, according to Linz and Stepan, as the
nation gets built alongside the state. This approach is best understood as
an ideal-type for the construction of the civic nation-state, though it does
raise first-principle questions about the quality of multiple political con-
structions that are not built in a sequential order. In fact, ultimately Linz
and Stepan, accept that the state takes priority. They consider the state
and democratization to be inextricably linked through citizenship: without a state, there can be no citizenship, without citizenship, there can be
no democracy.

According to Linz and Stepan, it is the fact that state- and nation-
building tend to be inseparable in practice that lies at the heart of the
post-communist "stateness" problem. They identify the "stateness problem" as one that arises "when there are profound differences about the
territorial boundaries of the political community's state and profound
differences as to who has the right of citizenship in that state."[71] Accordingly, state-building and nation-building are complementary logics virtually only when the following conditions are satisfied[72]: almost all residents
of a state identify with one subjective idea of the nation; the nation is virtually contiguous with the state; no significant irredenta is present; there
is only one nation in the state; and, there is low cultural diversity within
the state.

These ideal conditions reflect the conventional liberal argument about
the immense difficulties that multiethnicity creates for sustainable democracy, in particular when national minorities are *present* as opposed to
being *mobilized*. This begs the question whether and under what conditions policies of state- and nation-building and policies aimed at crafting
democracy can be overlapping. This question is not only critical for many
postcommunist states but also for the democracy-building projects in
Afghanistan and Iraq. Linz and Stepan conclude that a diverse society
makes any agreement on the fundamental nature of the state more difficult to achieve and sustain, though much depends on the nature of the
presence of other nations, for example, whether they are "awakened" or

"militant." In the case of the former, democracy can be consolidated "if crafted carefully"; in the case of the latter consolidation is difficult or impossible.[73] Where multiethnicity and multiple competing nationalisms are mobilized, Linz and Stepan argue, it is not that the absence of agreements about "stateness" before the creation of democratic institutions is "unsolvable," but rather that "complex negotiations, pacts, and possible territorial realignments and consociational agreements are often necessary" (though they do not elaborate on what these may be).[74] They regard democratic consolidation on the basis of such institutional arrangements as difficult but not impossible.

For theorists of nationalism and democratization, the diversity arising from multiethnic societies appears to be the single most important threat to the legitimacy of the state, its political stability, and an outcome of a successfully consolidated civic nation-state. Expressing skepticism about the prospects for democracy in divided societies is important, as is emphasizing the difficulty of building institutions conducive to multiethnic democracy, but equally so is the analysis of what is required in complex institutional engineering and policy-making to create stability in multiethnic states. Historically, of course, there have been highly volatile and violent means of dealing with multiethnicity in a state (such as genocide, ethnic expulsion, and regimes of control). Policies such as assimilation into the hegemonic group, or control strategies to repress and constrain nationalism, however, are not regarded as "conducive to democratic crafting."[75] Linz and Stepan single out "electoral sequencing" as an important stabilizer, but this is an overgeneralization of Spain's post-Franco transition. The experience of the collapse of communism in the USSR and Yugoslavia, they argue, suggests that holding the first democratic and legitimating "founding elections" at the statewide level, thus reinforcing the power and authority of the hegemonic group, rather than at the regional or local level, which may well empower minorities, may be an important factor in warding off ethnopolitical mobilization.[76] This is an argument for the imposition of power through majority rule rather than accommodation.

It seems indisputable that there will be less potential for conflict if the stateness problems are resolved as early as possible. It is surprising, therefore, given the focus of theory on the state and "stateness," and on the significance attached to an early arrangement of what is the state, that the question of institutional engineering to manage "stateness" problems is virtually sidelined from the analysis by Linz and Stepan. The challenge for any democracy or democratizing state is to accommodate differences in a stable, sustainable and morally acceptable way. A traditional principle of democracy is that the will of the majority should prevail. In ethnically polarized societies, however, where political loyalties are rooted in the ethnic ascription and floating voters are few, minorities may have little access to power and the "will of the majority," in practice, means majority dictatorship. This poses obvious problems for democratic stability and can foster the politics of antagonism. It can also produce violations of the fundamental ideas of political equality and equality of opportunity that are intrinsic to democracy.

Today, there is a well-established critique of the theories of nationalism and democratization for their respective failures to recognize the repertoire of institutional and policy mechanisms that can successfully manage multiethnicity in ways that are inherently compatible with democracy. Equally, traditional majoritarian democracy is seen as likely to heighten ethnic tensions, as hegemonic ethnic majorities privilege themselves and shut out ethnic minorities from access to power. The role of leadership and political "engineers" in "thwarting" and managing nationalist conflicts is regarded as of critical importance. The solutions that are generally recognized as normatively proper and functionally effective in terms of generating political stability fall into two main approaches: an institutionalist approach that focuses on constitutional and institutional design, in particular, forms of consociationalism, federalism, or autonomy arrangements, and the "group-differentiated rights" approach of multiculturalism popularized by Will Kymlicka.[77]

The most influential form of institutional design to manage "deeply divided" societies is undoubtedly consociationalism, which is a complex system devised by Arend Lijphart of institutionalized power-sharing based on the counterbalancing of group interests.[78] Horowitz, in contrast, emphasizes the danger of long-lasting segregation entailed in consociationalism, and instead proposes an entire package of conflict-reducing techniques and incentives for cooperation.[79] He distinguishes between distributive and structural means of conflictmanagement, though he himself is acutely aware of the potential overlap between the two: "Distributive policies aim to change the ethnic balance of economic opportunities and rewards. Structural techniques aim to change the political framework in which ethnic conflict occurs."[80] Much depends on whether the competing claims of different groups residing in the same territory are mobilized around "deep" divisions (usually race, ethnicity, and religion), compounded by ethnohistorical mythologies or socioeconomic grievances, and whether they are essentially domestically driven or involve spoiling external interference by foreign powers, diasporas, or irredentist states. While distributive policies rest on preferential treatment of or investment in an ethnic group and its territory, the main structural means of conflict-regulation involve the reshaping of territorial government (for example through federalism or autonomy), or the electoral system.

The experience of managing post-communist conflict in the Balkans, notably in the consociational-type of arrangements provided by the Dayton Accord of 1995 to bring peace to Bosnia-Herzegovina, has generated a growing current of criticism of consociational and federal forms of managing diversity. Such institutional arrangements are intended to allow an accumulation of interethnic trust and a gradual pluralist accommodation, but they are criticized for institutionalizing societal divisions in a manner that creates incentives for political polarization. They are perceived to be obstacles to the formation of "civic" nations, though it is clear that such a concept has minimal support in the region.[81] This critique is based on the absurd misunderstanding that majoritarian democracy can provide a fair rule of law regime in a deeply divided society. The consensus among experts on ethnic conflict is that recent comparative experience demonstrates that democracy in a "plural" society requires sophisticated institutionalized mechanisms, such as federalism and power-sharing devices, to ensure a more ethnically plural power structure in the organization and operation of the state.

The disintegration of the Soviet Union and Yugoslavia led to a surge in claims of self-determination and secession by national and ethnic groups, which were framed as a "struggle for democracy." The challenges came at a moment when state weakness was magnified by the overall context of the so-called "simultaneity dilemma" of wholesale reform in the political, economic, and social spheres. The fact that almost all the communist-era federations disintegrated (USSR, Yugoslavia) or dissolved (Czechoslovakia, Ethiopia) as part of the collapse of communism is taken as proof of the incompatibility between ethnified federalism, nationalism, and democracy. Brubaker observed that there is an inherent incompatibility between state integrity, democratization, and the institutionalized territorialization of ethnicity, which he termed "institutionalized multinationality." Ethnically denominated governing institutional structures, if territorialized, are most likely to act as a catalyst to mobilize and assert self-determination during a process of democratization. Similarly, Bunce claims that the ethnofederal design of these states in fact creates "subversive institutions" that have a corroding effect on state power that is magnified at times of regime crisis and transition. Thus, the communist form of federalism is seen as a suicidal institutional framework, for it unsuccessfully attempted to juggle a policy of homogenization on the one hand (the promotion of "Soviet" and "Yugoslav" identities) with, on the other hand, a policy of promoting national identities, including institutionalizing and territorializing many of these identities.[82]

The combination of federalism and territorialized national and ethnic identity, however, has generally worked well in other cases, notably in India, Canada, and Spain. Moreover, there was one important communist-era federation that did not break-up: the Russian Federation. The question of how to manage territorialized multiethnicity through a post-Soviet re-federalization posed immense dilemmas for the Russian leadership under Yeltsin and Putin. In an earlier chapter, I examined how asymmetric federalism was developed in the 1990s in an attempt to manage multiethnicity and the "stateness" issue, though it could not be reconciled with Chechnya's demand for secession. As we discussed previously, the key to understanding the relationship between the Soviet state as a multiethnic federation and its political stability or instability lies in the contingency of liberalization under Gorbachev. But the management of this institutional legacy by the successor states after the collapse also had a critical impact on conflict potential. One of the first acts of post-Soviet nationalizing states was to reorganize the state, and often this entailed a deinstitutionalization of the Soviet legacy of "institutionalized multiethnicity" by the elimination of ethnified autonomous units, and attempts to establish an ethnic cultural-linguistic, economic, and political hegemony.[83] The association of demography and territory is, of course, central to the realization of nationalist aspirations, but too often during the late Soviet era and in post-Soviet conflicts nationalism drove attempts to secure an ethnic hegemony by policies of forced ethnic expulsions, often on an immense scale.[84] In the case of Chechnya the Slavic and non-ethnic Chechens, perhaps as many as one third of the population, were forcibly expelled in the months following the Chechen "national revolution."

The principal dilemma in many post-communist states was how much power the center could delegate to manage multiethnicity and problems of "stateness" without endangering its internal cohesion and stability, and even external recognition. If the legitimacy of the state itself is insecure, giving autonomy to substate units may be perceived as weakening state consolidation and posing a threat to the hegemony of the dominant ethnic group. The deinstitutionalization of previously held and jealously guarded autonomies or attempts to otherwise secure an ethnic hegemony forced territorialized minorities to protect their interests through their own nationalist mobilizations, and in some cases this extended to a desire to exit the state by secession.

The Impulse for Secession

As with previous imperial collapses, Soviet liberalization and the end of empire under Gorbachev necessitated a readjustment of the international system. The bipolarization of global politics produced by the Cold War generated a basic geopolitical stability in Europe, while also transforming much of the developing world in the 1960s-1980s (parts of the Middle East, Africa, Asia, Latin America) into zones of superpower conflict and proxy wars, which often took a national and ethnic form. Here, there were cases aplenty of readymade conflicts that allowed the superpowers to engage. The situation was radically different in Europe, however, as the international agreements negotiated by the superpowers after the end of World War II established generally stable territorially demarcated zones of influence in Europe. The Helsinki Agreements of 1975 insulated the states in both zones from nonconsensual territorial changes. With a few exceptions, mainly the low-level internal conflicts in Northern Ireland, the Basque country, and Corsica, and the exceptional interstate crisis over Cyprus, the superpowers kept Europe free from nationalist or ethnic secessionist movements.

The end of the Soviet Union and the rise of nationalism threw this international order into confusion. With much hesitation, the international response to the collapse of communism followed the norms set during previous eras of decolonization, the most important of which was the recognition of secession under international law following the principle of *uti posseditis juris.* This principle had developed out of the experience of decolonization in Latin America, when the internal colonial boundaries of the Spanish empire became, by mutual consent, the international boundaries of the successor states (though they were subsequently reconfigured by war). *Uti posseditis juris* is inherently conservative, for it constrains when secession is possible by holding that new states may be formed on the basis only of the existing boundaries of the highest administrative units as established by the prior authority, in this case the colonial power. It discourages the unilateral redrawing of boundaries by secession or territorial seizure by threatening nonrecognition for such entities.[85]

Negotiated secession is not barred by international law, but unilateral secession is because of the requirement that the UN support the territorial integrity of its member-states—a principle enshrined in the UN Charter. By these means colonial practices are re-legitimized. The hardening of boundaries that may have been established for administrative convenience and without sensitivity to national or ethnic factors, and may not enjoy widespread current, let alone historic legitimacy, has often been proven flawed, as was all too evident from the numerous wars and conflicts that erupted in the new states of Africa and Asia after 1945.

During the era of decolonization, the priority for the UN was to facilitate self-determination and turn non-self-governing territories into independent states: in other words to build state capacity, where before it had been weak or nonexistent.[86] Exceptionally, disputed territories have been given an indeterminate status rather than statehood, for example, being placed under UN administration. Until the Kosovo crisis of 1999, such territories were very underdeveloped and overwhelmingly located outside Europe. Indeterminate and other kinds of special status for partitioned, occupied, or secessionist territories tend to be associated with the most protracted conflicts, including notably the conflicts between Israel and Palestine and neighboring Arab states, India and Pakistan over the division of Kashmir, Greece, Cyprus, and Turkey over Northern Cyprus, China and Taiwan, and the UK and the Republic of Ireland over Northern Ireland, among others.

Because the right to self-determination has been highly circumscribed in international practice and law, geographically confined, and temporally constrained, the prevailing international climate is, therefore, critical to the success of secession. There are four main aspects: first, the acceptance of the "morality" of the general principle; second, the acceptance of the "morality" of a particular claim; third, the recognition of a claim; and fourth, the international enforcement of a particular claim. Historically, the process is marked by a pattern whereby the first is generally accepted; the second is usually disputed but occasionally accepted; the third is rarely accepted; and the fourth is almost never enacted (Bangladesh, Bosnia-Herzegovina, East Timor, and probably Kosovo being significant exceptions).[87] To the above criteria we must add the role of the national interests of Great Powers who may be affected by the secession, and their capacity to block international action.

States are the basis of the international system. Not only does a state fulfill the Gellnerian logic of nationalism by making the political and territorial concepts of nation coincide, but statehood also traditionally confers certain benefits, including recognition of sovereign equality, territorial integrity, diplomatic relations and immunity, and international legal capacity and "personality." One of the theoretical core benefits of statehood is the protection from the use of force by other states (enshrined in Article 2 of the UN Charter). The most basic characteristic of secession is that it is a political act perpetrated against an existing state by one of its existing territorially demarcated units. In this sense, it is essentially not only an act that reshapes the domestic political order, but also an international act, as it is an attempt to reconfigure the existing international order. The history of international relations since the First World War demonstrates a close but inconsistent relationship between secession, which generally has been resisted by the international system, and self-determination, which periodically has been acknowledged. The recognition of secession in international practice falls into two main categories: first, territories which are parts of existing states, in respect to which self-determination is applied by the mutual agreement of the parties involved, and second, the highest level constituent units of an empire which has been, or is in the process of being, decolonized or dissolved, normally by agreement with the constituent units.[88] Historically, however, there have been many contested secessions.[89]

The key normative question for the claim to secede is what constitutes the legitimate territorial unit. In international practice, that unit is generally acknowledged to be the "state" or the colonial administrative unit, but in exceptional circumstances other territorial units within a state may be recognized as such. The concept of the "state" in the international system is governed by the Montevideo Convention on the Rights and Duties of States (1933), which defined a "state" as "a person of international law" which should possess "(a) a permanent population; (b) a defined territory; (c) a government; and (d) capacity to enter into relations with other states." As with many aspects of international law, the convention is ambiguous and minimalist; most important, it does not provide us with an answer to the questions: when does a state exist and, should the population of a state be indigenous to the defined state territory?[90] International lawyers refer to the "constitutive" and "declaratory" approaches to statehood. Under the former, recognition by existing states is necessary for the constitution of a new state, for without recognition the new entity cannot have legal personality, while under the latter approach recognition is not a requirement for statehood, but merely a statement by other states accepting a factual situation. International law has yet to reconcile the declaratory and constitutive approaches.[91]

While states and the international system generally oppose secession, this is not a logical reason for scholars of nationalist and ethnic conflict to do so. Most do, however. As is evident from Horowitz's skepticism about the recent more positivist approach to secession among international lawyers (in view of the experience of the post-communist conflicts in the Balkans and the Kosovo question in particular), there remains a deep resistance among theorists to secession as an instrument to correct problems of "stateness," ethnic conflict, and violence. Horowitz considers that "secession is almost never an answer to such problems and . . . is likely to make them worse."[92]

The question of secession becomes a major issue in the international order only during periods when the international system itself is in crisis. Secession and self-determination, consequently, came to be seen as processes that were difficult to prevent from escalating out of control, especially if they were regionally concentrated. These considerations were a long established part of international practice before the collapse of communism. The term "Balkanization," for example, which became ubiquitous in analyses of post-communist conflict to describe a general escalation of secession, was a historical term that emerged from the conflicts of that region in the first two decades of the twentieth century.

In practice, the history of international relations demonstrates that the criteria for statehood are operated differently depending on whether the case involves already constituted states or new entities claiming statehood. States can continue to exist even when they no longer meet the criteria.

For example, states may not have a government (e.g., present-day Somalia), or may not be recognized widely internationally (e.g., the Soviet "annexations" of the three Baltic states in 1940, Rhodesia, Transkei, the Taliban regime in Afghanistan until 2002), or international recognition may change (e.g., in 1971 the Republic of China (Taiwan) was expelled from the UN and replaced by the People's Republic of China), or may not exercise control over its territory (Bosnia and Herzegovina in 1992–95).

In the twentieth century there were three concentrated periods when self-determination was more broadly acknowledged or permitted: after the First and Second World Wars and after the fall of communism.[93] The collapse of communism gave rise to a host of secessionist claims, concentrated in the federal states of the USSR and Yugoslavia, only some of which have been recognized by the international system. Broadly, in the case of the USSR the international system followed the colonial-era doctrine of *uti posseditis juris*.[94] The international system did not recognize the declarations of "sovereignty" in the Soviet Union in 1990–91, *before* the collapse of communism. Gorbachev's equalization of the rights of Soviet "Union Republics" and "Autonomous Republics" (most of which are within Russia) in certain key respects created more confusion. For by endowing the latter with the right of secession in the event of the secession from the USSR of their host republic, he aimed a cannon at the territorial integrity of the state. In the case of Russia, there are ambiguities in the constitutional notions of "sovereignty" and "self-rule" (*suverenitet* and *samostoiatel'nost'*) in the sense that a claim to one or both is not necessarily equivalent to a claim to independence (*nezavisimost'*) per se. Even so, it is doubtful whether the demand to secede from the Russian Federation actually extended to any other case but Chechnya.

The response of the international system (the Western democracies in particular) was markedly cautious. It was only in the short period after the failure of the August 1991 coup and the formal Alma Aty Declaration of December 1991 (when all the former Union Republics declared that the USSR was defunct), that the Union Republic secessions were recognized by the international system. Thus, the fifteen Union Republics were recognized as independent new states, while assertions of "sovereignty" by former Soviet autonomous republics, and the attempt to secede by Chechnya, were not recognized. There were some remarkable anomalies, most obviously Russia's recognition of an independent Ukraine before the U.S. so acted, and the U.S. recognition of six former Soviet republics (Moldova, Turkmenistan, Azerbaijan, Tajikistan, Georgia, and Uzbekistan) with the proviso set by President George Bush Senior in his televised address to the American people on 25 December 1991 that the establishment of diplomatic relations would occur only "when we are satisfied that they have made commitments to responsible security policies and democratic principles." The international system was less consistent in its practice with regard to Yugoslavia. The key legal opinions that were issued by the EC's Badinter Commission on Yugoslavia of 1991–92 recognized the precedent of *uti posseditis juris* as a "preemptive" element of customary international law when empires or federal states dissolve. Equally, however, it controversially preemptively sanctioned the break-up of Yugoslavia with a tautological declaration that the state was already "in process of dissolution," at a time when arguably this was far from certain. In addition, in the case of the successor states to the former Yugoslavia, the EC made a radical departure from customary international law by employing political criteria, such as democracy and protection of national minorities, as factors that would be a basis of recognition, whereas no or much less specific conditions were set for the successor states to the USSR in late 1991.[95]

The recognition of the Union Republics as the successor states to the USSR had profound implications for conflict potential in the region. On the one hand, the decision of the international community to proceed with recognition and integration of the successor states was prompted only by the finality of the Soviet collapse and by fears of instability from an escalation of nationalist secession in what was termed the "Russian-doll" effect. Equally, by sanctioning the break-up of the communist-era federations, the international community recognized the key role of nationalism and the principle of national self-determination, while also affirming the importance of the "nation-state" in the international system. The recognitions were legally dubious within the terms of the constitutional arrangements of the USSR, given the amendments introduced under Gorbachev which had significantly diluted the powers of the Union Republic level and enhanced the powers of the autonomous units. The end result of this approach was that after 1991 secessionist Chechnya was consigned to an international limbo that served only to increase the potential for conflict with Russia. Even the post-Khasaviurt democratically elected Maskhadov government of 1997 was kept internationally isolated, with dire consequences for the stability of the territory. For although a considerable body of opinion inside and outside Russia did not dispute Chechnya's right to secession, though this was rarely stated openly, there was revulsion to *how* the Chechens asserted their right by violence, terrorism, hostage-taking, and so on.[96]

The international approach to the secession of Chechnya has an obvious comparison with that of Kosovo. After the war of 1999 Kosovo was placed under a UN administration while nominally remaining under Federal Republic of Yugoslavia sovereignty. The determination of the final status of Kosovo, which is currently being negotiated, will be a significant test for the doctrine of *uti posseditis juris*. The U.S. and EU are currently robustly driving the UN toward recognizing the secession of Kosovo, with or without the agreement of Serbia. This is a clear double standard compared with the absence of international moral or material support for the secession of Chechnya and its recognition as an "internal" matter for Russia. It suggests that *realpolitik* trumped *idealpolitik* as the U.S. and EU refused to put international cooperation and lucrative trade at risk by challenging Russia over Chechnya. Western governments have deluded themselves into thinking that an imposed secession in Kosovo without Serbia's agreement is "sui generis," can be contained and will not be a precedent for other conflicts. President Putin has repeatedly stated, however, that the outcome in Kosovo will establish "common principles" for dealing with the "frozen conflicts" in the Former Soviet Union, though whether he can insulate the question of Chechnya's status from that of Abkhazia, South Ossetia, and Transdnistria remains to be seen.

Conclusion: Rethinking Secession

The academic study of national and ethnic conflict tends to emphasize the rational and instrumental rather than the primordial nature of ethnicity, whereas policy-makers and media tend to emphasize the latter. Such conflicts may be driven by political, economic, or sociocultural interests, but the primary objective is to control territory and its governing institutions. Ethnic conflict, consequently, should be understood as primarily a power struggle over the state in the broadest sense—its political content and its economic, social, and cultural domains. Where one ethnic group exercises hegemonic control over the state, it may lead to a situation where the minority's calculation is that their interests cannot be met within the confines of the existing state. If such a minority group is territorialized, the calculation will be that its prospects for breaking with the state will be greater. But it is in these cases that we find demands for separate governing institutions, along a spectrum from autonomy to secession.

The interconnectedness of the concepts of nation, state, self-rule, ethnicity, and territory is central to the causes of nationalist and ethnic conflict. Theories of nationalism help us to understand the important linkages between modernity, state-building, and the construction and historical evolution of national identity, but they are less satisfactory in accounting for the political or institutional dynamics of contemporary nationalist mobilization and conflict. In contrast, theories of democratization, by focusing on the "stateness" problem, refocus attention on the political salience of identity and territorial issues in conflicts over the state, while offering little in the way of solutions. They make a values consensus on the basic parameters of statehood a precondition for a viable democratizing nation-state. When the state is in transition to democracy and characterized by multiethnicity, "stateness" problems are considered to be difficult to resolve.

This survey of current literature enables me to extract a consistent theme. The homogeneous nation-state is viewed as the most stable political unit, while multiethnicity is generally regarded as a force for instability. These theories are informed by Western liberalism's concern with homogenization, whether it is the role of the state and nation in the homogenization of the demos, or the a priori dictum that homogenization provides the best conditions for the success of democratization. The preference for homogenization is reinforced when we consider how mainstream theories address institutional mechanisms for managing multiethnicity. Mainstream theories of nationalism and democratization are opposed to consociationalism and other forms of institutionalized power-sharing, such as asymmetric federalism. Logically, it would seem that asymmetric federalism and secession could be answers to problems of homogeneity, assuming that ethnic minorities are territorialized, as such solutions would reinforce the homogenization of the pared-down state. Yet, asymmetric federalism is widely viewed as an infringement of liberal principles of equality at best, and as intrinsically destabilizing at worst. After all, one of the most widespread explanations for the collapse of the USSR stresses the role of its nationalities policy of "institutionalized multinationality" in the ethnification of politics and the constitutional crises that caused the collapse. The policy preferences suggested by the mainstream theories to resolve the homogenous versus heterogeneous dilemmas of a state's demographic content, paradoxically, appear to be a preference for "ending" them through the assimilation of minorities into the values of the hegemonic ethnic group, rather than managing them by institutional forms of multiculturalism and power-sharing or secession. Yet, it is precisely policies of hegemonic control and assimilation that lead to ethnic grievances and violent conflict.

The conflict in Chechnya is fundamentally a problem of secession. Historically, secession and the partition of the state have been important devices for conflict regulation. But states, the international system, and mainstream theories of nationalism and conflict regulation are inherently opposed to secession and consider it acceptable only under very exceptional political conditions. The tragedy of Chechnya is that its claims to the moral and legal rights to secession have been sacrificed to the interests of the Great Powers.

Conclusion

In his comparative study of state expansion and contraction, Ian Lustick observed that what "distinguishes a dominance relationship over a region 'inside' the state from a dominance relationship over a region 'outside' the state is the presence of a well-institutionalized belief within the dominant core that the region under consideration is immutably bound to it."[1] Policies of expansion and control and resistance to contraction originate in the way territory is appropriated and transfixed in political identity. The most useful starting point for understanding the conflict in Chechnya must be to examine the relationship between territory and identity. The conflict originated with the collapse of one state, the USSR, and the attempt to make a new one in most of its territory, the Russian Federation.

Whether one sees the USSR's collapse in terms of imperial disintegration or state implosion, this was a period of deep and general crisis for Russian identity. It was not just that the institutions of modern statehood were in flux, but Russian identity too was uprooted and directionless. The crisis in the USSR and Russia presented an opportunity for the political mobilization of a national identity in Chechnya that aspired to independence. Democracy, self-determination, independence, secession, freedom—if there was a spirit of the age in Europe and Eurasia in 1991, it was encapsulated in these terms. Chechnya's bid for secession in 1991, therefore, measured against the standards of the time, was neither extraordinary nor irrational. Dudaev did not mobilize Chechnya's national revolution in 1990–91, it mobilized him. Moreover, he was as much a product of the Estonian national revolution as he was of the Chechen struggle for self-determination.

Whether Chechnya's bid for secession had genuine mass support among the Chechen people is another matter. There is an argument, popular in some Russian circles, that the struggle for an independent Chechnya was a smokescreen for a coup d'état by a small criminal group, not a "national revolution." To deny the possibility of the aspiration for independence requires a denial of the very existence of a Chechen "nation." This argument rests on an implicit acceptance that Soviet identity had a currency that ran beyond the removal of the repressive apparatus of the CPSU. It is true that a large swathe of the ethnic Chechen Soviet elite in Chechnya remained loyal to a concept of Soviet identity, and then after the collapse, to Russian statehood. Undoubtedly, the political and territorial cleavages within Chechen society introduced a significant element of civil war into the conflict. Chechnya, after all, was the only part of the former Soviet Union except the Baltic States where there was an almost complete elite replacement after independence. The secessionist versus loyalist cleavage allowed Russia gradually to refine the policy of using Chechen proxies in its attempt to control Chechnya—the policy of Chechenization—and thus to turn the conflict into a continuum that ran from nationalist resistance to civil war. While this policy proved unworkable in the period 1991–94, Putin's relative military success since late 1999 has created space for Chechenization to take root during the second war. However, a focus on intra-Chechen rivalries is a distraction from the genesis of the conflict, which was fundamentally a struggle between Chechen secessionists who had power in Chechnya and Russian elites intent on restoring Russian hegemony over the whole territory of the former RSFSR.

Russian identity was so immutably bound with that of the Soviet Union that in many respects Russia's crucial role in its fall was an act of self-mutilation. Even within the Yeltsin "democratic' elite that seized power in late 1991, it was recognized that the collapse of the USSR could be a moment of self-destruction for Russia. For if the momentum of nationalist mobilization, matched by a loss of will for coercion on the part of the ruling Soviet elite, had caused the USSR to crumble, how could a multinational country like Russia avoid the same fate? There were only two possibilities for resolving the double crisis of state and identity. Russia could accept that its auto-decolonization was a logical consequence of the collapse of the USSR, or Russia must be remade. The issue was—on what territory?

International norms on decolonization gave Russia a major advantage by reinforcing its claim to sovereignty over the entire RSFSR territory inherited from the Soviet Union. The claim that the whole of this territory was "integral" to Russian statehood marked the Russian elites across the political spectrum and was broadly accepted internationally. The multinational nature of Russian society made it illogical to define this territory as an ethnonational space; rather the argument was posed in statist terms. Even Russian politicians who were sympathetic to Chechnya's demands for greater self-rule could not fathom the demand of successive Chechen leaderships for independence, nor could they countenance the challenge to Russia's territorial integrity and statehood, or the threat to its strategic position in the Caucasus that the loss of Chechnya would entail.

It may at first sight seem irrational to an outsider that a country such as Russia, which has almost twice the land mass of the United States and a population of 148 million, would be so concerned about a territory about the size of Connecticut with fewer than one million people. However, one cannot imagine the U.S. tolerating secession by Connecticut, in the unlikely event that this were to happen.

This kind of comparison does not invalidate Chechnya's aspiration for secession. I simply draw it to remind us once again of the implications of a territorial identity for state-building. By implication, a "dominant core' will resist, with force if necessary, the challenge to its territorial integrity, not because of the value of the territory per se (though a strategic dimension, as in Chechnya, will compound resistance to losing territory), but because the challenge is an attack on its identity. The conflict in Chechnya, consequently, began with a question about what Chechnya should be, thereby posing a challenge to what Russians think Russia is.

The causes of conflict are almost always complex, and it is often presumptive to identify any single factor or actor as predominant. If one asks the question—What is the conflict in Chechnya about?—the answer must vary over time. Historicist explanations, by focusing on the "unique" history and characteristics of Chechnya and the "ancient hatred" between Chechnya and Russia, tend to downplay the structural context of Soviet state collapse in which the demand for secession was quickly mobilized. Moreover, historicism cannot explain the undulating salience and marginalization of causes, actors, strategies, issues, and idioms during the conflict. There have been peaks and troughs of dialogue, negotiation, and mediation in the military conflict and diplomatic arenas. Because conflict is a process, what might have been the basis for compromise and a settlement at one stage may be made redundant by the conflict dynamics, as new issues and actors come to the fore. Chechnya impresses upon us the logic that a conflict transforms itself.

What is evident in the case of Chechnya, and this may well be a fundamental logic in any conflict process, is that over time there has been a radicalization of the protagonists. The question is do protracted conflicts induce radicalization or does radicalization produce a protracted conflict? In the case of Chechnya the shared conceptualization of the conflict of the early 1990s centered on secession. This "meta-conflict" has been steadily transformed by the protracted nature of the conflict itself. Certainly on the part of the Chechen resistance we can track a shift from the dominance of secular nationalism in the early to mid-1990s under Dudaev to a gradual Islamization, submergence of secular nationalism, and dominance of jihad under Basaev from the late 1990s on. The question of secession remains but is posed and legitimized by a different ideological frame.

Putin's radicalization, intransigence, and brutality are partly a reaction to what he views as the failure of Yeltsin's attempts to negotiate the integrity of Russian statehood. Putin claims that Khasaviurt signaled a genuine attempt by Russia to allow Chechnya to build an independent state, but the result was a power vacuum and Islamic radicalism.[2] One of his main goals on coming to power in Russia was to "cement Russian statehood." But we must not underplay the instrumentalization of the conflict for ulterior goals by Putin, and Yeltsin and Dudaev too. The conflict was a useful device for both sides in the president versus parliament institutional wars of the 1990s.

In Russia the policies of alternatively hammering the Chechens and making peace with the Chechens were operated almost like a switch depending on the political need and electoral cycle. Putin came to power in 2000 as a victorious "war president." When asked at a press conference in January 2006 to say what he considered the main achievements of his presidency, Putin put the question of Chechnya in first place: "We have strengthened the Federation, we have brought the Chechen Republic back within Russia's constitutional sphere and done this through legal means."[3]

The difference between Yeltsin and Putin is that Yeltsin, beyond pulling down the communist edifice, never had a vision for Russian state-building, nor the energy, clear head, good health, or commitment to be consistent in policy. Putin has adeptly exploited the conflict in Chechnya to win power and consolidate it in a wholly remade centralized state. The war to destroy Chechnya's secessionism has been employed by Putin as a battering ram to smash away the intricate institutional and informal foundations of the asymmetric federalism that was developed under Yeltsin to manage separatism within an integral concept of Russian statehood. The concept of autonomy as a form of ethnopolitical accommodation appears now to be regarded as appeasement and a betrayal of Russian "statehood." If Yeltsin's lure of asymmetric federalism was not palatable for Chechnya's secessionists, Putin's symmetrical federation repels. Putin's centralizing refederalization of Russia, consequently, is a recipe for prolonging the conflict in Chechnya.

The U.S. commander in Vietnam, General Westmoreland, infamously said of one operation that his forces "had to destroy the village in order to save it" from the enemy. Russia destroyed Chechnya so as to save it for Russian statehood. But what has been saved? For what has it been saved? At what cost? The conflict has resulted in massive loss of life, immense damage to the fabric of Chechen society, and wholesale destruction of the infrastructure of Chechnya. The "excesses" and disproportional use of force by Russia in Chechnya and its results, suggest that Russian policy has been genocidal in its consequences, if not in intent. The conflict has been costly in obvious human and economic terms for Russia, but there are also hidden costs such as the lurking problem of traumatized veterans for Russian society, the sporadic threat of terrorism, and the corrosion of Russia's democratization.

The impact of the war on Russia's democratization from 1991 has not been addressed in depth; rather, I have focused in particular on Yeltsin's and Putin's instrumentalization of the conflict to consolidate power. The "counterterrorism operation" since late 1999 has brought to a halt and seriously damaged democratization in Russia, helped undermine constitutional competitive politics and the rule of law, entrenched nationalist sentiment, severely constrained freedom of speech, and intensified racism against Chechens in particular and all Caucasian peoples in general. Putin spoke of granting the "widest possible autonomy" for Chechnya within the Russian state, yet even this promise sounds hollow as Chechnya remains at war, and Putin has invested wholly in a control strategy and a policy of Chechenization that depends on highly volatile and brutal local clients, such as the Kadyrovtsy.

The conflict has transformed Chechnya into a militarized society with strong paramilitary forces and no rule of law. Likewise, Russia's democratic institutions have been subordinated to a *siloviki* clique under Putin. If institutions are a major focus of the study of conflict, because they are catalysts and platforms for the mobilization of power and are critical for the prevention, management, or resolution of conflicts, then we must recognize that Chechnya and Russia are seriously institutionally debilitated. We are left, in both cases, with an increasingly authoritarian and personalized political order, where decision-making is distorted by very narrow information flows.

A "constructive ambiguity" in wordplay is often viewed in the field of conflict studies as a useful device to generate compromise. The major obstacle to a settlement of the conflict in Chechnya during the 1990s was the impossibility of reconciling Dudaev's insistence on independence with Yeltsin's claim to sovereignty. It was not that Dudaev was a nay-sayer; it was simply that for him the question of secession was non-negotiable and he insisted on clarity rather than ambiguity in any text. Moreover, whether such a device as "constructive ambiguity," which is after all a ruse and a delay to the thorniest questions, can provide a lasting basis for peace in a situation where a core principle must be compromised is questionable. Interim solutions—as Khasaviurt demonstrated—may only lead to further instability.

Postponing the most problematical issue, the question of status and secession, did not advance peace and stability in Chechnya. The ambiguities of peace-making left the de facto independent government of Maskhadov in a limbo, where neither Russia nor the international community was locked into a process of reconstruction and building state capacity which would have helped to stabilize Chechnya. The lesson of the successes of the peace process in 1996–97 is that in the absence of external supports, an independent Chechnya was and would be easy prey for subversion—notably by Islamists.

An Islamic element of religiosity in the Chechen national movement predated the wars with Russia and was developing in the period between secession in late 1991 and the outbreak of war in late 1994. It was war, however, that brought the radicalized Wahhabi Islamists under Basaev to dominance. In so doing, the conflict has brought a new kind of rationale to the fore. It is one that is uninterested in the secular territorial confines of the nation-state, but rather wages jihad in the name of a wider Caucasian religious state, or caliphate. Negotiations are unlikely because of the impossibility of reconciling these antithetical rationalizations: Russia's focus on the secular state goal of unity and the Islamists' deterritorialized ambitions for a politicized *ummah*. The challenge to Russian statehood has expanded from a territorial issue to an ideological one that has the potential to destabilize Russian republics in the North Caucasus and Volga regions where there are large populations of Muslims. When there is a perception that issues are non-negotiable, coercion becomes rational—even when it is apparent that this policy has demonstrably failed to deliver stability, security, or peace. To some extent Putin's relentless militarism is a mirror image of the ideologically intransigent position of Basaev. As the apogees of their respective historical forces, they reflect the dual radicalization of the conflict process.

The conceptualization and categorization of violence in conflicts is often under-theorized. Concepts and categories are important because they are the basis for the moral evaluation of any conflict: when is violence justified, and what kinds of violence are legitimate? Violent conflicts will be fought as much in the realm of idiom, in the mass media and culture, as in the fields and towns, as protagonists seek to frame the wider perception of the conflict according to their self-interest. The high level of politicization in the use of conflict idioms, such as the designations "freedom fighters' and "terrorists," makes it all the more important that we rigorously analyze categories in order to distinguish meaningfully between a struggle for national self-determination and an elite or criminal group's power grab.

The historical record of anticolonial nationalist struggles is scattered with ironies whereby yesterday's hunted "terrorist" resistance leaders are today's feted distinguished statesmen and women of independent states and former "freedom fighters." Even at the height of struggle, harsh and seemingly intransigent rhetoric from actors about non-negotiation tends to be a political epiphenomenon of any conflict. Often, the very same actors are secretly in active negotiating mode via "back channels." Assertions about non-negotiation are normal in the pre-negotiation phase, as the protagonists entrench and harden their positions in advance of bargaining and compromise. These are rational strategies for rational actors.

The killing of Maskhadov eliminated moderation from the Chechen secessionist movement. In fact, it is no longer, a recognizably secessionist movement of the traditional anticolonial secular nationalist type. The conflict process has deepened the complexity of the conflict in Chechnya to a level where secession is no longer understood as state boundaries, but is part of a wider globalized Islamist religious struggle. Negotiating an exit from such a conflict is immeasurably more difficult. Equally, Russia having constructed an Islamist bogeyman in Chechnya, has managed to give life to it by its brutal policies.

Theories of political violence suggest that terrorism may be legitimate if it is a "last resort' defense, and where there is no alternative, in particular in the presence of a threat of genocide. In this book, I have argued that there are grounds for understanding some of the terrorism by Chechen secessionists within this paradigm. Basaev's use of terrorism, however, emerged early in the conflict and has been a consistent strategy. His propensity to terrorism is unrelated to the harshness of Russia's military actions. Nevertheless, the primary motivation in his use of terrorism is retaliatory. From the time of the first war he framed his use of terrorism as a response to what he perceived to be Russia's genocidal war against Chechens; consequently, all means are legitimate and all Russians are legitimate targets. This justification became more prominent in Basaev's rhetoric over time. If we examine the acts of terrorism perpetrated by both sides, we often find that there is no wider strategic or political purpose, but simply the goal of revenge. Sometimes, as in suicide-attacks, the revenge may be motivated by personal rather than ideological factors, but we must not overstate this. Some of the large scale terrorist attacks (Budennovsk, Dubrovka, Beslan), however, did have political goals such as the withdrawal of Russian forces from Chechnya, the start of negotiations and the release of prisoners. A balanced assessment of the use of terrorism by Chechens demonstrates that it has been primarily a tactic used sporadically rather than systematically, and in reaction to Russian intervention. Terrorism, like Islamization, is a product of the conflict that has also had a significant impact on how the conflict has developed and been perceived.

While muted criticism and a more understanding approach from Western governments since 9/11 has made Chechnya less of an inconvenience in foreign affairs for Russia, it has also contributed to the hardening of Putin's policy, tilting it further toward the uncompromising strategy of coercion and control. Western states have persistently subordinated Chechnya to "bigger issues" of trade, energy supply, and international politics.

The hesitant international support for Maskhadov in 1997–99 was peripheralized after 9/11 by evidence that the Chechen resistance was linked to Al-Qaida. Putin maneuvered on the international stage like a seasoned actor, and successfully deflected international criticism of Russia's human rights abuses in Chechnya by opportunistically framing the conflict as part of the "global war on terrorism." Moreover, the kind of "excess" and over-reaction to "terrorism" that has been evident in Russian policy toward Chechnya has become a global phenomenon since 9/11. Governments in the advanced democracies are eroding civil liberties and securitizing the state in response to the "terrorist" threat. U.S. policy in Iraq and Afghanistan, the creation of its own "filtration" camps at Guantanamo, Abu Ghraib, and Bagram, the use of torture and the brutality of its response to the insurgencies, have seriously depleted any moral leverage that the Western democracies might have employed against Russia, assuming that they wished to.

The conflict in Chechnya is at an impasse. Events have demonstrated that Putin has been incapable of developing his Chechen policy beyond the war aims of 1999–2000: destroy the resistance, Chechenize and contain the conflict, while moving very slowly on political institutional development and reconstruction.[4] Attacks such as those at Beslan and Nalchik demonstrate that the containment policy has failed as jihad is spreading in the North Caucasus. Russian military and civilian casualties continue to mount, yet Putin's popularity over the period of the conflict has remained very high. The cycle of terror and counterterror has generated a steely acceptance of the costs of a long war of attrition, which is accentuating and reinforcing cleavages such as racism and sectarianism that comparative experience associates with the most intractable conflicts.

There is a pervasive pessimism among the "Chechen hands" in Russia about the future of the Chechnya conflict. Tishkov places some hope in the higher threshold or capacity of Chechen and Russian cultures to deal with extreme levels of violence, as such attitudes to death and loss might assist reconciliation.[5] Some Russians argue that Russia does not have a viable negotiating partner, and that consequently there is no solution.[6] The conflict process is continuing to change the configuration of the conflict. Leaders make an immense difference to the development of a conflict. Much as the killing of Maskhadov has removed a peace partner, the death of Basaev has removed a key controller of the insurgency. How will his removal affect the course of the conflict? Will it make the Islamist resistance more fragmentary and possibly even more dangerous for Russia? Could it open an opportunity for a revival of the endogenous secular nationalism of the early 1990s under Basaev's successor Udugov. A presidential alternance is due in Russia in early 2008, with Putin constitutionally obliged to step down. Will a new Russian president change policy on Chechnya? These are imponderables, but they demonstrate that, as much as the conflict process has transformed the nature of the conflict in Chechnya in the past, the dynamic continues. The only strategy that Russia has not so far attempted is outright independence and normalization of relations with Chechnya on a state-to-state basis. The sheer physical destruction of Chechnya and the ongoing trauma of its people makes independence an unthinkable prospect in the near term. Moreover, an independent Chechnya today would probably lead to open civil war between loyalists, nationalists, and Islamists and even wider regional instability.

The current outcome of the war in Chechnya offers grounds to validate theories of conflict regulation which almost universally oppose secession, whether on moral or practical grounds, as it is almost universally regarded as leading to a "domino effect" of collapsing states, a race to the lowest ethnic common denominator in state-building, and a source of further conflict. The proposed remedies for ethnic antagonisms are structural incentives to promote cross-cutting cleavages, such as power-sharing, autonomy, and federalism, or even all-out assimilation.[7] Equally, I would argue that the protracted "frozen conflicts" of the former Soviet Union, of which Chechnya is the most bloody example, indicate that the general reluctance in international politics, among policy-makers and in the conflict studies literature, to support secession as a conflict regulation device, needs to be reexamined. It is too categorical.

The question of secession is rising up the international political agenda again as the UN moves ahead with the final status talks over Kosovo. It seems likely that the secession of Kosovo will be given international approval irrespective of Serbian protests. If so, it will be the first international precedent since decolonization for the overriding of a state veto on secession. Putin has declared that such conflicts must be solved by "universal principles," equally applicable in all cases, and he sees international recognition of an independent Kosovo as a model for the settlement of the frozen conflicts of the Caucasus, in particular for Abkhazia and South Ossetia.[8] So far, Putin has not included Chechnya in this list, but if Kosovo is used as a model in the FSU, inevitably the question of Chechnya cannot be avoided.

Secession must be addressed on a case by case basis. In the case of Chechnya, if Russia had been less categorical and monopolistic over territory in the early 1990s, secession might have worked. It is extremely unlikely that a nationalist regime under Dudaev would have generated instability for the Russian Federation. With proper support from Russia and the international system, Dudaev might have been able to deliver a stable independent state. Russia's cooperation with Chechnya over the use of Basaev's Abkhazia Battalion demonstrates that there was potential for a stable relationship with Dudaev based on mutual interests. Oil resources would have made an independent Chechnya economically viable. Certainly, Dudaev was attentive to the problems of the weak state in Chechnya and devoted much of his time in government, when he was not fending off Russian aggression, to building state and societal capacity. That particular secular nationalist moment has passed, and with the rise of Islamism, the conflict in Chechnya has itself mutated its causes. As the second war enters its eighth year, the feasibility of either a military solution or a negotiated settlement are more remote than ever. The basic conditions for a negotiated peace such as trust, propitious timing, conducive domestic and international environments, and the presence of skilful mediation are not currently evident in the case of Chechnya. Moreover, Russia has eliminated the key moderate on the Chechen side, Aslan Maskhadov, who was the best hope as a partner for a stable peace.

Appendix 1

The Khasaviurt Russian-Chechen Agreement
Date: August 31, 1996
JOINT STATEMENT

We the undersigned,

Taking into consideration the progress achieved in the realization of the Agreement on the cessation of military actions;

Making efforts to achieve mutually acceptable preconditions for a political settlement of the armed conflict;

Acknowledging that the use or threat of armed force to settle disputes is unacceptable; Based on the generally accepted principles of the right of peoples to self-determination, the principles of equal rights, voluntariness and freedom of choice, the strengthening of national agreement and the security of peoples;

Expressing the intent to unconditionally defend the human rights and freedoms of citizens, regardless of national origin, religious denomination, place of residence or other differences, an end to acts of violence between political opponents, in accordance with the Universal Declaration of Human Rights of 1949 and the international covenant on Civil and Political Rights of 1966,

We have worked out Principles* for the determination of basis of relations between the Russian Federation and the Chechen Republic, on the basis of which further negotiation will take place.

Signed by

A. Lebed,
A. Maskhadov
S. Kharlamov,
S. Abumuslimov

In the presence of the Head of the OSCE Assistance Cooperation in the Chechen Republic, signed by T. Guldiman

*Principles for the determination of relations between the Russian Federation and the Chechen Republic

a. Agreement on the terms for relations between the Russian Federation and the Chechen Republic, to be decided in accordance with generally accepted principles and norms of international law, must be reached before 31 December 2001.

b. No later than 1 October 1996 a Joint commission will be formed from the representatives of State organs of the Russian Federation and the Chechen Republic, whose tasks will consist of:
1. control of the implementation of Decree no. 985 of the President of the Russian Federation of 25 June 1996 and preparation of proposals for the complete withdrawal of armed forces;
2. preparation of agreed upon measures to combat crime, terrorism and manifestations of national and religious conflict and control of their implementation;
3. preparation of proposals for monetary and budgetary relations;
4. preparation and creation by the Government of the Russian Federation of a program of rehabilitation of the economic infra-structure of the Chechen Republic;
5. control of the activities of organs of state power and other organizations in the supplying of food and medicine to the population.

c. The Laws of the Chechen Republic will be based on respect for human rights and rights of citizens, the right of peoples to self-determination, the principles of equality of peoples, the protection of peace, international harmony and security of civilians living in the territory of the Chechen Republic, regardless of their national origin, religious denomination or other differences.

d. The joint commission will undertake its work in accordance with mutual agreement.

Appendix 2

THE RUSSIAN-CHECHEN PEACE TREATY, 12 MAY 1997

Peace Treaty and Principles of Interrelation Between Russian Federation and Chechen Republic of Ichkeria

The esteemed parties to the agreement, desiring to end their centuries-long antagonism and striving to establish firm, equal and mutually beneficial relations, hereby agree:

1. To reject forever the use of force or threat of force in resolving all matters of dispute.

2. To develop their relations on generally recognized principles and norms of international law. In doing so, the sides shall interact on the basis of specific concrete agreements.

3. This treaty shall serve as the basis for concluding further agreements and accords on the full range of relations.

4. This treaty is written on two copies and both have equal legal power.

5. This treaty is active from the day of signing.

Moscow, 12 May 1997.

(Signed)

B. Yeltsin   A. Maskhadov

President of the Russian Federation   President of the Chechen Republic of
                                              Ichkeria

Source: http://www.chechnyamfa.info/legal/1.htm

Notes

Chapter 1. The Causes of Conflict

1. I discuss this literature and its implications for the study of the conflict in Chechnya at length in Chapter 6.

2. For academic accounts see Valery Tishkov, *Ethnicity, Nationalism and Conflict in and After the Soviet Union: The Mind Aflame* (London: Sage, 1997); and John B. Dunlop, *Russia Confronts Chechnya: Roots of a Separatist Conflict* (Cambridge: Cambridge University Press, 1998).

3. The most analytical of the journalistic accounts are those by Anatol Lieven, *Chechnya: Tombstone of Russian Power* (New Haven, Conn.: Yale University Press, 1998); and Carlotta Gall and Thomas De Waal, *Chechnya: A Small Victorious War* (New York: New York University Press, 1998). I do not underestimate the bravery required to report from a war-zone, particularly one as brutal as Chechnya, but the more impressionistic "eyewitness" journalistic accounts are generally as concerned with recounting the personal experiences of the reporters as they are with reporting the conflict. See Vanora Bennett, *Crying Wolf: The Return of War to Chechnya* (London: Macmillan, 1998); Sebastian Smith, *Allah's Mountains: Politics and War in the Russian Caucasus* (London: I.B. Tauris, 1998); Yo'av Karny, *Highlanders: A Journey to the Caucasus in Quest of Memory* (New York: Farrar Straus, 2000); Chris Bird, *To Catch a Tatar: Notes from the Caucasus* (London: John Murray, 2002); Thomas Goltz, *Chechnya Diary: A War Correspondent's Story of Surviving the War in Chechnya* (New York: St. Martin's Press, 2003); Anna Politkovskaya, *A Dirty War: A Russian Reporter in Chechnya* (London: Harvill, 2001); Anne Nivat, *Chienne de Guerre: A Woman Reporter Behind the Lines of the War in Chechnya*, trans. Susan Darnton (New York: Public Affairs, 2001); Brice Fleutiaux with Alexandre Levy, *Otage en Tchétchénie* (Paris: Robert Laffont, 2001); Andrew Meier, *Chechnya: To the Heart of a Conflict* (London: W.W. Norton, 2005).

4. John Baddeley, *The Russian Conquest of the Caucasus* (London: Longman, 1908). The c*herkesska* is the long black woolen military garment of the Cherkess people. The *kinzhal* is a traditional weapon, a curved dagger, carried extensively by men in the Caucasus in the pre-modern era. Anatol Lieven describes Baddeley as "a very balanced and neutral observer" of the region and cites the following insight from Baddeley's early twentieth-century excursion to explain late twentieth-century Chechen "banditry": "Cattle lifting, highway robbery, and murder were, in this strange code, counted deeds of honor; they were openly instigated by the

village maiden—often, by the way, remarkably pretty—who scorned any pretender having no such claims to her favor; and these, together with fighting against any foe, but especially the hated Russian, were the only pursuits deemed worthy of a grown man." Anatol Lieven, "Nightmare in the Caucasus," *Washington Quarterly* 23, 1 (2000): 153–54, citing Baddeley (1908), xxxvii.

5. Karny (2000), xvi acknowledges the influence of the film.

6. See for examples the maps in Karny (2000) and Bird (2002).

7. The Chechen word *taipa* is derived from the Arabic word *ta'ifa*, meaning group or community. For an analysis of the ethnographic debates on Chechen "clans," see Christian Dettmering, "Reassessing Chechen and Ingush (Vainakh) Clan Structures in the 19th Century," *Central Asian Survey* 24, 4 (2005): 470–71.

8. Sergei Arutiunov, "Ethnicity and Conflict in the Caucasus," in Fred Wehling, ed., *Ethnic Conflict and Russian Intervention in the Caucasus*, Policy Paper 16 (San Diego: Institute on Global Conflict and Cooperation, University of California, August 1995), 17, http://www-igcc.ucsd.edu/pdf/policypapers/pp16.pdf. Arutiunov is Professor of Anthropology and Director of the Caucasus Department, Institute of Ethnology, Russian Academy of Sciences. See also Dunlop (1998), 211–12. For other widely cited romanticized Russian-centered descriptions of traditional Chechen social organization, see Yan Chesnov, "Civilization and the Chechen," *Anthropology & Archaeology of Eurasia* 34, 3 (1995–96): 28–40.

9. Lieven (1998), 331–35, 339–45.

10. The word clann in Gaelic means an expanded kin group of blood lineage extending back over many generations.

11. The term "Vainakh" provides an overarching communal ethnic and linguistic identity for the Chechens and Ingush.

12. Ekaterina Sorianskaia, "Families and Clans in Ingushetia and Chechnya: A Fieldwork Report," *Central Asian Survey* 24, 4 (2005): 453–67.

13. For an example of this type of labeling see Zelimkhan Yandarbiev, Checheniia—Bitva za sovobodu (Lviv: Svoboda narodiv, 1996), 108. Doku Zavgaev was appointed party boss in Checheno-Ingushetia in 1989, and was the Russian-appointed president of Chechnya between October 1995 and December 1996; Salambek Khadzhiev was a former Soviet minister for the oil and petrochemicals industry and was Chairman of the pro-Russia Government of National Revival in Chechnya between January 1995 and October 1995; Vakha Arsanov was a former Soviet policeman who commanded a military unit during the Russo-Chechen war of 1994–96, was appointed Vice-President of Chechnya by Maskhadov in February 1997, and was linked to the spate of kidnappings in Chechnya in 1996–98. He refused to fight against Russian forces during the second war beginning in late 1999, and was reportedly killed in a shoot-out with Russian forces in Grozny in early 2005, though more recent reports in November 2006 claim that he is a prisoner of then prime minister of Chechnya Ramzan Kadyrov.

14. A tainted yet widely used source, for example, is the chapter by the ethnic Chechen émigré writer Abdurahman Avtorkhanov, "The Chechens and the Ingush During the Soviet Period and Its Antecedents," in Marie Bennigsen-Broxup, ed., *The North Caucasus Barrier: The Russian Advance Towards the Muslim World* (London: Hurst, 1992), 146–94. See also, in particular, the work of Chesnov and Artiunov, note 8 above. For a critique of this genre see Tishkov (1997), 186–87, and Valery Tishkov, *Understanding Violence for Post-Conflict Reconstruction in Chechnya* (Geneva: CASIN, January 2001), especially the section headed "Forging the Chechens from Ethnographic Trash,"56–60; and Tishkov, *Chechnya: Life in a War-Torn Society* (Berkeley: University of California Press, 2004), 219–21.

15. See Lieven (1998); Gall and de Waal (1998); Bennett (1998). Interviewees in Chechnya, on the other hand, tended to emphasize that "Today, there is not such respect for tradition"; see Lieven (1998), 26–29.

16. Lieven (1998), 327, 329–30. A rather unfortunate analogy, given that Achilles and Aeneas were on opposing sides in the Trojan War, both were military aggressors, and indeed, Aeneas was a military colonizer and the claimed mythological antecedent of Roman empire-builders.

17. Bird (2002), 232, 247, 253, 264–65, 282.

18. Edward Said, *Orientalism: Western Conceptions of the Orient* (Harmondsworth: Penguin reprint, 1995), 6–13. My use of the concept of Orientalism follows Said, who defined it as essentially a form of cultural power that counterposes "us" (the Western observer) against "them" (the "orientals").

19. Thus, Mt. Blanc in the Alps, not Mt. Elbrus in the Caucasus, was classified as the highest mountain in Europe. It is only after the fall of communism that one sees attempts to place the Caucasus within the definition of "Europe".

20. The classic English language historical narrative of the Russian colonial advance is Baddeley (1908). For recent studies of Muslim resistance see Bennigsen-Broxup (1992); Moshe Gammer, *Muslim Resistance to the Czar: Shamil and the Conquest of Chechnia and Daghestan* (London: Frank Cass, 1994); Anna Zelkina, *In Quest for God and Freedom: The Sufi Naqshbandi Brotherhood of the North Caucasus* (London: Hurst, 1999). For a nuanced treatment see the essay by Thomas Barrett, "Crossing Boundaries: The Trading Frontiers of the Terek Cossacks," in Daniel R. Brower and Edward J. Lazzerini, eds., *Russia's Orient: Imperial Borderlands and Peoples, 1700–1917* (Bloomington: Indiana University Press, 1997), 227–48.

21. See Susan Layton, "Primitive Despot and Noble Savage: The Two Faces of Shamil in Russian Literature," *Central Asian Survey* 10, 4 (1991): 31–45.

22. See Austin Lee Jersild, "From Savagery to Citizenship: Caucasian Mountaineers and Muslims in the Russian Empire," in Brower and Lazzerini, eds. (1997), 101–14.

23. Layton (1991), 43.

24. Zelkina (1999), 69–74, 123–34. Yermolov's name has been used as a logo of terror by Russian military forces during the current conflict, for example, by painting it on armored vehicles.

25. See Samuel P. Huntington, *The Clash of Civilizations and the Remaking of World Order* (London: Touchstone Books, 1998): 254–65.

26. The term *ghazavat* refers to a concept of Islamic "holy war" that is equivalent to jihad.

27. For the Imam Mansur see Alexandre Bennigsen, "Un mouvement populaire au Caucase du XVIIIe siècle: la guerre sainte de Sheikh Mansur (1785–1794): page mal connue et controversée des relations russo-turques," *Cahiers du Monde Russe et Soviétique* 5, 2 (1964): 159–205. For Shamil's role as a jihadist see Anna Zelkina, "Jihād in the Name of God: Shaykh Shamil as the Religious Leader of the Caucasus," *Central Asian Survey* 21, 3 (2002): 249–64. A "murid" is an adept or pupil of a Sufi order.

28. For studies of Sufism in the North Caucasus see Aleksandr Bennigsen and S. Enders Wimbush, *Mystics and Commissars: Sufism in the Soviet Union* (London: Hurst, 1985); Austin Lee Jersild, "Who Was Shamil? Russian Colonial Rule and Sufi Islam in the North Caucasus, 1859–1917," *Central Asian Survey* 14, 2 (1995): 205–23; and Zelkina (1999).

29. There are no reliable data on the numbers of the Chechen diaspora. Recent estimates indicate that there are as many as 100,000 in Turkey, 8,000 in Jordan,

5,000 in Egypt, 4,000 in Syria, and 2,500 in Iraq. See Wasfi Kailani, "Chechens in the Middle East: Between Original and Host Cultures," Caspian Studies Program, 2002, Belfer Center for Science and International Affairs, Kennedy School of Government, Harvard University), http://bcsia.ksg.harvard.edu/publication.cfm?ctype=event_reports&item_id=98.

30. For an account see Aleksandr Bennigsen, "Muslim Guerrilla Warfare in the Caucasus, 1918–1928," *Central Asian Survey* 2, 2 (1983): 280–94.

31. For a detailed account of the deportation see Dunlop (1998).

32. Alexander Solzhenitsyn. *The Gulag Archipelago*, vol. 3 (Boulder, Colo.: Westview, 1998), 402.

33. It was at this time that two steppe districts (Shelkovskii and Naurskii *raions*), mainly populated by ethnic Russians, were transferred to Checheno-Ingushetia from Stavropolskii Krai in an attempt to dilute the ethnic Chechen majority. The Prigorodny area of Ingushetia, which had been transferred to North Ossetia, was not returned to the newly restored republic—something that has remained a source of grievance for the Chechens and Ingush to the present day.

34. Suzanne Goldenberg, *Pride of Small Nations: The Caucasus and Post-Soviet Disorder* (London: Zed Books, 1994).

35. For an analysis of demographic changes see Dunlop (1998), 85–88.

36. Michael Rywkin, "The Communist Party and the Sufi Tariqat in the Checheno-Ingush Republic," *Central Asian Survey* 10, 1–2 (1991): 134.

37. See Aleksandr Bennigsen and S. Enders Wimbush, *Muslims of the Soviet Empire: A Guide* (Bloomington: Indiana University Press, 1986), 181ff; Rywkin (1991), 134–36.

38. Rywkin (1991), 145, note 14. This cites a speech by *obkom* secretary V. K. Foteev of October 13, 1985.

39. This norm was substantiated by quantitative analysis. See John H. Miller, "Cadres Policy in Nationality Areas: Recruitment of CPSU First and Second Secretaries in Non-Russian Republics of the USSR," *Soviet Studies* 29, 1 (1977): 3–36.

40. Rywkin (1991), 137–38.

41. See Donald L. Horowitz, *A Democratic South Africa? Constitutional Engineering in a Divided Society* (Berkeley: University of California Press, 1991), 2.

42. *Izvestiia*, 14 April, 1990: 1–2; 16 April 1990: 1–2; 3 May 1990: 1–2.

43. The law has also been employed as a justification for the secessions of other autonomous regions, such as the Autonomous Area of Nagorno-Karabagh from Azerbaijan.

44. For the RSFSR declaration of sovereignty see *Argumenty i fakty*, 16 June 1990: 1.

45. For the issue of local and regional "sovereignty" in 1990–92 see the study by Tomila V. Lankina, *Governing the Locals: Local Self-Government and Ethnic Mobilization in Russia* (Oxford: Rowman and Littlefield, 2004). Yeltsin's now legendary comment was made at meetings in Bashkortostan and Tatarstan.

46. Mikhail Gorbachev, *Memoirs* (London: Doubleday, 1996), 688. Gorbachev recalls the warning in the part of his memoirs that deal with the conflict in Chechnya.

47. From an account by Gorbachev's main legal advisor, Yuri Baturin, of the final negotiations leading to the signing of the treaty on 23 July 1991. See Yuri Baturin, "Chess-Like Diplomacy at Novo-Ogarevo. An Eye-Witness Account to the Drafting of the USSR Union Treaty of 1991," *Demokratizatsiia* 2, 2 (1994): 213. Baturin became one of Yeltsin's key advisors after the collapse of the USSR.

48. Gorbachev, *Zhizn' i reformy*, vol. 2 (Moscow: Novosti, 1995), 533–54. The statement was published in *Pravda*, 24 April 1991: 1.

49. The draft Union treaty was published in late June. See *Izvestiia*, 27 June 1991: 2.

50. For these discussions see Baturin (1994).

51. Chernobyl' sparked ecological protest movements that focused initially on nuclear issues and then quickly expanded into wider political issues; see Jane I. Dawson, *Eco-Nationalism: Anti-Nuclear Activism and National Identity in Russia, Lithuania, and Ukraine* (Durham, N.C.: Duke University Press, 1996).

52. For political developments in Chechnya during perestroika see Timur Muzaev, *Chechenskaia Respublika: organy vlasti i politicheskie sily* (Moscow: Panorama, 1995), 157–61; and his *V preddverii nezavisimosti* (Grozny: Groznenskii rabochii, 1994), 7–15.

53. Yandarbiev (1994), 9.

54. See Yandarbiev (1994), (1996).

55. For the secular basis of Yandarbiev's thinking on national identity at this time see his articles "Kavkazskost'" (1990), "Istoki (natsionnal'nyi vopros: problemy i suzhdeniia)" (May 1991), and "Suti i aspekty natsional'nogo edinstva" (June 1991) in Yandarbiev (1996), 387–418. Yandarbiev was assassinated by Russian FSB agents in Qatar in February 2004.

56. See Yandarbiev (1994), 27–30; Dunlop (1998), 92–93; Gall and de Waal (1998),82–83.

57. Tatarstan's declaration of 1990 is available on the web at http://www.tatar.ru/DNSID=4321f481771c57f4d8b8d312fe7c37ce&node_id=234

58. For the declaration of sovereignty see Muzaev (1995), 159–60; Tishkov (1997), 199–200.

59. See Alla Dudaeva, *Million pervyi* (Baku: Zeinalov & Synov'ia, 2002), 63–64. Dudaev, according to his wife, did not accept the position immediately but thought about it overnight.

60. See Muzaev (1995), 68. For Dudaev's career see Dunlop (1998), 97–98; Gall and de Waal (1998), 86–88.

61. Gall and de Waal (1998), 82; Lieven (1998), 58.

62. Yandarbiev (1994), 30–31. According to Galina Starovoitova, Dudaev provided a car and driver to take Yeltsin back to Moscow and avoid a security threat to his plane. See Gall and de Waal (1998), 88–89.

63. See Gail Lapidus, "Contested Sovereignty: The Tragedy of Chechnya," *International Security* 23, 1 (1998): 10, 15.

64. Reported by Baturin (1994), 214.

65. Tracey C. German, *Russia's Chechen War* (London: Routledge, 2003), 31.

66. Muzaev (1995), 130–31.

67. Dunlop (1998), 95; Gall and de Waal (1998), 92–93. Lieven describes the ignorance and embarrassment of Gantemirov on his being interviewed about his "Islamic" ideas in early 1992; Lieven (1998), 364. Dudaev, after a later rift with Gantemirov, declared him to be a "criminal"; see Aleksandr Sargin and Valerii Batuev, "Dzhokhar Dudaev: 'brat' siloi chechentzev—zanyatie bessmyslennoe," *Argumenty i fakty* 49, 7 (December 1994): 1.

68. For an account of Dudaev's seizure of power see Flemming Splidsboel-Hansen, "The 1991 Chechen Revolution: The Response of Moscow," *Central Asian Survey* 13, 3 (1994): 395–407. For a detailed discussion of the impact of the Chechnya issue in Russian politics in the early 1990s see William Hayden, "The

Political Genesis of Conflict in Chechnya, 1990–1994," *Civil Wars* 2, 4 (1999): 23–56. Tishkov reports secret testimony by the Russian head of the KGB in Chechnya at the time, Igor Kochubei, to the Russian Security Council in 1995 that claimed Dudaev's uprising was coordinated by telephone conversations between Dudaev, Khasbulatov and Aslanbek Aslakhanov (an influential Moscow-based Chechen politician who then headed the RSFSR Supreme Soviet's Committee on Legislative and Criminal Affairs, and later became Putin's appointee as president of Chechnya): Tishkov (1997), 201–2.

69. See Dunlop (1998), 106–7.

70. Chechen Electoral Commission data are reported in Dunlop (1998), 114.

71. For the decrees see *Izvestiia*, 5 November 1991: 2. For Dudaev's use of the term *nezavisimost'* see "Odinokii volk pod lunoi," *Izvestiia*, 1 November 1991: 8. A report in *Pravda* poked fun at Yeltsin's earlier encouragement for republics to "swallow" as much sovereignty as they wanted: "Suverenitet ne glotaetsia" (Choking on Sovereignty)," *Pravda*, 11 November 1991: 1.

72. *Izvestiia*, 1 November 1991: 8; 12 November, 1991: 1.

73. *Izvestiia*, 13 November, 1991: 1.

74. Valery Tishkov "Ethnic Conflicts in the Former USSR: The Use and Misuse of Typologies and Data." *Journal of Peace Research* 36, 5 (1999): 585.

75. Iurii Bespalov. "*Oruzhie sdali po prikazu moskvy*," *Izvestiia*, 14 January 1995; Valerii Yakov. "*Svidetelia luchshe ubrat'*," *Izvestiia*, 14 January 1995; Viktor Khlystun. "*Tochka zreniia. Pavel Grachev: 'Menia naznachili otvetstvennym za voinu'*," *Trud*, 15 March 2001.

76. Tishkov (1997), 207. For similar figures see Muzaev (1995), 28–29.

77. See Stasys Knezys and Romanas Sedlickas, *The War in Chechnya* (College Station: Texas A&M University Press, 1999), 36–38.

78. See Robert Seely, *Russo-Chechen Conflict, 1800–2000: A Deadly Embrace* (London: Frank Cass, 2001), 212–15. Rutskoi claimed that even weapons from the Trans-Baikal Military District were sold illicitly to Dudaev: see Tishkov (1997), 207.

79. Telephone interview with Dudaev, *Agence France-Presse*, 8 November 1991; *Nezavisimaia gazeta*, 12 November 1991: 3.

80. Testimony of Ruslan Khasbulatov and then Vice-President Aleksandr Rutskoi at the Public Hearings of the State Duma Commission on the Investigation of the Events in the Chechen Republic, 20 February 1995, reported in Tishkov (1997), 206. See also Dunlop (1998), 118–20.

81. See "Russia's Future:Whither the Flying Troika," *The Economist*, 7 December 1991: 19.

82. Yandarbiev famously articulated his anathema toward the Russians in verse. For example, his poems included lines such as "unwashed you were, and unwashed you remain," and reference to Russia as a "Bitch." See Yandarbiev (1996), 443, 486.

Chapter 2. Russia's Refederalization and Chechnya's Secession

1. These theories are discussed in Chapter 6.

2. The literature on the danger of an "ethnic" fragmentation and break-up of Russia is immense. For examples see Steven Solnick, "The Political Economy of Russian Federalism: A Framework for Analysis," *Problems of Post-Communism* (November/December 1996): 13–25; Solnick, "Will Russia Survive? Center and Periphery in the Russian Federation," in Barnett Rubin and Jack Snyder, eds.,

Post-Soviet Political Order: Conflict and State-Building (London: Routledge, 1998), 58–80; Solnick, "Is the Center Too Weak or Too Strong in the Russian Federation," in Valerie Sperling, ed., *Building the Russian State: Institutional Crisis and the Quest for Democratic Governance* (Boulder, Colo.: Westview Press, 2000), 137–56. Yeltsin's tolerant approach to decentralization was most criticized by those who wanted a strong center as a platform for the implementation of neoliberal economic reforms: see Daniel Treisman, "The Politics of Intergovernmental Transfers in Post-Soviet Russia," *British Journal of Political Science* 26 (1996): 299–335; Treisman, "Deciphering Russia's Federal Finance: Fiscal Appeasement in 1995 and 1996," *Europe-Asia Studies* 50, 5 (1995): 893–906; Treisman, "Fiscal Redistribution in a Fragile Federation: Moscow and the Regions in 1994," *British Journal of Political Science* 28 (1998): 185–209, and his book length treatment of the subject *After the Deluge: Regional Crises and Political Consolidation in Russia* (Ann Arbor: University of Michigan Press, 1999).

3. Tatarstan did briefly send a delegation to the Constitutional Assembly in July 1993, but it soon walked out when it became apparent that the proposed constitution would be highly symmetric and entrench ethnic Russian hegemony.

4. For an analysis of Russian federal relations that focuses on the stabilizing advantages of asymmetric federalism see James Hughes, "Managing Secession Potential in the Russian Federation," in James Hughes and Gwendolyn Sasse, eds., *Ethnicity and Territory in the Former Soviet Union: Regions in Conflict* (London: Frank Cass, 2002), 36–68.

5. See Jonathan Lemco, *Political Stability in Federal Governments* (New York: Praeger, 1991).

6. For the ethnodemographic structure see *SSSR v tsifrakh v 1989g.*, 23–25; *Argumenty i fakty* 13 (March 1991): 1.

7. The Federal Treaty of February 1992 recognized 20 ethnically designated "republics," 16 of which were inherited from the autonomous republics of the RSFSR (Bashkortostan, Buriatia, Checheno-Ingushetia, Chuvashia, Dagestan, Kabardino-Balkar, Kalmykia, Karelia, Komi, Marii El, Mordovia, North Ossetia-Alania, Sakha (Yakutia), Tatarstan, Tuva, Udmurtia), and four were upgraded from autonomous oblasts of the RSFSR (Adygeia, Altai, Karachai-Cherkess, Khakassia).

8. By 1994 the Russian population in these eleven republics was as follows: Karelia (73.6 percent), Buriatia (69.9 percent), Adygeia (67.9 percent), Mordova (60.8 percent), Altai (60.4 percent), Urdmutia (58.9 percent), Komi (57.7 percent), Sakha (Yakutia) (50.3 percent), Marii El (47.5 percent), Karachai-Cherkess (42.4 percent), Bashkortostan (39.3 percent). See V. A. Tishkov, ed., *Narody Rossii, Entsiklopediia* (Moscow: Bol'shaia Rossiiskaia Entsiklopediia, 1994), 433–35.

9. For debates about the role of the nomenklatura in the new structures see Olga Kryshtanovskaya and Stephen White, "From Soviet *Nomenklatura* to Russian Elite," *Europe-Asia Studies* 48, 5 (1997): 711–34; James Hughes, "Sub-National Elites and Political Transformation in Russia: A Reply to Krystanovskaya and White," *Europe-Asia Studies* 49, 6 (1997): 1017–36.

10. This argument is elaborated with case studies in Mary McAuley, *Russia's Politics of Uncertainty* (Cambridge: Cambridge University Press, 1997).

11. Lesotho, a British "protectorate" until independence in 1966, is surrounded by the Republic of South Africa, and effectively reverted to that status after a South African military intervention in September 1998.

12. The Russian Far East was briefly a nominally independent republic in 1919–22, though under Japanese occupation.

13. Laurence Hanauer, "Tatarstan and the Prospects for Federalism in Russia: A Commentary," *Security Dialogue* 27, 1 (1996): 82.

14. Boris Yeltsin, *Midnight Diaries* (London: Weidenfeld and Nicolson, 2000), 336.

15. In 1993–95 I participated in several Russo-American conferences on federalism held in Novosibirsk under the auspices of the USAID program and attended by leading specialists on federalism from Russia and the U.S. There was almost universal antipathy to the concept of "ethnic " autonomy and I was alone in proposing that an asymmetric federal model would be stabilizing for Russia.

16. See Graham Smith, "Russia, Multiculturalism and Federal Justice," *Europe-Asia Studies* 50, 8 (1998): 1397.

17. See Hughes, "Managing Secession Potential" (2002).

18. For a detailed discussion of the legislative changes and terminology see Jeffrey Kahn. *Federalism, Democratization and the Rule of Law in Russia* (Oxford: Oxford University Press, 2002), 83–122.

19. See Kahn (2002), 134–35.

20. See *Federativnyi Dogovor: Dokumenty, Kommentarii* (Moscow: Izdatel'stvo Respublika, 1992).

21. For the political bargaining around federal developments at this time see Hughes. "Managing Secession Potential" (2002); Darrell Slider, "Federalism, Discord, and Accommodation: Intergovernmental elations in Post-Soviet Russia," in Theodore Friedgut and Jeffrey Hahn, eds., *Local Power and Post-Soviet Politics* (Armonk, N.Y.: M.E. Sharpe, 1994), 239–69; Robert Sharlet, "The Prospects for Federalism in Russian Constitutional Politics," *Publius: The Journal of Federalism* 24 (1994): 115–27; Gail W. Lapidus and Edward W. Walker, "Nationalism, Regionalism, and Federalism: Center-Periphery Relations in Post-Communist Russia," in Gail Lapidus, ed., *Russia's Troubled Transition* (Cambridge: Cambridge University Press, 1995), 79–113.

22. See Hughes, "Managing Secession Potential" (2002); and Slider (1994), 247–48.

23. See James Hughes, "Regionalism in Russia: The Rise and Fall of Siberian Agreement," *Europe-Asia Studies* 46, 7 (1994): 1133–62.

24. See the work of a close advisor to president Shaimiev in Tatarstan, Raphael S. Khakimov, "Ob osnovakh asimmetrichnosti Rossiiskoi Federatsii," in Leokadiia M. Drobizheva, ed., *Asimmetrichnaia federatsiia: vzgliad iz tsentra, respublik i oblastei* (Moscow: Izdatel'stvo Instituta Sotsiologii RAN, 1998), 40.

25. The result of the constitutional referendum was almost certainly falsified by the Yeltsin administration. It legally required a 50 percent turnout of registered voters, which almost certainly did not occur. It is even doubted that the referendum secured the majority of votes. See Stephen White, Richard Rose, and Ian McAllister, *How Russia Votes* (Chatham, N.J.: Chatham House, 1997), 98–101, 126–29.

26. *Konstitutsiia Rossiiskoi Federatsii* (Moscow: Nauchnoe Izdatel'stvo, 1995), 266, 278–84.

27. For discussions of paid advertising in the 1993 election see James Hughes, "The 'Americanization' of Russian Politics: Russia's First Television Election, December 1993," *Journal of Communist Studies and Transition Politics* 10, 2 (1994): 125–50, and Ellen Mickiewicz, *Changing Channels. Television and the Struggle for Power in Russia* (Oxford: Oxford University Press, 1997), 154–64, 216.

28. *Konstitutsiia Rossiiskoi Federatsii*, 287.

29. Author's conversations with a senior presidential adviser on nationalities

and regional policy (and member of the presidential council) in Russia during various visits in 1994–96. Sergei Shakhrai, deputy prime minister for nationalities and regional policy, was the chief negotiator, although he was the leading proponent of equalized status for federal subjects.

30. *Konstitutsiia Rossiiskoi Federatsii*, 267.

31. See Kahn (2002), 151–57.

32. *Rossiskaia gazeta*, 18 February 1994; Mikhail N. Guboglo, ed., *Federalizm vlasti i vlast' federalizma* (Moscow: IntelTekh, 1997), 416–38. The treaty between the Russian Federation and Tatarstan, including the codicils, has been published on the official website of the Republic of Tatarstan: http://www.tatar.ru

33. *Segodnia* 17 February 1994, 31 May 1994.

34. As Yeltsin widened the bilateral treaty process to less powerful republics and regions, it became a more formulaic process. In general, the later treaties simply reproduced Article 72 of the 1993 Constitution, often verbatim. A presidential decree of 12 March 1996 established a standardized "rubber-stamp" format and a specific vocabulary for the later treaties. See *Sobranie zakonodatel'stva Rossiiskoi Federatisii* (Moscow: Iuridicheskaia literatura 1996): 12, 1058.

35. For the constitution of Tatarstan see *Konstitutsii Respublik v sostave Rossiiskoi Federatsii*, vol. 1. (Moscow: Izdanie Gosudarstvennoi Dumy, Izvestia, 1995).

36. Hughes, "Managing Secession Potential" (2002), 55.

37. *Vash Vybor* 5 (1993): 10.

38. Guboglo (1997), 652 et passim.

39. Galina Chinarikhina, "Dogovor kak sposob razgranicheniia polnomochii i predmetov vedeniia mezhdu subektami federativnykh otnoshenii v Rossii," *Vlast'* 9 (1996): 24.

40. *Rossiiskaia federatsiia* 3 (1995): 22–23.

41. Author's interview with Anatolii Sychev, then head of the Federation Council's Committee on Federal Affairs and Regional Policy, Novosibirsk, August 1997.

42. For the classic statement of this position see Juan Linz, "The Perils of Presidentialism," *Journal of Democracy* 1, 1 (1990): 51–69.

43. Guillermo O'Donnell, "Delegative Democracy," *Journal of Democracy* 5, 1 (1994): 55–69.

44. Donald Horowitz, "Democracy in Divided Societies: The Challenge of Ethnic Conflict," *Journal of Democracy* 4, 4 (1993): 18–38.

45. For the original statement of this thesis see Charles Tarlton, "Symmetry and Asymmetry as Elements of Federalism: A Theoretical Speculation," *Journal of Politics* 27, 4 (1965): 861–74.

46. For this argument see Svante E. Cornell, "Autonomy as a Source of Conflict: Caucasian Conflicts in Theoretical Perspective," *World Politics* 54, 2 (2002): 245–76; and his *Small Nations and Great Powers: A Study of Ethnopolitical Conflict in the Caucasus* (London: Curzon, 2001).

47. For Russian views see Irina Busygina, "Regional'noe izmerenie politicheskogo krisisa v rossii," *MEMO* 5 (1994): 5–17; Airat R. Aklaev. *Democratization and Ethnic Peace: Patterns of Ethnopolitical Crisis and Management in Post-Soviet Settings* (Aldershot: Ashgate, 1999); Mikhail A. Alexeev, ed., *Center-Periphery Conflict in Post-Soviet Russia: A Federation Imperiled* (London: Macmillan, 1999). For Western perspectives taking this approach see Joan DeBardeleben, "The Development of Federalism in Russia," in Peter J. Stavrakis, Joan DeBardeleben, and Larry Black, eds., *Beyond the Monolith: The Emergence of Regionalism in Post-Soviet Russia* (Washington, D.C.: Woodrow Wilson Center Press, 1997), 35–56; Kahn (2002), and the works cited in note 2.

48. See Christine I. Wallich, *Fiscal Decentralization: Intergovernmental Relations in Russia*, Studies of Economies in Transformation Paper 6 (Washington, D.C.: World Bank, 1992); Wallich, ed., *Russia and the Challenge of Fiscal Federalism* (Washington D.C.: World Bank, 1994); Wallich, "Reforming Intergovernmental Relations, Russia and The Challenge of Fiscal Federalism," in Bartlomiej Kaminski, ed., *Economic Transition in Russia and the New States of Eurasia* (Armonk, N.Y.: M.E. Sharpe, 1997), 252–76; Roy Bahl and Christine I. Wallich, "Intergovernmental Fiscal Relations in the Russian Federation," in Richard M. Bird, Robert D. Ebel, and Christine I. Wallich, eds., *Decentralization of the Socialist State* (Washington, D.C.: World Bank, 1995).

49. This was the view of Solnick (see note 2).

50. Peter Ordeshook, "Reexamining Russia: Institutions and Incentives," *Journal of Democracy* 6, 2 (1995): 46–60.

51. The term originated with the Spanish *fueros* of the Middle Ages, whereby the state gave certain localities preferential or exceptional powers enshrined in a charter or treaty. The term "federalism" itself, however, is derived from the Latin *foedus* meaning "treaty." See Daniel J. Elazar, *Exploring Federalism* (Tuscaloosa: University of Alabama Press, 1987), 59.

52. Irina A. Umnova, *Konstitutsionnye osnovy sovremennogo Rossiiskogo Federalizma* (Moscow: Delo, 1996), 80–82. The author was a legal specialist and Chief Consultant to the Russian Constitutional Court at this time, and the book was an official text for the Ministry of Justice.

53. Chinarikhina (1996), 20–25; Solnick (1998), 61.

54. Alfred Stepan, "Russian Federalism in Comparative Perspective," *Post-Soviet Affairs* 16, 2 (2000): 133–76.

55. See Smith (1998).

56. Andrei Shleifer and Daniel Treisman, *Without a Map: Political Tactics and Economic Reform in Russia* (Cambridge, Mass.: MIT Press, 2000), 135.

57. Ivo Duchacek, *Comparative Federalism: The Territorial Dimension of Politics* (New York: Holt, Rinehart and Winston, 1970).

58. See Janine R. Wedel, "Tainted Transactions: Harvard, the Chubais Clan, and Russia's Ruin," *National Interest* 59 (2000): 23–34.

59. See Gwendolyn Sasse, "The Theory and Practice of Conflict-Prevention in a Transition State: The Crimean Issue in Post-Soviet Ukraine," *Nationalism and Ethnic Politics* 8, 2 (2002): 1–26.

Chapter 3. A Secular Nationalist Conflict

1. See Eberhard Schneider, "Moscow's Decision for War in Chechnya," *Aussenpolitik* 46, 2 (1995): 157–67; Michael McFaul, "Eurasian Letter: Russian Politics After Chechnya," *Foreign Policy* 99 (1995): 149–68.

2. Gail Lapidus, "Contested Sovereignty: The Tragedy of Chechnya," *International Security* 23, 1 (1998): 13.

3. Matthew Evangelista, *The Chechen Wars: Will Russia Go the Way of the Soviet Union?* (Washington, D.C.: Brookings Institution Press, 2002), 6–9.

4. These positions are repeated throughout his latest work: Valery A. Tishkov, *Chechnya: Life in a War-Torn Society* (Berkeley: University of California Press, 2004). He argues that "over the course of three years [1991–94], an illegitimate, unconstitutional regime, backed by force, imposed itself on Chechnya as the result of an armed coup d'état" (68); "before 1991, Chechens had defined themselves as

Soviet citizens," and "neither their ethnic identity nor the fact of deportation constituted a central element of their identity" (219); "Foreign scholarship continues to be hampered by antipathy to 'neo-imperial,' or 'mini-imperial,' Russia and a justification of armed separatism in Chechnya" (226).

5. Tishkov was chairman of what was then the State Committee on Nationality Policy (Goskomnats) from March 1992 until his resignation in October 1992. The state committee was upgraded to a full-fledged Ministry for Nationalities and Regional Policy, and Tishkov was replaced by Sergei Shakhrai.

6. The "clash of personality" thesis was first reported by Tishkov in Valery A. Tishkov, Yelena Belyaeva, and Georgi Marchenko, *Chechenskii krizis* (Moscow: Business Roundtable of Russia Research Center, 1995), 29, 33. The conversation with Shaimiev is restated in Valery Tishkov, *Ethnicity, Nationalism and Conflict in and After the Soviet Union: The Mind Aflame* (London: Sage, 1997), 187.

7. Tishkov (1997), 214.

8. Interview with Galina Starovoitova, *Moskovskii komsomolets*, 29 January 1995.

9. From a speech by Khasbulatov of 11 September 1994 cited in Tishkov (1997), 217.

10. See John B. Dunlop, *Russia Confronts Chechnya: Roots of a Separatist Conflict* (Cambridge: Cambridge University Press, 1998), 215–19; Anatol Lieven, *Chechnya: Tombstone of Russian Power* (New Haven, Conn.: Yale University Press, 1998), 76; Carlotta Gall and Thomas De Waal, *Chechnya: A Small Victorious War* (New York: New York University Press, 1998), 145–46; Vanora Bennett, *Crying Wolf: The Return of War to Chechnya* (London: Macmillan, 1998), 313–14.

11. Dunlop (1998), 216.

12. The "evil Chechen" was a motif of Russian nineteenth-century literature, notably in the work of Lermontov. See Harsha Ram and Anna Wertz, *Prisoners of the Caucasus: Literary Myths and Media Representations in the Chechen Conflict* (Berkeley: Berkeley Program in Soviet and Post-Soviet Studies, University of California, 1999), 3–4.

13. For vignettes of Yeltsin in the 1990s see Aleksandr Vasil'evich Korzhakov, *Boris El'tsin: ot rassveta do zakata* (Moscow: Interbuk, 1997).

14. Boris Yeltsin, *Zapiski presidenta* (Moscow: Ogonek, 1994), 286; and his *The View from the Kremlin* (London: HarperCollins, 1994), 186.

15. Viacheslav Kostikov, *Roman s prezidentom: zapiski press-sekretaria* (Moscow: Vagrius, 1997), 111.

16. Aleksandr Sargin and Valerii Batuev, "Dzhokhar Dudaev: 'brat,' siloi chechentzev—zanyatie bessmyslennoe," *Argumenty i fakty* 49 (7 December 1994): 1.

17. *Moskovskie novosti* 29 March 1992

18. Given Russian antipathy to Chechens, it is rumored that Dudaev's mother forced him to put "Ossetian" as his ethnicity on his air force application form, in order to secure entry, thus demonstrating his pragmatic understanding of ethnic identity.

19. See Tishkov (1997), 200.

20. Lieven (1998), 148; Gall and de Wall (1998), 84.

21. Official Kremlin International News Broadcast, August 12, 1992; Sargin and Batuev (1994), 1.

22. Tishkov (2004), 80–82.

23. See, for example, Emil Pain and Arkadii Popov, "Chechenskaia tragediia," *Izvestiia*, 23–26, 7–10 February 1995; Dunlop (1998), 126–28.

24. In May 1992 Dudaev introduced a military draft for all eighteen-year-old men for a period of one and a half years; see *Itar Tass*, 5 May 1992.

25. Tishkov (1999), 585–86.

26. Tishkov (1997), 211–12.

27. *Kommersant* 101, 6 January 1992: 6.

28. See Robert Seely, *Russo-Chechen Conflict, 1800–2000: A Deadly Embrace* (London: Frank Cass, 2001), 212–15.

29. Lieven (1998), 74–75. Citing Russian sources, Lieven states that Dudaev's government took from between 300 million to one billion dollars from oil revenues, most of it extrabudgetary.

30. Zelimkhan Yandarbiev, *Checheniia—Bitva za sovobodu* (Lviv: Svoboda narodiv, 1996), 148–49, 251, 289–90. Yandarbiev claimed that two million tones of oil products worth about $230–250 million "disappeared" from the Grozneft accounts during the first six months of 1992 alone.

31. See the report by John Lloyd, *Financial Times* (London), November 12, 1991: 24; *Argumenty i fakty* (4 November 1991): 8. At a conference in Paris in July 2001, the author heard Valery Tishkov complain during a paper presentation about Dudaev's Islamism, based on the fact that he swore his oath of office on the Qur'an. Of course, the constitution did not exist when Dudaev was elected in October 1991, and we should no more attach significance to his swearing an oath on the Qur'an than we would to any politician doing so on the Bible.

32. *Konstitutsiia chechenskoi respubliki*, Grozny, 12 March 1992. For Russian and English language versions see Diane Curran, Fiona Hill, and Elena Kostritsyna, *The Search for Peace in Chechnya: A Sourcebook 1994–1996* (Cambridge, Mass.: Harvard University, John F. Kennedy School of Government. Strengthening Democratic Institutions Project, 1997), 101–41. A rather poor translation into English is available at http://www.oefre.unibe.ch/law/icl/cc01000_.html. For a Russian version, including amendments in 1996 and 1997, see http://www.chechen.org

33. International Alert, *Chechnia: Report of an International Alert fact-finding mission, September 24th–October 3rd 1992* (London: International Alert, 1992).

34. Article 4 was amended to make Islam the official state religion only in February 1999, see Chapter 4.

35. See Dzhokhar Dudaev, *Ternistii put' k svobode* (Vilnius, 1993), 141, cited in Tracey C. German, *Russia's Chechen War* (London: Routledge, 2003), 59.

36. Interview with Dudaev, Official Kremlin International News Broadcast, 12 August 1992.

37. Svante Cornell, *Small Nations and Great Powers: A Study of Ethnopolitical Conflict in the Caucasus* (London: Curzon, 2001), 215.

38. Dudaev's statement as reported in *Itar-Tass*, 31 March 1992.

39. Lieven (1998), 363.

40. These views were outlined in Dzhokhar Dudaev, *K voprosu o gosudarstvenno-politicheskom ustroistve v chechenskoi respubliki* (Grozny: Groznenskii rabochii, 1993), 3–16.

41. See *Sbornik ukazov presidenta chechenskoi respubliki s 1 iiulia 1992 g. po 31 dekabria 1992 g.* (Grozny: Kniga, 1993) and *Sbornik rasporiazhenii i postanovlenii presidenta chechenskoi respubliki* (Grozny: Kniga, 1993).

42. Boris Yeltsin, *Midnight Diaries* (London: Weidenfeld and Nicolson, 2000), 54.

43. See Huntington (1998), 245 (fig. 9.1), 276–77.

44. Aleksei Malashenko and Dmitrii Trenin, *Vremia Iuga: Rossiia v Chechne, Chechne v Rossii* (Moscow: Gendal'f, Carnegie Center Moscow, 2002), 73.

45. See Muzaev (1995), 165–66.

46. Yandarbiev (1996), 146–47.

47. See Galina Starovoitova, *Sovereignty After Empire: Self-Determination Movements in the Former Soviet Union* (Washington, D.C.: U.S. Institute of Peace, 1997), 11–15.

48. International Alert (1992).

49. Testimony of Gaidar to the Duma Commission of Investigation into events in the Chechen Republic, 20 February 1995, reported in Tishkov (1997), 210.

50. These episodes are reported, though with a negative assessment, in Tishkov (1997), 208–9, 213.

51. For a well-informed analysis of these attempts at negotiations see Märta-Lisa Magnusson, "The Negotiation Process between Russia and Chechenia—Strategies, Achievements, and Future Problems," in Ole Høiris and Sefa Martin Yürukel, eds., *Contrasts and Solutions in the Caucasus* (Aarhus: Aarhus University Press, 1998). The author was a co-rapporteur for the International Alert fact-finding mission of 1992 (see note 33).

52. Yandarbiev (1996), 127–28, 142–45.

53. Tishkov (1997), 213.

54. For a description of Dudaev's mental state see Lieven (1998), 65–70. Lieven attributes the unstable behavior to Dudaev's personality flaws rather than the pressure under which he was operating.

55. The term originated in the discussion that led to the 1993 Oslo Accords between Israel and the PLO. The concept was taken up by negotiators in other conflicts, most notably by Irish and British civil servants in the long build-up to the Belfast Agreement of 1998.

56. *Segodnia*, February 17, 1994.

57. Schneider (1995), 158–63.

58. *Argumenty i fakty* 49 (7 September 1994): 1.

59. Tishkov (1999), 586.

60. See Dmitrii Shevchenko, *Kremlevskie nravy* (Moscow: Kollektsiia Sovershenno sekretno, 1999); Korzhakov (1997), 371.

61. See the interview in *Izvestiia*, 21 August 1993.

62. See the interview in *Segodnia* 31 May 1994.

63. See the interview in *Moskovskie novosti* 31 July–7 August 1994.

64. Sargin and Batuev (1994), 1.

65. Viktor Khlystun interview with Grachev, *Trud*, 15 March 2001: 8.

66. For the decree and decision to invade see "President ne smog iskluchit vozmozhnost razreshenia voznikaushikh problem cherez nasilie v kakikh by to ni bylo formakh," *Moskovskie novosti* 63 (11–18 December 1994): 1.

67. Gall and de Waal (1998), 160. Reputedly, the comment was made by Lobov, the secretary of the Security Council, who drew comparisons between the invasion of Chechnya and President Clinton's plan to use military force against the military regime in Haiti in September 1994. In fact, the comparison was more of a rhetorical device, since the U.S. aim was to implement UN Security Council resolution 940 of 31 July 1994 which determined "to use all necessary means" to restore the democratically elected government of Jean-Bertrand Aristide, which had been overthrown in a military coup in January 1991. The military regime dissolved without a fight on 18 September, and U.S. forces were "invited" into Haiti to support the consolidation of the new Aristide government.

68. For the categorization of positions and their main adherents see Andrew Bennett, *Condemned to Repetition? The Rise, Fall, and Reprise of Soviet-Russian Military Interventionism, 1973–1996*, BCSIA Studies in International Security (Cambridge, Mass.: MIT Press, 1999), 306–10, 328–33.

69. Sergei Kovalev, *Proposals for a Peace Process*, 24 March 1995, http://asf.wdn.com/

70. For the role of television in the war see Mickiewicz (1997), 9–10, 244–63.

71. Kostikov cited in Gall and de Waal (1998), 154.

72. Starovoitova (1995): 13.

73. *Moskovskie novosti* 23–30 July 1995, 6.

74. For details of the military divisions see Viktor Khlystun interview with Grachev, *Trud*, 15 March 2001; Lieven (1998), 105–6.

75. For the decision of the Constitutional Court see T. G. Morshchakova, ed., *Konstitutsionnyi sud rossiiskoi federatsii, postanovleniia opredeleniia 1992–1996* (Moscow: Novyi Iurist, 1997), 609–28. For an analysis of the case decision see Paola Gaeta, "The Armed Conflict in Chechnya Before the Russian Constitutional Court," *European Journal of International Law* 7, 4 (1996): 563–70.

76. *Itar-Tass*, 23 October 1992; *Oil & Gas Journal*, 9 November 1992: 34; Yandarbiev (1996), 203.

77. For example, the murder of the Utsiev brothers, business associates of Dudaev's government, in London in February 1993 unleashed a storm of negative media comment about Chechnya. See Gall and de Waal (1998), 132–34.

78. See Paul Sampson, "Politics of the Pipeline," *Prospect* 17 (March 1997); Paul Klebnikov, *Godfather of the Kremlin: Boris Berezovsky and the Looting of Russia* (New York: Harcourt, 2000), 258–59, based largely on the views of Lebed. Lukoil came into conflict with Russian foreign policy when it was enticed by Azerbaijan's president Aliev to join the AIOC with a 10 per cent share in 1995. It sold its stake to Japan's Inpex in November 2002.

79. Viktor Khlystun interview with Grachev, *Trud*, 15 March 2001: 8.

80. Lebed comment in an interview with Klebnikov: see Klebnikov (2000), 41–42.

81. See Schneider (1995); Vladimir Mau, *Yeltsin's Choice: Background to the Chechnya Crisis* (London: Social Market Foundation, 1994).

82. Interview of Dudaev by Viktor Perushkin, *Argumenty i fakty* (December 7, 1994): 2.

83. For a study of the military conflict that is sympathetic to the Chechens see Stasys Knezys and Romanas Sedlickas, *The War in Chechnya* (College Station: Texas A&M University Press, 1999); and the numerous papers by Charles Blandy and others available from the UK Defence Academy at http://www.da.mod.uk/CSRC. One of the best collection of Russian journalist accounts and other documents is Oleg Panfilov and Aleksei Simonovg, eds., *Fond zashchity glasnosti, informatsionnaia voina v chechne: fakty, dokumenty, svidetel'stva, noiabr' 1994–sentiabr 1996* (Moscow: Prava cheloveka, 1997). For Western journalists' accounts of the 1994–96 war see Gall and de Waal (1998); Lieven (1998); Bennett (1998); Smith (1998); Karny (2000); Bird (2002). For journalistic classics of U.S. military involvement in Vietnam see Michael Herr, *Dispatches* (New York: Vintage Books, 1977), and Mark Baker, *Nam: The Vietnam War in the Words of the Men and Women Who Fought There* (New York: William Morrow, 1981).

84. One of the few works from the Chechen perspective is the recently published memoir of a medical doctor present in Grozny during the first war, Khassan Baiev, *The Oath: A Surgeon Under Fire* (New York: Walker, 2003).

85. "Eto ne Stalingrad 42-go: eto Grozny 95-go," *Literaturnaia gazeta*, 17 May 1995.

86. Lieven (1998), 108.

87. *Argumenty i fakty* 22 (30 May 2001).

88. *Izvestiia*, 4 September 1996.

89. John Dunlop, "How Many Soldiers and Civilians Died During the Russo-Chechen War of 1994–1996," *Central Asian Survey* 19, 3–4 (2000): 329–39. For further discussion of casualty figures see Chapter 5.

90. Muzaev (1995), 21–24. See also Charles H. Fairbanks, Jr., "Weak States and Private Armies," in Mark R. Beissinger and Crawford Young, eds., *Beyond State Crisis: Post-Colonial Africa and Post-Soviet Eurasia in Comparative Perspective* (Washington, D.C.: Woodrow Wilson Center Press, 2002), 129–60.

91. Yandarbiev (1996), 166–67, 211.

92. There are various estimates of the size of Chechnya's fighting force at this time. See Muzaev (1995), 19, and Knezys and Sedlickas (1999), 66.

93. This is an essential feature of the "new wars," thesis, for which see Mary Kaldor, *New and Old Wars: Organized Violence in a Global Era* (Cambridge: Polity Press, 1999).

94. See Fairbanks (2002), 130, 140–47.

95. Bird (2002), 150, 182, 191–92.

96. The most detailed analysis of the battle is provided by Knezys and Sedlickas (1999), 93–103. The horror of the battle from the Russian side is captured in an interview with its traumatized commander in Bird (2002), 180–81.

97. See Andrey Blinushov, A.Guryanov, O. Orlov, Ya. Rachinsky, and A. Sokolov, *By All Available Means: The Russian Federation Ministry of Internal Affairs Operation in the Village of Samashki: April 7–8, 1995*, trans. Rachel Denber (Moscow: Memorial Human Rights Center, 1996).

98. Bird (2002), 186. Due to the poor sound quality, Dudaev wrote the statements by hand and held them up to the screen.

99. "We will not fight in our territory," interview with Dzokhar Dudaev, Official Kremlin International News Broadcast, 12 August 1992.

100. For the plan see *Izvestiia*, 20 February 1996. Kovalev, Borshchev, Molostvov, and Rybakov had been horrified by what they found on a monitoring visit to Chechnya in December 1995.

101. For this and other peace proposals of this period see Curran et al. (1997), 81–91. For Shaimiev's role see also *Rossiiskaia gazeta*, 5 March 1996.

102. See Curran et al. (1997), 224. The continuing importance of the "Hague Initiative," to Shaimiev is suggested by the fact that details are still retained on the official server of Tatarstan: http://www.tatar.ru/00001219_d.html. The Hague dialogue was informed by a number of academic experts on Russia and ethnic conflict regulation, including: from Russia, Valery Tishkov; from the U.S., Bruce Allen, program director of Harvard University's Conflict Management Group, and Graham Allison and Fiona Hill from Harvard's Strengthening Democratic Institutions Project.

103. Apparently, Dudaev was lured into conducting negotiations by mobile phone and was tracked down and killed by a Russian air strike. This version was widely believed among the Chechens and is reported with some detail in Yandarbiev (1996), 378.

104. Gennadii Troshev, *Moia voina: Chechenskii dnevnik okopnogo generala* (Moscow: Vagrius, 2001), 121.

105. The Draft Treaty was published in *Rossiisskaia gazeta*, 31 May 1996: 4–5.

106. For alternate Russian views on the question of peace with Chechnya see the positive report in the liberal daily *Segodnia*, 28 May 1996: 1, and the extremely negative report in the main communist party daily *Sovetskaia rossiia*, 27 August 1996: 1.

107. Troshev (2001), 121–22.

108. Ibid., 124–29.

109. For the inconsistencies see the memoir of the former head of the Ministry of Defense Press Office, Viktor Baranets, *Eltsin i ego generaly: Zapiski polkovnika genshtaba* (Moscow: Sovershenno sekretno, 1998), 450–53.

110. As a condition of its application to join the Council of Europe, Russia was forced to accept the presence of an OSCE "Assistance Group," in Chechnya. It operated beginning 26 April 1995.

111. Author's interview with Tim Guldimann, 5 April 2006. A Russian journalist noted that the experience of the conflict in New Caledonia figured in the negotiations at Khasaviurt; see Il'ia Maksakov, "Aleksandr Lebed' nachal ocherednoi raund peregovorov," *Nezavisimaia gazeta*, 31 August 1996. Under the Matignon Accord of 1988, the French government and Kanak separatists agreed to end the conflict and postpone a decision on independence for ten years

112. For Lebed's version of what occurred during the negotiations see Aleksandr Barkhatov. *General Lebed', ili moia lebedinaia pesnia* (Moscow: Politburo, 1998), 98–107.

113. Later, out of government office and at a time when Russian relations with Chechnya were again tense, Lebed stated that "I believed and still believe in the good faith of Aslan Maskhadov." See Barkhatov (1998), 106.

114. Abumuslimov had studied History and German Language, and after the start of the second Russian-Chechen war in late 1999 he went into exile to Germany, where he organized a political office for the Chechen resistance.

115. Cited in Barkhatov (1998), 103.

116. Author's interview with Tim Guldimann, 5 April 2006.

117. For the text of the agreement see *Nezavisimaia gazeta*, 3 September 1996. It was also published with other documents relating to Russian-Chechen negotiations in 1994–97 in Ivan Rybkin, *Consent in Russia Consent in Chechnya* (n.p.: Lytten Trading and Investment, Abacus Trust and Management Services, 1998), 229–30.

118. See Anatolii Kulikov and Sergei Lembik, *Chechenskii uzel: khronika vooruzhennogo konflikta 1994–1996gg* (Moscow: Dom Pedagogiki, 2000), 261–62. See also Troshev's memoir (2001).

119. Rybkin (1998), 114–15.

120. Yeltsin's comments were made at a meeting with Russian media in the Kremlin on March 14, 1997, reported in *Nezavisimaia gazeta*, 15 March 1997: 1.

Chapter 4. Dual Radicalization: The Making of Jihad

1. I have previously discussed the process of dual radicalization in "Chechnya: Understanding the Causes of a Protracted Post-Soviet Conflict," *Civil Wars* 4, 4 (2001): 34–38.

2. Olivier Roy, "Afghanistan—War as a Factor of Entry into Politics," *Central Asian Survey* 8, 4 (1989): 50.

3. *Izvestiia*, 27 January 1997; *Itar-Tass*, 2 February 1997. There were 75 OSCE monitors, and more than 150 from Russia and other CIS states.

4. *Moscow News*, 30 January 1997. Run-off elections for the parliament were held until March 1997.

5. *Rossiiskaia gazeta*, 30 January 30 1997

6. *Argumenty i fakty* (25 January 1997).

7. The Chechen government claimed that 1,385 persons remained in these camps even six months after Khasaviurt. See *Nezavisimaia gazeta*, 15 March 1997.

8. Organization for Security and Co-operation in Europe, Annual Reports 1998 and 1999, http://www.osce.org/docs

9. See, for example, Paul Klebnikov's analysis of Berezovskii's relationship with Udugov, *Godfather of the Kremlin: Boris Berezovsky and the Looting of Russia* (New York: Harcourt, 2000), 260–66. For other details of alleged payments see John B. Dunlop, "'Storm in Moscow': A Plan of the Yeltsin Family to Destabilize Russia," (Washington, D.C.: Johns Hopkins School of Advanced International Studies, 8 October 2004), 36–38, www.sais-jhu.edu/programs/res/papers/Dunlop_paper.pdf

10. *Nezavisimaia gazeta*, 23 December 1997: 1.

11. Olivier Roy, *The Failure of Political Islam* (London: I.B. Tauris, 1994) and Roy (1989), 45.

12. See Olivier Roy, *Globalized Islam: The Search for a New Ummah* (New York: Columbia University Press, 2004), 62–64, 304–6.

13. I discuss Islamic radicalization in Chechnya in Hughes (2001), 34–36. For a similar and much more detailed exploration of the Islamization of the Chechen separatist movement, including key leaders, see Julie Wilhelmsen, "Between a Rock and a Hard Place: The Islamisation of the Chechen Separatist Movement," *Europe-Asia Studies* 57, 1 (2005): 35–59, and her paper: "When Separatists Become Islamists: The Case of Chechnya," FFI/RAPPORT-2004/00445 (Norwegian Defence Research Establishment), http://www.nupi.no/IPS/filestore/00445.pdf

14. This thesis is presented in Aleksei Malashenko and Dmitrii Trenin, *Vremia Iuga: Rossiia v Chechne, Chechne v Rossii* (Moscow: Gendal'f, Carnegie Center Moscow, 2002), 69–112 esp. 89–90.

15. Wahhabism is a radical, in the literal sense of "going back to roots," and militant Islamic movement that originated in the Arabian peninsula in the eighteenth century and seeks to restore a "pure" form of Islam based on the Qur'an through jihad. It is intolerant of other forms of Islam and regards Sufism as heresy.

16. Viktor Khlystun interview with Grachev, *Trud*, 15 March 2001: 8.

17. Zelimkhan Yandarbiev, *Checheniia—Bitva za sovobodu* (Lviv: Svoboda Narodiv, 1996), 172.

18. Interview with Basaev in Oleg Blotskii, "Terroristy pronikaiut v rossiiu za dengi," *Nezavisimaia gazeta*, 12 March 1996.

19. Igor Rotar, "Chechnia: po obe storony fronta," *Izvestiia*, 24 November 1995.

20. Anatol Lieven, *Chechnya: Tombstone of Russian Power* (New Haven, Conn.: Yale University Press, 1998), 35–38.

21. Kavkhaz Center, "Report About Ben Laden's Ties to Chechnya: Pack of Lies," 20 November 2004, http://www.kavkazcenter.com/eng/content/2004/11/20/3306.shtml. For the DIA report see http://www.judicialwatch.org/cases/102/dia.pdf

22. In July 2006 Udugov penned a rousing appeal to the resistance which included references to Khattab as one of the key figures in the resistance struggle and which ended with the slogan "the jihad continues". See http://www.kavkazcenter.com/russ/content/2006/07/11/45797.shtml

23. See Yandarbiev (1996), 281. The photograph dates from no later than 1995, and possibly earlier.

24. Interview with Basaev in Oleg Blotskii, "Terroristy pronikaiut v rossiiu za dengi," *Nezavisimaia gazeta*, 12 March 1996.

25. For the development of Islamic radical movements in Afghanistan in this period see Ahmed Rashid, *Taliban: The Story of the Afghan Warlords* (London: Pan Macmillan, 2001), 91–94, 132–34. Basaev would have been in Khost at a time when the Taliban were being sponsored by Pakistan (and the U.S.) to seize power in Afghanistan, and thus potentially secure the access routes to the energy resources of Central Asia and the Caspian.

26. Azzam ran the Makhtab al Khidmat (Services Center), which acted as the conduit for Islamic international assistance (especially Saudi) and Muslim Brotherhood influence on the Afghan Mujahidin. See Rashid (2001), 131; Steve Coll, *Ghost Wars: The Secret History of the CIA, Afghanistan, and Bin Laden, from the Soviet Invasion to September 10* (New York: Penguin, 2004), 153–58. The biography of Khattab is uncertain. For an "official" biography from the Chechen side see the main website for the Islamists of the Chechen resistance: http://www.kavkazcenter. com/eng/photo/amir_khattab/page1.shtml and http://www.kavkazcenter.com/ eng/content/2006/11/10/6355.shtml

27. There are no accurate data on the funding. Russian sources, usually based on intelligence sources, invariably exaggerate the sums involved. See Malashenko and Trenin (2002), 99–100.

28. Khattab's interest in Dagestan was also personal since he had married a Dagestani Dargin.

29. For Russian analysis of the raid and its implications see I. Rotar, "Chast" Musulman Gotova k Gazavatu" *Nezavisimaia gazeta*, 27 January 1998; "Organizatory Terakta v Buinakske Obeshaiut Prodolzhit' Voinu," *Nezavisimaia gazeta*, 29 January 1998; "Raduev Otmetilsia v Buinakske, " *Nezavisimaia gazeta*, 3 February 1998.

30. Radio Free Europe/Radio Liberty, Newsline, 17 November 1997.

31. "Chechnia na poroge na grazhdanskoi voiny, " *Trud*, 18 July 1998.

32. Article 4 was amended on 3 February 1997. See the revised constitution at http://www.chechen.org/content.php?catID=4

33. Georgi Derlugian. "Che Guevaras in Turbans: Chechens Versus Globalization," *New Left Review* 237 (1999): 3–27.

34. *Zaiavlenia presidenta chechenskoi respubliki ichkeria, sheikha Abdul-Khalima Sadulaeva*, 13 February 2006, http://www.kavkazcenter.com/russ/content/2006/02/ 13/42038.shtml

35. *Ukaz presidenta chechenskoi respubliki ichkeria, Abdul-Khalima Sadulaeva*, 9 March 2005, http://chechenpress.co.uk/news/2005/03/15/21.shtml

36. *Kommersant daily*, 26 August 2005.

37. For the decrees on the government reshuffle of 2 February 2006 see http:// www.chechenpress.co.uk/english/news/2006/02/06/01.shtml and http://www. chechen.org/content.php?catID=91
For the decree on further Islamization see *Zaiavlenia presidenta chechenskoi respubliki ichkeria, sheikha Abdul-Khalima Sadulaeva*, 13 February 2006, http://www. kavkazcenter.com/russ/content/2006/02/13/42038.shtml

38. Clifford Geertz, "The Integrative Revolution: Primordial Sentiments and Civil Politics in the New States, in Geertz, ed., *Old Societies and New States: The Quest for Modernity in Asia and Africa* (New York: Free Press, 1963), 124–26.

39. The changing idiom is traceable on the main official Chechen websites since 2000, http://chechenpress.co.uk/index.shtml; http://www.kavkazcenter. com/russ/

40. See http://www.kavkazcenter.com/eng/ebook.html

41. Interview with Basaev conducted by Andrei Babitskii, ABC Television, 28

July 2005, text at http://www.chechenpress.co.uk/english/news/2005/08/08/01.shtml

42. Anna Politkovskaia, "*Izmel'chennyi basaev,*" *Novaia gazeta,* 13 July 2006.

43. Gennadii Troshev, *Moia voina: Chechenskii dnevnik okopnogo generala* (Moscow: Vagrius, 2001), 142.

44. See Roy Allison, "The Chechnia Conflict: Military and Security Policy Implications," in Allison and Christoph Bluth, eds., *Security Dilemmas in Russia and Eurasia* (London: RIIA, 1998), 241–80.

45. See *Moskovskii komsomolets,* 5 November 1999; *Nezavisimaia gazeta,* 12 April 2000.

46. Sergei Kovalev, "Russia After Chechnya," *New York Review of Books* 44, 12 (1997).

47. See Dunlop (2004), 34–36.

48. For the resilience of political structures in Dagestan to the attack see Edward W. Walker, "Russia's Soft Underbelly: The Stability of Instability in Dagestan," Berkeley Program in Soviet and Post-Soviet Working Paper Series, Winter 1999–2000.

49. Vladimir Putin, "Russia at the Turn of the Millennium," 30 December 1999, at http://www.geocities.com/CapitolHill/Parliament/3005/poutine.html

50. See *Economist* (9 October 1999).

51. Subsequently, FSB defector Aleksandr Litvinenko, together with oligarch in exile Boris Berezovskii, both of whom were given political asylum in the UK, campaigned against Putin, including producing a book purporting to document FSB involvement in the apartment bombings. See Aleksandr Litvinenko and Iurii Fel'stinskii, *FSB vsryvaet rossiiu: Federal'naia sluzhba bezopasnosti—organizator terroristicheskikh actov, pokhishchenii i ubiistv,* 2nd ed. corrected and expanded (New York: Liberty Publishing House, 2004), http://terror99.ru/FSBSeconEdition.pdf. Berezovskii began to spread this version of events in the media from January 2002. Litvinenko died from poisoning in suspicious circumstances in London in November 2006.

52. See Robert Bruce Ware, "A Multitude of Evils: Mythology and Political Failure in Chechnya" in Richard Sakwa, ed., *Chechnya: From the Past to the Future* (London: Anthem Press, 2005), 94–96.

53. See Maskhadov's letter on the bombings, 11 February 2002 reproduced verbatim in Litvinenko and Fel'stinskii (2004), 253–54. Interview with Basaev by BBC Russia Service, cited verbatim in *CDI Johnson's Russia List,* 5 October 1999, http://www.cdi.org/russia/johnson/3544.html##4

54. See, for example, the statements by Vladimir Lukin, chairman of the Foreign Relations Committee of the State Duma and one of the leaders of the main pro-democracy party Yabloko, in late October 1999, *International Affairs* (Moscow) 45, 6 (1999): 107–10. Yabloko had been resolutely opposed to the first war.

55. Boris Yeltsin, *Midnight Diaries* (London: Weidenfeld and Nicolson, 2000), 344.

56. Vladimir Putin interview in *Focus* (Munich), 24 September 2001.

57. See Yuri Levada. "What the Polls Tell Us," *Journal of Democracy* 15, 3 (2004): 43–51. Intriguingly, Levada made no reference at all to the war in Chechnya when discussing Putin's rise or the erosion of Russian democracy. The correlation of Putin's popularity with his success in war against Chechnya was widely discussed at the time. See Richard Rose. "How Floating Parties Frustrate Democratic Accountability: A Supply-Side View of Russia's Elections" *East European Constitutional Review* 9, 1–2 (2000), and Peter Rutland, "Putin's Path to Power," *Post-Soviet Affairs* 16, 4 (2000): 313–54.

58. Opinion poll data accessed in February 2000 at the Levada Center, see http://www.levada.ru

59. In a televised election debate in late November 1999, economic liberal Anatoly Chubais revealed himself to be aligned with hard-line Russian nationalists when he called Yavlinskii a "traitor" for his opposition to the war in Chechnya. See *Komsomol'skaia pravda*, 27 November 1999, for extracts. After the renewal of war in late 1999, of the leading figures in the liberal/democratic forces only a few, such as Kovalev and Yavlinskii, were outspoken in their opposition to the war. Gradually, some rightists, notably Nemtsov, became vocal critics also.

60. For the results see http://www.russiavotes.org/

61. *Izvestiia*, 1 October 1999.

62. Iuliia Latynina in *Novaia gazeta*, 15 November 2002; *Komsomol'skaia pravda*, 13 November 2002: 3.

63. See Vladimir Putin, Annual Address to the Federal Assembly, 16 May 2003, and Annual Address to the Federal Assembly, 26 May 2004, http://www.kremlin.ru/sdocs/appears.shtml?type=63372

64. For a military account see Charles Blandy, *Chechnya: Two Federal Interventions: An Interim Comparison and Assessment* (Camberley: Royal Military Academy Sandhurst: Conflict Studies Research Centre, 2000/01), http://www.da.mod.uk/CSRC/documents/Caucasus/P29. This center has produced numerous publicly available working papers on military and security aspects of the war.

65. T. E. Lawrence, "The Evolution of a Revolt," *Army Quarterly* 1, 1 (1920): 1–21 at 8. U.S. Army Combined Arms Center Combat Studies Institute reprint available at: http://www-cgsc.army.mil/carl/resources/csi/csi.asp#reprints Lawrence's aphorism is the centerpiece for a recent study which stresses the superiority of British over U.S. counterinsurgency practices, see John A. Nagl, *Learning to Eat Soup with a Knife. Counterinsurgency Lessons from Malaya and Vietnam* (Chicago: University of Chicago Press, 2005).

66. See Lawrence (1920), 8. Lawrence observed, "but suppose we were an influence (as we might be), an idea, a thing invulnerable, intangible, without front or back, drifting about like a gas? Armies were like plants, immobile as a whole, firm-rooted, nourished through long stems to the head. We might be a vapour, blowing where we listed. . . . It seemed a regular soldier might be helpless without a target. He would own the ground he sat on, and what he could poke his rifle at."

67. The classic counterinsurgency studies are Frank Kitson, *Low-Intensity Operations: Subversion, Insurgency and Peacekeeping* (London: Faber and Faber, 1971), and Roger Trinquier, *Modern Warfare: A French View of Counterinsurgency* (New York: Praeger, 1964). The literature on insurgency and guerrilla warfare is vast but a useful introduction is Ian F. W. Beckett, *Modern Insurgencies and Counter-Insurgencies: Guerrillas and Their Opponents Since 1750* (London: Routledge, 2001).

68. Viktor Khlystun interview with Grachev, *Trud*, 15 March 2001: 8.

69. This is the conclusion drawn by Gil Merom, *How Democracies Lose Small Wars* (Cambridge: Cambridge University Press, 2003).

70. Lawrence (1920), 22.

71. For a study of the British counterinsurgency in Malaya see Richard Stubbs, *Hearts and Minds in Guerrilla Warfare: The Malayan Emergency, 1948–1960* (Oxford: Oxford University Press, 1989). For a study that focuses on the propaganda dimension of the counterinsurgency see Susan L. Carruthers, *Winning Hearts and Minds: British Governments, the Media and Colonial Counter-Insurgency, 1944–1960* (London: Leicester University Press, 1995).

72. The only major hiccup in the domestic propaganda war came in April 1952 when the Daily Worker published a photograph of a smiling British marine holding the severed heads of two insurgents. See Carruthers (1995), 110.

73. See Karl Hack, *Defence and Decolonisation in South-East Asia: Britain, Malaya and Singapore 1941–1968* (London: Routledge, 2000), 113–31.

74. For a balanced and comprehensively researched analysis of British policy in Kenya see the Pulitzer Prize-winning study Caroline Elkin, *Imperial Reckoning: The Untold Story of Britain's Gulag in Kenya* (New York: Henry Holt, 2005); for the number of detainees in Kenya and British attempts to "clean" incriminating evidence from the official records see xiii.

75. See *James S. Corum*, "How the British Defeated Insurgents in Malaya," *New York Times*, 6 February 2005, and Nagl (2005).

76. Minister of Defense Sergeev favored more allocations to "strategic" nuclear forces, while Chief of the General Staff Kvashnin sought prioritization of conventional forces and the war in Chechnya. In the summer of 2000, Kvashnin seems to have won the debate and Sergeev resigned. See Pavel Baev, "Chechnya and the Russian Military: A War Too Far?" in Sakwa (2005), 117–30.

77. Some suggest the war cost as much as $8 billion by 2001; see Miriam Lanskoy, "The Cost of the Chechen War," *Central Asia-Caucasus Analyst* (Johns Hopkins University), 7 November 2001, http://www.cacianalyst.org/view_article. php?articleid=65

78. For the effectiveness of "control" as a strategy in managing ethnic conflict see Ian Lustick, "Stability in Deeply Divided Societies: Consociationalism or Control," *World Politics* 31 (1979): 325–44.

79. Stathis N. Kalyvas, *The Logic of Violence in Civil War* (Cambridge: Cambridge University Press, 2006), 171.

80. These reasons for abandoning resistance to Russia were spelled out by Kadyrov in an interview with Anna Politkovskaia of 24 July 2000. In particular he stressed that he wanted to "save my nation" and "root out" Wahhabism. Politkovskaia (2001), 192–201.

81. *See Human Rights Center Memorial, Chechnia 2004 god. Pokhishcheniia i ischeznoveniia liudei, 7 February 2005*, http://www.memo.ru/hr/hotpoints/caucas1/index.htm

82. For detailed reports that demonstrate the consistency of the policies of torture, kidnapping, and disappearances over time see Human Rights Watch, "The 'Dirty War' in Chechnya: Forced Disappearances, Torture, and Summary Executions," *Human Rights Watch* 13, 1 (D) (March 2001), http://www.hrw.org/ reports/2001/chechnya/ and "Widespread Torture in the Chechen Republic." Human Rights Watch Briefing Paper for the 37th Session U.N. Committee against Torture (13 November 2006), http://hrw.org/backgrounder/eca/chechnya1106/ chechnya1106web.pdf; Human Rights Center Memorial, Chechnya 2004: "New" Methods of Anti-Terror. Hostage taking and repressive actions against relatives of alleged combatants and terrorists (17 March 2005), http://www.memo.ru/ hr/hotpoints/caucas1/msg/2005/03/m33236.htm. Two fascinating accounts of the human realities of the war on the ground in Chechnya are Anne Nivat, *Chienne de Guerre: A Woman Reporter Behind the Lines of the War in Chechnya*, trans. Susan Darnton (New York: Public Affairs, 2001), and Anna Politkovskaia, *A Dirty War: A Russian Reporter in Chechnya* (London: Harvill, 2001). Nivat provides detailed anecdotal accounts of the *zachistki* and kidnapping for ransom, see 217–18.

83. Human Rights Center Memorial, "'Voluntary Surrender' of Magomed Khambiev," 10 March 2004, http://www.memo.ru/eng/memhrc/texts/01new404. shtml The arrests were also intended to intimidate the political activities of

Magomed's brother and Chechen Minister of Health Dr. Omar Khambiev, living in exile in Western Europe.

84. Politkovskaia (2001), 73.

85. As of 31 December 2002, there were, according to UNHCR, some 103,000 IDPs in Ingushetia, 142,000 within Chechnya itself, 8,000 in Dagestan, and 40,000 in other regions of the Russian Federation. See UNHCR Newsletter *UN in Russia*, January–February 2000, http://www.unrussia.ru/eng/NewsletterFeb 2000Page6.htm; Parliamentary Assembly Council of Europe, *The Humanitarian Situation of the Chechen Displaced Population*, Doc. 10282l, 20 September 2004, http://assembly.coe.int/Documents/WorkingDocs/doc04/EDOC10282.htm; Médicins sans Frontières, *The Trauma of Ongoing War in Chechnya: Quantitative Assessment of Living Conditions, and Psychosocial and General Health Status Among War Displaced in Chechnya and Ingushetia*, August 2004, http://www.uk2.msf.org/reports/Chechnyareport.pdf; John B. Dunlop. "Russian Federation: The Situation of IDPs from Chechnya," UNHCR WRITENET Paper 11 (2002).

86. Politkovskaia (2001), 59–62.

87. BBC Monitoring of World Broadcasts, 30 September 2001, from an interview on TV6.

88. Valery A. Tishkov, *Understanding Violence for Post-Conflict Reconstruction in Chechnya* (Geneva: CASIN, 2001), 584.

89. Putin's comments were made at a meeting with Head of the Administration of Chechnya Akhmed Kadyrov, Kremlin, 27 March 2003, http://www.kremlin.ru/appears/2003/03/27/1922_type63378_41982.shtml

90. The attack caused hundreds of casualties among Russian troops and local police and militia. See Liz Fuller, "Russia: Basaev Says He Planned Nalchik Raid," Radio Free Europe/Radio Liberty, News and Analysis, 17 October 2005, http://www.rferl.org/featuresarticle/2005/10/0d20ee94-5883-4082-bed1-d5557b4a52fc.html. For Basaev's comments on the raid see his email address to "Kavkaz-Tsentr," 17 October 2005, http://www.kavkaz.org.uk/russ/content/2005/10/17/38543.shtml

91. Vladimir Putin, Annual Address to the Federal Assembly, April 18, 2002, http://www.kremlin.ru/sdocs/appears.shtml?type=63372

92. For this designation see Sergei Kovalev, "Putin's War," *New York Review of Books* 47, 2 (2000): 4–8.

93. Pavel Baev, "Instrumentalizing Counter-Terrorism for Regime Consolidation in Putin's Russia," *Studies in Conflict and Terrorism* 27 (2004): 339–40.

94. For the recentralizing trends under Putin see James Hughes, "From Refederalization to Recentralization," in Stephen White et al., eds., *Developments in Russian Politics 5* (London: Macmillan, 2001), 128–46; David Cashaback, "Risky Strategies? Putin's Federal Reforms and the Accommodation of Difference in Russia," *Journal on Ethnopolitics and Minority Issues in Europe* 3 (2003): 1–32, http://www.ecmi.de/jemie/special_3_2003.html

95. The districts are Central, North West, North Caucasus, Volga, Urals, Siberia, and Far East.

96. PBS Newshour, 1 July 2003 http://www.pbs.org/newshour/bb/media/july-dec03/russia_07-01.html

97. Kovalev (2000), 8.

98. Human Rights Center Memorial, *The Chechen Republic: Consequences of "Chechenization" of the Conflict*, 2 March 2006, http://www.memo.ru/hr/hotpoints/caucas1/index.htm

99. The nature of "death squads" is explored in Bruce B. Campbell and Arthur

D. Brenner, eds., *Death Squads in Global Perspective: Murder with Deniability* (Basingstoke: Palgrave Macmillan, 2002).

100. Meeting between Putin and Aimani Kadyrova and Ramzan Kadyrov, 21 August 2005, http://www.kremlin.ru/appears/2005/08/21/1735_type63378_92688.shtml

101. Yevgenia Borisova, "Putting Chechnya Back Together Again," *Moscow Times*, 7 October 2002: 12.

102. Médicins sans Frontières (2004), 33.

103. Report of meeting between Putin and Kadyrov on Kadyrov's personal website http://www.ramzan-kadyrov.ru/press.php?releases&press_id=318&month=08&year=2006

104. Bulletin of the Accounts Chamber 7 (67) / 2003, http://www.ach.gov.ru/eng/bulletins/2003–7.php; Interview with Riabukhin, "Stealing Has Its Reasons," *Kommersant vlast'*, 14 May 2005.

105. See Liz Fuller, "Tug of War for Control of Chechnya's Oil Revenues Continues," Radio Free Europe/Radio Liberty, Newsline 10, 224, Part 1 (6 December 2006), http://www.rferl.org/newsline/

106. Ministry of Foreign Affairs of the Chechen Republic of Ichkeria, The Russian-Chechen Tragedy: The Way to Peace and Democracy: Conditional Independence Under an International Administration (February 2003), 40, http://www.chechnya-mfa.info/. Even earlier, in November 1999, Maskhadov spoke of the need for an international peace-keeping force in Chechnya, *Groznenskii rabochii*, 10 November 1999.

107. *Kommersant daily*, 8 February 2005: 4.

108. See Musa Muradov, "Kontrpropaganda: Aslan Maskhadov prodolzhaet mirit'sia. A emu predlagaiut sdat'sia," *Kommersant daily*, 8 February 2005: 4. The Russian government issued a legal warning to *Kommersant* for publicizing "terrorist" views.

109. *Komsomol'skaia pravda*, 12 November 2002: 3.

Chapter 5. Chechnya and the Meaning of Terrorism

1. See Evangelista (2002), 144–50, 178–89.

2. For the "asymmetric inderdependency" of the EU and Russia see James Hughes, "The EU's Relations with Russia: Partnership or Asymmetric Interdependency?" in Nicola Casarini and Costanza Musu, eds., *The EU's Foreign Policy in an Evolving International System: The Road to Convergence* (London: Palgrave, 2007).

3. For the predominance of political over economic criteria in the release of the IMF funds see Randall W. Stone, *Lending Credibility: The International Monetary Fund and the Post-Communist Transition* (Princeton, N.J.: Princeton University Press, 2002), 138–46.

4. Bill Clinton, *My Life* (New York: Knopf, 2004).

5. See Lapidus (1998), 32–45.

6. Strobe Talbott, *The Russia Hand: A Memoir of Presidential Diplomacy* (New York: Random House, 2002), 126.

7. *Washington Post*, 23 April 1996; see also Talbott (2002), 204–5.

8. Talbott (2002), 361.

9. When Maskhadov traveled abroad he used, as Dudaev had, his old Soviet passport.

10. Talbott (2002), 181–82.

11. For a discussion of the limitations to international involvement in the Chechnya case see Emil Pain, "Armed Conflict in Kosovo and Chechnya: A Comparison," *Forced Migration Monitor* 25 (September 1998): 1–6; Ekaterina Stepanova, "Kosovo and Chechnya: Illogical Parallels," *Security Dialogue* 3, 1 (2000): 135–41.

12. This argument is developed in Alexei G. Arbatov, *The Transformation of Russian Military Doctrine: Lessons Learned from Kosovo and Chechnya*, Marshall Center Papers 2 (Garmisch-Partenkirchen: George C. Marshall European Center for Security Studies, July 2000), http://www.marshallcenter.org/site-graphic/lang-en/page-coll-mcp-1/. Arbatov notes (20–21): "The main lesson learned is that the goal justifies the means. The use of force is the most efficient problem solver, if applied decisively and massively. Negotiations are of dubious value and are to be used as a cover for military action. Legality of state actions, observation of laws and legal procedures, and humanitarian suffering are of secondary significance relative to achieving the goal. Limiting one's own troop casualties is worth imposing massive devastation and collateral fatalities on civilian populations. Foreign public opinion and the position of Western governments are to be discounted if Russian interests are at stake. A concentrated and controlled mass media campaign is the key to success."

13. For the "doctrine" of "conditional non-interference" see Blair's speech to the Chicago Economic Club, 24 April 1999, http://www.pm.gov.uk/output/Page1297.asp. Blair stated that "the principle of non-interference must be qualified in important respects. Acts of genocide can never be a purely internal matter. When oppression produces massive flows of refugees which unsettle neighboring countries then they can properly be described as 'threats to international peace and security.' When regimes are based on minority rule they lose legitimacy—look at South Africa."

14. This policy has not been without critics in the U.S., for which see the editorial "Why Chechnya Is Different," *Washington Post*, 4 October 2001.

15. See PACE, Order no. 506, and Resolution 1055, February 2, 1995, http://assembly.coe.int/default.asp

16. Reports and documents relating to the activities of PACE may be found on the Council of Europe website http://assembly.coe.int/default.asp. See, in particular, PACE, Opinion No. 193, 25 January 1996.

17. The most reluctant to sign were Austria, Sweden, Finland, and Portugal, whose ratification followed the Russian-Chechen truce of August 1996 and peace treaty of May 1997.

18. European Council, Presidency Conclusions, Helsinki 10/11 December 1999, Declaration on Chechnya, http://europa.eu.int/council/off/conclu/dec99/annexII. The EU also took the opportunity to impose a self-interested form of sanctions by cutting import quotas for Russian steel products by 12 percent in March 2000.

19. The visit provoked a storm of protest from critics of Putin's policy in Chechnya within Russia and internationally. It also seriously damaged the pretence of Labor's "ethical foreign policy," *The Guardian*, 11 March 11 2000, http://www.guardian.co.uk/ethical/article/0,2763,192041,00.html

20. For the Swedish work plan see http://eu2001.se/static/pdf/program/ordfprogram_eng.pdf. See also Swedish Presidency Conclusions, Goteborg European Council, 15–16 June 2001, http://ue.eu.int/ueDocs/cms_Data/docs/pressData/en/ec/00200-r1.en1.pdf. Leif Pagrotsky, Sweden's Minister for Foreign Trade was particularly active in pushing the EU-Russia agenda.

21. *The Guardian*, 26 September 2001.

22. This is evident at the symbolic level in *topoi*: a "Dudaev Street" in the Ukrainian city, Lviv, A "Dudaev Square" in the Lithuanian capital, Vilnius, and a "Dudaev Circus" in the Polish capital, Warsaw.

23. Data provided by ECHO, the EU Humanitarian Aid department, http://europa.eu.int/comm/echo/field/russia/echo_en.htm. See also data on TACIS at http://europa.eu.int/comm/europeaid/projects/tacis/index_en.htm

24. For the text see http://www.globalsecurity.org/military/library/news/1999/12/991208-chechen-usia1.htm

25. For a statement of Russia's position see the article by foreign minister Sergei Lavrov, "Reform Will Enhance the OSCE's Relevance," *Financial Times*, 29 November 2004.

26. Author's interview with Lord Frank Judd, (UK) House of Lords, 24 January 2006.

27. See Hughes (2007). Germany's preference for bilateralism in the relationship with Russia is evident in the growing energy ties between the two countries. In January 2006 Germany decided to proceed with Russia to construct the North European Gas Project without consulting its EU partners.

28. PACE, Human Rights Violations in the Chechen Republic: The Committee of Ministers' Responsibility vis-à-vis the Assembly's Concerns, Resolution 1479 (2006), adopted January 25, 2006, http://assembly.coe.int/Main.asp?link=/Documents/AdoptedText/ta06/ERES1479.htm#P15_177 For Mr. Bindig's report see http://assembly.coe.int/Main.asp?link=/Documents/WorkingDocs/Doc05/EDOC10774.htm

29. Useful documentation on the judgements and problems of enforcement may be found at http://www.londonmet.ac.uk/research-units/hrsj/ehrac/ehrac-litigation/judgments.cfm and http://www.londonmet.ac.uk/research-units/hrsj/ehrac/ehrac-litigation/enforcement-of-chechen-judgments.cfm

30. According to the *Tyndall Report*, which monitors the main U.S. television media, for the year 2005 in the news summaries by three main channels the time allocated to the conflict in Chechnya was 2 minutes out of a total of 14,529 minutes. In the period 2000-present Chechnya has never been a lead story, even during the Dubrovka and Beslan attacks, http://www.tyndallreport.com/index.php3

31. Vladimir Putin, Press conference at the Kremlin, 6 February 2004, http://www.kremlin.ru/appears/2004/02/06/1949_type63380_60388.shtml

32. For the kind of uncompromising critique that such negotiations can provoke see the attack on the Bush administration in the Op-Ed by Diana West, "Tea with Terrorists," *Washington Times*, 1 July 2005. She argued that "it represents a ghastly capitulation to terrorists and a strategic victory for terrorism, living proof that it's possible to kill and behead and hack and dismember and terrify your way to a peace parlay with the U.S.A."

33. National Security Concept of the Russian Federation *Rossiiskaia gazeta*, 18 January 2000. For the concept of "asymmetric warfare" see Joint Chiefs of Staff, *The National Military Strategy of the United States of America: A Strategy for Today; A Vision for Tomorrow* (2004), 4–5, 13–14. Unclassified version, http://www.defenselink.mil/news/Mar2005/d20050318nms.pdf

34. See, for example, news reports on the main Chechen resistance websites, http://www.kavkaz.org.uk/; http://chechenpress.co.uk

35. *The Times*, 6 March 1981: 1

36. This publication is now updated annually by the Office of the Coordinator for Counterterrorism within the Department of State. The entire collection of U.S. POGT reports from 1976 to the present are digitized and available at

http://www.mipt.org/Patterns-of-Global-Terrorism.asp, and those from 1995 at http://www.state.gov/s/ct/rls/pgtrpt/. U.S. "domestic terrorism" is covered by the FBI, and its reports are available at http://www.fbi.gov/publications.htm

37. U.S. Department of State, Office of the Coordinator for Counterterrorism, *Fact Sheet*, Foreign Terrorist Organizations (FTOs), Washington, D.C., 11 October 2005, http://www.state.gov/s/ct/rls/fs/37191.htm

38. POGT Report 1997, http://www.state.gov/www/global/terrorism/1997Report/1997index.html; Fact sheet released by the Office of the Coordinator for Counterterrorism, 8 October 1997, http://www.state.gov/www/global/terrorism/fs_terrorist_orgs.html#designation

39. POGT Report 2003, http://www.state.gov/s/ct/rls/pgtrpt/2003/31759.htm

40. "O bor'be s terrorizmom" (On the Fight Against Terrorism) (1998), Russian Federation Federal Law No. 130-FZ, 25 July 1998 *Rossiiskaia gazeta*, 4 August 1998. For the UK definition in the Terrorism Act (2000) see http://www.legislation.hmso.gov.uk/acts/acts2000/20000011.htm. For the U.S. definition in the Patriot Act (2001) see http://files.findlaw.com/news.findlaw.com/cnn/docs/terrorism/hr3162.pdf

41. See "O bor'be s terrorizmom" (1998), Article 19.

42. *O protivodeistvii terrorizmu, Federal'nye zakony, Nezavisimaia gazeta*, 14 February 2006: 2.

43. This was the charge laid against the head of the Russian-Chechen Friendship Society, Stanislav Dimitrievskii, who was sentenced to two years imprisonment in February 2006.

44. Council Framework Decision of 13 June 2002, *On Combating Terrorism*, http://europa.eu.int/eur-lex/pri/en/oj/dat/2002/l_164/l_16420020622en00030007.pdf

45. For resolution 1373 see http://www.un.org/Docs/scres/2001/sc2001.htm. The Declaration on Measures to Eliminate International Terrorism (1994) is at http://www.un.org/documents/ga/res/49/a49r060.htm; the International Convention for the Suppression of Terrorist Bombings (1997) and International Convention for the Suppression of the Financing of Terrorism (1999) are at http://untreaty.un.org/English/Terrorism.asp

46. The most recent Security Council resolution 1566 (2004) on "Threats to international peace and security caused by terrorist acts" does not go farther in defining terrorism than the previous conventions and declaration. See http://www.un.org/Docs/sc/unsc_resolutions04.html. See also United Nations, Report of the Policy Working Group on the United Nations and Terrorism, 2002, http://www.un.org/terrorism/a57273.htm

47. United Nations, Report of the Policy Working Group.

48. For the text of the decision of the Danish Ministry of Justice see http://www.tjetjenien.dk/congress/extradition.html

49. Zakaev was defended by two leading UK law firms, Doughty Street chambers and Matrix chambers (the latter being the law firm of Cherie Booth Q.C., UK prime minister Tony Blair's wife). The full text of the judgment is available at http://zakaev.ru/turnover/papers/50592.html

50. Protocol Additional to the Geneva Conventions of 12 August 1949, and Relating to the Protection of Victims of Non-International Armed Conflicts (Protocol II) (1978), Articles 1, 4, and 13 at http://www.unhchr.ch/html/menu3/b/94.htm

51. Anne Applebaum, "Two-Faced Chechnya Policy," *Washington Post*, 30 June 2004: 21 and the editorial, "A Good Decision," *Washington Post*, 10 August 2004: 18.

52. Press Release of the Russian Ministry of Foreign Affairs, *O predostavlenii*

politicheskogo ubezhishcha vlastiami SSHa I. Akhmadovy, 6 August 2004, http://www.ln.mid.ru/brp_4.nsf/sps/3766DA652AA1E753C3256EE800421EDA

53. The list was drawn up by the Security Council Committee established pursuant to paragraph 6 (d) of resolution 1267 (1999). For the list and resolution see http://www.un.org/Docs/sc/committees/1267/1267ResEng.htm and http://www.unis.unvienna.org/unis/pressrels/2003/sc7809.html

54. *Nezavisimaia gazeta,* 27 February 2004: 1.

55. *RIA-Novosti,* 26 February 2004.

56. The deputy chief of the Russian Interior Ministry's department for the struggle against organized crime and terrorism, Nikolai Ovchinnikov, told an international seminar on the prevention of terrorism held in Moscow in June 2005 that there were about 500 "terrorist and extremist" organizations operating worldwide. *Itar Tass,* 27 June 2005.

57. *Rossiiskaia gazeta,* 4 March 2006: 1.

58. Putin's comments were made at a press conference following his talks with the Spanish prime minister José Luis Rodríguez Zapatero, Madrid, 9 February 2006, http://www.kremlin.ru/appears/2006/02/09/0039_type63374type63377type63380_101410.shtml

59. See *Rossiiskaia gazeta,* 28 July 2006.

60. Alex P. Schmid and Albert J. Jongman with Michael Stohl et al., *Political Terrorism: A New Guide to Actors, Authors, Concepts, Data Bases, Theories and Literature,* 2nd ed. (Amsterdam: North-Holland, 1988).

61. See Michael Howard, "Constraints on Warfare," in Michael Howard, George I. Andreopoulos, and Mark R. Shulman, eds., *The Laws of War: Constraints on Warfare in the Western World* (New Haven, Conn.: Yale University Press: 1994), 1–11; Karma Nabulsi, *Traditions of War: Occupation, Resistance and the Law* (Oxford: Oxford University Press, 1999), 4–18. Goya graphically portrayed the brutality of this type of warfare in his "El Segundo de Mayo 1808," "El Tercero de Mayo 1808," and the suite of etchings "Los disastres de la guerra."

62. The literature on the subject of terrorism is immense and growing fast after 9/11. The literature analyzed here is employed to illustrate the wider genre. For the views of a political scientist see Paul Wilkinson, *Terrorism Versus Democracy: The Liberal State Response* (London: Frank Cass, 2001). For the views of historians see Charles Townshend, *Terrorism: A Very Short Introduction* (Oxford: Oxford University Press, 2002), and Ian F. W. Beckett. *Modern Insurgencies and Counter-Insurgencies: Guerrillas and Their Opponents Since 1750* (London: Routledge, 2001). For the views of a criminologist see Grant Wardlaw, *Political Terrorism: Theory, Tactics and Counter-Measures* (Cambridge: Cambridge University Press, 1989). For the views of political theorists and philosophers see Ted Honderich, *After the Terror* (Edinburgh: Edinburgh University Press, 2003); Michael Walzer, *Arguing About War* (New Haven, Conn.: Yale University Press, 2004); R. G. Frey and Christopher W. Morris, *Violence, Terrorism, and Justice* (Cambridge: Cambridge University Press, 1991); and the special issue on terrorism of the *Journal of Ethics* 8, 1 (2004). For the views of a security specialist see Bruce Hoffman, *Inside Terrorism* (New York: Columbia University Press, 1998). For a study of terrorism as a social movement see Michel Wieviorka, *The Making of Terrorism* (Chicago: University of Chicago Press, 2004).

63. *See United Nations, Office of the High Commissioner for Human Rights,* Geneva Convention relative to the Protection of Civilian Persons in Time of War (1950), *Geneva: United Nations 1997–2002* http://www.unhchr.ch/html/intlinst.htm

64. See the contradiction in Hoffman (1998), 25, 186.

65. Alex P. Schmid, "Terrorism and the Use of Weapons of Mass Destruction: From Where the Risk?" in Max Taylor and John Horgan, eds., *The Future of Terrorism* (London: Frank Cass, 2000), 106–32.

66. See Andrew Silke, "The impact of 9/11 on research on terrorism" in Magnus Ranstorp ed., *Mapping Terrorism Research* (Abingdon: Routledge, 2007): 76–93. While observing the huge outpour of studies into Al-Qaida, Silke notes that research into the I.R.A. has actually increased after 9/11 and the peace process in Northern Ireland, 84.

67. Wilkinson (2001), 12–13; Paul Wilkinson, *Terrorism and the Liberal State* (London: Macmillan, 1977), 48–49. For similar definitions see Wardlaw (1989), 16; Hoffman (1998), 14–15.

68. Wilkinson (2001), 13, 218–19; Wilkinson (1977), 49, 53.

69. Wardlaw (1989), 2–3.

70. Wievorka (1983), xxix–xxxi, 297.

71. See Andrew Silke, "Becoming a Terrorist," in Silke, *Terrorists, Victims, and Society: Psychological Perspectives on Terrorism and Its consequences* (Chichester: Wiley, 2003), 39–44.

72. See, for example, the approach of one of the most established "terrorism experts": Walter Laqueur, *The New Terrorism: Fanaticism and the Arms of Mass Destruction* (London: Phoenix Press, 2001), 81–97.

73. For critiques of attempts to pathologize "terrorists" see John Horgan, "The Search for the Terrorist Personality" in Silke (2003), 3–28; and Silke, "Becoming a Terrorist." Horgan notes that the "rigour of research pointing to either explicit or implicit abnormality, or to the existence of a 'terrorist personality,' is such that its propositions are built on unsteady empirical, theoretical and conceptual foundations" (23). For a comprehensive analysis of the debates on what makes a "terrorist" see John Horgan, *The Psychology of Terrorism* (London: Routledge, 2005).

74. Silke, "Becoming a Terrorist," 51.

75. See Robert A. Pape, *Dying to Win: The Strategic Logic of Suicide Terrorism* (New York: Random House, 2005); Ami Pedazhur, *Suicide Terrorism* (Cambridge: Polity, 2005).

76. Honderich (2003), 98–99, 185–86. Honderich's primary case is the justification of Palestinian terrorism against "neo-Zionism."

77. In his early work Walzer argued that the threat must be "enslavement or extermination," (my emphasis) see Michael Walzer, *Just and Unjust Wars: A Moral Argument with Historical Illustrations* (New York: Basic Books, 1977): 254. In his later work, the justification had changed to "political and physical extinction," (my emphasis) see Walzer (2004), 54.

78. See Wilkinson (1977), 53.

79. John B. Dunlop, "How Many Soldiers and Civilians Died During the Russo-Chechen War of 1994–96," *Central Asian Survey* 19, 3–4 (2000): 339.

80. Memorial *biulleten'* no. 28, 2004. http://www.memo.ru/about/bull/b28/; Memorial, *Chechnya, 2004 god. Pokhishcheniia i Ischeznoveniya lyudei*, 7 February 2005, http://www.memo.ru/hr/hotpoints/caucas1/index.htm

81. Associated Press, 16 May 2001, 17 February 2003, and 26 February 2006. The Russian Ministry of Defense figures are reported in "Skorbnaia statistika," *Krasnaia zvezda*, 12 August 2005, and are challenged in *Novaia gazeta*, 15 August 2005.

82. According to figures provided by Karel de Roy of UNICEF office in Russia, *Interfax*, 6 December 2005.

83. Valery A. Tishkov, "Ethnic conflicts in the Former USSR: The Use and Misuse of Typologies and Data," *Journal of Peace Research* 36, 5 (1999): 581–82.

84. The lower figure was cited by Taus Djabrailov, the head of Chechnya's pro-Moscow interim parliament and reported in *Nezavisimaia gazeta*, 16 August 2005. He claimed that 30,000–40,000 Chechens had been killed, but the bulk were ethnic Russians and others killed in the bombardment of Grozny in January 2005. The higher figure was stated by Dukvakha Abdurakhmanov, a deputy prime minister in the Kremlin-controlled Chechen civilian administration, *BBC Monitoring International Reports*, 26 June 2005.

85. The data on attacks were extracted from a quasi-official Russian website on terrorism designed by the Foundation for Effective Politics, a group close to the Kremlin: see http://www.antiterror.ru/in_russia/81051648 We can reasonably assume that this maximizes the number of incidents. Attacks listed on the site have been excluded by me if they can be attributed to criminal gang wars or other non-Chechen groups; and from Memorial *biulleten'* no. 28, 2004, http://www.memo.ru/about/bull/b28/

86. For the events at Budennovsk and Kizliar see Gall and de Wall (1998), 256–75.

87. The responsibility of the authorities, whether central or local, is still much debated. The 30-page report by the North Ossetian Parliamentary Commission into the Beslan events presented by deputy parliament speaker Stanislav Kesaev on 29 November 2005 contradicted some aspects of the official account of events given by federal authorities. The report blamed "shortcomings in the activities of the forces," FSB, Ministry of Internal Affairs, Ministry for Emergency Situations), http://www.pravdabeslana.ru/dokl.htm. The Federal Parliamentary Commission under Alexander Torshin, a Federation Council deputy speaker, in its preliminary report of 28 December 2005, rejected attempts to blame federal forces for the incident and shifted blame on to the lack of vigilance of the local authorities, http://www.pravdabeslana.ru/torshintez.htm For thorough analyses of these two incidents see the reports by John B. Dunlop, "The October 2002 Moscow Hostage-Taking Incident," Parts I–III, *RFE-RL Organized Crime and Terrorism Watch*, 18 December 2003, 8 January 2004, and 15 January 2004; and "Beslan: Russia's 9/11?" (American Committee for Peace in Chechnya and Jamestown Foundation, October 2005), http://www.peaceinchechnya.org/reports/Beslan.pdf.

88. See John Reuter, "Chechnya's Suicide Bombers: Desperate, Devout or Deceived" (Washington, D.C.: American Committee for Peace in Chechnya, 16 September 2004), 1–33, http://www.peaceinchechnya.org/reports/SuicideReport/SuicideReport.pdf

89. Personalistic motives are stressed in John Reuter, "The Calculus of Chechnya's Suicide Bombers," *Chechnya Weekly* (Jamestown Foundation) 6, 2 (13 January 2005), http://www.jamestown.org/publications_details.php?volume_id=409&issue_id=3195&article_id=2369088, and Cerwyn Moore, "Post-Modern War, Genocide and Chechnya: The Case of Female Suicide Attacks as a Problem for International Law and International Relations theory," *International Criminal Law Review* 5, 3 (2005): 485–500. For a focus on the political motivations in suicide attacks see the works cited in note 45 above.

90. Mia Bloom, "Mother. Daughter. Sister. Bomber," *Bulletin of the Atomic Scientists* 61, 6 (2005): 54–62. See also her book length study *Dying to Kill: The Allure of Suicide Terror* (New York: Columbia University Press, 2005).

91. See Iuliia Iuzik, *Nevesty Allakha. Litsa i sud'by vsekh zhenshchikhin-shakhidok vsorvavshikhsia v rossii* (Moscow: Ultra kul'tura, 2003).

92. Silke, "The Psychology of Suicidal Terrorism," in Silke (2003), 105.

93. Pape (2005), 64–76; Pedahzur (2005), 125–51. Pape and Pedazhur provide rigorous and balanced analysis of suicide attacks over time and stand in sharp contrast to the more sensationalist journalistic books on the phenomenon that have been spawned by 9/11. For an example of the latter see Christopher Reuter, *My Life Is a Weapon: A Modern History of Suicide Bombing* (Princeton, N.J.: Princeton University Press, 2004).

94. See Iuzik (2003).

95. See the datasets used in the works cited in notes 88 and 89 above.

96. Whereas Dudaev applauded Basaev's "heroism," he regarded the bus hijackers as criminals.

97. This is the general view of the political class in Russia. For an academic analysis that is sympathetic to the Russian position see Irina Mukhina, "Islamic Terrorism and the Question of National Liberation, or Problems of Contemporary Chechen Terrorism," *Studies in Conflict and Terrorism* 28 (2005): 515–32.

98. See p. 27 above.

99. *Moskovskie novosti,* 29 March 1992

100. Interview with Dudaev, Official Kremlin International News Broadcast, 12 August 1992.

101. Interview with Basaev, *Nezavisimaia gazeta,* 12 March 1996.

102. Ibid. and interview, *Izvestiia,* 25 April 1996.

103. Thomas Goltz. *Azerbaijan Diary: A Rogue Reporter's Adventures in an Oil-Rich, War-Torn, Post-Soviet Republic* (Armonk, N.Y.: M.E. Sharpe, 1998), 426–27.

104. *Segodnia,* 25 July 1995: 2.

105. Aleksandr Sargin and Valerii Batuev, "Dzhokhar Dudaev: 'brat" siloi chechentzev—zaniatie bessmyslennoe," *Argumenty i fakty* 49 (7 December 1994): 1.

106. A broadcast of Ekho Moskvy reported in BBC Summary of World Broadcasts, 11 March 1995.

107. *The Independent* (London), 26 March 1995, 13.

108. Interview with Basaev, *Nezavisimaia gazeta,* 12 March 1996.

109. See Margaret Wilson, "The Psychology of Hostage-Taking," in Silke (2003), 55–76.

110. Interview of President Abdul-Khalim Sadulaev for *Gazeta Wyborcza,* posted 14 September 2005, http://www.chechenpress.co.uk/english/news/2005/09/14/01.shtml

111. Interview with Maskhadov, 22 September 2003, published in *Novaia gazeta,* 2 October 2003.

112. Interview with Basaev, "Jihad Is Only Starting to Flare up in Ichkeria," *Kavkaz Center,* 9 June 2003.

113. As General Shamanov told Politkovskaia, civilians caught up in firefights were assumed "to be people connected in one way or another with the bandits." Politkovskaia (2001), 182. See also chapter 4 page xx above.

114. Interview with Zakaev, June 15, 2003, http://www.grani.ru/War/Chechnya/m.35505.html

115. Interview with Maskhadov, *Le Monde,* 4 October 2003, http://www.kavkaz.org.uk/russ/content/2003/10/06/11627.shtml

116. Interview with Maskhadov, 22 September 2003.

117. See http://www.kavkaz.org.uk/russ/content/2004/08/14/24674.shtml and http://www.kavkaz.org.uk/russ/content/2005/01/01/28350.shtml

118. Interview with Basaev by Andrei Babitskii, shown on ABC television (USA), July 28, 2005; extracts posted at Chechenpress.info, 8 August 2005, http://www.chechenpress.co.uk/english/news/2005/08/08/01.shtml

119. Statement by President Maskhadov, 23 September 2004, http://www. chechnya-mfa.info/print_news.php?func=detail&par=123 (on Beslan)

120. Last letter of President Aslan Maskhadov, 25 February 2005, http://www. chechnya-mfa.info/print_news.php?func=detail&par=131

121. Interview with Basaev broadcast on Channel 4 Television (UK), 3 February 2005. Basaev appeared on film wearing a black tee-shirt with the logo "anti-terrorist" in Russian. For extracts see http://www.kavkaz.org.uk/russ/content/2005/02/03/29868.shtml; Interview of Basaev by Andrei Babitskii, shown on ABC television (USA), July 28, 2005; extracts posted 8 August 2005, http://www.chechenpress.co.uk/english/news/2005/08/08/01.shtml

122. Igor Rotar, "Chechnya: po obe storony fronta," *Izvestiia*, 24 November 1995.

123. Walzer (1977), 198.

Chapter 6. Chechnya and the Study of Conflict

1. See Ted Robert Gurr, *Minorities at Risk: A Global View of Ethnopolitical Conflicts* (Washington, D.C.: U.S. Institute of Peace Press, 1993); and Ted Robert Gurr, "Ethnic Warfare on the Wane?" *Foreign Affairs* 79 (2000): 52–64.

2. For a broad representation of the diverse approaches to post-Soviet conflicts see the following collections: Alexei Arbatov, Abram Chayes, Antonia Handler Chayes, and Lara Olson, eds., *Managing Conflict in the Former Soviet Union* (Cambridge, Mass.: MIT Press, 1997); Barnett Rubin and Jack Snyder, eds., *Post-Soviet Political Order: Conflict and State-Building* (London: Routledge, 1998); James Hughes and Gwendolyn Sasse, eds., *Ethnicity and Territory in the Former Soviet Union: Regions in Conflict* (London: Frank Cass, 2002); Zoltan Barany and Robert G. Moser, eds., *Ethnic Politics After Communism* (Ithaca, N.Y.: Cornell University Press, 2005).

3. James D. Fearon and David D. Laitin, "Ethnicity, Insurgency and Civil War," *American Political Science Review* 97, 1 (2003): 75–76.

4. Rogers Brubaker and David Laitin. "Ethnic and Nationalist Violence," in Rogers Brubaker, *Ethnicity Without Groups* (Cambridge, Mass.: Harvard University Press, 2004), 115.

5. Ernest Gellner, *Nations and Nationalism*, 5th ed. (Oxford: Blackwell, 1983), 35.

6. Ernest Gellner, *Thought and Change* (London: Weidenfeld and Nicolson, 1964), 169.

7. Ernest Gellner, *Nationalism* (London: Weidenfeld and Nicolson, 1997), 72.

8. See Benedict Anderson, *Imagined Communities: Reflections on the Origin and Spread of Nationalism* (London: Verso, 1983).

9. Gellner (1997), 96.

10. Anthony Smith, *National Identity* (London: Penguin, 1991), 13.

11. For an evaluation of the continuing importance of Gellner's work see Brendan O'Leary, "On the Nature of Nationalism: A Critical Appraisal of Ernest Gellner's Writings on Nationalism," *British Journal of Political Science* 27, 2 (1997): 191–222; O'Leary, "Gellner's Diagnoses of Nationalism: A Critical Overview *or* What Is Living and What Is Dead in Gellner's Philosophy of Nationalism?" in J. A. Hall, ed., *The State of the Nation: Ernest Gellner and the Theory of Nationalism* (Cambridge: Cambridge University Press, 1998), 40–90.

12. Few Sovietologists expected a nationalist implosion of the USSR, and among the most unequivocal advocates in writing of the stability thesis were Gail Lapidus,

"Ethnonationalism and Political Stability: The Soviet Case" *World Politics* 36, 4 (1984): 555–80; and Mary McAuley, "Nationalism and the Soviet Multiethnic State," in Neil Harding, ed., *The State in Socialist Society* (London: Macmillan, 1984): 179–210. Among the notable exceptions that predicted the collapse along ethnonational lines were Walker Connor, *The National Question in Marxist-Leninist Theory and Strategy* (Princeton, N.J.: Princeton University Press, 1984); Hélène Carrère d'Encausse, *L'empire éclaté: la reévolte des nations en U.R.S.S* (Paris: Flammarion, 1978); and Robert Conquest, ed., *The Last Empire: Nationality and the Soviet Future* (Stanford, Calif.: Hoover Institution Press, 1986).

13. Donald L. Horowitz, "How to Begin Thinking Comparatively About Soviet Ethnic Problems," in Alexander J. Motyl, ed., *Thinking Theoretically About Soviet Nationalities. History and Comparison in the Study of the USSR* (New York: Columbia University Press, 1992), 11–13.

14. Gellner (1964).

15. Ernest Gellner, "Nationalism in the Vacuum," in Motyl (1992), 250.

16. Horowitz (1992), 14.

17. See S. N. Eisenstadt, "Center-Periphery Relations in the Soviet Empire: Some Interpretive Observations" in Motyl(1992), 205, 220–22; Rogers Brubaker, *Nationalism Reframed: Nationhood and the National Question in the New Europe* (Cambridge: Cambridge University Press, 1996); Valerie Bunce, *Subversive Institutions: The Design and the Destruction of Socialism and the State* (Cambridge: Cambridge University Press, 1999).

18. Eric Hobsbawm focuses more on the refusal of the Soviet regime to apply force rather than the power of nationalist movements; see Eric Hobsbawm, *Nations and Nationalism Since 1780: Programme, Myth and Reality* (Cambridge: Cambridge University Press, 1990), 168.

19. See Mark Beissinger, *Nationalist Mobilization and the Collapse of the Soviet State* (Cambridge: Cambridge University Press, 2002).

20. See Michael Ellman and Vladimir Kontorovich, "Overview," in Michael Ellman and Vladimir Kontorovich, eds., *The Disintegration of the Soviet Economic System* (London: Routledge, 1992), 1–39; Alexander Dallin, "The Causes of Collapse," *Post-Soviet Affairs* 8, 2 (1992): 279–302.

21. Ronald Suny, "The Revenge of the Past: Socialism and Ethnic Conflict in Transcaucasia," *New Left Review* 184 (1990): 5–34.

22. Gellner (1997), 86, 104.

23. See, for example, the contributions in David A. Lake and Donald S. Rothchild, eds., *The International Spread of Ethnic Conflict: Fear, Diffusion, and Escalation* (Princeton, N.J.: Princeton University Press, 1998).

24. Beissinger (2002), 25.

25. See Joseph Rothschild, *Ethnopolitics: A Conceptual Framework* (New York: Columbia University Press, 1981).

26. See Smith (1991).

27. Francisco J. Gil-White, "How Thick Is Blood? The Plot Thickens . . . : If Ethnic Actors Are Primordialists, What Remains of the Circumstantialist/Primordialist Controversy?" *Ethnic and Racial Studies* 22, 5 (1999): 789–820; Francisco J. Gil-White, "Are Ethnic Groups Biological 'Species' to the Human Brain? Essentialism in Our Cognition of Some Social Categories," *Current Anthropology* 42, 4 (2000): 515–55.

28. See the critical assessment by Donald L. Horowitz, "The Primordialists," in Daniele Conversi, ed., *Ethnonationalism in the Contemporary World: Walker Connor and the Study of Nationalism* (London: Routledge, 2002), 72–82.

29. Clifford Geertz, "The Integrative Revolution: Primordial Sentiments and Civil Politics in the New States," in Clifford Geertz, ed., *Old Societies and New States: The Quest for Modernity in Asia and Africa* (New York: Free Press, 1963), 105–57, esp. 128–29, 154–57.

30. There is a vast literature on the role of the media in agenda-setting. For studies which focus on the media's role in conflict see for example, Philip M. Seib, ed., *Media and Conflict in the Twenty-First Century* (New York: Palgrave, 2005); Tim Allen and Jean Seaton, eds., *The Media of Conflict: War Reporting and Representations of Ethnic Violence* (London: Zed Books, 1999). For a critical examination of the "CNN effect" see Peter Viggo Jakobsen, "Focus on the CNN Effect Misses the Point: The Real Media Impact on Conflict Management is Invisible and Indirect" *Journal of Peace Research* 37 (2000): 131–143. The U.S. led invasion of Iraq is perhaps the most glaring example of media distortion of recent times, see David Miller ed., *Tell Me Lies. Propaganda and Media Distortion in the Attack on Iraq* (London: Pluto Press, 2004).

31. "The Caucasus: Where Worlds Collide, " *Economist,* 19 August 2000: 19–23

32. Jack Snyder, *From Voting to Violence: Democratization and Nationalist Conflict* (New York: Norton, 2000), 226.

33. Roger D. Petersen, *Understanding Ethnic Violence: Fear, Hatred, and Resentment in Twentieth-Century Eastern Europe* (Cambridge: Cambridge University Press, 2002). He defines emotions in the context of ethnic violence as "switches" that are "a mechanism that triggers action to satisfy a pressing concern" (17).

34. Georg Elwert, "Intervention in Markets of Violence," in Jan Koehler and Christoph Zuercher, eds., *Potentials of (Dis)Order: Explaining Conflict and Stability in the Caucasus and in the Former Yugoslavia* (Manchester: Manchester University Press, 2003), 219–42.

35. For a discussion of the theories see John Darwin, *The End of the British Empire: The Historical Debate* (Oxford: Blackwell, 1991).

36. For a comprehensive critique of Kedourie's *Nationalism* see Brendan O'Leary, "In Praise of Empires Past: Myths and Method of Kedourie's Nationalism," *New Left Review* 18 (2002): 106–30.

37. Mark R. Beissinger, "The Persisting Ambiguity of Empire," *Post-Soviet Affairs* 11, 2 (1995): 155. The contentiousness of the term "empire" in the Soviet context is also evident from the reply to Beissinger by Ronald Grigor Suny, "Ambiguous Categories: States, Empire, and Nations," *Post-Soviet Affairs* 11, 2(1995): 185–96.

38. Elie Kedourie, *Nationalism,* rev. ed. (London: Hutchinson, 1961): 108–10, 138–39.

39. For the most effusive statement of support see Niall Ferguson, *Empire: How Britain Made the Modern World* (London: Allen Lane, 2003); and his *Colossus: The Price of America's Empire* (London: Penguin, 2004). For a critique of recent works that associate the U.S. with empire, see Alexander J. Motyl, "Empire Falls" *Foreign Affairs* 85, 4 (2006).

40. Michael W. Doyle, *Empires* (Ithaca, N.Y.: Cornell University Press, 1986), 45; Ernest Gellner, *Nations and Nationalism,* 5th ed. (Oxford: Blackwell, 1983), 1.

41. See, for example, the essays in W. H. Morris-Jones and Georges Fischer, eds., *Decolonisation and After: The British and French Experience* (London: Frank Cass, 1980), especially Dennis Austin, "The Transfer of Power: Why and How," 3–34.

42. The serious decolonization conflicts of the British Empire were in Ireland, Palestine, India, Kenya, Cyprus, Malaya, Aden, and Northern Ireland; in the French empire, they were in Vietnam and Algeria; in the Portuguese, they were in Angola and Mozambique.

43. A recent article compared Putin's policy on Chechnya with De Gaulle's exit from empire; see Matthew Evangelista, "Is Putin the New De Gaulle? A Comparison of the Chechen and Algerian Wars" *Post-Soviet Affairs* 21, 4 (2005): 360–77.

44. When the British government hosted the annual visiting delegation of Russian military and security officers in January 2004, it arranged a program that was tailored to imparting to the Russians the benefits of the British model of counterterrorism. According to the International Institute for Strategic Studies the program included a visit to OPTAG (the Operational Training and Advisory Group) of the MOD to learn first-hand how British soldiers are trained for peace support operations, briefings by MOD officials in Whitehall, and a two day stay in Belfast organized by the Northern Ireland Office, which included a visit to military units and briefings on "approaches taken by the British Armed forces under police primacy in handling terrorist threats and threats to public order," http://www.iiss.org/programmes/russia-and-eurasia/conferences/conferences-2004/russian-mod-senior-officials-visit-iiss. Whether the Russians have anything to learn from a model that spent twenty-five years trying to defeat the IRA by military force is another question.

45. For perspectives on the collapse of the Soviet Union as an "empire" see Karen Dawisha and Bruce Parrot, eds., *The End of Empire? The Transformation of the USSR in Comparative Perspective* (Armonk, N.Y.: M.E. Sharpe, 1997); Dominic Lieven, *Empire: The Russian Empire and Its Rivals* (London: John Murray, 2000).

46. For a discussion of the measures taken by Yeltsin and his team to disengage rapidly from the former Soviet republics in late 1991 see Jerry Hough, *Democratization and Revolution in the USSR, 1985–1991* (Washington, D.C.: Brookings Institution Press, 1997), 466–69.

47. See Neil Malcom, Alex Pravda, Margot Light, and Roy Allison, *Internal Factors in Russian Foreign Policy* (Oxford: Oxford University Press, 1996), 53–55, 63–64, 68.

48. For sympathetic, though not uncritical, assessments of the Clinton-era approach see Thomas Carothers, *Aiding Democracy Abroad: The Learning Curve* (Washington, D.C.: Carnegie Endowment for International Peace, 1999), 75–92; Michael Cox, "Wilsonianism Resurgent? The Clinton Administration and the Promotion of Democracy," in Michael Cox, G. John Ikenberry, and Takashi Inoguchi, eds., *American Democracy Promotion* (Oxford: Oxford University Press, 2000), 218–42; Margot Light, "Exporting Democracy," in Karen E. Smith and Margot Light, eds., *Ethics and Foreign Policy* (Cambridge: Cambridge University Press, 2001). For an example of the messianism of "idealpolitik" under Clinton see Strobe Talbott, "Democracy and the National Interest," *Foreign Affairs* 75, 6 (1996): 47–63, which not only makes a full commitment to the democratic peace theory, but also declares the lineage of Clinton's policy to be with Roosevelt, Wilson, the Founding Fathers, and Pericles, among others.

49. The obvious contradictions are evident from Vice-President Cheney's infamous "Vilnius speech" of 4 May 2006, when he criticized Russia and Belarus for lack of progress on democratization, while failing to mention the dynastic authoritarianism of Central Asia. The following day, during a visit to Kazakhstan, Cheney expressed his "admiration" for the rule of President Nazarbaev; see http://www.whitehouse.gov/news/releases/2006/05/20060504-1.html and http://www.whitehouse.gov/news/releases/2006/05/20060505-4.html (accessed 8 August 2006).

50. Edward D. Mansfield and Jack Snyder, "Democratization and the Danger of War," *International Security* 20, 1 (1995): 5. The authors used statistical evidence

to demonstrate that newly democratizing states were more warprone than either long-established democracies or stable autocracies.

51. Snyder (2000), 352.

52. Ibid., 32.

53. Ibid., 226.

54. Mary Kaldor, *New and Old Wars: Organized Violence in a Global Era* (Cambridge: Polity Press, 1999).

55. Beissinger (2002), 305–6.

56. Max Weber, "Politics as a Vocation," in *From Max Weber: Essays in Sociology*, ed. H. H. Gerth and C. Wright Mills (London: Routledge and Kegan Paul, 1974), 83.

57. Ibid., 78.

58. Christoph Zürcher and Jan Koehler, "Introduction," in Koehler and Zürcher (2003), 8.

59. Elwert (2003), 219, 230.

60. Lake and Rothchild (1998), 8, 11–23.

61. Beissinger (2002): 17.

62. Allen Feldman, *Formations of Violence. The Narrative of the Body and Political Terror in Northern Ireland* (Chicago: University of Chicago Press, 1991), 20–21.

63. See Mark R. Beissinger and Crawford Young, eds., *Beyond State Crisis? Post-Colonial Africa and Post-Soviet Eurasia in Comparative Perspective* (Washington, D.C.: Woodrow Wilson Center Press, 2002). This collection illustrates the point that it is generally easier to identify the key elements for comparison than to systematically compare and analyze them.

64. Brubaker (1996), 63; Claus Offe, *Varieties of Transition: The East German and East European Experience* (Cambridge: Polity Press, 1996), 50–81.

65. The euphemism "ethnic cleansing" masks three strategies that may or may not be found together: genocide, expulsion, and coercive assimilation. What these strategies have in common is a preference for ethnic homogenization.

66. For one of the few studies of conflict potential in the FSU that did not materialize see the analysis of the Crimean question in post-Soviet Ukraine by Gwendolyn Sasse, "The Theory and Practice of Conflict-Prevention in a Transition State: The Crimean Issue in Post-Soviet Ukraine" *Nationalism and Ethnic Politics* 8, 2 (2002): 1–26; and her forthcoming monograph *The Crimea Question: Identity, Transition, and Conflict* (Cambridge. Mass.: Harvard University Press, 2007). Sasse explains how the deliberative elite bargaining process itself defused the potential for violence.

67. See the individual case studies of different outcomes in post-Soviet states in James Hughes and Gwendolyn Sasse, eds., *Ethnicity and Territory in the Former Soviet Union: Regions in Conflict* (London: Frank Cass, 2002).

68. See Charles Tilly, ed., *The Formation of National States in Western Europe* (Princeton, N.J.: Princeton University Press, 1975), 602, 607.

69. Gellner (1983), 4.

70. Gellner (1983), 43–50. See also his essays on various country cases of nationalism in *Encounters with Nationalism* (Oxford: Blackwell, 1994).

71. Juan Linz and Alfred Stepan, *Problems of Democratic Consolidation: Southern Europe, South America, and Post-Communist Europe* (Baltimore: John Hopkins University Press, 1996), 16.

72. Ibid., 25. In particular, they reflect the notion of the "proper unit" for democracy as set out by Robert Dahl, *Democracy and Its Critics* (New Haven, Conn.: Yale University Press, 1989), 207–9.

73. Linz and Stepan (1996), 36, table 2.1.

74. Ibid., 25–26.

75. Ibid., 31.

76. Juan Linz and Alfred Stepan, "Political Identities and Electoral Sequences: Spain, the Soviet Union, and Yugoslavia" *Daedalus* 121 (1992): 123–39.

77. For a critique of the theories see Brendan O'Leary, "On the Nature of Nationalism: A Critical Appraisal of Ernest Gellner's Writings on Nationalism," *British Journal of Political Science* 27, 2 (1997): 191–222 and his "Nationalism and Ethnicity: Research Agendas on Theories of Their Sources and Their Regulation," in Daniel Chirot and Martin Seligman, eds., *Ethnopolitical Warfare: Causes and Consequences and Possible Solutions* (Washington, D.C.: American Psychological Association, 2001), 37–48. For a discussion of the relative merits and problems of federalism as a solution see John McGarry and Brendan O'Leary, "Introduction: The Macro-Political Regulation of Ethnic Conflict," in John McGarry and Brendan O'Leary, eds., *The Politics of Ethnic Conflict Regulation* (London: Routledge, 1993), 1–40, and John McGarry and Brendan O'Leary, "Federalism as a Method of Ethnic Conflict Regulation," in Sid Noel, ed., *From Power-Sharing to Democracy: Post-Conflict Institutions in Ethnically Divided Societies* (Montreal: McGill-Queen's University Press, 2005), 263–96. For multiculturalism see Will Kymlicka, *Multicultural Citizenship: A Liberal Theory of Minority Rights* (Oxford: Oxford University Press, 1995).

78. See Arend Lijphart, *Democracy in Plural Societies: A Comparative Exploration* (New Haven, Conn.: Yale University Press, 1977). Consociationalism has four main features: a grand coalition government guaranteeing the representation the main segments of the divided society; a proportional representation electoral system; community autonomy (a degree of self-government of ethnic communities over certain issues); and constitutional vetoes for minority groups in power. For an evaluation of its effectiveness see Brendan O'Leary, "Debating Consociation" in Noel, ed. (2005), 3–43.

79. Donald Horowitz. *Ethnic Groups in Conflict* (Berkeley: University of California Press, 1985), 6–7, 18, 33.

80. Ibid., 596.

81. Vesna Bojcic, Mary Kaldor, and Ivan Vejvoda, *Post-War Reconstruction in the Balkans: A Background Report for the European Commission,* SEI Working Paper 14 (Brighton: Sussex European Institute, 1995). Institutionalized power-sharing is also seen as an obstacle to democratization in the former Soviet Union; see Philip G. Roeder, "Peoples and States After 1989: The Political Costs of Incomplete National Revolutions," *Slavic Review* 58, 4 (1999): 873–76.

82. See Brubaker (1996), 26; Bunce (1999); Connor (1984).

83. For case studies that relate post-Soviet conflicts to changes in the organization of state institutions, and the de-institutionalization of Soviet-era "institutionalized multiethnicity" see Hughes and Sasse (2002).

84. For a recent study of the role of the demographic factor in the conflicts in the Caucasus see Monica Duffy Toft, *The Geography of Ethnic Violence: Identity, Interests and the Indivisibility of Territory* (Princeton, N.J.: Princeton University Press, 2003).

85. For the most comprehensive study of *uti posseditis* and the international legal aspects of self-determination and secession see Antonio Cassese, *Self-Determination of Peoples: A Legal Reappraisal* (Cambridge: Cambridge University Press, 1998).

86. Articles 1(2) and 55 of the UN Charter (1945) enshrined the "principle" (not the "right") of "self determination of peoples." The term "peoples," however,

is not a defined category, thus casting doubt over who can legitimately claim this right. Adopted just as the era of decolonization was accelerating, Chapters XI and XII of the UN Charter stipulated that colonial powers should promote "self-government" of "territories" not ethnic groups, thus reaffirming the norm for colonial administrative demarcations to become the basis for new states; see Morton H. Halperin and David J. Scheffer, eds., *Self-Determination in the New World Order* (Washington, D.C.: Carnegie Endowment for International Peace, 1992), 20; Louis B. Sohn, "The Concept of Autonomy in International Law and the Practice of the United Nations," *Israel Law Review* 15, 2 (1980): 185–88; Thomas D. Musgrave, *Self-Determination and National Minorities* (Oxford: Clarendon Press, 1997): 62–90.

87. As it proved impossible to get UN agreement on a satisfactory definition of "self-government," the shift from principle to enforceable right of "self-determination" in international law came very gradually. In a UN resolution of 1960 the right of self-determination of all "peoples" was again restated. In 1966 self-determination was included in two UN International Covenants of Human Rights, which marked important steps on the way to the general recognition of the legally binding character of the clause: the International Covenant on Civil and Political Rights and the International Covenant on Economic, Social, and Cultural Rights. Only in 1976, with the entry into force of these two international covenants, "self-determination" became a legal right. The first article of both covenants declared "All peoples have the right of self-determination." The binding legal effect, however, was accompanied by a number of ambiguities, most importantly over defining "peoples." See Ruth Lapidoth, *Autonomy: Flexible Solutions to Ethnic Conflicts* (Washington, D.C.: U.S. Institute of Peace Press, 1997), 19–23.

88. Benedict Kingsbury, "Claims by Non-State Actors in International Law," *Cornell International Law Journal* 25, 3 (1992): 487.

89. For competing "moral" claims, see Allen Buchanan, *Secession: The Morality of Political Divorce from Fort Sumter to Lithuania and Quebec* (Boulder, Colo.: Westview Press, 1991).

90. James Crawford, *The Creation of States in International Law* (Oxford: Clarendon Press, 1979).

91. Colin Warbrick, "State and Recognition in International Law," in Malcolm D. Evans, ed., *International Law* (Oxford: Oxford University Press, 2003), 205–67.

92. Donald Horowitz, "The Cracked Foundations of the Right to Secede," *Journal of Democracy* 14, 2 (2003): 5.

93. See Lapidoth (1997); Hurst Hannum and Richard B. Lillich, "The Concept of Autonomy in International Law" in Yoram Dinstein, ed., *Models of Autonomy* (New Brunswick, N.J.: Transaction Books, 1981), 215–54.

94. For a discussion of the issues of secession and international relations in the post-Soviet context see Hughes and Sasse (2002), 12–20.

95. See Badinter Arbitration Commission. Opinion No. 1, 29 November 1991, *European Journal of International Law* 3 (1992): 182; Roland Rich, "Recognition of States: The Collapse of Yugoslavia and the Soviet Union," *European Journal of International Law* 4 (1993): 36–65; Richard Caplan, *Europe and the Recognition of New States in Yugoslavia* (Cambridge: Cambridge University Press, 2005).

96. See Richard Sakwa, "A Just War Fought Unjustly," in Bruno Coppieters and Richard Sakwa, eds., *Contextualizing Secession: Normative Studies in Comparative Perspective* (Oxford: Oxford University Press, 2003), 156–86.

Conclusion

1. Ian S. Lustick, *Unsettled States, Disputed Lands: Britain and Ireland, France and Algeria, Israel and the West Bank-Gaza* (Ithaca, N.Y.: Cornell University Press, 1993), 447.

2. Putin interview, *New York Times*, 4 October 2003, http://www.kremlin.ru/eng/speeches/2003/10/04/1345_53478.shtml

3. Putin, press conference, Kremlin, January 31, 2006, http://www.kremlin.ru/appears/2006/01/31/1310_type63380type63381type82634_100848.shtml

4. Tolstoy's ascription of Nicholas I's approach to the Poles, that he "hated them in proportion to the harm he had done them," seems appropriate for Putin's attitude to the Chechen resistance. The quote is from *Hadji Murat.*

5. Valery Tishkov, "Ethnic Conflicts in the Former USSR: The Use and Misuse of Typologies and Data." *Journal of Peace Research* 36, 5 (1999), 582

6. Radio Free Europe/Radio Liberty interview with Emil Pain, 15 October 2005, http://www.rferl.org/featuresarticle/2005/10/b543d3da-1542-4d26-952d-0bbda79d0edd.html

7. These remedies are proposed by Horowitz, Lijphart, McGarry and O'Leary, and Cornell respectively.

8. Putin, press conference, Kremlin, 31 January 2006, http://www.kremlin.ru/appears/2006/01/31/1310_type63380type63381type82634_100848.shtml

Bibliography

Newspapers and Other Media

Agence France Presse
Argumenty i fakty
BBC Monitoring International Reports
BBC Summary of World Broadcasts
Bulletin of the Atomic Scientists
The Economist
Financial Times
Focus (Munich)
The Guardian
Groznenskii rabochii
The Independent (London)
Interfax
Itar-Tass
Izvestiia
Kommersant daily
Kommersant vlast'
Komsomol'skaia Pravda
Krasnaia zvezda
Literaturnaia gazeta
Memorial biulleten'
Moskovskie novosti
Moskovskii komsomolets
Moscow News
Moscow Times
New York Times
Nezavisimaia gazeta
Novaia gazeta
Official Kremlin International News Broadcast
Oil & Gas Journal
Pravda
Prospect
Radio Free Europe/Radio Liberty
Rossiiskaia federatsiia

Rossiiskaia gazeta
Segodnia
Sovetskaia rossiia
The Times (London)
Trud
Vash Vybor
Vlast'
The Washington Post
The Washington Times

Books, Articles, Documents

Aklaev, Airat R. *Democratization and Ethnic Peace: Patterns of Ethnopolitical Crisis and Management in Post-Soviet Settings.* Aldershot: Ashgate, 1999.
Alexeev, Mikhail A., ed. *Center-Periphery Conflict in Post-Soviet Russia: A Federation Imperilled.* London: Macmillan, 1999.
Allen, Tim and Jean Seaton, eds. *The Media of Conflict: War Reporting and Representations of Ethnic Violence.* London: Zed Books, 1999.
Allison, Roy. "The Chechnia Conflict: Military and Security Policy Implications." In Roy Allison and Christoph Bluth, eds., *Security Dilemmas in Russia and Eurasia.* London: Royal Institute of International Affairs, 1998. 241–80.
Anderson, Benedict. *Imagined Communities: Reflections on the Origin and Spread of Nationalism.* London: Verso, 1983.
Arbatov, Alexei G. *The Transformation of Russian Military Doctrine: Lessons Learned from Kosovo and Chechnya.* Marshall Center Papers 2. Garmisch-Partenkirchen: George C. Marshall European Center for Security Studies, July 2000. http://www.marshallcenter.org/site-graphic/lang-en/page-coll-mcp-1/
Arbatov, Alexei G., Abram Chayes, Antonia Handler Chayes, and Lara Olson, eds. *Managing Conflict in the Former Soviet Union.* Cambridge, Mass.: MIT Press, 1997.
Arutiunov, Sergei. "Ethnicity and Conflict in the Caucasus." In Sergei Arutiunov, Andranik Migranian, Emil Payin, and Galina Starovoitova, *Ethnic Conflict and Russian Intervention in the Caucasus. Institute on Global Conflict and Cooperation. IGCC Policy Papers.* (August 1, 1995): 15–18. http://repositories.cdlib.org/igcc/PP/PP16.
Avtorkhanov, Abdurahman. "The Chechens and the Ingush During the Soviet Period and Its Antecedents." In Marie Bennigsen Broxup, ed., *The North Caucasus Barrier: The Russian Advance Towards the Muslim World.* London: Hurst, 1992. 146–94.
Baddeley, John. *The Russian Conquest of the Caucasus.* London: Longman, 1908.
Badinter Arbitration Commission. Opinion No. 1, 29 November 1991. *European Journal of International Law* 3 (1992): 182.
Baev, Pavel. "Instrumentalizing Counter-Terrorism for Regime Consolidation in Putin's Russia." *Studies in Conflict and Terrorism* 27 (2004): 337–52.
———. "Chechnya and the Russian Military: A War Too Far?" In Richard Sakwa, ed., *Chechnya: From Past to Future.* London: Anthem Press; Sterling, Va.: Stylus Publishers, 2005. 117–30.
Bahl, Roy and Christine Wallich. "Intergovernmental Fiscal Relations in the Russian Federation." In Richard M. Bird, Robert D. Ebel, and Christine I. Wallich, eds., *Decentralization of the Socialist State.* Washington, D.C.: World Bank, 1995.

Bahry, Donna. *Outside Moscow: Power, Politics, and Budgetary Policy in the Soviet Republics.* New York: Columbia University Press, 1987.

Baev, Pavel. "Chechnya and the Russian Military: A War Too Far?" In Richard Sakwa, ed., *Chechnya: From Past to Future.* London: Anthem Press, 2005.Sakwa (2005), 117–30.

Baiev, Khassan. *The Oath: A Surgeon Under Fire.* New York: Walker, 2003.

Baker, Mark. *Nam: The Vietnam War in the Words of the Men and Woman Who Fought There.* New York: William Morrow, 1981.

Baranets, Viktor. *Eltsin i ego generaly: Zapiski polkovnika genshtaba.* Moscow: *Sovershenno sekretno,* 1998.

Barany, Zoltan and Robert G. Moser, eds. *Ethnic Politics After Communism.* Ithaca, N.Y.: Cornell University Press, 2005.

Barkhatov, Aleksandr. *General Lebed', ili moia lebedinaia pesnia.* Moscow: Politburo, 1998.

Barrett, Thomas. "Crossing Boundaries: The Trading Frontiers of the Terek Cossacks." In Daniel R. Brower and Edward J. Lazzerini, eds., *Russia's Orient: Imperial Borderlands and Peoples, 1700–1917.* Bloomington: Indiana University Press, 1997. 227–48.

Baturin, Yuri. "Chess-Like Diplomacy at Novo-Ogarevo. An Eye-Witness Account to the Drafting of the USSR Union Treaty of 1991." *Demokratizatsiia* 2, 2 (1994): 212–21.

Beckett, Ian F. W. *Modern Insurgencies and Counter-Insurgencies: Guerrillas and Their Opponents Since 1750.* London: Routledge, 2001.

Beissinger, Mark R. "The Persisting Ambiguity of Empire." *Post-Soviet Affairs* 11, 2 (1995): 149–84.

———. *Nationalist Mobilization and the Collapse of the Soviet State.* Cambridge: Cambridge University Press, 2002.

Beissinger, Mark R. and Crawford Young, eds. *Beyond State Crisis? Post-Colonial Africa and Post-Soviet Eurasia in Comparative Perspective.* Washington, D.C.: Woodrow Wilson Center Press, 2002.

Bennett, Andrew. *Condemned to Repetition? The Rise, Fall, and Reprise of Soviet-Russian Military Interventionism, 1973–1996.* Cambridge, Mass.: MIT Press, 1999.

Bennett, Vanora. *Crying Wolf: The Return of War to Chechnya.* London: Macmillan, 1998.

Bennigsen, Alexandr. "Un mouvement populaire au Caucase du XVIIIe siècle: la guerre sainte de Sheikh Mansur (1785–1794). Page mal connue et controversée des relations russo-turques." *Cahiers du Monde Russe et Soviétique* 5, 2 (1964): 159–205.

———. "Muslim Guerrilla Warfare in the Caucasus, 1918–1928." *Central Asian Survey* 2, 2 (1983): 280–94.

Bennigsen, Alexandre and S. Enders Wimbush. *Mystics and Commissars: Sufism in the Soviet Union.* London: Hurst, 1985.

———. *Muslims of the Soviet Empire: A Guide.* Bloomington: Indiana University Press, 1986.

Bennigsen-Broxup, Marie, ed. *The North Caucasus Barrier: The Russian Advance Toward the Muslim World.* London: Hurst, 1992.

Bespalov, Iurii. "Oruzhie sdali po prikazu moskvy." *Izvestiia,* 14 January 1995.

Bird, Chris. *To Catch a Tatar: Notes from the Caucasus.* London: John Murray, 2002.

Blandy, Charles. *Chechnya: Two Federal Interventions: An Interim Comparison and Assessment.* Camberley: Royal Military Academy Sandhurst, Conflict Studies Research Centre, 2000/01. http://www.da.mod.uk/CSRC/documents/Caucasus/P29

Blinushov, A. et al. *By All Available Means: The Russian Federation Ministry of Internal Affairs Operation in the Village of Samashki, April 7–8, 1995.* Moscow: Memorial Human Rights Center, 1996.

Bloom, Mia. "Mother. Daughter. Sister. Bomber." *Bulletin of the Atomic Scientists* 61, 6 (2005): 54–62.

———. *Dying to Kill: The Allure of Suicide Terror.* New York: Columbia University Press, 2005.

Bojcic, Vesna, Mary Kaldor, and Ivan Vejvoda. *Post-War Reconstruction in the Balkans. A Background Report for the European Commission.* SEI Working Paper 14. Brighton: Sussex European Institute, 1995.

Breuilly, John. *Nationalism and the State.* 2nd ed. Manchester: Manchester University Press: 1993.

Bronshteyn, Karen, ed. *The 1989 USSR Census: A Bilingual (Russian/English) Companion Guide to the Microfiche Edition.* Minneapolis: Eastview, 1994.

Brubaker, Rogers. *Nationalism Reframed: Nationhood and the National Question in the New Europe.* Cambridge: Cambridge University Press, 1996.

Brubaker, Rogers and David Laitin. "Ethnic and Nationalist Violence." In Rogers Brubaker, ed., *Ethnicity Without Groups.* Cambridge, Mass.: Harvard University Press, 2004. 88–115.

Buchanan, Allen. *Secession: The Morality of Political Divorce from Fort Sumter to Lithuania and Quebec.* Boulder, Colo.: Westview Press, 1991.

Bunce, Valerie. *Subversive Institutions: The Design and the Destruction of Socialism and the State.* Cambridge: Cambridge University Press, 1999.

Busygina, Irina. "Regional'noe izmerenie politicheskogo krisisa v rossii." *MEMO* 5 (1994): 5–17.

Campbell, Bruce B. and Arthur D. Brenner, eds. *Death Squads in Global Perspective: Murder with Deniability.* Basingstoke: Palgrave Macmillan, 2002.

Caplan, Richard. *Europe and the Recognition of New States in Yugoslavia.* Cambridge: Cambridge University Press, 2005.

Carothers, Thomas. *Aiding Democracy Abroad: The Learning Curve.* Washington, D.C.: Carnegie Endowment for International Peace, 1999.

Carrère d'Encausse, Hélène. *L'empire éclaté: la révolte des nations en U.R.S.S.* Paris: Flammarion, 1978.

Susan L. Carruthers. *Winning Hearts and Minds. British Governments, the Media and Colonial Counter-Insurgency 1944–1960.* London: Leicester University Press, 1995.

Cashaback, David. "Risky Strategies? Putin's Federal Reforms and the Accommodation of Difference in Russia." Journal on Ethnopolitics and Minority Issues in Europe 3 (2003): 1–32. http://www.ecmi.de/jemie/special_3_2003.html

Cassese, Antonio. *Self-Determination of Peoples: A Legal Reappraisal.* Cambridge: Cambridge University Press, 1998.

Chesnov, Yan. "Civilization and the Chechen." *Anthropology & Archaeology of Eurasia* 34, 3 (1995–96): 28–40.

Chinarikhina, Galina. "Dogovor kak sposob razgranicheniia polnomochii i predmetov vedeniia mezhdu subektami federativnykh otnoshenii v Rossii." *Vlast'* 9 (1996): 20–25.

Clinton, Bill. *My Life.* New York: Knopf, 2004.

Coll, Steve. *Ghost Wars: The Secret History of the CIA, Afghanistan, and Bin Laden, from the Soviet Invasion to September 10.* New York: Penguin Press, 2004.

Colomer, Josep M. "The Spanish 'State of Autonomies': Non-Institutional Federalism." *West European Politics* 21, 4 (1998): 40- 52.

Colton, Timothy J. "Boris Yeltsin, Russia's All-Thumbs Democrat." In Timothy

Colton and Robert C. Tucker, eds., *Patterns in Post-Soviet Leadership*. Boulder, Colo.: Westview Press, 1995. 49–74.

Connor, Walker D. *The National Question in Marxist-Leninist Theory and Strategy*. Princeton, N.J.: Princeton University Press, 1984.

Conquest, Robert, ed. *The Last Empire: Nationality and the Soviet Future*. Stanford, Calif.: Hoover Institution Press, 1986.

Coppetiers, Bruno and Richard Sakwa, eds. *Contextualizing Secession: Normative Studies in Comparative Perspective*. Oxford: Oxford University Press, 2003.

Cornell, Svante. *Small Nations and Great Powers: A Study of Ethnopolitical Conflict in the Caucasus*. London: Curzon, 2001.

———. "Autonomy as a Source of Conflict: Caucasian Conflicts in Theoretical Perspective." *World Politics* 54, 2 (2002): 245–76.

Cox, Michael. "Wilsonianism Resurgent? The Clinton Administration and the Promotion of Democracy." In Michael Cox, G. John Ikenberry, and Takashi Inoguchi, eds., *American Democracy Promotion*. Oxford: Oxford University Press, 2000. 218–42.

Crawford, James. *The Creation of States in International Law*. Oxford: Clarendon Press, 1979.

Curran, Diane, Fiona Hill, and Elena Kostritsyna. *The Search for Peace in Chechnya: A Sourcebook 1994–1996*. Cambridge. Mass.: Harvard University, John F. Kennedy School of Government Strengthening Democratic Institutions Project, 1997.

Dahl, Robert. *Democracy and Its Critics*. New Haven, Conn.: Yale University Press, 1989.

Dallin, Alexander. "The Causes of Collapse." *Post-Soviet Affairs* 8, 2 (1992): 279–302.

Darwin, John. *The End of the British Empire: The Historical Debate*. Oxford: Blackwell, 1991.

Dawisha, Karen and Bruce Parrot, eds. *The End of Empire? The Transformation of the USSR in Comparative Perspective*. Armonk, N.Y.: M.E. Sharpe, 1997.

Dawson, Jane I. *Eco-Nationalism: Anti-Nuclear Activism and National Identity in Russia, Lithuania, and Ukraine*. Durham, N.C.: Duke University Press, 1996.

DeBardeleben, Joan. "The Development of Federalism in Russia." In Peter J. Stavrakis, Joan DeBardeleben, and Larry Black, eds., *Beyond the Monolith: The Emergence of Regionalism in Post-Soviet Russia*. Washington, D.C.: Woodrow Wilson Center Press, 1997. 35–56.

Derlugian, Georgi. "Che Guevaras in Turbans: Chechens Versus Globalization." *New Left Review* 237 (1999): 3–27.

Dettmering, Christian. "Reassessing Chechen and Ingush (Vainakh) Clan Structures in the 19th Century." *Central Asian Survey* 24, 4 (2005): 469–89.

Dmitrieva, Olga. "Politicheskie igri vokrug budzheta." *Moskovskie novosti* 28 (1993): 8–9.

Doyle, Michael W. *Empires*. Ithaca, N.Y.: Cornell University Press, 1986.

Duchacek, Ivo. *Comparative Federalism: The Territorial Dimension of Politics*. New York: Holt, Rinehart, 1970.

Dudaev, Dzhokhar. *Ternistii put' k svobode, Pravitelstvennye dokumenty Chechenskoi Respubliky, stat'y, intervju*. Vilnius, 1993.

———. *K voprosu o gosudarstvenno-politicheskom ustroistve v chechenskoi respubliki*. Grozny: Groznenskii rabochii, 1993.

Dudaeva, Alla. *Million pervyi*. Baku: Zeinalov & Synov'ia, 2002.

Duffy Toft, Monica. *The Geography of Ethnic Violence: Identity, Interests and the Indivisibility of Territory*. Princeton, N.J.: Princeton University Press, 2003.

Dunlop, John B. *Russia Confronts Chechnya: Roots of a Separatist Conflict*. Cambridge: Cambridge University Press, 1998.

———. "How Many Soldiers and Civilians Died During the Russo-Chechen War of 1994–1996." *Central Asian Survey* 19, 3–4 (2000): 329–39.

———. *Russian Federation: The Situation of IDPs from Chechnya*. UNHCR WRITENET Paper 11 (2002).

———. "'Storm in Moscow': A Plan of the Yeltsin Family to Destabilize Russia." Washington, D.C.: Johns Hopkins School of Advanced International Studies, 8 October 2004: 1–52. www.sais-jhu.edu/programs/res/papers/Dunlop_paper.pdf

EastWest Institute. *Federal Budget and the Regions: Analyzing Fiscal Flows*. Moscow: Dialogue-MSU, 1999.

Eisenstadt, Shmuel N. "Center-Periphery Relations in the Soviet Empire: Some Interpretive Observations." In Alexander J. Motyl, ed., *Thinking Theoretically About Soviet Nationalities*. New York: Columbia University Press, 1992. 205–23.

Elazar, Daniel J. *Exploring Federalism*. Tuscaloosa: University of Alabama Press, 1987.

Elkin, Caroline. *Imperial Reckoning: The Untold Story of Britain's Gulag in Kenya*. New York: Henry Holt, 2005.

Ellman, Michael and Vladimir Kontorovich. "Overview." In Michael Ellman and Vladimir Kontorovich, eds., *The Disintegration of the Soviet Economic System*. London: Routledge, 1992.

Elwert, Georg. "Intervention in Markets of Violence." In Jan Koehler and Christoph Zuercher, eds., *Potentials of (Dis)Order: Explaining Conflict and Stability in the Caucasus and in the Former Yugoslavia*. Manchester: Manchester University Press, 2003. 219–42.

European Council. Presidency Conclusions, Helsinki 10/11 December 1999, Declaration on Chechnya. http://europa.eu.int/council/off/conclu/dec99/annexII

Evangelista, Matthew. *The Chechen Wars: Will Russia Go the Way of the Soviet Union?* Washington, D.C.: Brookings Institution Press, 2002.

———. "Is Putin the New De Gaulle? A Comparison of the Chechen and Algerian Wars." *Post-Soviet Affairs* 21, 4 (2005): 360–77.

Fairbanks, Charles H., Jr. "Weak States and Private Armies." In Mark R. Beissinger and Crawford Young, eds., *Beyond State Crisis? Post-Colonial Africa and Post-Soviet Eurasia in Comparative Perspective*. Washington, D.C.: Woodrow Wilson Center Press, 2002. 129–60.

Fearon, James D. and David D. Laitin. "Ethnicity, Insurgency, and Civil War." *American Political Science Review* 97, 1 (2003): 75–90.

Federativnyi Dogovor: Dokumenty, Kommentarii. Moskva: Izdatel'stvo Respublika, 1992.

Feldman, Allen. *Formations of Violence: The Narrative of the Body and Political Terror in Northern Ireland*. Chicago: University of Chicago Press, 1991.

Ferguson, Niall. *Empire: How Britain Made the Modern World*. London: Allen Lane, 2003.

———. *Colossus: The Price of America's Empire*. London: Penguin, 2004.

Fleutiaux, Brice, with Alexandre Levy. *Otage en Tchétchénie*. Paris: Robert Laffont, 2001.

Frey, R. G. and Christopher W. Morris. *Violence, Terrorism and Justice*. Cambridge: Cambridge University Press, 1991.

Fuller, Liz. "Tug of War for Control of Chechnya's Oil Revenues Continues."

Radio Free Europe/Radio Liberty, Newsline 10, 224, Part 1 (6 December 2006). http://www.rferl.org/newsline/

Gaeta, Paola. "The Armed Conflict in Chechnya Before the Russian Constitutional Court." *European Journal of International Law* 7, 4 (1996): 563–70.

Gall, Carlotta and Thomas de Waal. *Chechnya: A Small Victorious War.* New York: New York University Press, 1998.

Gammer, Moshe. *Muslim Resistance to the Czar: Shamil and the Conquest of Chechnia and Daghestan.* London: Frank Cass, 1994.

Geertz, Clifford. "The Integrative Revolution: Primordial Sentiments and Civil Politics in the New States." In Clifford Geertz, ed., *Old Societies and New States: The Quest for Modernity in Asia and Africa.* New York: Free Press, 1963. 105–57.

Gellner, Ernest. *Thought and Change.* London: Weidenfeld and Nicolson, 1964.

———. *Nations and Nationalism.* 5th ed. Oxford: Blackwell, 1983.

———. "Nationalism in the Vacuum." In Alexander J. Motyl, ed., *Thinking Theoretically About Soviet Nationalities.* New York: Columbia University Press, 1992. 243–54.

———. *Encounters with Nationalism.* Oxford: Blackwell, 1994.

———. *Nationalism.* London: Weidenfeld and Nicolson, 1997.

German, Tracey C. *Russia's Chechen War.* London: Routledge, 2003.

Gil-White, Francisco J. "How Thick Is Blood? The Plot Thickens . . . : If Ethnic Actors Are Primordialists, What Remains of the Circumstantialist/Primordialist Controversy?" *Ethnic and Racial Studies* 22, 5 (1999): 789–820.

———. "Are Ethnic Groups Biological 'Species' to the Human Brain? Essentialism in Our Cognition of Some Social Categories." *Current Anthropology* 42, 4 (2000): 515–55.

Goldenberg, Suzanne. *Pride of Small Nations: The Caucasus and Post-Soviet Disorder.* London: Zed Books, 1994.

Goltz, Thomas. *Azerbaijan Diary: A Rogue Reporter's Adventures in an Oil-Rich, War-Torn, Post-Soviet Republic.* Armonk, N.Y.: M.E. Sharpe, 1998.

———. *Chechnya Diary: A War Correspondent's Story of Surviving the War in Chechnya.* New York: St. Martin's Press, 2003.

Gorbachev, Mikhail. *Zhizn i reformy.* 2 vols. Moscow: Novosti, 1995.

———. *Memoirs.* London: Doubleday, 1996.

Guboglo, Mikhail N., ed. *Federalizm vlasti i vlast' federalizma.* Moscow: IntelTekh, 1997.

Gurr, Ted Robert. *Minorities at Risk: A Global View of Ethnopolitical Conflicts.* Washington, D.C.: U.S. Institute of Peace Press, 1993.

———. "Ethnic Warfare on the Wane?" *Foreign Affairs* 79 (2000): 52–64.

Hack, Karl. *Defence and Decolonisation in South-East Asia: Britain, Malaya and Singapore 1941–1968.* London: Routledge, 2000.

Halperin, Morton H. and David J. Scheffer with Patricia L. Small. *Self-Determination in the New World Order.* Washington, D.C.: Carnegie Endowment for International Peace, 1992.

Hanauer, Laurence. "Tatarstan and the Prospects for Federalism in Russia: A Commentary." *Security Dialogue* 27, 1 (1996): 81–86.

Hannum, Hurst and Richard B. Lillich. "The Concept of Autonomy in International Law." In Yoram Dinstein, ed., *Models of Autonomy.* New Brunswick, N.J.: Transaction Books, 1981. 215–54.

Hayden, William. "The Political Genesis of Conflict in Chechnya, 1990–1994." *Civil Wars* 2, 4 (1999): 23–56.

Herr, Michael. *Dispatches.* New York: Vintage Books, 1977.

Hobsbawm, Eric. *Nations and Nationalism Since 1780: Programme, Myth and Reality.* Cambridge: Cambridge University Press, 1990.

Hoffman, Bruce. *Inside Terrorism.* New York: Columbia University Press, 1998.

Honderich, Ted. *After the Terror.* Edinburgh: Edinburgh University Press, 2003.

Horgan, John. "The Search for the Terrorist Personality." In Andrew Silke, ed., *Terrorists, Victims, and Society: Psychological Perspectives on Terrorism and its Consequences,* Chichester: Wiley, 2003. 3–28.

———. *The Psychology of Terrorism.* London: Routledge, 2005.

Horowitz, Donald L. *Ethnic Groups in Conflict.* Berkeley: University of California Press, 1985.

———. *A Democratic South Africa? Constitutional Engineering in a Divided Society.* Berkeley: University of California Press, 1991.

———. "How to Begin Thinking Comparatively About Soviet Ethnic Problems." In Alexander J. Motyl, ed., *Thinking Theoretically About Soviet Nationalities: History and Comparison in the Study of the USSR.* New York: Columbia University Press, 1992. 9–22.

———. "Democracy in Divided Societies: The Challenge of Ethnic Conflict." *Journal of Democracy* 4, 4 (1993): 18–38.

———. "The Primordialists." In Daniele Conversi, ed., *Ethnonationalism in the Contemporary World: Walker Connor and the Study of Nationalism.* London: Routledge, 2002. 72–82.

———. "The Cracked Foundations of the Right to Secede." *Journal of Democracy* 14, 2 (2003): 5–17.

Hough, Jerry. *Democratization and Revolution in the USSR, 1985–1991.* Washington, D.C.: Brookings Institution Press, 1997.

Howard, Michael. "Constraints on Warfare." In Michael Howard, George I. Andreopoulos, and Mark R. Shulman, eds., *The Laws of War: Constraints on Warfare in the Western World.* New Haven, Conn.: Yale University Press, 1994: 1–11.

Hughes, James. "Regionalism in Russia: The Rise and Fall of Siberian Agreement." *Europe-Asia Studies* 46, 7 (1994): 1133–62.

———. "The 'Americanization' of Russian Politics: Russia's First Television Election, December 1993." *Journal of Communist Studies and Transition Politics* 10, 2 (1994): 125–50.

———. "Russia's Federalization: Bilateral Treaties Add to Confusion." *Transition* 2, 19 (1996): 39–43.

———. "Sub-National Elites and Political Transformation in Russia: A Reply to Krystanovskaya and White." *Europe-Asia Studies* 49, 6 (1997): 1017–36.

———. "Chechnya: Understanding the Causes of a Protracted Post-Soviet Conflict." *Civil Wars* 4, 4 (2001): 11–48.

———. "Managing Secession Potential in the Russian Federation." In James Hughes and Gwendolyn Sasse, eds., *Ethnicity and Territory in the Former Soviet Union: Regions in Conflict.* London: Frank Cass, 2002. 36–68.

———. "From Federalisation to Recentralisation." In Stephen White et al., eds., *Developments in Russian Politics 5.* London: Macmillan, 2001. 128–46.

———. "The Peace Process in Chechnya." In Richard Sakwa, ed., *Chechnya: From Past to Future.* London: Anthem Press, 2005. 265–87.

———. "The EU's Relations with Russia: Partnership or Asymmetric Interdependency?" Nicola Casarini and Costanza Musu eds., *The EU's Foreign Policy in an Evolving International System: The Road To Convergence,* Palgrave, London: 2007 forthcoming.

Hughes, James and Gwendolyn Sasse, eds. *Ethnicity and Territory in the Former Soviet Union: Regions in Conflict.* London: Frank Cass, 2002.

———. "Comparing Regional and Ethnic Conflicts in Post-Soviet Transition States." In James Hughes and Gwendolyn Sasse, eds., *Ethnicity and Territory in the Former Soviet Union: Regions in Conflict.* London: Frank Cass, 2002. 1–35.

———. "Conflict and Accommodation in the FSU: The Role of Institutions and Regimes." In James Hughes and Gwendolyn Sasse, eds., *Ethnicity and Territory in the Former Soviet Union: Regions in Conflict.* London: Frank Cass, 2002. 220–40.

Human Rights Center Memorial. *Chechnia 2004 god. Pokhishcheniia i ischeznoveniia liudei,* 7 February 2005. http://www.memo.ru/hr/hotpoints/caucas1/index.htm

———. *The Chechen Republic: Consequences of "Chechenization" of the Conflict.* 2 March 2006. http://www.memo.ru/hr/hotpoints/caucas1/index.htm

Human Rights Watch. "The 'Dirty War' in Chechnya: Forced Disappearances, Torture, and Summary Executions." *Human Rights Watch* 13, 1 (D) (March 2001). http://www.hrw.org/reports/2001/chechnya/

———. "Widespread Torture in the Chechen Republic." Human Rights Watch Briefing Paper for the 37th Session U.N. Committee against Torture (13 November 2006). http://hrw.org/backgrounder/eca/chechnya1106/chechnya1106web.pdf

Huntington, Samuel. *The Clash of Civilizations and the Making of World Order.* London: Touchstone Books, 1998.

Informatsionnaia voina v chechne: Fakty, dokumenty, svidetel'stva, noiabr' 1994–sentiabr' 1996. Moscow: Fond zashchity glasnosti, 1997.

International Alert. *Chechnia: Report of an International Alert Fact-Finding Mission, September 24th–October 3rd 1992.* London: International Alert, 1992.

Itogi vsesoiuznoi perepisi naseleniia 1989 goda. Gosudarstvennyi komitet SSSR po statistike. Imprint. Minneapolis: East View Publications, 1992.

Iuzik, Iuliia. *Nevesty Allakha. Litsa i sud'by vsekh zhenshchikhin-shakhidok vsorvavshikhsia v rossii.* Moscow: Ultra kul'tura, 2003.

Jakobsen, Peter Viggo "Focus on the CNN Effect Misses the Point: The Real Media Impact on Conflict Management Is Invisible and Indirect." *Journal of Peace Research* 37 (2000): 131–43.

Jersild, Austin Lee. "Who Was Shamil? Russian Colonial Rule and Sufi Islam in the North Caucasus, 1859–1917." *Central Asian Survey* 14, 2 (1995): 205–23.

———. "From Savagery to Citizenship: Caucasian Mountaineers and Muslims in the Russian Empire." In Daniel R. Brower and Edward J. Lazzerini, eds., *Russia's Orient: Imperial Borderlands and Peoples, 1700–1917.* Bloomington: Indiana University Press, 1997. 101–14.

Joint Chiefs of Staff. *The National Military Strategy of the United States of America: A Strategy for Today, a Vision for Tomorrow.* Washington, D.C.: Department of Defense, 2004. http://www.defenselink.mil/news/Mar2005/d20050318nms.pdf

Kahn, Jeffrey. *Federalism, Democratization and the Rule of Law in Russia.* Oxford: Oxford University Press, 2002.

Kaldor, Mary. *New and Old Wars: Organized Violence in a Global Era.* Cambridge: Polity Press, 1999.

Kalyvas, Stathis N. *The Logic of Violence in Civil War.* Cambridge: Cambridge University Press, 2006.

Karny, Yo'av. *Highlanders: A Journey to the Caucasus in Quest of Memory.* New York: Farrar Straus, 2000.

Kedourie, Elie. *Nationalism.* Rev. ed. London: Hutchinson, 1961.

Khakimov, Raphael S. "Prospects of Federalism in Russia: A View from Tatarstan." *Security Dialogue* 27, 1 (1996): 71–76.

———. "Ob osnovakh asimmetrichnosti Rossiiskoi Federatsii." In Leokhadiia M. Drobizheva, ed., *Asimmetrichnaia federatsiia: vzgliad iz tsentra, respublik i oblastei.* Moscow: Izdatel'stvo Instituta sotsiologii RAN, 1998. 37–48.

Kingsbury, Benedict. "Claims by Non-State Actors in International Law." *Cornell International Law Journal* 25, 3 (1992): 481–97.

Kitson, Frank. *Low-Intensity Operations: Subversion, Insurgency and Peacekeeping.* London: Faber and Faber, 1971.

Klebnikov, Paul. *Godfather of the Kremlin: Boris Berezovsky and the Looting of Russia.* New York: Harcourt, 2000.

Khlystun, Viktor. "*Tochka zreniia. Pavel Grachev: 'Menia naznachili otvetstvennym za voinu'.*" *Trud,* 15 March 2001.

Knezys, Stasys and Romanas Sedlickas, *The War in Chechnya.* College Station: Texas A&M University Press, 1999.

Koehler, Jan and Christoph Zuercher, eds. *Potentials of (Dis)Order: Explaining Conflict and Stability in the Caucasus and in the Former Yugoslavia.* Manchester: Manchester University Press, 2003.

Konstitutsii respublik v sostave Rossiiskoi Federatsii. Vols. 1, 2. Moscow: Izvestiia, 1996.

Konstitutsiia Rossiiskoi Federatsii. Moscow: Nauchnoe Izdatel'stvo, 1995.

Korzhakov, Aleksandr Vasil'evich. *Boris El'tsin: ot rassveta do zakata.* Moscow: Interbuk, 1997.

Kostikov, Viacheslav. *Roman s prezidentom: zapiski press-sekretaria.* Moscow: Vagrius, 1997.

Kovalev, Sergei. *Proposals for a Peace Process.* 24 March 1995. *http://asf.wdn.com/*

———. "Russia After Chechnya." *New York Review of Books* 44, 12 (17 July 1997): 27–31.

———. "*Putin's War.*" New York Review of Books *47, 2 (10 February 2000): 4–8.*

Kryshtanovskaya, Olga and Stephen White. "From Soviet *Nomenklatura* to Russian Elite." *Europe-Asia Studies* 48, 5 (1997): 711–34.

Kulikov, Anatolii and Sergei Lembik. *Chechenskii uzel: khronika vooruzhennogo konflikta 1994–1996gg.* Moscow: Dom Pedagogiki, 2000.

Kymlicka, Will. *Multicultural Citizenship: A Liberal Theory of Minority Rights.* Oxford: Oxford University Press, 1995.

Lake, David A. and Donald S. Rothchild, eds. *The International Spread of Ethnic Conflict: Fear, Diffusion, and Escalation.* Princeton, N.J.: Princeton University Press, 1998.

Lankina, Tomila V. *Governing the Locals: Local Self-Government and Ethnic Mobilization in Russia.* Oxford: Rowman and Littlefield, 2004.

Lapidoth, Ruth. *Autonomy: Flexible Solutions to Ethnic Conflicts.* Washington, D.C.: U.S. Institute of Peace Press, 1997.

Lapidus, Gail. "Ethnonationalism and Political Stability: The Soviet Case." *World Politics* 36, 4 (1984): 555–80.

———. "Contested Sovereignty: The Tragedy of Chechnya." *International Security* 23, 1 (1998): 5–49.

Lapidus, Gail W. and Edward W. Walker. "Nationalism, Regionalism, and Federalism: Center-Periphery Relations in Post-Communist Russia." In Gail Lapidus, ed., *Russia's Troubled Transition.* Cambridge: Cambridge University Press, 1995. 79–113.

Laqueur, Walter. *The New Terrorism: Fanaticism and the Arms of Mass Destruction.* London: Phoenix Press, 2001.

Lavrov, Sergei. "Reform Will Enhance the OSCE's Relevance." *Financial Times* 29 November 2004.

Lawrence, T. E. "The Evolution of a Revolt." *Army Quarterly* 1, 1 (1920): 1–21. U.S. Army Combined Arms Center Combat Studies Institute reprint, http://www-cgsc.army.mil/carl/resources/csi/csi.asp#reprints

Layton, Susan. "Primitive Despot and Noble Savage: The Two Faces of Shamil in Russian Literature." *Central Asian Survey* 10, 4 (1991): 31–45.

Lemco, Jonathan. *Political Stability in Federal Governments.* New York: Praeger, 1991.

Levada, Yuri. "What the Polls Tell Us." *Journal of Democracy* 15, 3 (2004): 43–51.

Lieven, Anatol. *Chechnya: Tombstone of Russian Power.* New Haven, Conn.: Yale University Press, 1998.

———. "Nightmare in the Caucasus." *Washington Quarterly* 23, 1 (2000): 145–59.

Lieven, Dominic. *Empire: The Russian Empire and Its Rivals.* London: John Murray, 2000.

Light, Margot. "Exporting Democracy." In Karen E. Smith and Margot Light, eds., *Ethics and Foreign Policy.* Cambridge: Cambridge University Press, 2001. 75–92.

Lijphart, Arend. *Democracy in Plural Societies: A Comparative Exploration.* New Haven, Conn.: Yale University Press, 1977.

Linz, Juan. "The Perils of Presidentialism." *Journal of Democracy* 1, 1 (1990): 51–69.

Linz, Juan and Alfred Stepan. "Political Identities and Electoral Sequences: Spain, the Soviet Union, and Yugoslavia." *Daedalus* 121 (1992): 123–39.

———. *Problems of Democratic Consolidation: Southern Europe, South America, and Post-Communist Europe.* Baltimore: John Hopkins University Press, 1996.

Litvenenko, Aleksandr and Iurii Fel'stinskii. *FSB vsryvaet rossiiu: Federal'naia sluzhba bezopasnosti—organizator terroristicheskikh actov, pokhishchenii i ubiistv.* 2nd ed. corrected and expanded. New York: Liberty Publishing House, 2004, http://terror99.ru/FSBSeconEdition.pdf

Lustick, Ian. "Stability in Deeply Divided Societies: Consociationalism or Control." *World Politics* 31 (1979): 325–44.

———. *Unsettled States, Disputed Lands: Britain and Ireland, France and Algeria, Israel and the West Bank-Gaza.* Ithaca, N.Y.: Cornell University Press, 1993.

Magnusson, Märta-Lisa. "The Negotiation Process Between Russia and Chechenia—Strategies, Achievements and Future Problems." In Ole Høiris and Sefa Martin Yürukel, eds., *Contrasts and Solutions in the Caucasus.* Aarhus: Aarhus University Press, 1998.

Malashenko, Aleksei and Dmitrii Trenin. *Vremia Iuga: Rossiia v Chechne, Chechne v Rossii.* Moscow: Gendal'f, Carnegie Center Moscow, 2002.

Malcolm, Neil, Alex Pravda, Margot Light, and Roy Allison. *Internal Factors in Russian Foreign Policy.* Oxford: Oxford University Press, 1996.

Mansfield, Edward D. and Jack Snyder. "Democratization and the Danger of War." *International Security* 20, 1 (1995): 5–38.

Matvieva, Anna. *The North Caucasus: Russia's Fragile Borderland.* London: Royal Institute of International Affairs, 1999.

Mau, Vladimir. *Yeltsin's Choice: Background to the Chechnya Crisis.* London: Social Market Foundation, 1994.

McAuley, Mary. "Nationalism and the Soviet Multiethnic State." In Neil Harding, ed., *The State in Socialist Society.* London: Macmillan, 1984: 179–210.

———. *Russia's Politics of Uncertainty.* Cambridge: Cambridge University Press, 1997.

McFaul, Michael. "Eurasian Letter: Russian Politics After Chechnya." *Foreign Policy* 99 (1995): 149–68.

McGarry, John and Brendan O'Leary. "Introduction: The Macro-Political Regulation of Ethnic Conflict." In John McGarry and Brendan O'Leary, eds., *The Politics of Ethnic Conflict Regulation*. London: Routledge, 1993. 1–40.

———. "Federalism as a Method of Ethnic Conflict Regulation." In Sid Noel, ed., *From Power-Sharing to Democracy: Post-Conflict Institutions in Ethnically Divided Societies*. Montreal: McGill-Queen's University Press, 2005. 263–96.

Médicins sans Frontières. *The Trauma of Ongoing War in Chechnya: Quantitative Assessment of Living Conditions, and Psychosocial and General Health Status Among War Displaced in Chechnya and Ingushetia*. Amsterdam: Médicins sans Frontières, August 2004. http://www.uk2.msf.org/reports/Chechnyareport.pdf

Meier, Andrew. *Chechnya: To the Heart of a Conflict*. London: W.W. Norton, 2005.

Merom, Gil. *How Democracies Lose Small Wars*. Cambridge: Cambridge University Press, 2003.

Mickiewicz, Ellen. *Changing Channels: Television and the Struggle for Power in Russia*. Oxford: Oxford University Press, 1997.

Miller, David ed., *Tell Me Lies. Propaganda and Media Distortion in the Attack on Iraq*. London: Pluto Press, 2004.

Miller, John H. "Cadres Policy in Nationality Areas: Recruitment of CPSU First and Second Secretaries in Non-Russian Republics of the USSR." *Soviet Studies* 29, 1 (1977): 3–36.

Ministry of Foreign Affairs of the Chechen Republic of Ichkeria. *The Russian-Chechen Tragedy: The Way to Peace and Democracy: Conditional Independence Under an International Administration*. February 2003, http://www.chechnya-mfa.info/

Moore, Cerwyn. "Post-Modern War, Genocide and Chechnya: The Case of Female Suicide Attacks as a Problem for International Law and International Relations Theory." *International Criminal Law Review* 5, 3 (2005): 485–500.

Morris-Jones, W. H. and Georges Fischer, eds. *Decolonisation and After: The British and French Experience*. London: Frank Cass, 1980.

Morshchakova, T. G., ed. *Konstitutsionnyi sud rossiiskoi federatsii, postanovleniia opredeleniia 1992–1996*. Moscow: Novyi Iurist, 1997.

Motyl, Alexander J., ed. *Thinking Theoretically About Soviet Nationalities*. New York: Columbia University Press, 1992.

———. "Empire Falls." *Foreign Affairs* 85, 4 (2006).

Mukhina, Irina. "Islamic Terrorism and the Question of National Liberation, or Problems of Contemporary Chechen Terrorism." *Studies in Conflict and Terrorism* 28 (2005): 515–32.

Musgrave, Thomas D. *Self-Determination and National Minorities*. Oxford: Clarendon Press, 1997.

Muzaev, Timur. *Chechenskaia Respublika: Organy Vlasti i Politicheskie Sily*. Moscow: Panorama, 1995.

Nabulsi, Karma. *Traditions of War: Occupation, Resistance, and the Law*. Oxford: Oxford University Press, 1999.

Narody Rossii, Entsiklopediia, Bol'shaia Rossiiskaia Entsiklopediia. Moscow, 1994

Nivat, Anne. *Chienne de Guerre: A Woman Reporter Behind the Lines of the War in Chechnya*. Trans. Susan Darnton. New York: Public Affairs, 2001.

"O bor'be s terrorizmom" (On the Fight Against Terrorism). Russian Federation Federal Law No. 130-FZ, 25 July 1998 *Rossiiskaia gazeta*, 4 August 1998.

O'Donnell, Guillermo. "Delegative Democracy." *Journal of Democracy* 5, 1 (1994): 55–69.

O'Leary, Brendan. "On the Nature of Nationalism: A Critical Appraisal of Ernest

Gellner's Writings on Nationalism." *British Journal of Political Science* 27, 2 (1997): 191–222.

———. "Gellner's Diagnoses of Nationalism: A Critical Overview *or* What Is Living and What Is Dead in Gellner's Philosophy of Nationalism?" In J. A. Hall, ed., *The State of the Nation: Ernest Gellner and the Theory of Nationalism*. Cambridge: Cambridge University Press, 1998. 40–90.

———. "Nationalism and Ethnicity: Research Agendas on Theories of Their Sources and Their Regulation." In Daniel Chirot and Martin E. P. Seligman, eds., *Ethnopolitical Warfare: Causes, Consequences and Possible Solutions*. Washington, D.C.; American Psychological Association, 2001. 37–48.

———. "In Praise of Empires Past: Myths and Method of Kedourie's Nationalism." *New Left Review* 18 (2002): 106–30.

———. "Debating Consociation." In Sid Noel, ed., *From Power-Sharing to Democracy: Post-Conflict Institutions in Ethnically Divided Societies*. Montreal: McGill-Queens University Press, 2005. 3–43.

Offe, Claus. *Varieties of Transition: The East European and East German Experience*. Cambridge: Polity Press, 1996.

Ordeshook, Peter. "Reexamining Russia: Institutions and Incentives." *Journal of Democracy* 6, 2 (1995): 46–60.

Pain, Emil. "Armed Conflict in Kosovo and Chechnya: A Comparison." *Forced Migration Monitor* (New York: Open Society Institute) 25 (September 1998): 1–6. http://www.osi.hu/fmp/html/fm_monitor_98_toc.html

Panfilov, Oleg and Aleksei Simonov, eds. *Fond zashchity glasnosti, informatsionnaia voina v chechne: fakty, dokumenty, svidetel'stva, noiabr' 1994–sentiabr 1996*. Moscow: Prava cheloveka, 1997.

Pape, Robert A. *Dying to Win: The Strategic Logic of Suicide Terrorism*. New York: Random House, 2005.

Parliamentary Assembly Council of Europe. *Human Rights Violations in the Chechen Republic: The Committee of Ministers' Responsibility vis-à-vis the Assembly's Concerns*. Committee on Legal Affairs and Human Rights, Rapporteur: Mr. Rudolf Bindig, Report, Doc. 10774, December 2005.

Pedahzur, Ami. *Suicide Terrorism*. Cambridge: Polity Press, 2005.

Petersen, Roger D. *Understanding Ethnic Violence: Fear, Hatred, and Resentment in Twentieth-Century Eastern Europe*. Cambridge: Cambridge University Press, 2002.

Politkovskaya, Anna. *A Dirty War: A Russian Reporter in Chechnya*. London: Harvill, 2001.

Protocol Additional to the Geneva Conventions of 12 August 1949, and Relating to the Protection of Victims of Non-International Armed Conflicts (Protocol II) (1978). http://www.unhchr.ch/html/menu3/b/94.htm

Ram, Harsha. *Prisoners of the Caucasus: Literary Myths and Media Representations of the Chechen Conflict*. Working Papers Series. Berkeley: Berkeley Program in Soviet and Post-Soviet Studies, University of California, 1999.

Rashid, Ahmed. *Taliban: The Story of the Afghan Warlords*. London, Pan Macmillan, 2001.

Reuter, Christopher. *My Life Is a Weapon: A Modern History of Suicide Bombing*. Princeton, N.J.: Princeton University Press, 2004.

Rich, Roland. "Recognition of States: The Collapse of Yugoslavia and the Soviet Union." *European Journal of International Law* 4 (1993): 36–65.

Roeder, Philip G. "Peoples and States After 1989: The Political Costs of Incomplete National Revolutions." *Slavic Review* 58, 4 (1999): 873–76.

Rose, Richard. "How Floating Parties Frustrate Democratic Accountability: A

Supply-Side View of Russia's Elections" *East European Constitutional Review* 9, 1–2 (2000).

Rothschild, Joseph. *Ethnopolitics: A Conceptual Framework.* New York: Columbia University Press, 1981.

Roy, Olivier. "Afghanistan—War as a Factor of Entry into Politics." *Central Asian Survey* 8, 4 (1989): 43–62.

———. *The Failure of Political Islam.* London: I.B. Tauris, 1994.

———. *Globalized Islam: The Search for a New Ummah.* New York: Columbia University Press, 2004.

Rubin, Barnett and Jack Snyder, eds., *Post-Soviet Political Order: Conflict and State-Building.* London: Routledge, 1998.

Rutland, Peter. "Putin's Path to Power." *Post-Soviet Affairs* 16, 4 (2000): 313–54.

Rybkin, Ivan P. *Consent in Russia, Consent in Chechnya.* N.p.: Lytten Trading and Investment, Abacus Trust and Management Services, 1998.

Rywkin, Michael. "The Communist Party and the Sufi Tariqat in the Checheno-Ingush Republic." *Central Asian Survey* 10, 1–2 (1991): 133–45.

Said, Edward. *Orientalism: Western Conceptions of the Orient.* Harmondsworth: Penguin, 1995.

Sakwa, Richard. "A Just War Fought Unjustly." In Bruno Coppetiers and Richard Sakwa, eds., *Contextualizing Secession: Normative Studies in Comparative Perspective.* Oxford: Oxford University Press, 2003. 156–86.

———, ed. *Chechnya: From Past to Future.* London: Anthem Press, 2005.

Sargin, Aleksandr and Valerii Batuevi. "Dzhokhar Dudaev: brat' siloi chechen-tzev—zanyatie bessmyslennoe." *Argumenty i fakty* 49 (7 December 1994): 1.

Sasse, Gwendolyn. "The Theory and Practice of Conflict-Prevention in a Transition State: The Crimean Issue in Post-Soviet Ukraine." *Nationalism and Ethnic Politics* 8, 2 (2002): 1–26.

———. *The Crimea Question: Identity, Transition, and Conflict.* Cambridge. Mass.: Harvard University Press, 2007.

Sbornik rasporiazhenii i postanovlenii presidenta chechenskoi respubliki. Grozny: Kniga, 1993.

Sbornik ukazov presidenta chechenskoi respubliki s 1 iiulia 1992 g. po 31 dekabria 1992 g. Grozny: Kniga, 1993.

Schmid, Alex P. "Terrorism and the Use of Weapons of Mass Destruction: From Where the Risk?" In Max Taylor and John Horgan, eds., *The Future of Terrorism.* London: Frank Cass, 2000. 106–32.

Schmid, Alex P. and Albert J. Jongman, with Michael Stohl et al. *Political Terrorism: A New Guide to Actors, Authors, Concepts, Data Bases, Theories and Literature.* 2nd ed. Amsterdam: North-Holland, 1988.

Schneider, Eberhard. "Moscow's Decision for War in Chechnya." *Aussenpolitik* 46, 2 (1995): 157–67.

Seely, Robert. *Russo-Chechen Conflict, 1800–2000: A Deadly Embrace.* London: Frank Cass, 2001.

Seib, Philip M., ed. *Media and Conflict in the Twenty-First Century.* New York: Palgrave, 2005.

Sharlet, Robert. "The Prospects for Federalism in Russian Constitutional Politics." *Publius: The Journal of Federalism* 24 (Spring 1994): 115–27.

Shevchenko, Dmitrii. *Kremlevskie nravy.* Moscow: Kollektsiia Sovershenno sekretno, 1999.

Shleifer, Andrei and Daniel Treisman. *Without a Map: Political Tactics and Economic Reform in Russia.* Cambridge, Mass.: MIT Press, 2000.

Silke, Andrew, ed. *Terrorists, Victims, and Society: Psychological Perspectives on Terrorism and Its Consequences.* Chichester: Wiley, 2003.

———. "Becoming a Terrorist." In Silke, ed., *Terrorists, Victims, and Society,* 29–54.

———. "The Psychology of Suicidal Terrorism," in ibid., 93–108.

———. "The impact of 9/11 on research on terrorism." In Magnus Ranstorp ed., *Mapping Terrorism Research.* Abingdon: Routledge, 2007: 76–93.

Slider, Darrell. "Federalism, Discord, and Accommodation: Intergovernmental elations in Post-Soviet Russia." In Theodore Friedgut and Jeffrey Hahn, eds., *Local Power and Post-Soviet Politics.* Armonk, N.Y.: M.E Sharpe, 1994. 239–69.

Smith, Anthony. *National Identity.* London: Penguin, 1991.

Smith, Graham. "Russia, Multiculturalism and Federal Justice." *Europe-Asia Studies* 50, 8 (1998): 1393–1412.

———. *The Post-Soviet States: Mapping the Politics of Transition.* London: Arnold, 1999.

Smith, Sebastian. *Allah's Mountains: Politics and War in the Russian Caucasus.* London: I.B. Tauris, 1998.

Snyder, Jack. *From Voting to Violence: Democratization and Nationalist Conflict.* New York: W.W. Norton, 2000

Sobranie zakonodatel'stva Rossiiskoi Federatisii. Moscow: Iuridicheskaia literatura, 1996.

Sohn, Louis B. "The Concept of Autonomy in International Law and the Practice of the United Nations." *Israel Law Review* 15, 2 (1980): 185–88.

Solnick, Steven. "The Political Economy of Russian Federalism: A Framework for Analysis." *Problems of Post-Communism* (November/December 1996): 13–25.

———. "Will Russia Survive? Center and Periphery in the Russian Federation." In Barnett Rubin and Jack Snyder, eds., *Post-Soviet Political Order: Conflict and State-Building.* London: Routledge, 1998. 58–80.

———. "Is the Center Too Weak or Too Strong in the Russian Federation?" In Valerie Sperling, ed., *Building the Russian State: Institutional Crisis and the Quest for Democratic Governance.* Boulder, Colo.: Westview Press, 2000. 137–56.

Solzhenitsyn, Alexander. *The Gulag Archipelago.* Vol. 3. Boulder, Colo.: Westview Press, 1998.

Sorianskaia, Ekaterina. "Families and Clans in Ingushetia and Chechnya. A Fieldwork Report." *Central Asian Survey* 24, 4 (2005): 453–67.

Splidsboel-Hansen, Flemming. "The 1991 Chechen Revolution: The Response of Moscow." *Central Asian Survey* 13, 3 (1994): 395–407.

SSSR v tsifrakh v 1989g. Moscow: Finansy i statistika, 1990.

Starovoitova, Galina. "Is Democracy Possible in Russia After Chechnya?" In Sergei Arutiunov, Andranik Migranian, Emil Payin, and Galina Starovoitova, *Ethnic Conflict and Russian Intervention in the Caucasus Institute on Global Conflict and Cooperation. IGCC Policy Papers.* (August 1, 1995): 9–14. http://repositories.cdlib.org/igcc/PP/PP16.

———. *Sovereignty After Empire: Self-Determination Movements in the Former Soviet Union.* Washington, D.C.: U.S. Institute of Peace, 1997.

Stepan, Alfred. "Russian Federalism in Comparative Perspective." *Post-Soviet Affairs* 16, 2 (2000): 133–76.

Stepanova, Ekaterina. "Kosovo and Chechnya: Illogical Parallels." *Security Dialogue* 31, 1 (2000): 135–37.

Stone, Randall W. *Lending Credibility: The International Monetary Fund and the Post-Communist Transition.* Princeton, N.J.: Princeton University Press, 2002.

Strange, Susan. "The Defective State." *Daedalus* 124, 2 (1995): 55–74.

Stubbs, Richard. *Hearts and Minds in Guerrilla Warfare: The Malayan Emergency, 1948–1960.* Oxford: Oxford University Press, 1989.

Suny, Ronald Grigor. "The Revenge of the Past: Socialism and Ethnic Conflict in Transcaucasia." *New Left Review* 184 (1990): 5–34.

———. "Ambiguous Categories: States, Empire, and Nations." *Post-Soviet affairs* 11, 2 (1995): 185–96.

Suverennyi Tatarstan. Moscow: Insan, 1997.

Talbot, Strobe. "Democracy and the National Interest." *Foreign Affairs* 75, 6 (1996): 47–63.

———. *The Russia Hand: A Memoir of Presidential Diplomacy.* New York: Random House, 2002.

Tarlton, Charles. "Symmetry and Asymmetry as Elements of Federalism: A Theoretical Speculation." *Journal of Politics* 27, 4 (1965): 861–74.

Tilly, Charles, ed. *The Formation of National States in Western Europe.* Princeton, N.J.: Princeton University Press, 1975.

Tishkov, Valery A., ed. *Narody Rossii, Entsiklopediia.* Moscow: Bol'shaia Rossiiskaia Entsiklopediia, 1994.

———. *Ethnicity, Nationalism and Conflict in and After the Soviet Union: The Mind Aflame.* London: Sage, 1997.

———. "Ethnic Conflicts in the Former USSR: The Use and Misuse of Typologies and Data." *Journal of Peace Research* 36, 5 (1999): 571–91.

———. *Understanding Violence for Post-Conflict Reconstruction in Chechnya.* Geneva: Centre for Applied Studies in International Negotiations (CASIN), 2001.

———. *Chechnya: Life in a War-Torn Society.* London: University of California Press, 2004.

Tishkov, Valery A., Yelena Beliaeva, and Georgi Marchenko. *Chechenskii krizis.* Moscow: Business Roundtable of Russia Research Center, 1995.

Tolz, Vera. "Forging the Nation: National Identity and Nation Building in Post-Communist Russia." *Europe-Asia Studies* 50, 6 (1998): 993–1022.

Townshend, Charles. *Terrorism: A Very Short Introduction.* Oxford: Oxford University Press, 2002.

Treisman, Daniel. "Deciphering Russia's Federal Finance: Fiscal Appeasement in 1995 and 1996." *Europe-Asia Studies* 50, 5 (1995): 893–906.

———. "Fiscal Redistribution in a Fragile Federation: Moscow and the Regions in 1994." *British Journal of Political Science* 28 (1998): 185–209.

———. "The Politics of Intergovernmental Transfers in Post-Soviet Russia." *British Journal of Political Science* 26 (1996): 299–335.

———. *After the Deluge: Regional Crises and Political Consolidation in Russia.* Ann Arbor: University of Michigan Press, 1999.

Trinquier, Roger. *Modern Warfare: A French View of Counterinsurgency.* New York: Praeger, 1964.

Troshev, Gennadii. *Moia voina: Chechenskii dnevnik okopnogo generala.* Moscow: Vagrius, 2001.

Umnova, Irina A. *Konstitutsionnye osnovy sovremennogo Rossiiskogo Federalizma.* Moscow: Delo, 1996.

United Nations, *Report of the Policy Working Group on the United Nations and Terrorism,* 2002, New York: United Nations, 2002. http://www.un.org/terrorism/a57273.htm

———. *Office of the High Commissioner for Human Rights,* Geneva Convention relative to the Protection of Civilian Persons in Time of War (1950), *Geneva: United Nations 1997–2002.* http://www.unhchr.ch/html/intlinst.htm

U.S. Department of State, Office of the Coordinator for Counterterrorism. *Country*

Reports on Terrorism 2004. Washington, D.C.: Department of State, April 2005. http://www.state.gov/s/ct/rls/c14812.htm

———. *Fact Sheet: Foreign Terrorist Organizations (FTO's).* Washington, D.C.: Department of State, 11 October 2005.

Walker, Edward W. "Russia's Soft Underbelly: The Stability of Instability in Dagestan." Berkeley Program in Soviet and Post-Soviet Working Paper Series, Winter 1999–2000. http://socrates.berkeley.edu/~bsp/publications.html

Wallich, Christine I. "Fiscal Decentralization, Intergovernmental Relations in Russia." Studies of Economies in Transformation Paper 6. Washington, D.C.: World Bank, 1992.

———, ed. *Russia and the Challenge of Fiscal Federalism.* Washington, D.C.: World Bank, 1994.

———. "Reforming Intergovernmental Relations: Russia and the Challenge of Fiscal Federalism." In Bartlomiej Kaminski, ed., *Economic Transition in Russia and the New States of Eurasia.* Armonk, N.Y.: M.E. Sharpe, 1997. 252–76.

Walzer, Michael. *Just and Unjust Wars: A Moral Argument with Historical Illustrations.* New York: Basic Books, 1977.

———. *Arguing About War.* New Haven, Conn.: Yale University Press, 2004.

Warbrick, Colin. "State and Recognition in International Law." In Malcolm D. Evans, ed., *International Law.* Oxford: Oxford University Press, 2003. 205–67.

Wardlaw, Grant. *Political Terrorism: Theory, Tactics, and Counter-Measures.* Cambridge: Cambridge University Press, 1989.

Ware, Robert Bruce. "A Multitude of Evils: Mythology and Political Failure in Chechnya." In Richard Sakwa, ed., *Chechnya: From the Past to the Future.* London: Anthem Press, 2005: 79–115.

Weber, Max. "Politics as a Vocation." In *From Max Weber: Essays in Sociology,* ed. H. H. Gerth and C. Wright Mills. London: Routledge and Kegan Paul, 1974. 77–128.

Wedel, Janine R. "Tainted Transactions: Harvard, the Chubais Clan and Russia's Ruin." *National Interest* 59 (2000): 23–34.

White, Stephen, Richard Rose, and Ian McAllister. *How Russia Votes.* Chatham, N.J.: Chatham House, 1997.

Wievorka, Michel. *The Making of Terrorism.* 1983. Chicago: University of Chicago Press, 2004.

Wilhelmsen, Julie. "When Separatists Become Islamists: The Case of Chechnya." FFI/RAPPORT-2004/00445. Oslo: Norwegian Defense Research Establishment. http://www.nupi.no/IPS/filestore/00445.pdf

———. "Between a Rock and a Hard Place: The Islamisation of the Chechen Separatist Movement." *Europe-Asia Studies* 57, 1 (2005): 35–59.

Wilkinson, Paul. *Terrorism and the Liberal State.* London: Macmillan, 1977.

———. *Terrorism Versus Democracy: The Liberal State Response.* London: Frank Cass, 2001.

Wilson, Margaret. "The Psychology of Hostage-Taking." In Andrew Silke, ed., *Terrorists, Victims, and Society: Psychological Perspectives on Terrorism and Its Consequences.* Chichester: Wiley, 2003. 55–76.

Yakov, Valerii. "*Svidetelia luchshe ubrat'.*" *Izvestiia,* 14 January 1995.

Yandarbiev, Zelimkhan. *V preddverii nezavisimosti.* Grozny: Groznenskii rabochii, 1994.

———. *Checheniia—bitva za sovobodu.* Lviv: Svoboda Narodiv, 1996.

Yeltsin, Boris. *Zapiski presidenta.* Moscow: Ogonek, 1994.

———. *The View from the Kremlin.* London: HarperCollins, 1994.

———. *Midnight Diaries.* London: Weidenfeld and Nicolson, 2000.

Zelkina, Anna. *In Quest for God and Freedom: The Sufi Naqshbandi Brotherhood of the North Caucasus.* London: Hurst, 1999.

———. "Jihād in the Name of God: Shaykh Shamil as the Religious Leader of the Caucasus." *Central Asian Survey* 21, 3 (2002): 249–64.

Zürcher, Christoph, Koehler, Jan. "Introduction." In Christoph Zürcher and Jan Koehler, eds., *Potentials of Disorder: Explaining Conflict and Stability in the Caucasus and in the Former Yugoslavia.* Manchester: Manchester University Press, 2003. 1–40.

Index

Acknowledgments

This book has been in germination for about a decade. Some time in the late 1990s I was struck by the fact that the burgeoning literature on Chechnya, much of it produced by journalists who had reported the first war, tended toward two explanations for the conflict. The first was a form of historicism, emphasizing the historical roots of the contemporary conflict between Chechnya and Russia. The second was more contingent, focusing on the political expediency for Yeltsin of a "short victorious war." Moreover, there was a huge investment from the Russian side into framing the idiom of the conflict in terms of a struggle against "bandits," "terrorism," and "Islamic fundamentalism." The literature did not seem to me to offer a satisfactory explanation for what had turned one of the most peaceful parts of the Soviet Union into one of the deadliest conflicts of the post-Soviet era. It seemed to me clear that the origins of the conflict lay in the recent upheaval caused by the collapse of the Soviet Union and the demand for national self-determination.

Considering the alternative positive "heroic" and negative "criminal" stereotypes of the Chechens that characterized writing and reporting of the conflict, the old adage "one person's terrorist is another's freedom fighter" seemed appropriate. I perceived the growing Islamist radicalization of the Chechen side to be the result not the cause of the violence. These ideas formed the basis of an essay, "Chechnya: The Origins of a Protracted Conflict," which was published in *Civil Wars* 4. Later, after further study of the comparative political science literature on conflict, I wrote a chapter on the attempts at peacemaking in Chechnya, published in the collection of essays edited by Richard Sakwa, *Chechnya: From Past to Future*. These two essays formed the starting point of my study of the conflict in Chechnya, which rejects the "historicist" thesis.

To understand and explain this conflict, I have drawn on a wide range of source materials, including government documents, journalists' reports, and materials from the Chechen resistance, but I have applied my discretion to their interpretation. As much as possible I have relied on the leading protagonists to speak for themselves, through their own writings, interviews, and statements. Most of the analysis rests on published material and web-based sources. I have also interviewed some key actors who played a critical role at key moments.

I owe much to the friends and colleagues in the UK, Russia, Europe, and North America who have commented on early drafts of the work in progress or whose own work helped to shape my thinking on the subject of Chechnya. I owe most to my friends and colleagues Gwendolyn Sasse, Margot Light, and John Sidel at LSE, Brendan O'Leary of the University of Pennsylvania, Anna Zelkina of the School of Oriental and African Studies, and Neil Melvin, formerly Senior Political Advisor to the High Commissioner on National Minorities of the OSCE and currently at the Centre for European Policy Studies in Brussels. I would like also to thank Olga Levitsky, who provided research assistance in the final stage of the manuscript preparation. My greatest debt is to Frank Wright (died February 1993), who taught me political science during my undergraduate studies at Queen's University Belfast in the late 1970s. Frank was a prize-winning scholar from Oxford who came to Queen's at the height of the violence in 1973 and threw himself into efforts at peacemaking and reconciliation in Northern Ireland. From him I learned to appreciate the roles of historical tradition, context, and especially comparison in the analysis of violent conflict. Most important, he taught me that the dispassionate exploration and analysis of the causes of conflict precedes the finding of a way out of the violence.